BUSINESS POLICY AND PARTICIPATIVE DECISION-MAKING

WILSON ESSIEN

authorHOUSE®

AuthorHouse™
1663 Liberty Drive
Bloomington, IN 47403
www.authorhouse.com
Phone: 1 (800) 839-8640

Published by AuthorHouse 07/02/2019

ISBN: 978-1-5462-4350-2 (sc)
ISBN: 978-1-7283-1123-4 (hc)
ISBN: 978-1-5462-4349-6 (e)

Library of Congress Control Number: 2018906164

Print information available on the last page.

CONTENTS

PREFACE

The glue between efficient productivity and profitability is great decision-making. I do not think that a farmer has ever sown rice and harvested corn. In computers, the most common language is GIGO, meaning garbage in, garbage out. Usually, the decisions we make are our personalities, and yet very few people accept responsibility for their actions, their failures in business, or in any endeavor in which they have failed. They desire to blame others without remembering GIGO.

I have articulated the mystery that surrounds the lone decision-maker or the CEO who enjoys lonely decision-making and blaming his or her failures on the engineer or the accountant in his company. The new name for decision-making is participative decision-making. In this, the senior officers take part, but separately—the engineers, accountants, supervisors, workers and maintenance people form another group. Both platforms must have a dialogue format; there must be a writer or clerk, a vote taken on each discussion for its authenticity or viability, and in the end, the senior officers must compare their notes with the second group so that amendments can be made where necessary. The final product is now ready to be presented before the board of directors as a formal decision for the company. In a smaller company, this activity stops with the owner, but the owner must understand that two heads are usually better than one.

The CEO and his group must not be taken over by egos; the only time for pride in business is when business is doing well financially. Even then, business needs a lot of careful activity because "pride goes before a fall." It is good to entrust the CEO with the decision-making responsibility, but it is the biggest risk a business can take because business is a collection of ideas. Therefore, it a discipline of collective learning and inquiry.

Any student, manager, or business owner who wants to use participative decision-making skills in his or her business or as a consultant in participative decision-making should attend a workshop at least twice and read about participative decision-making thoroughly and practice it from case studies.

ACKNOWLEDGEMENTS

This book is the product of many years of empirical research findings, literature reviews, eyewitness accounts, Internet exploration and development. I would like to thank all those individuals who made the entire research and development process interesting and possible for me.

I want to thank my good friend, Dr. Asuquo Unda, for updating me on Biase politics.

I also want to thank my very good friend and a native of my hometown of Ikun, Chief (Dr.) Uno A. Uno for updating me on the economy and administration of our homeland, Ikun.

Thanks to all those who bought my Strategic Management, my managerial handbook , and the Woodpecker Story. It is this encouragement that keeps me writing, researching and analyzing my eyewitness accounts in order to keep up this high standard.

I sincerely thank my family for understanding and knowing that I could not be there with them as much as they wanted me because as a scholar, I have to work on the research and development of new ideas for the future generations.

I thank Almighty God for giving me good health and insatiable urge to doing things for the benefit of others.

CHAPTER 1
DIALOGUE – DEFINITION

1. Definitions
2. The Power of Dialogue
3. Dialogue: A Working Definition
4. Dialogue Versus Consensus
5. Why Dialogue?
6. Characteristics of Pure Dialogue and Communication
7. How to Start a Dialogue
8. Numbers
9. Duration
10. Leadership
11. Teamwork as a Decision-Making Process
12. Task Force

CHAPTER 1

DEFINITIONS

"Dialogue, the discipline of collective learning and inquiry, is a process for transforming the quality of conversation and the thinking that lies behind it" (Isaac, 1993, p. 24). Dialogue is concerned with providing a space within which such attention can be given. It allows a display of thought and meaning that makes possible a kind of collective perceptions, prejudices, and the characteristic patterns that lie behind an individual's thoughts, opinions, beliefs, and feelings, along with the roles he or she tends habitually to play. It also offers an opportunity to share these insights (Bohm, Factor, & Garrett, 1991, p. 3).

The Power of Dialogue

Often complex issues require intelligence beyond that of any single individual; yet, in the face of complex, highly conflicting issues, teams typically break down, revert to rigid positions, and cover up deeper views. The result is a watered-down compromise and tenuous commitment. Dialogue, however, is a discipline of collective learning and inquiry. It can serve as a cornerstone for organizational learning by providing an environment in which people can reflect together and transform the ground out of which their thinking and acting emerges. Dialogue is not merely a strategy for helping people talk together; in fact, dialogue often leads to new levels of coordinated action without the artificial,

1

often tedious, process of creating action plans and using consensus-based decision-making. Dialogue does not require agreement; instead, it encourages people to participate in a pool of shared meaning, which leads to aligned action (Isaacs, 1993).

Dialogue: A Working Definition

In dialogue as we use the term, people gradually learn to suspend their defensive exchanges and probe further into the underlying reasons for why those exchanges exist. However, this probing into the underlying reasons is not the central purpose of a dialogue session; the central purpose is simply to establish a field of genuine meeting and inquiry, which we call a container, a setting in which people can allow a free flow of meaning and vigorous exploration of the collective background of their thoughts, their shared attention, and rigid features of their individual and collective assumptions. Dialogue can be initially defined as a sustained collective inquiry into the processes, assumptions, and certainties that encompass everyday experience (Isaacs, 1993).

Dialogue Versus Consensus

In consensus building, according to Isaacs (1993), people seek some rational means to limit options and focus on the ones that are logically acceptable to most people. Often, the purpose of the consensus approach (the root of the word means "to feel together") is to find a view that reflects what most people in a group can "live with for now."

This assumes that shared action will arise out of a shared position. This assumption is questionable. While consensus approaches may create some measure of agreement, they do not alter the fundamental patterns that led people to disagree at the outset. Consensus approaches generally do not have the ambition of exploring or altering underlying patterns of meaning (Isaacs, 1993).

Further, Isaacs (1993) finds that dialogue seeks to have people learn how to think together, not just in the sense of analyzing a shared problem, but also in the sense of surfacing fundamental assumptions and gaining insight into why they arise. Dialogue can thus produce an environment where people are consciously participating in the creation of share meaning. Through this, they begin to discern their relationships to a larger pattern of collective experience; only then can the shared meaning lead to new and aligned action.

For example, in the early 1960s the Eastern Nigerian government established a farm settlement that they called Erei Farm Settlement, land owned by Ikun and Erei. At a point, disagreement ensued between management and the settlers. The settlers' union and management could not talk to each other without shouting and name calling. The disagreement lasted for more than two years. The fact was that the disagreement began taking a toll on how each side worked. Both management and the settlers' union knew that the premier (governor) was overdue for a visit; so, the senior manager met with the chairman of the settlers' union and asked the chairman to meet with him for lunch. The request was accepted, and during lunch they ate and drank very little. They were still skeptical about each other, but they managed to talk a little bit about their differences on the job. The meeting was very cordial. Each individual went home thinking about the meeting and what really took place and wondered why they had not shouted at each other.

A few days later the chairman of the settlers union called the senior manager and thanked him for the lunch and requested general meeting between the settlers union and management. The manager quickly accepted, and they set an agenda.

On the day of the meeting, the senior manager and the chairman greeted each other and laughed about a few jokes; members couldn't believe what was going on, but I believe that a tone setting for the meeting was a big factor for its success. When the meeting began, some of the settlers union started shouting while one of the managers was talking. The chairman quickly asked the settlers to hold on and hear what the speaker had to say; the same thing occurred in the management team. Any manager would shout while a settler was speaking; the senior manager would then ask the individual to stop interrupting until the settler had completed what he/she was saying. Both the management team and the settlers union at this point realized that a new frontier was emerging and that the old ways of doing business were over or close to being over. So, the quick and annoying ways of responding was ceasing.

Both the management team and the settlers union realized that the new frontier was encouraging everyone to participate in a pool of shared meaning, which would ultimately lead them to aligned action. The meeting was adjourned and a new date was set. As they left the hall, each member was thinking about the meeting; in fact, they were impressed and could not wait to attend the next meeting.

In fact, the next meeting was even more futuristic than others in that members from all sides of the issues gradually learned to suspend their defensive exchanges and began to probe further into the underlying reasons for why these exchanges occurred. The central point here is simply to establish a field of genuine meeting and inquiry (called a container)—a setting in which people are allowed a free flow of meaning and vigorous exploration of the collective background of their thought, their shared attention, and the rigid features of their individual and collective assumptions.

The field of genuine meeting and inquiry was the brain child of both the chairman of the settlers union and the management team. They were both right when their long-desired dream was reached, and later when the premier visited the settlement, he was very happy at the all-around improvement of the farm settlement and attributed the improvements to the efficiency of both management and the settlers union.

Another clear example in dialogue is in the Arab Spring uprising that occurred in Syria and Jordan. The people of Syria refused to give up their quest for freedom because President Assad did whatever he liked in Syria; his iron-hand administration had reached a boiling point. Of course, Assad's administration is not an inclusive government. He does not communicate effectively with the citizens of Syria, let alone conduct business on a dialogical level.

On the other hand, the nearby country of Jordan, which is very inclusive of its citizens in running its administration, remains free of serious uprisings and violence. I am not saying that Jordan is free of problems; of course, no country is. You can see President Obama and his advisors in the situation room. The element of dialogue exists in every democratic environment. The fact is that anytime someone does that which is repugnant to another person's sense of justice it is always on a short-term basis; it is not forever. That is what President Assad is seeing today. Dialogue is not only necessary in business; it is also required in politics even within a family.

Remember the settlers in Erei-Ikun farm settlement from the time they had the meeting because the settlers union and the management now talk to each other with respect and listen attentively when the other speaks. That is what dialogue does for a dysfunctional organization.

Why Dialogue?

Dialogue is concerned with providing a space within which such attention can be given. It allows a display of thought and meaning that makes possible a kind of collective perceptions, prejudices, and the characteristic patterns that lie behind the individuals' thoughts, opinions, beliefs, and feelings, along with the roles they tend to play habitually (Bohm, Factor, & Garrett, 1991, p. 3).

Characteristics of Pure Dialogue and Communication

Dialogue Discussion/Debate

Dialogue	Discussion/Debate
1. Seeing the whole among the parts	Breaking issues/problems into parts
2. Seeing the connections between the parts	Seeing distinctions between the parts
3. Inquiring into assumptions	Justifying/defending assumptions
4. Learning through inquiry and disclosure	Persuading, selling, telling
5. Creating shared meaning among many	Gaining agreement on one meaning

(Ellinor & Gerard, 1998, p. 21)

How to Start a Dialogue

Suspension of thoughts, impulses, judgments, etc. lies at the very heart of dialogue. It is one of is most important new aspects. It is not easily grasped because the activity is both unfamiliar and subtle. Suspension involves attention, listening and looking, and is essential to exploration. Speaking is necessary, of course, for without it, there would be little in the dialogue to explore.

But the actual process of exploration takes place during listening—not only to others, but also to oneself. Suspension involves exposing one's reactions, impulses, feelings, and opinions in such a way that they can be seen and felt within one's own psyche and also be reflected back by others in the group. It does not mean repressing, suppressing, or even postponing them. It means simply giving them serious attention so that their structures can be noticed while they are actually taking place (Bohm, Factor, & Garrett, 1991, p. 6).

Numbers

A dialogue works best with between twenty and forty persons or employees facing one another in a single circle. A group of this size allows for the emergence and observation of different sub-groups or subcultures that can help reveal some of the ways in which thought operates collectively. This is important because the differences between such subcultures are often unrecognized causes of failed communications and conflicts. Smaller groups, on the other hand, lack the requisite diversity needed to reveal these tendencies and generally emphasize more familiar, personal and family roles and relationships (Bohm, Factor, & Garrett, 1991, p. 7).

Between twenty and forty people or employees may constitute a good number with which to begin a dialogue, but the hindrance could be space and the required number of employees. In a small business with less than ten employees with enough space a dialogue can be started and if well-disciplined could achieve just as much or more in some cases, This is true for the following reasons.

1. Understanding is quick, much like a small class.
2. If the aim of the dialogue were to create a solution to a problem, the aim might be defeated because of the perspectives, which may turn the meeting into a political rally.
3. In business, we have business cultures; therefore, business solutions may require business culture and not very much about the contributions of subcultures.
4. The leader of a larger group of forty may require both skills and talents to get such dialogical inquiry to a successful end.

My aim in this brief addition is to let the reader understand that dialogue is used in context, depending on the desired achievements. In business, you may not be required to reveal anything, but it may be necessary when one is dealing with religious matters. Dialogue creates understanding for the decision-making process in any discipline.

Duration

A dialogue needs some time to get going. It is an unusual way of participating with others, and some sort of introduction is required in which the meaning of the whole actually can be communicated. However, even with a clear introduction when the group begins to talk together, the group may often experience confusion, frustration, and a self-conscious concern as to whether or not it is actually engaging in dialogue.

It would be very optimistic to assume that a dialogue would begin to flow or move toward any great depth during its first meeting. It is important to point out that perseverance is required. The more regularly the group can meet, the deeper and more meaningful will be the territory explored (Bohm, et al., 1991, p. 8).

Leadership

A dialogue is essentially a conversation between equals. Any controlling authority no matter how carefully or sensitively applied will tend to hinder and inhibit the free play of thought and the often delicate and subtle feelings that would otherwise be shared. "Dialogue is vulnerable to being manipulated, but its spirit is not consistent with vulnerability. Hierarchy has no place in dialogue" (Bohm, et al., 1991, p. 8).

Finally, Bohm, et al. (1991) found that in the early stages some guidance is required to help the participants realize the subtle differences between dialogue and other forms of group, processes. At least one, or preferably two, experienced facilitator are essential. Their role should be to occasionally point out situations that might seem to be sticking points for the group; in other words, to aid the process of collective perception, but these interventions should never be manipulative or obtrusive. "Leaders are participants just like everyone else. Guidance, when it is felt to be necessary, should take the form of 'leading from behind," and preserve the intention of making itself redundant as quickly as possible" (Bohm, et al., 1991, p. 9).

Teamwork As a Decision-Making Process

Teamwork for decision making is a process, but the process is made up of three components One component is often mistaken for another. Let us examine them in the following order:

1. Task Force
2. Working As a Team or in a Team
3. Teamwork

Task Force

Former U.S. President Jimmy Carter now travels to different parts of the United States organizing citizen volunteers to build family homes free of charge to deserving non-homeowners. Upon satisfactory completion of the building, the volunteers are released, as former President Carter and his staff move on to a different community and render the same type of service with builders and volunteers in the new community. So, the difference here is that the organization has no permanent builders even though they are in the business of building homes.

Another example is what I saw in South Africa where miners were trapped underground by an accident. The government sent in volunteers from different parts of the world to use their expertise in rescuing the miners from the underground trap. After removing the miners from underground, the South African government thanked the volunteers for their assistance and let them return to their homes around the world. The service here is known as task work because it involves an event or

9

catastrophe that has occurred that needs immediate attention. It does not matter if the service people are paid or not, but the fact is the service people were not retained as employees.

A task force may not be the best option for problem solving, though the service people might be insured within the period of service, but they are in no way treated as employees, which might have been very expensive. A task force sometimes is used unconsciously in that if a neighbor's dog falls in a pit and cannot get out, a good neighbor or a passer-by may start doing something to help rescue the dog. Many more neighbors may also join in the project. Eventually, the dog's life may be saved, while all the helpers go back to their places feeling good for a successful rescue. It is a task because you want the dog out of the pit before you leave and all the helpers think that way. It is that type of thinking that forces one to work very hard and creatively to bring the dog out of the pit.

The spirit of a task force, to me, seems as the oldest or one of the oldest ways for humans to help one another. Think about the Stone Age where wild animals could easily kill people, but for some reason humans came quickly together with objects and chased away the animals. I think that this idea of coming together to help was a gradual creation of working as a group or in a group.

A task force today is in some cases very sophisticated. Think about what former President Carter is doing in building homes for the underprivileged. Think about the miners in South Africa who were rescued by people from around the world. The fact is that a task force, working as a group or in a group or teamwork, use these methods of solutions to problems, but the methods are different from one another and therefore must be differentiated for clarity of purpose.

With the little-known facts about former President Jimmy Carter, we understand that he worked with a group of volunteers; he has no permanent volunteers, though there is no known law prohibiting permanent volunteering. The workers may receive some rewards, but none known as salaries. The volunteers are from many professions who simply go to a location and know what to do. It could be interpreted that the ultimate aim of volunteering is to make a difference in solving a problem. Therefore, the mindset of task force volunteers is a far different than those who work in groups or as a group, even in teamwork, because they are not motivated by financial rewards or from any nobility that may differentiate them from the rest of the world, but success based on humility. These humble people may not necessarily have any religious affiliation, but they know that it is good to be good.

There is a drawback; nothing may be perfect on our planet; in some cases:

1. Implements for the job may be faulty;
2. Fewer people may be available to get the job done than is needed;
3. Information may be scanty;
4. Financial difficulties may delay the project; and
5. Uniformity of purpose may be based on the fact that the volunteers only do what they are asked to do. Although they may have some say, especially the professionals, but that may not be the type of basic principles of what the organizers intended to achieve. Volunteers must be aware of what they are volunteering for, and there must be a clear exit in case an individual decides to opt out of the project.

CHAPTER 2
WORKING IN A GROUP

CHAPTER 2

WORKING IN A GROUP

Working in A Group or As A Group

Working in a group or as a group is an offspring of civilization; it is quite different from a task force, which is some voluntary undertaking. Working in or as a group is employment arranged in departments; for instance, a finance department or a human resources department, etc. In most cases these are professionals.

These employees have different assignments meant for the same result. This could be called a division of labor. The US Postal Service is another example; some employees sell stamps; some stamp envelopes; some run sorting machines, and some employees deliver letters and packages. The aim of all of these people is to make sure that a letter or package is delivered properly. The employees work in groups to accomplish their task.

We may have a ministry of education, but a lot needs to be done to make it meaningful. The employees work individually or mostly in groups going from the primary school, secondary school, and college or universities, including all the boards and school superintendents. All of these people are part of the ministry of education headed by the Secretary of Education or Minister of Education who coordinates all the factors necessary for the departmental success.

These are employees who work for a salary; they may or may not live their job, but since they receive paychecks regularly, they just like it for the incentive. Some may not be specialists on what they do, but they have the minimum qualifications with the hope of being trained on the job. Employees in most cases work in clean and equipped offices where they truly work as a group or team because they produce just one product. The American football sport, the soccer team, the basketball team—all of them and much more work as a group or as a team. They want to defeat their opponents on the field or court as a group, but they don't practice teamwork.

Government offices and businesses of all kinds with more than ten employees can practice both working as a team or a group and teamwork. However, a business-like basketball team may only practice working as a group or team and not teamwork because although they may have a staff of more than ten individuals, the staff members are not players, and as such, they may not know what problems the players have on the field. This is because teamwork has to do with the decision-making process. You make decisions on what you know very well. If the players tried to form teamwork, that might be tantamount to being decision-makers forming teamwork deciding for themselves what they think is the problem; that is self-serving.

The team decision-making process, analysis, and research is a lot easier if the company is losing money and no one in the company can figure out why.

The decision-making process is a very powerful tool; therefore, it must be done with those independent of the decision-makers other than that the decision-makers may look like judges and witnesses.

Working as a team is very commonly done in society and often mistaken as teamwork. Working as a team or in a group is simply a division of labor in the workplace. Working as a team or group and task work are not decision-making elements or processes, but teamwork is clearly a decision-making process. What I have been analyzing is to show how task work and working as a team or working in a group are different from each other and from teamwork itself Rather, dialogue and teamwork constitute the decision-making process while task work and working as a team make up the job itself motivated by a division of labor.

Teamwork As A Decision-Making Process

This is a group of people working together for efficient decision making. The members may have distinct identities but work together in a coordinated and mutually supportive way, open, and expressive, with any disagreements being resolved promptly. The members are understanding and accepting, listening, sharing information, and ultimately having great decision-making skills. Members of the Erei Farm Settlement between Erei and Ikun and the management of the farm settlement had to agree to settle down and analyze their situation (Tjosvold, et al., 1995).

Teamwork is a means of generating new ideas or creating solutions when information is highly disbursed initially among several individuals and/or when some mutual stimulation is needed among members to be fully creative. It can serve as a critical liaison or coordination function among several departments in organizations whose work is, to some degree, interdependent. In meetings members also dialogue instead of just communicating. In dialogue, thoughts are often suspended, meaning that no one is expected to have a preconceived idea of what should be right or wrong about issues to be discussed. Team members have to understand the connections between or among the parts that are connected in order to make a decision workable. Every assumption is carefully examined every question answered while the pros and cons of other suggestions are examined before a recommendation based on the facts is made. More often than not, the winning recommendations are often the best recommendations to be implemented. The company can still fail if the implementations are carried out wrongly or ignored.

A case in point is that of Bassey and Sons, a private, limited liability manufacturing company. The company manufactures office equipment, paper, chairs, and tables. They monopolized the industry for years in Calabar; in fact, they forgot all about any competition, but suddenly sales went down 15%. The company began experiencing confusion because employees were not sure any more if they would maintain their jobs. The company was semi-medium in size, had 15 members in each department, and had four departments. Each department had a team leader and a manager. Each manager wrote to his members regarding precisely what was occurring in the company with no one knowing why it was happening or how to solve the issues.

The general manager scheduled a general meeting of the four departments where he divided the company into two teams, Team "A" made up, of departments one and two, while departments three and four became Team "B." Team "A" was managed effectively by two leaders and two managers as was Team "B." Team members were taught how to use dialogue in a decision-making process.

Figure 1

Engineers	Finance Human Resources				Sales	Team A				
1	2	3	4	5	6	7	8	9	10	11
12	13	14	15							

2 | |

Team | | Secretary

Leaders | |

	16	17	18	19	20	21	22	23	24	25	26	27
		28	29	30									

Sales   Finance HR   Engineers

Manager	Manager

Two Managers

Remember that the general manager simply merged departments one and two into Team "A" and departments three and four into Team "B" in the interest of the teamwork decision-making process. After the process was completed, the team members would go back to their respective departments. Teamwork as a decision-making process is expensive in that those concerned in the process are also employees of the company, and so productivity during this process slows down. Yet, the employees are paid normal salaries and more in order to keep the members happy and stronger during this process. Let's see Team "B."

<u>Figure 2</u>

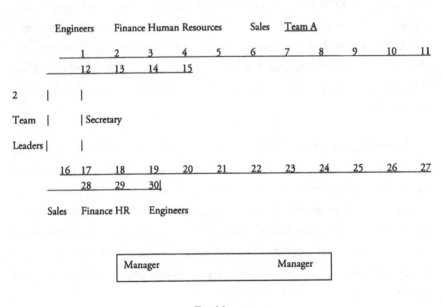

Two Managers

You can see that the teams are intermingled with professionals and workers. We must take note that during the process everybody is equal. If one is said to be, or even thought to be, superior, then that conflicts with the doctrine of non-reprisal during and after the process. In complete equality, the company may divided the teams into micro teams and macro teams.

Micro Team – this talks about or considers questions on "how should it be decided, what enterprises should operate; what goods and services should be produced; what techniques of production should be used; at what prices should goods be sold; on what terms should products be sold; and how should income be distributed amongst the members of society. Emphasis is given to the question of how consumers can maximize their utility or satisfaction given their tastes and levels of income (Peterson, 1986).

Macro Team – this team is concerned with the aggregate decision-making process or the company as a whole. The team considers what determines total employment and production, consumption, investment in raising productive capacity, and how much a country imports and exports. It questions what causes booms and slumps in the short term and what determines the long-term growth rate of the economy, the general level of prices, and the rate of inflation. The term considers how the government could influence the economy through monetary and fiscal policies.

Both micro and macro teams are mainly used by the government. All members are professionals—no workers—with long deliberations; recommendations may be too academic and may have no bearing at all on the required solutions. Even though academics are very important in our analytical maturity, individual ego is always the barrier. Companies mainly need mixed teams; that is both professionals and workers who do the job every day and can figure out where the "shoe does or does not fit."

Setting

Let us go back to Figures 1 & 2 where professionals and workers sit together as equals deliberating and asking questions where needed. The round or spherical outlook of the setting makes it possible for each individual to pay attention to the point that every other member is making. Therefore, the following elements must be present in a teamwork setting for it to be effective.

1. It has to be conducted about a round or spherical table.
2. A business team may not be more than 50 members.
3. There must be a secretary or a recorder that takes down most of the things said.
4. The team leader must be the moderator.
5. Disagreements must be treated maturely; that is, these should be done in the form of questioning to clarify issues, rather than shouting and arguing in a disorderly manner.
6. There must be a long list of recommendations.
7. The list of recommendations must be reduced to a shorter list in the form of elimination by substitution. Those similar, one much more meaningful must be substituted. However, both long and short lists must be handed over to the team leader or the manager. The manager, in turn, must let the decision-makers see both lists.
8. The team leader or manager or both must be near the decision-makers to answer any questions or to explain any necessary points.
9. Decision-makers must make the decisions available as soon as possible to avoid corrupt reasoning that may not be connected with what the company desires to achieve. Decisions delayed are decisions denied.
10. If the short list of recommendations are meaningful enough, they should be adopted as the regulations of the company.

Participative Decision-Making Process

Teams can exist hand-in-hand with the hierarchical system where the president and chief executive officers are at the top, followed by the senior executive offices, the mangers, team leaders, workers, and other leaders. I call this the participative decision-making process.

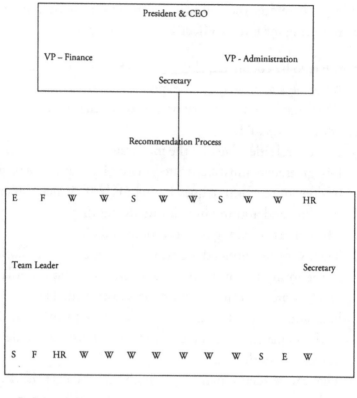

E = Engineers   F = Finance   W = Worker   S = Sales

HR = Human Resources

The participative decision-making process has been proven time and time again as the best way of making a company's decisions, and from my eye-witness account, I agree that this style of decision-making is definitely a nearly perfect method of decision-making.

Leadership Skills

Team members will be put into various leadership roles, including those of team leader, technical mentor, systems integrator, and liaison. These leadership roles require skills of informal influence, meeting management, and communication that are similar to, but more sharply honest than, those required of a member who is not in a leadership role.

Leadership in the technical integration process, for example, might require a broad technical knowledge to allow the leader to translate across the world views of various contributors. Leaders also need to be skilled at the kinds of processes that enable a team to move through the process of divergent information and the building of convergence around a shared direction. Some leaders may need to learn models and tools for this (Mohrman, et al., 1995).

Integration of Dialogue and Teamwork

We gladly say that this type of decision-making process is done by the use of teamwork because dialogue is a given since a meeting may not proceed if we did not talk to each other, and this art of talking to each other is known as dialogue. In order for teamwork to produce a meaningful decision-making process, a basic training in dialogue must be taught to the team members, especially on how to begin a dialogue. If the team members understand dialogue well, then it becomes a discipline of collective learning and inquiry, which apparently makes team meetings run smoothly with clear thinking and analysis that result in great recommendations for the company.

Otherwise, we may expect to have the following:

1. Team meetings become pep rallies.
2. No one understands what the other is saying because of noise.
3. No one understands the point the other is making.
4. One or two members may monopolize the talking, which invalidates the idea of equality among members.
5. Recommendations reached may be below average for solving problems.
6. Team meetings could become a waste of time and money.
7. Some members could feel less productive and therefore not worthy of being in the meeting.

8. The principle of collective accountability could have been an abuse of the system and misrepresentation.
9. If teamwork and dialogue are not properly integrated and procedures followed properly, consequent recommendations made may not fit the norms of the intended great outcome.

Characteristics of Dialogue and Teamwork

Dialogue	**Teamwork**
1. Suspension of thoughts, impulses, and judgments.	1. Listening and observing
2. Attention	2. Attention
3. Learning from one another	3. Explaining and telling what you know
4. Inquiry into assumptions	4. Analyzing the assumptions
5. Gaining agreement on facts	5. Accepting agreements based on reasonable alternatives
6. Contribute to making recommendations	6. Make recommendations
7. Deeper thinking on issues	7. Experts shared more lights on issues

Understanding the Basics of Your Job

In order to be a good team member, one has to understand what one does on the job; for instance, the BART policeman who killed Oscar Grant might not be a killer, but at the time of an emergency he became confused as to what tool to use to subdue Mr. Grant if that was even necessary. The policeman pulled out a gun unprofessionally and before it was over, Mr. Grant was dead simply because the policeman did not understand the basis of his job.

An individual like this BART policeman who killed Mr. Grant might not be a good team member for the decision-making process.

The policeman could have been more careful about his job, known different tools that he carried out daily, and how and when to use each of them. This could have been the type of person who could contribute to a team decision-making process. I am not saying the policeman was crazy, but he might not have been competent enough to be on a team.

CHAPTER 3
CASE STUDIES

1. Definition of Case Studies
2. Team Meetings
3. Program Director
4. Discussions
5. Discussions on Third Day and Beyond
6. Assumptions
7. Deliberations
8. Long List Deliberations
9. Short List Deliberations
10. Submission

CHAPTER 3

CASE STUDIES

Definition of Case Studies

A case study is the explanation of what a writer is talking about. Sometimes writing about something may make sense, but the understanding of the concept may need further explanation. Therefore, a case study is a story the author uses to make the concept clearer to the reader. Most of my friends who read my books enjoy reading the stories I have told about the cases, and students cannot have enough examples, for instance, Effiong and Eward in my recent book, <u>The Strategic Management</u>, who were two brothers beginning their lives after their university education.

Effiong was not sure what he was doing was an academic exercise, but he was just trying to do his best for his family. Eventually, his approach brought about unintended consequences that is now one of the core approaches for strategic management. Effiong may have been a very smart man, but he was just looking for a way to achieving his goal as a house owner. Now, it has become a case we have to study in a bid to expanding our horizon on strategic management.

Another case in point is the case of a post office in the southern part of the United States. Before entering the facility, there was a security booth which ran seven days a week and three shifts a day. At the front of the booth there was a sign stating, "No Pedestrian Traffic." One day a trucker ran out of the facility to take care of something important to him. He knew he was not going to be able to run back in; otherwise, he would be violating the "No Pedestrian Traffic" rule. He knew he must either be given a lift back in or go through the front desk back to his dock.

For some reason known to the security guard, he ran after the trucker and made a citizen's arrest and detained the trucker for two hours. The "No Pedestrian Traffic" rule meant that if you ran or walked out of the facility, you must not run or walk back in. If one did that, he must be arrested for breaking the "No Pedestrian Traffic" rule, but the fact is the trucker did not try to come back in.

The development was that the trucker sued the security guard, the security company, and the post office for an unlawful arrest and detention. Both sides retained high-powered attorneys; in the end, the case was settled out of court with an undisclosed amount to the trucker. Understanding the basics of your job is very important; you do not have to be an expert in your company, but just knowing the basics can go a long way to avoiding many problems.

You can read the next case in point from the main textbook, <u>The Strategic Management</u>, in detail. A company that was profitable became very unprofitable; both management and the workers wondered what had happened. They could not figure it out until they resorted to a teamwork approach. Then, a certain employee told the team that from a certain hour to a certain hour the machines ceased operating and the stoppage could last for two hours beginning around midnight, even though the machine made the usual noises and appeared to be operating, but the job was not being done. It took careful observation over time to figure out that the work was not being accomplished. On that note, the meeting was adjourned to make the careful observations of the equipment.

At a few minutes before midnight, the team gathered around the plant to observe what would happen. At exactly midnight, the equipment was still running but at a much slower pace. The team then discovered that it took a certain rate of speed to accomplish the work. The team then decided to put off the plant for two hours. Then, all breaks were rearranged—the short and the lunch breaks. The same went for those who worked on the day shifts. At mid-day, a two-hour long break was allowed as a cooling off period, and all the short-term and lunch breaks were made to fall within that two-hour timeframe.

Remember that in this case the company did not go through channels of approval because the need to remedy the situation was critical. Employees and management were afraid of losing the entire company due to low productivity and consequently low revenue. However, what really made this situation interesting was that the company did not need to spend money for anything. Perhaps if the situation has required any type of expenditure, the normal level of approval could have been needed. By the way, the individual who told the team about his observation was instantly promoted to a managerial position.

Understanding the basics of your job can be a stepping stone for creativity. A case in point is Steve Jobs; while he did not invent companies, he understood the basics of the computer. Mr. Jobs observed deeply that he could build a computer his own way and make it much better and called it Apple. Vision always comes from knowing the basics. The participative decision-making process works much better when you know the basics; that is why it is important to use long-standing employees as team members. However, this premise may not work all the time because some new employees may be very smart and inquisitive about what is new to them. But employees who may have been working for a particular company for a number of years may be preferred because of their experience.

Employees who have been in one particular company for years may know the names of most of their co-workers, the store room, different equipment they use daily, and how the equipment works. Teamwork/dialogue is, therefore, saying what you know to a group of people for analysis and discussion, which enables the team to learn and inquire deeply for more meaning. It is when analysis, discussion, questions, answers, and deeper inquiry have been done sufficiently that there can be recommendations made on the issue. Argument and loud talking are completely forbidden or not allowed in a teamwork setting unless you call it a pep rally. As I stated earlier, this process of decision-making is called teamwork because it is a team endeavor. However, remember that wherever teamwork exists, dialogue is a given because teamwork uses dialogical settings for deliberations. (You may need my strategic management book for more information about dialogue.) Knowing the basics of our job not only helps anyone participate in discussions and analysis, but it also creates some fulfillment in a vacuum not known to have existed.

In colleges and universities, this principle of knowing your basics may be based on theory but still helps a great deal during discussions and analysis. However, if the school has financial problems and would like teamwork recommendations to be made on the issues. Of course, the school must have lunchrooms, libraries, other facilities, staff, and professors. The team can look into all of that and be able to come up with unnecessary expenditures or even look into what the school can do to generate some revenues other than school fees. So, it is not all theory. Students may benefit more because they get to study the principles and write examinations about them, expecting to see such cases in practical terms. This is much like law students studying the law and case history and only to see such cases during practice. In school, it works much better because as I said earlier if you read your lesson before going to class, you must contribute sensibly in class discussions. This is not a miracle. In a teamwork setting, if you can look at your facility with your eyes open and observe well, your accuracy may not be like the student of teamwork, but you surely will make valuable contributions in discussions with your team.

Team Meetings

The team leader should always remain with the team during meetings for orderly organization according to the rules of the company.

Program Director

The director should explain the rules and procedures of the company's decision-making process. He/she shall distribute the case study to the participants; the participants will be allowed to ask questions for clarification and may be allowed to take the case study home for more reading in preparation for team discussions.

Discussions

At this time, the team members must have a full understanding of the case study; this is yet the second day of meetings. General discussions of the case are encouraged by the team leader, and on this day, a secretary is appointed by the team leader. He/she writes down all agreements reached. A tape recorder is also allowed in the meeting, but on the second day, nothing is written down. Any member who wants a point of clarification on the case will be allowed to offer questions, after long discussions, explanations, and more questions and answers by any member who seems to have understood the case. Still, nothing is written down, the tapes are not to be used for anything; this is a period of demonstrations.

Discussions on Third Day and Beyond

From this point on, agreements that are reached should be written down and tapes should be viewed when needed. Discussions could go on for weeks until agreements on all fronts are reached. No questions or statements should be regarded as less important. Every question or statement should be examined, analyzed, pros and cons figured out, and facts clearly separated from fiction. This procedure must be repeated each time unfamiliar questions or statements are made. When enough analysis is made on a subject and each salvaged, the team should then move on.

Assumptions

All assumptions should be reviewed and reanalyzed. No consensus is allowed; consensus is what you can live with for now. It does not solve the underlying problems. Team discussions and deliberations are painstaking ways of making recommendations for final decision-making. Any time the team is stressed after long hours of discussion, the team should close for the day and relax so members can have fresh minds the following day. The team should remain as long as it takes to have everything done right. The goal here is to make great recommendations for final decision-making. Great decisions, if kept as made, could mean a well-managed and profitable business.

Deliberations

The written discussions should be reviewed, and if needed, more questions should be asked, satisfactory answers given by anyone who knows or either the team leader or the manager or the individual who asked to throw more light on the discussion. However, both the manager and the team leader should play no part in the deliberations. The deliberations should take as long as possible, within a reasonable timeframe. The participants should learn to listen and remember that dialogue is a discipline of collective learning and inquiry. Members should suspend thoughts, impulses, and judgments to enable them to inquire into their own assumptions.

Long List Deliberations

Every reasonable statement made should be on the list, including assumptions made on certain issues in the case, but the long list should represent the case study. All the participants should try to say something; in a dialogue setting, nothing is irrelevant. The team has to look at everything that might be a breakthrough; one never knows. So, no idea should be treated lightly until proven unworthy by the team. If any idea does not sound right, the team should go back, analyze it, bring up its pros and cons, and have more discussions until proven unworthy to make the list or otherwise. The long list should be numbered but not necessarily in order of the case, but should make sense when one is reading it through.

Short List

The short list should be the summary of the long list. It should be about three-quarters of the long list or less. Remember that consensus is not allowed at any point of the proceedings because consensus is what you can live with for now, but team deliberations are the long-term solution.

If there are more than 20 participants, the team leader could split the group into two parts on the same case; it might be interesting to see what each team could come up with. In the end, the two teams should come together to compare their short lists. If there are slight differences, both teams should analyze the two lists and be able to combine the lists with no consensus by either team. Instead of consensus, both team should go over the process in a careful dialogical process, and both teams will come to agreement based on the facts. Please note that splitting the team should be based on available space, equipment, convenience, company anticipated benefits, and other resources that may be necessary. Do not split a team and create a substandard team because that may mean garbage in and garbage out (GIGO).

Submission

If the company or organization had just one team for the process, the team then submits its short list to the team leader, who, with or without comments, submits it to the CEO and the team of final decision-makers. If they had a dual team process for the same subject, the two short lists should be submitted to the team leader who finally submits, with or without comments, to the CEO and the team of decision-makers. Note that if there was a dual team process on the same subject, the two teams must have just one team leader.

The reasons for one team leader include:

1. Uniformity of information;
2. Recommendations will be direct to the case study instead of reflecting two rigid ideologies because of egos;
3. It may be a lot easier for a leader to admit guilt and make necessary corrections instead of two leaders blaming each other, since that may be tantamount to disrupting the entire process.

CHAPTER 4
DECISION-MAKING

CHAPTER 4

THE CEO AND THE FINAL DECISION-MAKING TEAM

The CEO and his/her team of senior officers could invite both the team leader and the manager to explain how rigorous the decision-making process had been with the team. The executive officers will now understand what the team went through in order to get to the short list before them. With the most respected document on the table, they may add or remove some sentences or phrases or simply write a decision using the list or reject the list by voting it down. The CEO could override the votes if the executives deviate too much from the team's short list because the final decision rests with the CEO. However, in most cases, the short list is adopted, and the final decisions are written with the short list ideas, with some modifications where required.

Straight Line Analysis

What I call straight-line analysis is seeing something for the first time without a deeper look and simply deciding on what you think that it means (stereotype). Sometimes one may be invited to testify before the team; for some reason he/she may become nervous and start mixing words and saying things before thinking. At that point you are passing your own judgment on the individual. This is premature; the judgment does not represent what you saw. Eventually, your recommendations will be off the point.

Straight-line analysis is responsible for many people going out of business because they quickly write off legitimate advice and brand information from other people as incredible because of some educational standard, how the individual looks, the company or association. They come up with reasons unconnected with the advice given, but all have to do with the class system. Such business people always convince themselves that they were being careful about running their businesses badly, not knowing that their management style is more toxic.

Straight-line analysis is much more prevalent in any society than we think. Most disagreements in political parties are done by such an analysis. For example, the Speaker of the House of Representatives might say if the bill the President is asking for includes any mistakes. Then, of course, it is dead on arrival. The Speaker did not say the bill would be read and if there was any value the House might salvage. We will do that.

Teamwork as it concerns the decision-making process works in every human endeavor, providing we want it to work. In the beginning of this book, I talked about dialogue and how to begin dialogue, which included, among others, suspensions of thoughts, impulses, and judgments. Remember that the essence of being a team member is to gather information. The information we gather is what is known as *data*, and data is very essential for making recommendations that alternately comes down to decision-making. Of course, in a straight-line analysis, no rigorous procedure is required; you just look at the person or thing and make your judgment. Of course, the chances of having to make a good judgment is very remote.

Another example of straight-line analysis is that when an individual meets someone in the library or wherever and falls in love at first sight. The individual met the person and immediately began talking with him/her. The other individual said nothing to you but only looked at you. This individual is actually making a straight-line analysis of you. He/she might be saying:

1. Who is this person?
2. I've never met this person, yet he/she wants to go out with me.
3. He may be a womanizer or she may be a vamp.
4. I don't think she/he is any good; otherwise he/she could have talked to me in a friendly manner the first time.
5. Maybe he/she is an abuser.

But the facts about this person are that he/she just completed an MD degree and is working towards a PhD. He/she comes from a very conservative family and is well behaved and has never been in trouble. The other person may be a third-year college student and well-mannered also, but somewhat more conservative than the first person.

The fact here is that this could have been a match "made in heaven" but perhaps this is my own straight-line analysis about this "could have been" couple. Straight-line analysis may work well if an idea about the person he/she is referring to or is talking about is well known, but by no means is straight-line analysis a habit always worth imitating. No student should go to class the first day and assess the worth of the teacher; in the final analysis, the teacher might turn out to be one of the best teachers the student has ever had. Always give someone a chance. You might feel disappointed the first day in class; perhaps even the first month, but as time draws near to the end of the semester, you may begin seeing other characteristics of the teacher that you had not appreciated fully before. This is what I call "package analysis." You may be surprised grading the teacher higher than what you had in mind before. The straight-line analysis is based on the following:

1. Fear of the unknown;
2. Misrepresentation of facts;

3. Lack of enough research or findings;
4. Lack of self-confidence;
5. Low self-esteem;
6. Complete ignorance of a situation; and
7. Lack of courage and self-discipline.

Package Analysis

Package analysis is based on:

a) Having known the person well, perhaps being born in the same village or neighborhood and attending primary schools together.
b) What the person has become as a grown person.
c) Even in package analysis, some elements of straight-line analysis may be included since it is difficult to know someone that well, including what he/she does in their private life, unless the individual has written a biography or referenced information on a social media such as Facebook.

The team leader should always direct the team to avoid unnecessary analysis, especially of someone asked to testify before the team. Remember that the job of the team is to make recommendations, but a wrong analysis will always give you wrong recommendations meaning that the team has been wasting the company's time and money.

Out-of-Meeting Discussions

After the team's daily deliberations, please do not discuss personal findings with a teammate, which would be tantamount to consensus building and making a coalition that would divide free understanding of the case. The team should be free and fair from any disruptions. If a team member is confused about anything, he/she should frame it in the form of a question for the team to hear where possible answers may be given by team members or the team leader. Instead of making public misunderstandings private gossip, simply ask questions and have them cleared up once and for all. The questions asked and the answers given may not only help you but also others may benefit from them, too. Avoid out-of-meeting discussions; it is divisive and creates a dysfunctional team and renders any recommendations made by the team unworthy of accomplishing the task. Remember that the company or any institution spends a lot of resources organizing teamwork as a decision-making process.

No team member should waste time thinking about what the CEO and other members of the decision-making group will think about the team's recommendations if only the team has done its best. The following must be considered the team's best:

1. The team must be very attentive during deliberations.
2. Team members must ask questions and expect the right answers or answers that fit logically to the question(s).
3. The team must spend a lot of time analyzing statements made and answers given.
4. No member should consider any questions or answers irrelevant until proven irrelevant by the team.
5. Witnesses should not be treated as criminals; rather, they should be made to feel at home or free in order for them to open up and be forthcoming with what they know about the case or incident.
6. Before new discussions begin on the following day, there has to be a recap of the previous day's meeting in the interest of continuity and to enable someone who was not there to catch up.
7. Except for extreme cases, absenteeism must never be allowed; when absenteeism is allowed, before the new meeting commences, the team leader must sit down one on one with the absentee member and recap the important facts.
8. The team may allow the member who was absent to ask a few questions for clarification.
9. Absenteeism should not exceed two meeting days. Any more than that, the member should be asked to step down as a team member.

10. Some professional analysis may not be easy; in such cases, the team leader looks for outside assistance, who then may be able to explain the situation and make it easier for team members to understand. Understanding is the core of the analysis; the fact is that if the case is not understood, the analysis will be wrong and ultimately, the recommendations will be wrong. That is why package analysis is important, too.

Problems Among Team Members

Any problems among team members must be treated promptly by the team leader; in fact, that is one of the core duties of the team leader. The team leader must always be fair in dealing with team members. It is a fact that problems are part of human existence; therefore, the team leader must always be prepared to show his/her expertise in solving problems among members. Team members should always talk to the team whenever they feel something is going wrong; finger pointing should be avoided. Any problem observed by a member should be framed as a question or questions; answer or answers given will keep the potential member in the know that what he/she did or said should not repeat itself again or is the right thing to do. Peaceful coexistence is the nucleus for fair and creative recommendations. No team leader should do everything to avoid problems; otherwise, problems will be "driven down."

A driven-down conflict means that the conflict is still there in the individuals' minds waiting to come out again at another time when conditions permit. Team members should always be encouraged to come forward with complaints that they may have. They should know the following:

1. That coming forward with their complaints will not cause them to be labeled "trouble makers."
2. That they will be helping the team focus on the issues before it instead of having divided minds.

3. That conflicts resolved will be tantamount to free and creative minds, which will help the team make great recommendations for great decision-making.
4. That once the root causes of a particular problem is found, every team member will take precedence from there. Therefore, the verdicts will serve as examples for future conflicts and may even deter conflict from happening in the first place.
5. That sometimes conflict helps us adjust from our comfort zone if conflicts did not come up just for the sake of conflict. Everybody learns from constructive conflict.

Irony of Team Conflict

Inasmuch as conflict may provide a learning environment, we should remember that the team was formed to provide solutions to problems by coming up with recommendations to the senior officials for decision-making. If they now turn against themselves because they lack the discipline of remaining together as a team, then such a team may not be viable as a team for making recommendations for decision-making.

The team leader should look out for team members who may find it difficult to remain peaceful with fellow members. Such members should be taken out of the team before they infect others on the team. A peaceful team is a creative one and is bound to making respectful recommendations. In most cases, teams that make effective recommendations always see their recommendations accepted by the decision-makers as the company's final decisions and may become very sustainable for years to come.

The team leader should encourage members to ask questions on what they do not know or are confused about. If what someone does not know stays with that person for long, the person tends to begin believing what he/she had in mind. This could build up until it tends to become gossiping and a larger conflict involving many team members occurs.

In that case, the team has to be dissolved and new members appointed. Conflict has to be settled promptly to keep it from spreading.

The team leader must not only coordinate the activities of the team, but he/she must also make sure that instability does not set in during the team's meetings. The team leader must always be free and fair with all members. The team leader must be careful about her/his credibility. The leader's credibility is a big part of creating great recommendations. The leader takes credit for the success of the team, and, of course, he/she receives the blame for the team's failure. A team must laugh and cry together; that is the nucleus of collective accountability.

Take a good look at President Obama's economic team. Whether exaggerated or not, the team has seriously been damaged because trust has been lost. I mean trust among the team members and with the president. A team that is damaged may require a miracle to reorganize and function very well again. One of the actors on the president's economic team was quoted as saying, "No one is home." That means the economic team does not understand what they are supposed to be doing. Like any other team, they deliberate, ask questions, analyze the situation, and ask those who are supposed to testify to do so without prejudice. At a point in time, they come up with a long list of recommendations and finally come up with their short list of recommendations, which they have to present to the secretary, who then takes the short list of recommendations to the president.

The CEO With His Team

In the example of the president of the United States, the president then sits with his top economic advisors, including the Secretary of the Treasury. The setting has to be the same with the economic advisors, the round table conference. Then, they take each item on the short list of recommendations, analyze them, make any points of clarifications, ask the Secretary of the Treasury if there is anything he/she does not know, and then they send for the team leader.

The president's team may accept all of the short list of recommendations or accept some and reject others, or reject all of them. When a certain number of the recommendations or all of them are rejected, the process begins again with some of the team members, all of them, or a completely new team to reexamine the case.

The team must work independently of the president (or the CEO); if the president interferes during the team's deliberations, then the final decision may have lost its basis for unbiased and clear decision-making because the president has become a judge and a witness. The president may be capable of doing it all, but this is not about him/her; it is about the entire country (or company). The final decision must represent the best interests of all concern, not just a segment of the company (or country) the president knows very well. The short list must be well documented, but that may not even be accepted by the Secretary of the Treasury, let alone the president's team. "No one is home" is uncalled for; it merely shows ignorance on the part of the economic team.

The economic team is appointed by the president; they work for the president, much like any economic team works for a company's CEO, but in either case, the team is given the freedom of non-interference by their boss. The team has to make independent recommendations; otherwise, such recommendations may lose any legitimacy that they may have had. The principles of the freedom of non-interference by any leader makes the team's recommendations appear legitimate and free of any political pressure. The principle of non-interference enables team members to write their recommendations the way they understand the case.

The principle of non-interference enables the team members to concentrate on their tasks rather than watching to see where mistakes will come from, so that they can use such mistakes in a profitable way. The non-interference principle promotes creativity because members are less stressed and more ready to work harder and do more research for better findings. This principle also promotes accountability because when individuals go wrong, they have no one else to blame but themselves; however, when they are right, they receive the credit.

Also, non-interference plainly clarifies the division of labor–the team that made the recommendations and the team that makes the decisions. If the recommendations are great, the president then understands that he/she made excellent appointments, but if the recommendations are poor, then the president knows he/she has to dissolve the team and appoint new people to do the job.

Decision-Making By One Person

If an entrepreneur who works alone wants to make complicated decisions must first have a setting like the team has. He/she must sit in a ventilated office with no distractions from phone calls, and the businessperson must know the case very well. He/she takes up a clean exercise book, clearly analyzes the case, and maintains objectivity, meaning that he/she must not simply analyze the case to favor her/his prior thinking. Whenever he/she becomes tired, he/she either calls it a day, meaning leaving the work for the day, or simply rests for the time being and comes back later in the day. The entrepreneur must not think of finishing the job in a day or possibly even in a month. Ancient philosophers in Calabar once said, "If you cook very fast, there are possibilities of eating raw food." After a long internal argument, he/she begins working on long-term recommendations that may take quite a few days before the individual can begin writing down the short-term recommendations by selecting the main points from the long list.

Short List Analysis. The points taken from the long list that represent the short list are re-analyzed to be doubly sure that the points actually represent the short list. If any point does not fit, the pint has to be taken out and a replacement inserted. This is the period of elimination by substitution because this is the position of the analysis the CEO has to see with his team. Therefore, it has to be as professional as possible. In this case, an individual is playing all the parts; the actor must be serious to act well. In the end, he/she comes up with a sustainable result from where he/she can come up with a great decision.

The exercise can be nerve-wracking if an entrepreneur is doing all the analysis alone up to the decision-making. The fact is that he/she saves a lot of money because it is expensive to build a team and keep them until they come up with sustainable recommendations. A determined entrepreneur can complete the exercise alone, but if it could be possible that he/she could have others to assist, let them take the advantage of this assistance because "two heads are better than one" or many hands do light work. In any case, the team or the entrepreneur must know how to use dialogue for deliberations during the recommendation-making process.

Whether working as a group or individually, the basics of dialogue are required because it sets the tone and the procedure of deliberations. Dialogue brings up the professionalism that is required of such organizations. Teamwork can blend easily with dialogue if the basics of the two are understood.

CHAPTER 5
CASE ANALYSIS

CHAPTER 5

CASE ANALYSIS

Case One: Soap Manufacturing Company

Mr. John's company was established 25 years ago, and servicing was done yearly. It is a soap manufacturing company; the locals patronized the company, and for years business was booming for them. They had just two salespeople, more than 20 engineers, one general manager, three managers, three supervisors, and about 70 other employees. The company traded publicly at $40/share. For reasons unknown to management, the customers began cutting back on their purchases, profits began to fall, and for the first time, the company had to lay off employees.

Management met on several occasions trying to figure out what had happened to their product sales. They realized that a similar company had been established about five miles away from their site with prices lower than John's, and that company had delivery service at a very low price. The company was called The People's Soap, and they had about 15 salespeople. Their sales team was very aggressive; they talked to all the local stores soliciting orders. John's company then understood that they now had strong competition. The People's Soap knew that John's company was seriously gasping for air, meaning that John's company was in great difficulty in terms of sales. But The People's Company even then kept the pressure on. Uphill now, John's company is still looking for strategies to combat this strong competition.

1. Could you please help John's company compete with their competitor?
2. Do you think that The People's Soap will ever slow down their aggressive sales strategy?
3. Analyze the situation and come up with your long list and submit your short list to your chief executive officer and his team of decision-makers.

Case Two: Saint Joseph's High School

Saint Joseph's High School is known for its high academic standards. In about 40 years, over 90 percent of its students have enrolled in colleges and universities. To be specific, more than 50 percent of the professionals in town were the products of Saint Joseph's High School. Students were from many towns and big cities. Admission to Saint Joseph's signified success in life.

However, in the past five years a few public schools have tried to surpass Saint Joseph's academic standard. Saint Joseph's High School couldn't figure out what went wrong. The principal finally summoned a team meeting. The team was made up of teachers from the school, staff members, and other personnel. They were told about the past glory and how they were above the competition they had, and what was happening today. The principal concluded, "I want to know why." One teacher was appointed as team leader.

The case was not easy; they had to know what other schools had been doing to make them great competitors, especially a few public schools, which had been laughingstocks in the past. Saint Joseph's thought perhaps they were the best forever as far as academic competition was concerned within the district.

47

The team read about the school's greatness and what they had done to get there over and over. The team also read about other schools and what they had been doing to close the gap between them and Saint Joseph's. Saint Joseph's team analyzed every situation that was presented to them and came up with an unusually long list, and from that a short list was compiled for the CEO and his decision-making team. The CEO in this case was the principal of the school. The principal thanked the team for working the long hours and promised to come up with decisions as soon as possible for implementation.

1. Can you help Saint Joseph's High School?
2. Submit your findings to the principal.

Case Three: Paul's Motor Company

Mr. Paul, a great entrepreneur who lived in central London, owned 60 busses operating on different routes. His business had been very profitable for over 25 years. His company had a rule that "no driver is allowed to take off without first seeing proof of payment from passengers and if any passenger fails to pay, assuming they have 100 seats and only one passenger occupying one seat fails to pay, the rest should be left to stay in their seats, but the bus would not move until the lone passenger pays his/her fare but will never try to put him/her out and move on with the other 99 passengers."

The policy went on for a while until Paul's Motors started seeing more competition. Passengers who thought Paul's Motors was very time consuming opted for other companies. The practice went on for a few years, but as years went by the revenue continued to diminish. The company then started experiencing financial hardship. Paul's Motors turned to private business consultants whose advice yielded no dividends until they turned to a team approach. The team quickly took shape. The team leader quickly gave out Paul's team members the company's history encompassing triumph and tribulation until other motor companies were established to compete with them.

Analysis and deliberations were carefully made. It took them a few weeks to come up with the long list. The team members went through the long list again with a run-through analysis from where they had the short list, which they presented to the CEO and the decision-making team for the final decision-making.

1. Can you help Paul's Motor Company?
2. Submit your recommendations to the CEO, both long and short lists.

Definition

Teamwork as a decision-making process is a process where employees, managers, and professionals team up and regard themselves as equals, deliberate, analyze the issues to figure out the core problems, deliberate on the core problems, and analyze the findings to come up with recommendations. The recommendations are composed of long and short lists. The short list is presented to the CEO and his team, but they could also ask to see the long list.

Decision-Making

The decision-makers usually are the CEO and his/her senior officers, the vice presidents, account managers, senior engineers, the sales manager, and others. The CEO may bring in those who may be knowledgeable about decision-making in a team-based organization. They analyze the short list they received from the team, the senior officers; then, most deliberate, ask questions, support their analysis with documents and may invite some of the team members for questioning. This is another rigorous undertaking in the end where they come up with a long list of their findings and select their short list from their long list. The team's short list is compared with the CEO's short list team. The team's short list may be modified or both short lists may form a coalition or one modified short list may be required for the company's solution to the problem. A rule is therefore made following the solution of the case. The information about all that is displayed on the company's notice board.

Case Four: The Best Manager in a District

There was a general manager serving in a printing press manufacturing company who was considered the best in the business by his CEO. The general manager laid off three employees in a month and consecutively for five months including a few engineers. The general manager has no patience for complaints made in every department of the company. Consequently, his ability to lead because of his impatience in the workplace became questionable. However, the CEO under the whole cloud refused to let him go (fire him).

Productivity began going down, revenue went down drastically, shareholders were not paid for a period of over a year. Complaints mounted and the products were no longer competitive in the marketplace. The board of directors invited the CEO to testify. It seems that every employee in the company knew what was the cause of the decline of productivity and revenue, but the CEO was the odd man out. They finally took a vote, and unanimously he was asked to leave, so the axe fell on the CEO and not the general manager. A new CEO was employed as soon as possible. Within the week, the CEO summed up a meeting of the executives where he asked the general manager to only discipline employee and not to let any employee go until the CEO had the chance to hear the whole story.

The general manager returned to work much more subdued and tried to make friends, but he was very much hated by the employees because he had been a tyrant for many years disturbing employees at the workplace. The employees' opinions were divided. Some said the general manager could have been let go; some wanted both the general manager and the former CEO be let go. Together. Even then, both productivity and revenue were still not improved after six months. The blame was still focused on the general manager, employees blamed the general manager for the company's low morale. Some employees told their supervisors that seeing the general manager still managing the company is much like bringing Hitler back to manage the Jews. Of course, the result would be too bad. It was said everywhere in the company that the general manager had got to be fired, but the new CEO had no grounds for releasing the general manager. This is because all that happened before the new CEO was hired.

All of the gossip became rather wild because it spread very rapidly and finally reached the ears of the Board of Directors' chairman. A meeting was convened wherein the Board finally directed that the general manager be transferred to a substation and to head the station. The whole scenario sounded like a promotion, but the employees loved the story because the general manager was no longer with them at the main office. The fact is that the general manager learned his lesson; he never let anybody go; he worked very hard and became a father figure instead of a tyrant. In fact, both productivity and revenue increased to record highs to the extent that some of the general manager's former employees were transferred to be with him. This time there was no animosity because the employees over there had job security because business was good for them. The Board of Directors became convinced that while the company was united as one, it was better for the branches to have autonomous administrations.

The new CEO took the idea of making the branches of the company autonomous very personally; he regarded the move as a vote of no confidence in him; however, he knew the main company was not doing well financially. So, he decided that a team be set up to look into what happened and how the situation could be remedied. A team was organized, orientation begun, and a few days later the case was distributed to the participants for study.

Questions

1. Do you think that the CEO was right in forming a team for the study?
2. Where do you think the team will focus: poor business or autonomous administration for the branches of the company?

Case Five: A Case of Strategic Management

We saw the protests in Oakland, California about income inequality in the United States. We saw the same protests around the world, but specifically in Oakland, California, the police and the mayor at first wanted the encampment near the city hall removed because it was a dreadful spectacle for the city such as Oakland and all of the negative publicity that went with it. However, removing the protesters was not well received in the court of public opinion. The same event was happening in San Francisco across the bay, but San Francisco refused to use force in removing the protesters.

So, Mayor Quan of Oakland tried another course of action. She even asked government employees to join the protest. It was peaceful at first, but it turned very ugly in the end. There were confrontations with the police, windows were broken, many protesters were arrested, and bottles were thrown at the police. There was about $2 million in damages. It became a state of anarchy in the end.

Let us now assume that the Oakland City Council has ordered a team to look into whether the mayor of Oakland made the best decision by supporting the protesters, preparing long and short lists of recommendation with a copy given to each member of the city council and the Alameda County Supervisors, including the President of the Board of Supervisors.

Questions

1. Oakland is not the wealthiest city in California. Why do you think Oakland was chosen for such international exposure?
2. Why do you think Oakland Mayor Quan changed her mind to support the protesters?
3. Why were the protesters protesting? Or do you think that they had no agenda?
4. What type of people vandalized Oakland—Ex-convicts, criminals from other cities, states, or the country?
5. Do you have sympathy for Oakland Mayor Quan? Why or why not?

Employees Participating in the Decision-Making Process

Every Thursday morning the CEO asked for different employees to meet with him/her in the discussion room. In the room, participants were free to ask questions, tell stories about what they thought should be done for the company to grow, and what competitors were doing, which perhaps the company should do also. After about two hours, they returned to their workplaces. In the meeting they had a secretary who wrote down important facts for the executives to review.

In most cases, the lower ranking participants would say after the meeting that they had many things to say but that many had been disciplined for speaking their minds, and instead of risking losing their jobs, they would like to say those things that the executives would like to hear. Because of the able leadership of the CEO, the company has been able to employ three engineers. But the irony is that the company broke even last quarter and paid no dividends to investors for the past two quarters. Worst of all, this particular company had been rumored to be seeking Chapter 11 bankruptcy for fear of what the Board of Directors might do.

However, with the news spreading all over the company, the Board of Directors sent for the CEO to find out what was going on. The CEO told the board that he had no idea, but that the fact was the company had not been profitable for about two years, even though sometimes they broke even but nothing more than that. The CEO told the board that he had been asking the employees to participate in the decision-making process; yet, all to no avail. The Board of Directors then asked the CEO to return to his office and to report for a final meeting on the subject in two weeks.

The Board of Directors began research on its own; they invited a handful of employees who told the Board that every Thursday the CEO had invited employees into the discussion room just to say what he wanted to hear; otherwise, they would get punished for speaking their mind on what that person knew well. They mentioned a few employees who were released for saying what they thought would help the company to rebound financially as well as product quality even though the CEO knew that the company had not been making profits for some two years. The research and findings from the employees were done behind closed doors. The CEO had no idea what was going on. In the second meeting with the Board, the CEO brought in who he thought was going to testify that every Thursday the employees had a meeting with the CEO to discuss what the company should be doing to compete in a global market.

When the meeting started, the CEO quickly brought in his witness; the witness to the Board that the company cannot succeed with one person but that it takes every person in the company to work very hard together to realize some profits. The CEO's witness told the board that the meeting was a scam because the CEO is only interested in hearing what he wanted to hear. The witness expressed some surprise at why the CEO asked him to be his witness, knowing that he always told the truth. The witness then told the board that he had a wife and three children and in about five years' time his oldest son would be leaving for college and that the family's only hope was in the company the witness worked for. The CEO's witness contended that he was going to be the last person to witness the demise of the company, which was his only hope, without saying anything. The witness then turned to the CEO and asked him simply to leave if he disliked the company. Then, turning to the Board, the witness said, "I end my testimony."

There were no questions asked, including none by the CEO. The Board simply thanked the witness for shedding more light on the problem. There was a long silence until the chairman of the board called the CEO by his real name and told him that he was fired and that the board would be giving him a police escort to take out his personal belongings from his office.

Even as I am writing this, many companies still conduct employee participation in the decision-making process simply in order to know what the employees think about them (the executives). Whatever they think is your opinion, could determine the future of the employee. Many of the CEOs or executives do not really think much about the company because even if the CEOs were let go, they have a handsome amount of money (or golden parachute) for having been there as the CEO. Having said this, CEOs are great, think about the company, and follow the dreams they had for the company to the benefit of the investors, employees, and customers, even though the end never justifies the means.

Questions, Answers, Clarifications

Unlike interrogations or fact finding operations by a Board of Directors from the CEO, team clarifications on issues are extremely important. The clarifications must be satisfactory to at least two-thirds of the team members; otherwise, until a satisfactory clarification is made, it does not matter who gives the clarification. True answers are always clear and justified and can withstand any kind of analysis. Teams derive their findings from intense deliberations, questioning, answers, and analysis.

Deliberations. After going through the case study or the problems in forming a team in the first place, the team members talk about how an individual thinks about the case and argue back and forth. This could take a few minutes, which is not recorded.

The team leader has to be the umpire. After the noise and communication aspects have been brought to an end by the team leader, the dialogical aspects begin. This is also the recorded aspects of the deliberations. A member of the team speaks while others listen and ask questions later; answers are given until the team is satisfied.

Questions. If a member or members are not satisfied with any clarification or answers that are given, then questions are asked until the points are clarified. Team members cannot move forward if the answers are unclear or fuzzy because that may be tantamount to unclear recommendations. It is a painstaking exercise in the interest of the organization. Neither the team leader nor the CEO is allowed to tamper with the team exercise; otherwise, the process could be declared null and void, and that would mean everyone has wasted their time and the company's resources. This could also cause negative responses from investors and the Board of Directors, which could cost the CEO her/his job. The team must be run in a very democratic way in order to succeed in its endeavors. Any elements of rigidity in control renders the system invalid as a decision-making process. Let's look at the following case in point.

There was a man who owned a cereal processing plant. In the beginning he was making great profits and was even going to go public with the company, meaning he was about to sell shares to any person who would buy them. But then the company began experiencing some sales problems, the warehouse was full, very few customers wanted the cereal produced, and no increase in orders.

The owner of the cereal processing plant organized a team to investigate the sales problems of the company. Even as the organization was about to begin deliberations, they found it was getting harder for salaries to be paid. So the team members worked hard to come up with answers to stop the downward spiral of the company and its increasing losses.

However, as the team was working, the owner was also restless, and therefore impatient for results from the team's activities. The owner started giving directives to the team and even replaced some of the team members for insubordination and being unwilling to take advice from the owner. Some team members even stayed away from the meeting and began looking for work elsewhere. Sooner or later, the company was put up for sale. Some of the team members and other employees left because they thought dictatorship had no room in modern management and as such, their present company was headed for disaster.

Answers. Answers may not always come from eyewitness accounts. It could be merely an opinion, but in a democratic society everyone is entitled to an opinion. However, the policymakers should overly stress their own opinions; otherwise, if the policy fails, they go down with it. They might even be called different names including dictator, such as the business owner who tried to show his strength, but to his dismay, the team knew what it was doing and refused to take chances.

Analysis. An analytical ability is the number one tool for the team to use in order to understand why things happen and what to do about it. It is like taking a car apart so as to know the nuts and bolts that do not fit or that may be broken or other things that may have gone wrong within the automobile.

A case analysis is almost the same, but in an analysis one has to know where to look, the right questions to ask, and how to evaluate the answers. Answers have to fit the case perfectly with no room for second-guessing whether the answers or part of the answers were made up. Case analysis is very sensitive, and by being sensitive, I mean that there are suspicions in the very information given until team members are convinced without any reasonable doubt. This is much like a "suspect" is innocent until proven guilty. So, if a business owner interferes during a team's analysis and its deliberations, that might create more suspicion amongst team members, and some team members might leave thinking that such a company has no future in the face of the competitive global economy.

CHAPTER 6
IMF POLICIES IN NIGERIA

1. IMF Policies in Nigeria
2. Reducing Public Expenditures
3. Eliminating Subsidies
4. Devaluing the Currency
5. Conforming the Free Trade Policies
6. Removing Barriers to Foreign Investment and Ownership
7. Selection of Team Managers
8. Deliberation Analysis
9. Long List Analysis
10. Analysis
11. The Power of Collective Thinking
12. Dialogue
13. The Power of Dialogue
14. The Practice of Dialogue
15. Levels and Stages of Dialogue
16. Initial Guidelines for Dialogue
17. Submission
18. Dialogue and Organizational Learning
19. Organizational Learning

CHAPTER 6

IMF POLICIES IN NIGERIA

The policy of having an open, liberal economy, privatization of public utilities, and devaluation of the local currency prescribed for Nigeria by the International Monetary Fund (IMF) has been described as harmful to the country's economic development.

Former Director of Budget and Planning in the Federal Ministry of Finance, Chief Onwali-Kuye, made this observation while delivering a lecture entitled, "Nigeria' Relationship with the IMF: The Way Forward" at the July meeting/luncheon of Financial Houses Association of Nigeria (FHAN).

According to Chief Onwali-Kuye, continuous and massive naira devaluation, excessive mopping up of liquidity by the Central Bank, liberalization of imports by which all manner of goods and services are imported without regulations, privatization of all major government corporations, except those bought by Nigerians, and other measures that stem from the policy prescription of the IMF will not move the nation forward.

Chief Onwali-Kuye (2002) urged the federal government of Nigeria to critically evaluate the advice of the IMF, accept those found consistent with Nigeria's restructuring programs, and ignore those that are negative. Quoting the author of *The Mystery of Capital*, Omonwale stated that the IMF's regular solution that prescribes the removal of barriers to trade by lowering tariffs, balancing budgets by governments, raising interest rates, and devaluation of currency by the Central Bank transferring the little investable capital in developing countries to the West and the United States of America, stressing that this is evident in the fact that there has not been a single success story among countries that have implemented these policy prescriptions of the IMF.

Chief Omonwale (2001), the former chairman of Icon Limited (Merchant Bank) commended the suspension of IMF staff supervision of the country's economic program, saying that it is a blessing in disguise. Chief Omonwale (2002) stated, "The monitoring activities of the IMF staff sometimes negate the sovereignty of the country being supervised. In many respects, the supervision becomes humiliating to the government and the people."

Babajido Komolate (2002) argued, according to Chief Omonwale, that the way forward for the Nigerian economy after the suspension of IMF supervision and monitoring of the government's economic programming is for the federal government to adopt a *closed economy.*"

Babajido Komolate (2002) commented that Chief Omonwale said it has become imperative to adopt a closed economy in view of the observations of a distinguished former IMF economist, Mr. George Soros, who stated that globalization creates a very uneven playing field between the industrialized and underdeveloped economies. Hence world governments and institutions should find ways to encourage individual countries to follow policies that promote economic growth that does not rely on "market disciplines," stressing that we (IMF) do not have the mechanism for providing incentives and leveling the playing field.

This position, according to Omonwale, behooves Nigeria to adopt therefore measures that will protect its nascent industries and agriculture even if the measures include absolute banning of undesirable products, stressing that Nigeria should not feel shy in using a prohibiting program as rich and industrialized countries have found the measures appropriate in protecting and utilizing their resources.

Even as I am writing this book, one must make sure that my information is current and correct. One of my observations about Nigeria is that the citizens are always proud of being Nigerians, but many of them cannot explain this phenomenon: "It is truly in every Nigerian that the country could accomplish anything that it wants to do. Though tribes and languages may differ but in brotherhood and sisterhood they stand." Nigerians are a very resilient people. They have been pushed down by constant military takeovers until the rest of the world has begun doubting what a Black African could achieve in life. Many animals began having longer life expectancies than many Nigerians did. The pride of being a Nigerian has almost been forgotten.

This pride, as I could see, originated from the classroom, as they believed in academics. Just by passing standard six, one could teach to work competently in any office. I remember when different countries were visiting Nigeria just for the interest of knowing how to plant oil palm, rubber, and cocoa trees. After the devastating civil war, military regimes followed, schools were left to decay, and citizens fled to the West. Nigerians became refugees and once again, Africans had no hope, but they believed that their homeland was the only place they could live a suitable life. When the first civilian administration came into being, many Nigerians returned to their homes, although once again they were disappointed by another military takeover. The military authorities called in the International Monetary Fund later and measures were set up including:

1. Reducing public expenditures;
2. Eliminating subsidies;
3. Privatizing state enterprises;
4. Devaluing the currency;
5. Conforming to "free" trade policies; and
6. Removing barriers to foreign investment and ownership.

Reducing Public Expenditures.

Even though Nigeria was a strong supporter of capitalism, there were many loopholes in the laws to accommodate the weaker citizens. The laws allowed everyone to struggle through innovation and hard work to acquire as much wealth as possible, but many citizens were unable to care for themselves. The government realized these points and decided to put in more money or public expenditures, for example, education. During the colonial period in Nigeria, high school tuition was £80 (eighty pounds) a year whereas a holder of a bachelor's degree was earning £720 or seven hundred and twenty pounds a year, and they were the upper middle class of course, next to politicians and government contractors. Under this canopy, one could simply imagine how many poor people one could have in a community. In fact, many people didn't even know they were poor as much as they didn't go hungry every day. The people I knew were peasant farmers who harvested all they needed for food from their farms, hunted for food in groups, and went to family lakes to catch fish for food. Most only needed salt to complete their delicious cooking, and for that commodity, they may simply sell some of their crops or catch of fish in exchange for salt and kerosene. The only help from the government was building more high schools to enable communities to help those who could not afford to live in dormitories and those who could come to school from their homes or stayed with relatives. These were called day students, and later with the help of the government—I mean regional governments and the central government.

Therefore, with much of this type of help from the government, communities began adhering to the government instructions and even voted during elections. However, the IMF asked them to curtail such assistance. None of the communities in Nigeria received the order kindly. Remember that I began by pointing out how proud Nigerians were in their native country. They demonstrated and asked the federal government to reject the loan. Also, remember that the government was a military one; they were not facing elections, and so they took the loans, and then abject poverty began, leases, and other difficulties descended upon the citizens of Nigeria. It was a nightmare.

The same thing happened in other countries with austerity. Here in Nigeria, hearing about the reduction in government assistance was like asking every Nigerian to carry 5000 pounds of gouri; it is too heavy and eventually no one can carry it. The only way would be for the people to revolt and that was what happened. The country ran into roadblocks. The soldiers were unable to begin killing the citizens, but the citizens realized that the austerity measures had come to stay. Eventually they started absorbing the reduction of public expenditures for whatever that meant. At the right time for the soldiers, they started enforcing whatever reduction of public expenditures they wanted.

Eliminating Subsidies

Many farmers planted cash crops, especially cocoa, but in order to compete with the rest of the world, they needed some subsidies. Otherwise, even the production of chocolate for local consumption might be difficult or impossible; so cocoa farms in Nigeria were left quite open for international competition with no subsidies for the local farmers. It was generally believed that the IMF was not in Nigeria to remedy any kind of situation, but rather to undo the forgotten harm in the colonial administrations. Cash crop farmers complained endlessly against the IMF. The civilian population truly despised the soldiers. People called the soldiers *every name in the book*; these included ignorant individuals with no college or university degrees as well as others.

The fact here is that the soldiers themselves did not know the deal they were entering into. Most military officers, when polls were taken, sided with the civilians because Nigerians had never seen anything like the proposals being made by the IMF. Therefore, they didn't know nor could predict the results. The ruling military leaders knew that doing nothing could have been worse. The civilian experts who worked for the military did a long-term cost benefit analysis; yet, the military was not sure about anything done for them because many top military officers were listening to the educated civilians. The whole point here is based on the fact that Nigerians are a very proud people. It looked very much like a nightmare for foreigners who came to Nigeria and tell Nigerians what to do and even to inspect what they did in order to be doubly sure that Nigerians conformed with instructions given in this case, the elimination of subsidies.

One thing I know is that Nigerians are never a violent people, no matter how annoyed they may be on a particular subject. They can talk or write a book to make someone look stupid, but life is always guaranteed except in very unusual circumstances such as politics, and even politics are not so deadly. However, in the case of the elimination of subsidies, everybody was against this, including the colonialists. Even the British, as every country that took the IMF loan was subjected to obeying such rules; therefore, Nigeria could not have been an exception. In the end, subsidies were reduced, but not dramatically.

The tension lessened; chocolate production, palm fruit, groundnuts, and other cash crops were not seriously disrupted for local industries meant for local consumption. Peasant cash crop farmers were no longer rich, but they still lived comfortably. One funny thing to add to all of these items—even though both soldiers and civilians never had experience in Structural Adjustment Programs (SAP), I am happy to report that the farmers are still in business more than ever. I remember when U.S. President William J. Clinton visited Nigeria and expressed optimism on how great a country Nigeria would be if they could diversify their portfolio.

In fact, weeks ago Nigeria's statistical experience revealed that the country is far more diversified than previous figures had suggested. Oil and gas, frequently thought to account for one-third of Nigeria's overall economy, actually accounted for less than 15 percent of Gross Domestic Product (GDP). The agricultural portion of the GDP had similarly dropped from 37% to 22%. Most national statistics agencies release their findings every three or four years to ensure it remains an accurate measure of the size of the country's economy Nigerians had not done in 25 years (Mail and Guardian, p. 3).

In Nigeria, structural adjustment programs (SAPs) in some enterprises are more welcome than in others such as the Nigerian Electric Power Authority (NEPA). NEPA supplies every Nigerian with power, light, assuming that if it was privatized power would be very expensive for many people, and the essence of capitalism might be defeated because if the locals cannot afford electricity, local industries might be missing a link in the chain of progress. This could mean no progress at all in Nigerian industrialization. However, the irony in all of this thinking and analysis is that most of the things objected to being done actually happened. Building a large dam with no maintenance, NEPA was worse off and on, and no industry could survive under those conditions coupled with the anarchy and public humiliation Nigerians went through with their military government.

Well, the majority of the nation thought that privatizing electric power would make things worse and never gave it a lot of thought; however, anything worse than NEPA meant no existence at all. Newspapers began writing about privatizing some of the so-called public industries and that this would do the country more good than harm. Remember that citizens had stopped demonstrating about the reduction of public expenditures and the elimination of subsidies. Therefore, the idea of privatization of state industries came up and many had no opinion about it; some accepted the idea, citing NEPA's problems, and a few were against it. People truly talked about this for months, and a few industries were privatized, but NEPA was not. In fact, the military said that state enterprises were to be privatized, but no one could figure out which ones were privatized, and in fact, it seemed the government merely reduced expenditures across the board on public enterprises.

However, public enterprises such as the palm and rubber estates were simply abandoned, left to decay, and thousands of employees were left jobless to fend for themselves. Nigerian citizens were found in almost every country of the world doing all types of jobs, most of which were below their value, but no one cared, provided that they could eat and live. Education, meaning academics, was forgotten. At some point, IMF was fighting a losing battle because those who had an economic sustainable education were almost completely out of the country. The military was trying, but they were not trained to rule. The Western world became fed up with the Nigerian military. The only source of revenue was the oil, which was mainly for private pockets. Oil dealers made billions of dollars illegally.

Of course, education during the military rule had no outstanding value and could not support a competitive economy. Like other demands made by the IMF in order to qualify for the loan, these were quietly accepted. All of the IMF's demands were not really accepted, but when the citizens ceased demonstrating, the military then felt Nigerians must have accepted the program. The truth was that Nigerians wanted things to remain the way they had always been if only the oil revenue could be managed well and used in developing public programs and in encouraging private business to grow and prosper.

Privatization in the public view then was simply to hand over the enterprise to the well-to-do people who paid taxes to the military government, and who as usual embezzled the money as they were doing with the oil revenue. The military was so foreign to Nigerians even though the soldiers were their own sons and daughters. Trust was a remote commodity. The military tried harder to gain the trust and respect of the citizens, but to no avail because they wanted the military to protect the country from foreign invasion, not to rule the country because the military could not do both successfully. The people believed in the separation of powers.

Devaluing the Currency

Devaluing the Nigerian currency was a procedure or policy used by the IMF before the loan was to be given to any country. Finally, the loan was given. The amount was about $7 billion at an interest rate of over 15%. Immediately, a cup of garri that had been sold at 5 Kobos per cup was now sold at 75 naira per cup, and buying even a tee shirt was a luxury. People began dying like ants; life expectancy had no meaning (meaning that people were dying sooner and life expectancy was much shorter). The irony is that each time a country's currency is devalued, education, business, and everything that made life worthwhile is affected. Nigeria became an under developing country.

Most of the educated elite had left the country in search of a better life; most of them started doing work such as that of security guards. I was too ashamed seeing my people doing anything to survive. I remembered how proud they had always been. Most of them were academic doctors educated in Britain, some at home, and others in the United States of America. Gradually, the military became aware of the fact that they were not meant to rule (nor capable of it) but to serve their country. The aim of devaluation of a currency was to enable a country to sell its products, but Nigeria had nothing to sell, other than the oil and gold that by then meant nothing because the money made from these products were for individual pockets. The idea of devaluing a country's currency and still hope that the country will eventually recover is an idea beyond human thinking. I am sounding like money is everything, but of course, it is not. However, look at someone with no home, shelter, or clothing to wear and protect their bodies; just imagine the thinking of the decisions that such a person can make.

Human beings are used to certain levels of comfort; i.e., most of the food we eat must be cooked. Deviation from that norm is tantamount to poor living. Farming today is more complicated than one might imagine. A farmer has to buy tools that are appropriate for the work; one has to think and plan regarding when to do specific tasks such as when to harvest. If the farming is for family consumption, the ingredients required to make the harvest palatable must be added. All of these things require money. One truly needs money for the basics in life. However, when your income becomes an opportunity cost, life becomes very miserable or uncomfortable. By "income becoming an opportunity cost", I mean, for example, if you earn $30.00 a month, while your housing costs $10.00, food is $15.00 and transportation is $5.00. Your job is 25 miles from where you live. You, therefore, cannot walk 50 miles every day, meaning walking 25 miles to work and 25 miles back from work. Therefore, you only have money for rent, food, and transportation. You do not have food, clothing and shelter. The result is an individual either pays rent, buys food, and pays for transportation or one buys clothes and has a social life, but paying rent, buying food, and paying for transportation are *opportunity costs* to buying clothing and social activities.

Therefore, when the Nigerian currency was devalued, millions of people had *opportunity costs* because they had money for needs with no money at all for wants, or they either paid for their wants and went without their needs because they could not afford both needs and wants. In this case, needs are *opportunity costs* to wants or wants are *opportunity costs* for needs. Currency devaluation brings so much inflation where fewer goods are available for sale while too much money is available to buy the goods. At the time of the Nigerian currency devaluation, inflation was about 100 percent. Citizens simply lived to eat because that was just what the inflated money could do.

Conforming to *Free Trade* Policies

On the surface, *free trade policies* sound very good, but free in this case means no hindrances. Free trade is like two or more boxers fighting; it is against the law for a qualified heavyweight to fight a featherweight boxer because one might kill the other. If gravity were not defied, the heavyweight would certainly win. Free trade is better done by equals; if not, one must have an advantage, meaning that the one with an advanced economy will certainly be in the most advantageous position. I call that *dumping economic practice*" because the one with an advantage sells goods at a much lower price than the one without the advantage. The most alarming aspect in the whole process is that the one without an advantage will, in the end, cease producing because price and quality will push them out of business.

Returning to our discussion on the Nigerian economy, that is exactly what happened to Nigeria. Other economies were producing for Nigeria and already inflation had taken over the value of the naira. Therefore, at this point Nigeria paid in oil and gas and not money because the country had no foreign reserves; so, it was trade by barter, meaning give me oil and gas when I will give you soap to wash your clothes or to bathe. Nigeria had returned to the old days of bartering. Trade was free and no duties were charged. It was a country of lawlessness. Young people looked for what to eat or how to survive. Parents were unable to control their children, and some parents simply stopped having children because that was tantamount to abuse of children because it takes money to raise children, and without resources to raise a child in the right way, many parents considered that *abuse*. Trade is based on cultures, not just one culture; therefore, when other cultures ae excluded from the equation, the name of such trade is no longer world trade. It might be called *trade* based on the policies of the International Monetary Fund (IMF). I could not tell whether the IMF was helping Nigeria or Nigeria was helping the IMF.

Nigerians knew what was coming; they demonstrated with no fear of guns; many citizens thought it was better to give up life than to live as less than human. Foreign goods and food were rationed to citizens as if they were in refugee camps, not knowing they were in their own homes. The policy went on for some time. The country's military became more foreign than the foreign goods, and they knew it. In the end, the military knew that politics and elections were the better way of selecting leaders and rulers.

Removing Barriers to Foreign Investment and Ownership

Removing the barriers to foreign investment might be fantastic because foreigners will invest in Nigeria; the issue here is that many educated people had left the country. Many of those still in Nigeria were poor and barely had a good education; therefore, it might mean that the investors would come with their own employees. The IMF might mean well for Nigeria, but the idea of the removal of barriers does not sound like running a country properly. You may own your investments if you can pay your taxes. The fact here is that a country wants to borrow money and, of course, have to pay it back. Let us understand one thing—for example, your household has borrowed money for your daughter's tuition for the next semester. Remember that the third semester is in January, and another school year begins. So, how are you prepared to pay for the tuition for that year? In this example, say, your grandmother who died left you with a lake where you may catch a lot of fish and sell; a yearly catch would pay for your daughter's tuition for two years. However, the fact that you simply allowed anyone to fish in your lake with no fees and you are just a peasant fisherman or farmer with no other sources of income means that if you charged fees for fishing in your lake, then you would have a barrier to fishing in your lake or you might rent out the lake for a specific sum, which could help pay the tuition, but you did neither.

This example is much like the IMF barrier removal, but asking you to borrow money which you have to pay back when your infant industries no longer exist, with more than 60% unemployment in the country, constant unrest and lawlessness, young people with no respect for personal and public properties, teachers not paid for six months or more, and parents who are unable to control their children. Of course, today we are talking about the same country, the United States, which has the largest and richest economy in the world. The IMF should understand this large economy did not start as Great Britain or even France, but today is the largest and richest economy in the world. I think that the IMF is mistaken in wanting its debtors to attain a developed culture overnight. The only help the IMF could have rendered Nigeria would have been to go back to a democratic system. Ironically, today Nigeria is the largest economy in Africa and very democratic because they have been able to get back to their own culture that resonated stability and progress.

Selection of Team Members

The ideal team members are those who work for the same plant or office, or an experienced person in the subject with a university or college degree may be acceptable, but whoever is accepted must be willing to learn.

Copies of the cases must be distributed to the parties concerned and must be given a day or two to read and digest the subject material.

Deliberations

The team talks carefully and in depth about the subject matter. Members may ask questions directing them either to the team leader or to any member who can answer acceptably. At this point, the secretary who has been handpicked by the team leader writes down any idea that appears to be acceptable. The deliberations could last longer, but the team leader must always remind the team how to deliberate in an ideal way. Remember that during the period of unwritten deliberations, the team leader or anyone well educated on the teaching of dialogue must conduct a few classes on dialogue. From time to time, members must discipline themselves with the basics of dialogue. Remember that dialogue is a discipline of collective learning. Every deliberation on an ideological format is based on learning from one another or from the team leader. Therefore, a dialogue is defined as a discipline of collective learning and inquiry. Team deliberation must never be rushed nor lay blame on anyone for anything that might go wrong. The team has to take responsibility for the actions and discussions of the team. Before a team member is selected, he/she must know that the team has a collective responsibility for any deliberations that are made and any actions that are taken.

Long List Analysis

Remember that the team has a secretary who writes down the important items and thoughts spoken during the deliberations. Those factual analyses make up what I call "long list analysis." *Long List Analysis* is very important because it includes everyone's contributions; it is very flexible because it could be modified or left as it is. The facts are all over the written deliberations, but not well arranged, but we have to remember that the team has conducted a few classes on dialogue, so they are somehow conversant with the dialogue process and how it operates during deliberations, including providing a space within which attention can be given. It allows a display of thought and meaning that makes possible a kind of collective perception, prejudices, and characteristic patters that lie behind individuals' thoughts, opinions, beliefs, and feelings, along with the roles he/she tend to play habitually. It also offers an opportunity to share those insights (Bohm, Factor, & Garrett, 1991, p. 3).

With all that in mind, let us go back to the IMF's policies in Nigeria. We have to pick up the main points and deliberations or talk. Let us talk about the following:

1. Do you think that the IMF policies are bad for Nigeria, and why?
2. Do you think that the IMF's policies are good for Nigeria, and why? If not, why not?
3. What was the purpose of the loan?
4. Did Nigeria achieve that purpose? If not, why not?
5. Has any country ever achieved their goals for the loans they received from the IMF? If not, why not?
6. The former Director of Budget and Planning in the Federal Ministry of Finance, Chief Onwakir Kuye, observed that the policy prescriptions of the IMF would not move Nigeria forward/ What are those policy prescriptions? Why won't they move Nigeria forward or why are the IMF's prescriptions bad for Nigeria?

7. Chief Omonwale stressed that undesirable imports may be banned absolutely for the protection of the country's nascent industries. Is Chief Omonwale right? If so, why or why not?

8. The IMF economist, Mr. George Soros, was quoted as saying that "globalization created a very open playing field between the industrialized and underdeveloped economies." Mr. Soros urged the world governments and institutions to promote economic growth, which does not rely on "market disciplines." Do you think that Mr. Soros is correct? If not, why not?

9. Do you think that the world environment is a way the world economy works? If so, why have they not done anything to alleviate the suffering of many people? Alternatively, what should they do? (Show professionalism in every answer.)

10. Do you think that the suspension of IMF staff supervision was the right thing to do and why?

Analysis

All the questions generated from the case have to be analyzed carefully, although all of these questions may not carry equal weight and take up the same amount of time. Nothing, however, should be taken for granted. The primary points should be written down by the secretary. In the end, the secretary has to read aloud what he or she has put down, after which a vote is taken. A simple majority vote for the item means that the long list is adopted. Fifty-one percent constitutes a simple majority. However, when the long list is adopted, all the team members are accountable for everything on the list. That is called the principle of accountability.

Let us begin our analysis with Question #1: Do you think that the IMF policies are bad for Nigeria, and why? The answer I give is no, the policies are not good for the people of Nigeria because the IMF directs the use of funds, and they want open markets. The IMF knows that business transactions are primarily based on culture and that every country has a unique culture. However, the IMF wants every business to be conducted in either the American or the British cultures. We know that there is nothing like the European culture or the Western European culture since all of them do not even speak the same language. As I see it, culture derives its meaning from the language people speak or the beliefs that they hold, religious affiliations and even the culture of food we eat among other factors.

It is true that no country may benefit from the IMF loan especially going through the process as a humiliating way of getting the loan. The IMF economist, Mr. George Soros, was quoted as saying that globalization creates a very uneven playing field between developed economies and undeveloped economies. If both economies are subjected to the same economic rules, then, of course, one has to rely on the other as such economic inequality continues. Eventually, the economies of the developing nations become a drag on the developed nations' economies. At this juncture, no country wins. I think it at this time that globalization is not globally understood as much as people think. Every country still looks for the best of its citizens, especially the elected leaders. This may be the right thing to do particularly in previous years. However, in a global economy, we may be thinking locally, but we need the uneven playing field to become more level because countries need global success, which is the only sustainable economy globalization can offer. We have to understand that if the developed countries recognize that the world is playing on a different playing field and still want the world economy to be directed by the global market discipline, then we have to understand that the world is still living with the global economy or something might be wrong. Mr. George Soros helped us understand that the IMF executives have no power to rearrange a loan or even give directives to the contributing nations.

Looking back at what is happening in the world today, we have many Nigerian look-alikes today, includes Greece, Spain, Italy, and a host of other countries. If many Western countries are Nigerian look-alikes economically, do we now attribute the blame to the leaders of those countries? I do not think so, but what I think is that no leader really understands the global leadership track. Sometimes countries enjoy protectionism when the country has advantages in protectionism, and other times, the country may become an advocate of open-market operations. I could say that there is no known trait in global economy where resources like money travel at almost the speed of light. I have always maintained that a business or an economy today contains acts and strategies. In the past, countries depended upon traits like friendliness, diplomacy, prestige, adaptability, and so on. Even Mr. George Soros of the IMF said his organization has no idea on how to find things much better other than what the investors ask them to do. I think this says it all—that the IMF's policies are not even fair to Nigeria.

In business and economics, we have tried for years to point at character analyses of leadership traits by skin and other human differences, but all to no avail. We have to see what is happening in the market daily and adjust quickly where needs are revealed.

Let us revisit *dialogue* as collective learning and inquiry.

The Power of Collective Thinking

The way people talk together in organizations is rapidly being acknowledged as a dialogue to the creation and management of knowledge. According to Alan Webber, former editor of the *Harvard Business Review*, conversation is the means by which people share and often create what they know. Therefore, the most important work in the new economy is creating conversation. (Webber, 1993). Dialogue, the discipline of collective learning and inquiry, is a process for transforming the quality of conversation and the thinking that underlies it (Isaacs, 1993).

Dialogue

Dialogue is the discipline of collective learning and inquiry. It can serve as a cornerstone for organizational learning by providing an environment in which people can reflect together and transform the platform from which their thinking and acting emerges (Isaacs, 1993).\

Isaacs (1993) contended that dialogue is not merely a strategy for helping people talk together; in fact, dialogue often leads to new levels of coordinated action without the artificial and often tedious process of creating action plans and using consensus-based decision-making. Dialogue does not require agreement; instead, it encourages people to participate in a pool of shared meaning, which leads to aligned action.

A case in point is the long dispute between management and the union of Erei/Ikun Farm Settlement in Nigeria. This case is discussed in more detail in my <u>Strategic Management</u> book. The relationship in this case was so bad that the two sides could not greet each other. Their meetings always involved name-calling and lack of respect for each other. However, one day the general manager invited the union leader for morning coffee; the union leader accepted, and they really had a good time instead of not talking to one another. They even went as far as discussing some of the topics that they had been avoiding such as should the settlers' production be inspected monthly or yearly or should the inspections be limited to the accounting books. They found pleasure in discussing these topics and much more. By the end of this meeting, they were very excited about setting a date for another meeting. Before they left, they had drafted basic orders for the general manager and the union leader to sign.

At the meeting that had been set up, the written and signed order was distributed to the participants. The meeting hall became very quiet; some of the participants looked around to the right and the left thinking that they might have entered another meeting in error, but both the general manager and the union leader were sitting right in front of them. Those who came to the meeting to create trouble were disappointed; others who thought there was going to be more drama were asking themselves, "Why the change? Who brought about the change?" Others said, "We now have leaders that are really serious about their jobs of managing the Erei/Ikun Farm Settlement. Participants spent more time praising the two leaders in such a way that before they got down to the real business of settlement, it was already time to adjourn.

The next meeting was scheduled immediately. The leaders and settlers felt very good about the upcoming meeting. Some shopped for better things to wear; some came with their cameras. At the meeting, many of them made new friends; it was clearly a very civilized meeting. Discussion or dialogue was the style of the meeting. Settlers who refused to join the union began considering joining the union; it became a starting point of a real good time in the Erei/Ikun Farm Settlement.

The truth about the world class dialogue was that the then governor of Eastern Nigerian, Dr. M. I. Okpara, had intimated that he would visit the Erei/Ikun Farm Settlement. Then, of course, the fragmentation of management in the farm settlement might be considered by the governor as lapses in management by the general manager. Even though others might view that as selfish, after the visit by the governor, no settler ever wanted to go back to days of disrespect for one another in the farm settlement.

The governor was pleased at the welcome the settlers gave him and was particularly pleased with the settlers and management celebrating and dancing together. The governor also saw that productivity in the farm had risen and that the settlers were looking healthier. Tribal dances were played; all groups mixed with each occasion, and the governor concluded that the farm was the most integrated organization in Eastern Nigeria. He asked all government corporations, private and other entities in Eastern Nigeria to come to the Erei/Ikun Farm Settlement and learn from how management and the union could work together for the good of everyone. Dr. Okpara was actually called *Premier* but chose the work of a governor. Then, the prime minister was in charge of the federal republic of Nigeria's work, while the *Premier* was in charge of a region (such as Eastern Nigeria). At the time, Nigeria was divided into three regions, plus the federal territory—the Eastern Region, Western Region, the Northern Region, and the Federal Territory of Lagos. Today, Nigeria has 32 states, and more are said to be in the works.

Dr. Okpara, who by trade was a medical doctor, strategically told the Erei/Ikun Farm Settlement that his government was going to give the settlement £50 million for road improvements within the farm area and a £100 million loan at 0% interest for small loans to the settlers who needed them. By then, Nigeria was still using the British pound sterling. This was because the Erei/Ikun Farm Settlement had become the most stable large organization in the region with high productivity, and as a role model, the farm settlement deserved a handsome reward. Dr. Okpara also promised the same or more to companies that would try to emulate the management style of the Erei/Ikun Farm Settlement. Settlers and business people were overjoyed, and, in turn, thanked the premier of Eastern Nigeria for his able leadership.

News of the premier's visit to the farm settlement spread like wildfire; the visit was properly covered by every major newspaper in the region. Corporations, public and private, worked so hard to be at the same management level as the Erei/Ikun Farm Settlement because of the monetary rewards the premier had promised to companies in the region. Some companies made it through, but whatever happened, the region succeeded "big time" because competition was at its peak. Many companies became very productive; yet, again, Premier Dr. Okpara rewarded them by giving them more money and promised to do more. Dr. Okpara was very popular in the Eastern Region of Nigeria. He toured the region asking every organization to converse effectively with each other and with their unions and that like the Erei/Ikun Farm Settlement productivity would go up.

Alan Webber (1993), former editor of the *Harvard Business Review*, said that the way people talk together in organizations is rapidly being acknowledged as central to the creation and management of knowledge and that conversation is the mean s by which people share and often create what they know. Therefore, "the most important work in the new economy is creating conversations."

The *Harvard Business Review* (1993) asked, "What is so new about the new economy?" Their answer was, "Dialogue," the discipline of collective learning and inquiry that is a process for transforming the quality of conversation and thinking that lies beneath it.

The Power of Dialogue

William Isaacs (1993) states that complex issues require intelligence beyond that of any single individual. Yet, in the face of complex, highly conflictual issues, teams typically break down, refer to rigid positions, and cover up deeper views. The results are then watered-down compromises and tenuous commitment. Dialogue, however, is a discipline of collective learning and inquiry that can serve as a cornerstone for organizational learning by providing an environment in which people can reflect together and transform the ground out of which their thinking and acting emerges.

William Isaacs (1993) also said that dialogue is not merely a strategy for helping people talk together; in fact, dialogue often leads to new levels of coordinated action without the artificial, often tedious, process of creating action plans and using consensus based decision-making. Dialogue does not require agreement; instead, it encourages people to participate in a pool of share meaning which leads to aligned action.

Even though the former premier of Eastern Nigeria, Dr. Okpara, did not ask companies in the region to practice using dialogue in their decision-making process, rather he asked companies, large or small, to form the habit of talking with one another because those individuals who are not involved in conversation will likely think that he/she is not important or may think the company does not consider them as contributors in terms of knowledge. This may lead to those individuals having low self-esteem problems. Dr. Okpara realized that solving problems together not only brings about economic progress, but also brings about healthy living amongst the participants because a group of healthy minds makes great decisions.

When Alan Webber, former editor of the *Harvard Business Review*, was talking about the power of collective thinking, Dr. Okpara had already commented on the power of collective decision-making in the 1960s. The generational gap between the two men reveals that academics and politics have seen that two heads are better than one when it comes to decision-making. Not only that, but Dr. Okpara and Alan Webber understood what an economic situation would be like if economic decision-making would be left to a chief executive officer with perhaps only one or two senior officers. Today's business is global and complicated; therefore, the situation calls for more hands to analyze deeply and come up with acceptable findings that are more accurate. I became fascinated with thinkers like Alan Webber and Dr. Okpara because they talked about economics, business, or both. Well, as a business scholar. I have to concentrate on what I think will throw more light on my profession. However, before I came across Alan Webber's and Dr. Okpara's comments, there were other systems thinkers like J. Krishnamurti, David Bohm, Donald Factor, Peter Garrett, and many others. Some of them talked about religion, while others had their philosophies based in other disciplines, though based on dialogue. The aim of dialogue is to create a special environment where a different kind of relationship among participants can come into play, one that reveals both high energy and high intelligence (Isaacs, 1993).

The Practice of Dialogue

William Isaacs (1993) commented that the pivotal challenge lies in producing dialogue in practical settings. Dialogue poses a paradox in practice; while it seeks to allow greater coherence among a group of people (remember this does not necessarily imply agreement), it does not impose this. Indeed, dialogue comes up and explores the very mechanisms by which people attempt to control and manage the meanings of their interactions. People often come to a dialogue with the intention of understanding their fundamental concerns in a new way.

Isaacs (1993) further stated that in contrast with more familiar modes of inquiry, it is helpful to begin without an agenda and without a *leader*, although a facilitator is essential, and without a task or decision that needs to be made. This is done by deliberately trying not to *solve* familiar problems in a familiar way, and dialogue opens a new possibility for shared thinking (*The Systems Thinker*, (4)3).

One particular story illustrates the power of this kind of exchange. In Ubagara, which consists of Ikun, Biakpan, Etono I, and Etono II, all the villages combined are considered as a clan. The clan has always been a part of the old Calabar bordering with villages that have different dialects. The clans have always had land disputes. These disputes had always been very disturbing to the British during colonial rule of Nigeria. By the way, the four village clan is also known as Ubaghara. The people of Ubaghara never agreed on anything; they only agreed to disagree.

One day the United Nations dispatched four letters to Ubaghara, each one assigned to a different village. It contained instructions concerning road construction in Ubaghara; Ubaghara was informed that the road was going to pass through the old Ikun road or the colonial road. On a specified date, the United Nations' officials showed up. The meeting continued for a time, and then one of the UN officials asked, "How are you doing?" The participants sat in groups of four, just as in their villages. The Ikun group said they liked the plan; the Biakpan group said they approved the plan, and both Etono I and Etono II also liked the plan. No one believed what was going on. Usually, if the Ikun people like something, the Biakpan people would not like it. These rivalries began after the death of Chief Uno Egim of Ikun, who was the paramount ruler of Ikun, Ubaghara, and beyond. One might have called him a dictator, but the British liked him. Ikun was also the seat of the colonial administration in the region and the headquarters for the Church of Scotland Mission in the region. However, the death of Chief Uno Egim and the beginning of Nigerian independence rendered colonial Ikun ineffective; hence, rivalries sprang up throughout the region.

Because of the rivalries in the region, the situation made any "yes" vote look like Ikun wasn't a factor in the vote. Therefore, every village had a reason or reasons for their vote. The striking point here is that the participants in any Ubaghara meeting, which never had an agenda, agreed on a direction, although for different reasons. The point worth noting is that Ikun people and Chief Uno Egim were not bad people, but it was a different period in history. Some larger villages could have eliminated the smaller villages; killing could have become rampant, but Chief Egim's administration made it possible for the smaller villages to coexist with the larger communities.

Levels and Stages of Dialogue

Dialogue requires creating a series of increasingly conscious environments in which a special kind of *cool inquiry* can take place. The environments that we call *containers* may develop as a group of people becomes aware of the requirements and the discipline needed to create them. A container may be understood, then, as the sum of the assumptions, shared intentions, and beliefs of a group. These create a collective *atmosphere* or climate. The core of the theory of dialogue builds on the premise that changes in people's shared attention can alter the quality and level of inquiry that is possible.

The evolution of a dialogue among a group of people consists of both levels and stages. These tend to be sequential, although once one moves through a stage, one can return to it. Passing through a level usually involves facing different types of individuals and collective crises. The process is demanding and, at times, frustrating but also deeply rewarding (Isaacs, 1993.

Initial Guidelines for Dialogue

1. Suspend Certainties;
2. Listen to Your Listening;
3. Slow Down the Inquiry;
4. Be Aware of Thought; and
5. Maintain Peripheral Attention (Isaacs, 1993, p. 3).

Suspend Certainties. A participant who attends the meeting with a certainty of a case is said to have carried baggage into the meeting place. That may mean knowing the case beforehand or being biased and not following or knowing how to conduct a dialogue. I call the hall in which the dialogue takes place *the hall of collective thinking.* One has to basically suspend everything one has thought one knows and assume the role of a listener, ask questions when questions are required. Do not allow your thoughts to perish with you; say what you think; no one will laugh at you. If one speaks out, other participants will want to know more. However, if one says what one thinks out of certainty, responses to that may begin to be negative towards the person being so certain in their opinions. Fellow participants may be suspicious that you have already heard the case and may a solution from the individual who is so certain. Suspension of certainty is required to enable the system to take its course. Dialogue is supposed to be unfolded as the discussion proceeds. The discussion should create questions of who, what when, and why. All of these create reasons for dialogue. These are not signs for a pep rally. They are signs of the real business of dialogue. Therefore, the professor or instructor in charge of teaching decision-making should make sure that the basic ways of conducting dialogue are clear; otherwise, the situation might get out of hand very quickly and what one finds is noisy communication and dissent that serves no real purpose.

Certainty on a subject like dialogue makes no sense because whatever you are examining might not be where most of the other participants are thinking, and you may be the odd person out in the whole case. It is always excellent to hear what others have to say to enable you to modify your thoughts before you become that *odd person out*. A proverb in my native Calabar, Nigeria says, "If you are very fast in cooking, your food might not be well done." Therefore, if you jump quickly onto a topic in dialogue, without first evaluating your facts, you may not know what you are discussing. Life itself is full of uncertainties; so, if one is always certain about things, it may be a risk not worth taking. In order to be on the same page as your teammates, it is advisable to *look before you leap*.

Listen to Your Listening. A great participant must listen to whatever others are saying to understand their point in the conversation. You do not have to talk before you understand; your lips should not be faster than your mind. Otherwise, again, you may become the odd man out. This is not a pep rally; one has to listen so that one can participate intelligently. Remember that one wants to know "why, what, and how" of an issue. If the questions are answered clearly, then, of course, one may ask other questions for clarification or to throw more light on the conversation, and this may bring in a question into the conversation.

If you want others to listen to what you have to say, you must also listen to what the other participants are saying. Otherwise, you may talk, hear, and understand yourself while the other participants only listen and understand themselves, which means the value of any dialogue is completely lost. This is an academic exercise and therefore understood; otherwise, you cannot analyze what you do not understand, and all that can be done only by listening, questioning, and having input. Otherwise, your input will be *garbage in, garbage out*. One has to open one's ears and pay attention to what others are saying in order to enable you to understand the points that are being made about the issues under discussion.

Listening does apply when you are conducting dialogue. At one point in time, President Reagan was known as *the great communicator*, but without listening, he had nothing to communicate because he could not have had material worthy of responses because he was not listening.

Listening is a vital part of adulthood. As a parent, one has to listen to one's children or one may be giving vague or ineffectual advice that may be nonsense. Therefore, listen to your listening is therefore a vital part in conducting dialogue if one is to contribute during discussions. You know that equality of the participants is important and must be maintained. Speaking of the equality of the participants, it is not the position that each participant holds or the academic standard one has that makes the dialogue, but the fact that all the participants are to be heard, judged, critiqued, and accepted with no fear or favor towards any participant that makes the principle of equality a vital part of a dialogue.

A good listener is a great contributor, and his or her advice in the meeting is always an asset because he/she is a good listener and is able to summarize quickly, isolate facts from fiction, and come up with accurate or nearly accurate predictions or analyses.

As in politics, a good listener is a good person to be with because she/he is able to know how the customers react or what they want, and can then change the direction of the company's production accordingly. By listening, we have to avoid what I call *selective listening*. A case to illustrate this is in my former company, Wilson Maintenance, where I had a cleaning operation in a law firm. Unfortunately, the lawyers who had been good friends from college suddenly began having altercations, and these grew to the point that one of the partners moved to another location. One day, one of my employees said something that could have made a difference in the dispute, but the lawyer he was talking to was not listening. Therefore, he did not understand what my employee was saying.

Listening is very important; perhaps the testimony of my employee in this case could have made a difference. Many students have failed examinations because they have refused to listen to the instructor teacher. A good listener does much better in a logical setting where he or she is always regarded as an excellent contributor in whatever decision-making setting. He or she goes straight to the point because they understand the case.

Slow Down the Inquiry. It is important to find out what really happened while at the same token some fact-finding is unnecessary and time consuming. Some findings become very personal and antagonizing and may even develop into a blame game. In that case, the team leader should remind the team members of their mission. The inquiry should be about what happened, why it happened, and what should be done about it. Inquiry should not be emotional fact finding. Inquiry should be done with the utmost suspension of the baggage that may give the participants divided attention and feelings of despair. In some cases, people begin dialogue with the intention of doing things that they are worried about in a different way; yet, more is said than done.

Inquiry should begin without the following:

1. An agenda;
2. Leader but with a facilitator;
3. No task (decision-making);
4. Do not try to solve; deliberate;
5. Possibility for shared thinking not dictation.

1. Agendas do not maintain a plan for conducting a dialogue; dialogue evolves as the conversations go on. I do not say this deliberation will be complete after a few minutes or one hour. The conversation will wind down by itself, and the facilitator will then ask for the session to move on.

2. Leadership. This may have political and domineering overtones that may defeat the spirit of dialogical equality. Participants may be afraid to speak out and fear retribution from individuals who may be their bosses at their workplace. Facilitators are equal to every other participant, and therefore there is no fear of repercussions whatsoever. At this juncture, the conversation becomes as free as freedom itself.

3. <u>No Task or Decision-Making</u>. The participants are not given time to accomplish anything; they deliberate, and they make no decisions. Dialogical organizations work hand in hand with hierarchical organizations because the final decisions are made by management of the organization. However, management may implement exactly what the dialogue or deliberations submit to them, or management may reject all of the submissions or modify the deliberations. More often than not, management does not reject all of the submissions; they modify the contents and the ideas or if problems persist, management may take the blame and may not take it kindly. Therefore, in order to share blame in case things go wrong, modification is usually the name of the game. But the dialogical deliberations are always within the margin of error, meaning the deliberations are always nearly correct.

The CEO (Chief Executive Officer) and his executives have their own group; they deliberate also. They have to have their own decisions ready to compare with the deliberations and recommendations made by the dialogue group. The executives must know what the dialogue group has said. The group's ideas must never be brushed aside for any reason. In most situations, executives made their decisions on a long list and short-term basis, which may or may not balance with long-term effectiveness.

The United States and the rest of world have just come out of an economic catastrophe that could have brought the world to a standstill and here we go again. The last time the housing bubble was one of the ingredients that kindled the fire (as the expression goes). This time realtors all over the world may be blamed for being greedy. My friend was pre-approved for a $285,000 loan for the purpose of purchasing a residence. No sooner had my friend begun celebrating, than the realtor called him demanding to know if he could produce twenty percent of the asking price as a down payment. If the buyer has no way of having such an amount, then he or she will have two mortgages to pay, and when he or she can no longer afford such payments, then they will have to default on the loan, eventually bringing down the mortgage value of the entire neighborhood. Another *bubble* is on the horizon. Now, we see how a small real estate firm's commission could grow to become a nightmare to the mortgage industry. This means that the profitability of the realtor never balances with the long-term effectiveness of his or her own business.

The Banks should have a dialogical meeting with the realtors, meaning that the realtors should have dialogue with the banks. The realtors should take note of the following:

1. Listen to the bankers;\
2. Slow down the inquiry;
3. Maintain peripheral attention during deliberations that take place before them.

My point here is for both the banks and the realtors to be on the same page when doing business with the public. Again, this point is the banks may want the consumer to make a down payment of about 3.5% of the loan while the realtor may want 20% down. In most cases, the 20% is borrowed with a high interest rate, and sometimes the 20% might be interest only loan, which compounds the problem for the borrower. This reminds me of the last economic downturn that occurred in 2008 before Mr. Obama took office as president of the United States.

Now, I can emphatically say that the bubble began from the grass roots, which eventually affected the big banks. It is unbelievable that a neighborhood realtor could be one of the causes of an economic downturn, but it actually happened. Since everyone is viewing the big banks, the small realtor gets away with *murder*, so to speak. The questions are: How did the loans get to the big banks? Who did what? If we can trace action from there, we could begin to see how the housing bubble began in the United States. Again, here we can say that the realtors' profits do not balance with the economic effectiveness of the country.

4. <u>Do not try to solve problems</u>. Just deliberate and recommend. The dialogue team, as I call them, must understand at least the preliminary part of dialogue or how dialogue is used for conversations. They must read and understand the issues as given to them by their leaders. The team must talk about the case, analyze it, and ask questions. The person recording the information must put down all relevant facts. Everything must be reviewed and corrected. Facts must be rewritten, followed by elimination by substitution. In this case, facts may be duplicated, so some lines may be cancelled out while some facts may not fit into the analysis. The whole deliberation is then copied for all participants to point out the irrelevant facts. After which, the recommendations are made from the deliberations.

<u>Submission</u>. The leader or the facilitator then submits the recommendations to the CEO and his team of final decision-makers. This team consists of high-ranking officers and professionals who then compare their findings with the recommendations made by the dialogue team. The decision-makers may accept or modify both findings that now become the final decision.

5. <u>Shared Thinking</u>. From the recommendations to the final decision-making group, no dictation is allowed; everything is about shared thinking and participation in the deliberations. If any part of the findings is found to be dictated, then the final decision may be nullified, and the process starts again from the beginning. Shared thinking and deliberations are the core of dialogue. If one of the participants objects to something said, then he or she should be allowed to say their version that may bring counter reactions from other participants. If the participant is still dissatisfied, the entire group should examine that person's objection until the majority agrees to it. Remember that there is no consensus. Consensus is what you can live with for now, but does not alter the underlying causes of the problems in the first place. Shared

thinking is a shared understanding and is the basis for democratic decision-making.

Be Aware of Thought. Do not enter the deliberations with an ill-conceived notion, meaning do not enter the meeting room with the attitude of "I know what happened" before you have heard what has happened. If you do, the consequence may well be appearing as a joke and useless. Carrying thought into the meeting room is even against the practice of dialogue. Entering the room with what caused the problems will make you appear to be a judge and a witness. We have been advised that in order to develop- the highest level of dialogue, we have to suspend our thoughts about what we think might be the root causes of the issues at hand and how the problems can be solved even before the draft of the case is presented. This might be an example of how talk can affect a conversation.

Thoughts tantamount to pre-judging that causes more problems than it solves. Even in courts, the judge must hear from both sides to enable him make a verdict; otherwise, it is not a balanced judgment. It would be a one-sided judgment, which probably would be overturned on appeal. I know it is not an easy task for a human being to engage in a problem-solving deliberation with an open mind, especially when the CEO is involved or in a case of embezzlement or perhaps a case involving a superior officer. However, that does not help in finding out anything but deepens the misery.

Prejudice is a next-door neighbor to prejudging, meaning analyzing something negatively. Again, no one wins because prejudging is based on short-term profitability, which doesn't balance with long-term effectiveness. People have been sent to prison for offenses they did not commit, but some of these cases have been quickly overturned, while others take a long time to find out the truth. The fact is that truth will always be known. Many companies fail because of impatience; they don't have the patience to do what is known as due diligence—the time consuming deep analysis to discover the hidden parts. That is why the facilitator's advice is important to keep the team on the right path. The fact is that during the dialogue process, many minds may be changed until the process is completed. I know that time is money, but thought is an element of new ideas and in some cases an element of failure. However, *time* and great thinking make a perfect business.

    <u>Maintain Peripheral Attention</u>. *Little by little* said a thoughtful boy I will employ learning a little every day. If one pays a little attention daily on the decision-making process before the decision is made, one learns so much by the time the decisions are made. One becomes so deficient in decision-making process, especially in the use of dialogue in decision-making. In decision-making, paying attention does not mean one did so because of the little experience one has had. One may have had a lot of experience in the process and procedure of conducting dialogue, but all other things might be variable, meaning that the cases and the analyses may be different while the procedure and process of dialogue remains constant.

In Conducting Dialogue

Cases	Variable
Analysis	Variable
Procedure	Constant
Processes	Constant

Case: Why does the company have low sales?
Analysis: Product quality, competition, fewer sales personnel
Procedure: Setting what needs to be done
Processes: Suspension of thought; maintaining attention; asking appropriate questions

Dialogue and Organizational Learning

    Years ago, as a young man growing up with my parents and my grandfather (or *Grandpa* as I called him), I was with my grandfather who was one of the local rulers. People went to *Grandpa* for settlement of minor disputes. He charged nothing; he merely united friends, brothers, sisters, spouses and families. Some would come to *Grandpa* laughing with the hope of peaceful settlement, but for various reasons, they had stopped talking to each other. When they tried to talk, they began shouting at each other just as if they were fighting. I asked *Grandpa* to tell me what could cause people to behave like that, and he would laugh and tell me, "Son, this is what I call a breakdown in communication; they should not use this method in settling their disputes. Rather, they should use what I called dialogue" "You see, "my *Grandpa* would continue, "People understand issues differently, even though they hear the same things Mr. A, told the audience. Mr. A, by the way, is the right source of the story. I asked him, "*Grandpa*, is that also a breakdown in communication?" He said, "Son, that is true and much more than that, but listen or watch and hear what I will do in the next few days."

Grandpa separated the disputants and talked to them individually and collectively. I thought what he was doing was building the formulation of their dispute the way each of them would understand it. Whatever my grandfather was doing, it worked for him and the people he served. However, today situations are much more complicated than in my grandfather's time, although the results may be nearly the same. My contention here is that in my grandfather's time it took people of influence to bring people together for discussions even without being paid. To be candid, the Ikun system had been like that for over five centuries; however, my grandfather's system was more about settling disputes rather than decision-making because it required a lot of agreement, which is difficult in conducting dialogue in the modern age.

Even though much work has been done in bringing the system to where it is today, we still have a lot of work to do for future generations. Edgar H. Schein (1993) in a paper he wrote said, "Clearly, we need ways of improving our thought processes, especially in groups where the solution depends upon people reaching a common formulation of the problem. It is for this reason that governments, communities, and organizations are focusing increasing attention on the theory and practice of dialogue." Proponents of dialogue claim that it holds promise as a way of helping groups reach higher levels of consciousness, and thus be more creative and more effective. At the same time, the uninitiated may view dialogue as just one more form of communication technology or nothing more than a new variation of sensitivity training (Schein, 1993).

Schein (1993) also commented that all problem-solving groups should begin with a dialogue format to facilitate the building of sufficient common ground and mutual trust to make it possible to tell what is on one's mind.

I do understand Schein's definition of dialogue, but dialogue in any shape is a positive idea for public and private organizations. It is interesting to note that Mr. Schein's emphasis is on building trust and knowing the ideological differences one may have with his or her would-be business partners. This means that building a lucrative business could be a result of trusting one another and knowing the ideological differences one may have with a business associate in a particular business. You both may proceed to a further step if both of you are comfortable with each other. However, dialogue as a *collective learning and inquiry* may look a lot different from Mr. Schein's idea of dialogue because dialogue as collective learning has the following characteristics:

1. Requires a lot more to participate;
2. Results may be the goal here;
3. Deliberations must be intensive;
4. Questions are asked by anyone on the team.
5. Answers are given by anyone on the team.
6. Long-list deliberations are written down by the team's clerk.
7. A facilitator is always standing by to correct and redirect the team to the goal that brought them together in the first place.

8. The team's clerk writes a short list. A lot of questions and answers are asked and given.
9. Finally, the team sends the short list to the decision-making team headed by the CEO.
10. The decision-making team also follows the same procedures and then compares their own short list with that which has been submitted by the team. The facilitator cannot tamper with the team's deliberations; otherwise, the short list is null and void, and the process has to begin again.\
11. If both the short list of the decision-making team and the submission team have many differences, some members of the submission team, including the facilitator, may be asked to appear before the decision-making team to explain how the team arrived at the short list that was submitted.
12. If both teams have similar short lists, the team's short list may be adopted as the decision of the company, or if the short lists only have minor differences, the final decision-making team may modify the differences, which may or may not be accepted by the CEO. If the team does not have enough support to overrule the CEO's decision, the final decision making team may be dissolved and a new group of final decision-makers be appointed. If that happens again, the CEO must resign. The CEO's short list automatically becomes the law of the company, but must never conflict with the law of the land; if it does, the law of the land takes precedence.

Usually Mr. Schein's idea comes in the form of partnership agreements. When the agreement is drawn up, all the opposing factors must be modified or the process stops right there. I remember when I invited my friend to my mortgage loan office in downtown San Francisco. I asked him if he was open to becoming a partner in a maintenance business with me. Without hesitating, he said, "Yes." He asked me right then what his title was going to be. I told him that he was going to be the chairman while I was going to be the president and CEO. He objected emphatically and told me that he wanted to be president and CEO. I told him that our positions and titles would be interchangeable. He said he desired to be the first president and CEO. I asked him why, and he could not come up with a convincing fact. I told him I have been managing my own business for over ten years; I had connections and more contact, and besides, I had an MBA. He was not convinced, and I realized he would not be a serious partner at all. Since he left my office, we have not heard from each other.

Since I mentioned the dream of owning a maintenance business to one of my friends before, my friend called a week later and told me he found a maintenance business for sale. I went with him to review the business. I made a feasibility study on the business, found that it was feasible. I bought the business and assumed ownership with my own management style immediately. In a few weeks, I had quite a number of contracts, and the number of my employees grew from five to fifteen. Then, I realized that in some cases the end of a partnership agreement goes with friendship, but that might have an isolated incident.

Dialogue differences and trust may not be seen quickly; they might be in process. The first test of a one-on-one style of dialogue is when serious profits are made and then there is the question of how to spend the money and who owns what in the division of the money. Dialogue in a stressful situation is really a true measure of one-on-one dialogue expressions. Therefore, dialogue may or may not be a true measure of what your partnership in the months to come or may make you feel good at the outset. Dialogue might also give you a false sense of trustworthiness in business. In any environment where money is made, one should be ready for the unpredictable events, which may or may not have anything to do with dialogue.

Organizational Learning

Dialogue at the executive level is not enough for organizational learning to occur. The process of communicating across hierarchical levels of an organization will require further dialogue because of the likelihood that different strata operate with different assumptions. If the initial learning has occurred in groups below the executive level, as is often the case, the problem of creating a dialogue across hierarchical strata is even more essential because it is so easy for the higher level to undermine the learning of the lower levels (Schein, 1993).

I have no problem with hierarchical organizations; a dialogue organization can exist hand-in-hand with a hierarchy. The fact is some hierarchical organizations live very much in the past; they have the information; they give you the order to carry it out because the executives think they know it all, whereas those who actually do the work daily are the lower level employees. It is like wearing your shoes, but another person will tell you that your shoes are bothering you; it makes no sense. Similarly, a corporation without a CEO is like a country without a president or a prime minister. You have to blame someone when something goes wrong and praise someone for the good work.

CHAPTER 7
BUSINESS OR ORGANIZATIONAL POLICY

CHAPTER 7

BUSINESS OR ORGANIZATIONAL POLICY

Definition

Business or organizational policy is a defense course of action adopted by a company for the sake of what is great to do or courteous to do in the name of good business. The policy may be the brainchild of handpicked participants who deliberated and sent their deliberations to a group of policymakers of the company who also held their own deliberations, which the policymakers may accept the submitted documents, reject, or modify. If the deliberations are great, the policymakers adopt the documents to become the policy of the company. If the deliberations are modified, these also become the company's policy. However, if the deliberations from the submissions and the ones from the policymakers are not acceptable, the procedure begins again.\

Therefore, business and organizational policy is an adopted course of action for effective management. Remember that the submitted deliberations are made available by the participants who were trained in how to use dialogue for discussions. Questions are asked and answers are given by the facilitator or by any of the participants. The clerk for the deliberations has written down the deliberations, of which he or she is also a participant and elected by the rest of the participants for the work of clerk. The deliberations team has both a short-term deliberation and a long-term deliberation. Short-term deliberations are derived from the long-term ones by the procedure I call elimination by substitution. Amongst two similar deliberations, one has to be eliminated. The policymakers group consists of the CEO, the Chief Financial Officer (CFO), Chief Engineer, and other high-ranking officers, and some people from other companies may be asked to participate and be paid for their assistance.

Making a decision in today's economy has become very complicated because of the worldwide competition. In the interest of our discussion, I will refer to the submission by a group as a lower level decision-making, while the CEO's group will be known as the upper level decision-making. The lower level is also made up of professionals and specialists in various disciplines, and there is representation by ordinary workers. The company should not forget to inform its employees to participate if they think they have relevant contributions to be made.

A Case In Point. There was a company that had low production problems, and as such, smaller income. The customers were worried, and the Board of Directors became very concerned. Therefore, both levels of decision-makers were appointed to investigate the issues. After a series of dialogue questions and answers, deliberations were drawn up and the short list had been sent to the upper level decision-makers. When the whole room was quiet, one of the employees stopped by; one of the managers thought he was a troublemaker and shouted, "Hey, how can I help you?" The employee spoke to the gathering of the executives, "Please, sirs, I have something to say about the subject you are discussing. The CEO responded, "Please, go on." The employee then told the officers that he had been documenting what had been happening in the plant. He told them that for about three months after 2:00 p.m. the engine would be running but the productivity would be nearly zero.

The employee further asked the CEO to allow him to tell his personal story. The CEO again responded, "Go on." The employee told the group that he had worked for the company for over 25 years and the he had a wife and three children, two boys and one girl, and that most of the three months each time he got home, he began weeping because he thought the dream he had for his children was dying. He said that he couldn't go to college because there was nobody to sponsor him. However, his children and his job had renewed his hope. The employee said he could not tell anybody because he thought someone might ask him to keep quiet.

On that note, the CEO adjourned the meeting and asked all those attending to meet with him at the plant at about 1:30 p.m. They assembled at the plant and observed the output with the young man who had told his story. It turned out the story was true, and by this time, they had spent over $15 million on the plant. The CEO personally thanked the employee. Now, every break they can possible take starts from 2:00 p.m. Productivity picked up and so did revenue. The young man received multiple promotions and remained an example for the company.

Thereafter the CEO became a believer in participative decision-making. He became very respectful towards the employees and would always want to hear their opinions on issues. On that premise, the CEO created an opinion box where everyone had access to place his or her ideas. The decisions the CEO and his executive team could not go any further because the hidden obstacle had been found and the problem solved Sometimes, it takes just one dedicated employee to save an entire company. Already, a lot of money had been spent just to come up with a solution, yet all to no avail. The employee was right by not telling anyone about what he had uncovered because he might have been prevented from seeing the executives. Even though the problem had been identified and solved, the idea of a solution by participation remained the company's policy.

<u>Workshop</u>. Another component of my study is the practical part that simplifies what I have been talking about. The workshop is

divided into two groups—the upper level made up of the CEO and other executives, while the other group is the lower level made up of professionals, workers, specialists, and the like. Therefore, a workshop could be defined as a group of people who meet from time to time for a study in a specialized discipline in search of better outcomes.

An example would be a workshop on how to increase productivity. Members of the workshop team might either be employees of the company or selected from other companies or institutions, but must have both practical and academic knowhow on subject of the discussions. Besides that, a copy of the discussions is given to each team member as a homework assignment. Much emphasis is placed on knowing what this assignment is all about because one simply cannot effectively participate in what you do not understand. The manager or facilitator of the team knows that all team members need to be on the same platform of understanding before the team can proceed to the next level of deliberations on the case. Again, having a good grip on what the case is about will enable members to ask relevant questions. If the leader allows the process to proceed when just a few of the members clearly understand the case, then, of course, the analysis will not have the intended results as such, and the short and long-term deliberations would be skewed and probably would be rejected at the upper level, and the whole process would have to begin again.

Instances such as not knowing the case study very well before beginning deliberation speak much about the leaders overseeing the process. We can see that the process itself is very expensive even when all things are equal. Therefore, in the case of starting all over, this would mean financial loss for the company. Bearing with the subject is primary and that knowing the case study is tantamount to knowing or understanding the subject matter. As much as we understand the financial costs in beginning the process again, we should also understand more that not starting the process gain will bring in more financial disruption than ever before because the company's policies may be erroneous and that may bring the needed revenues down to the point of the company going out of business. Business policy, participative decision-making, and workshop are powerful combinations and sensitive in decision-making because any mistakes could further cost the company.

However, mistakes are different from differences of opinion. Mistakes—the facilitator may authorize the team to go on with its deliberations or discussions when these are not yet grounded in dialogue, the members don't understand the situation, they cannot ask the right questions, and give off-the-topic answers. Otherwise, most of the things said or done in due course may be dominated by mistakes.

The Case	Members 1	Members 2	Members 3
Facilitator Sentences or Words	Mistakes	Opinion	Correct answers or Questions
This is about collective learning	Listen to me; your talk is irrelevant.	Talk one after the other.	Collective learning and inquiry
What is dialogue?	Common Sense	Learning	Collective learning and inquiry
How many levels do we have on this case?	1 ½	3	2
What is the case we are having now?	About husband and wife.	Profit	Lost revenue
What are the names of the levels in this case	Great Level	Highest Level	Lower and Upper Levels

Is this a manufacturing company?	We are talking about high school.	Sales Company	Manufacturing Company
Are the lower and upper levels of this meeting funded by the government or the company itself	I think that the government is responsible for what is going on here.	I think that a bunch of millionaires are helping.	The company we work for is paying the bills

We can see from every column in the previous figure that the questioner was the facilitator, the boss of the lower level. He asked members 1, 2, and 3 the same question although he applied shields to prevent the others from hearing the answers given by other members. The answers were very different, indicating that the eight members on the Mistakes column (1) never truly read the case study because they had no right to do so and the members on column (2) barely read or understood the case study. In a case such as that, the entire figure is taken to the upper level to let the CEO and his staff know that the lower level members were not ready for the project. In that case, the members may either start again from the beginning or be replaced. The third column remains intact because the members did their assignments perfectly well.

It could also be read across. Reading across, let's look at question four:

What is the case we are having now?	About husband and wife.	Profit	Lost revenue

In this case, we can see that the standard deviation of answers given by Members 1 and 2 are star gazing, meaning that the differences in the answers given are far apart and that could come from the fact that they never read the text or they read the text without understanding it. This is an issue that the facilitator must not react alone; the facilitator must refer the matter to the upper level management because it may entail additional expenditures. The upper level with the CEO participating may decide to give members 1 and 2 a second chance to read the text or be excused from the team. All things being equal, deliberations begin from where the long and short-term lists are derived and are sent to the upper level where the lower level's version can be rejected or accepted, and/or modified or accepted in its entirety as the by-laws of the company or organization.

What Is Our Business?

Sometimes we need to be reminded about what we are doing or intending to do. This will keep us in line. Here we want to formulate a business policy because we have begun to lose ground to our competition and because we no longer understand what we are doing. For the past decade, we dominated the profitability of the industry, and now we are struggling to break even. What might have caused this to happen? Can we figure out how to get back to where we were?

The answer to the question of whether we can regain our momentum is, of course, yes. This reminds me about my dissertation research. Many of the companies I visited had abandoned the feasibility study they had made before starting their businesses. The fact is that since management is an artistic work, when they use one or two other methods of management in making profits, the managers completely forget about the feasibility study drawn up earlier, which had given the hope of being a successful business owner or manager. Now, going back to the dusty feasibility study, the manager has no idea what the earlier ideas were. The ideas that made him profits have been overused, and the company is running out of ideas.

The question "What is our business?" now becomes very important because one has forgotten what one is supposed to be doing. There are many other reasons besides forgetting what you were meant to be doing simply because you made a one-time profit and felt that was the only way to make profits. Remember that what you were meant to be doing is included in your feasibility studies, which may include the following:

1. Location of the business;
2. How to obtain raw materials, if applicable;
3. How decisions could be made;
4. What the product is;
5. The usefulness of the product;
6. The audience;
7. The causes of the decision-making;
8. Detailed analysis of facts about income and expenditure;
9. Expansion and contraction; and
10. Competition.

Location of the Business. This could be where the business is situated or where the decision is made. The site of the business is very important; a good location may curtail a number of decisions to be made. This means that you may have fewer decisions to make, following the fact that you may have fewer financial problems. Many people believe that "if your car is not broken, you should not try to fix it," or you may create more problems. Following this adage, companies or businesses tend to save money at good locations because of having fewer problems. A case in point is the Sunrise Company I founded. The company with which I was dealing had over 1500 employees and was owned by the City and County of San Francisco. Sunrise Vending is at the tail end of retail. The company sells candy removed from their bags or containers into canisters of the machines. The machine contains three canisters, and the customers simply slide one quarter and turn the handle clockwise when the quarter has been entered. The candy comes out in quantities set by the company that manufactures the machine. The candy could be M&Ms or Cashew Nut or any other candy that can be of the appropriate size for the machine. Any country's coin that is of the size of a US quarter could also buy the candy from the same machine.

The interesting aspect of this situation is the rate of turnover; after about two weeks of filling the six canisters with candy, someone has to go back and clear the canisters because they are completely empty. The business was good from every angle; the rate of turnover was as great as the customer participation in deciding what they needed or wanted. Therefore, I always bought the right candy for the customers. The turnover might be important, but another big factor is proximity to the sources of candy. If Sunrise's purchasing source of candy was very difficult, this could be a big obstacle in supplying the customers with what they wanted. This very location is about ten minutes away from where candy is sold wholesale.

Other factors are important, but transportation was another factor that gave me the strength to work harder. Truck rentals were nearby; our drivers might go and get the truck or if the trucking company received more money, they could send their own drivers to make the delivery. Although some of my customers' locations might not be easily accessible, but there were vehicles to get to those locations as needed. Locations are very important for a business, but it is more so for some companies than others; it all depends on the type of company and product the company sells. What I am talking about is PG&E (as an example) might not necessarily be located where my Sunrise candy machines provide candy products, while PG&E processes electricity and gas. Gas, electricity, and candy are not really comparable as products to be sold at the same location. Location is a big part of doing business in either sales or manufacturing.

A friend of mine owns a manufacturing company in a remote area of California. It is not easy for an individual to go there and buy just a few of the products unless he or she was a wholesale buyer equipped with the necessary transport to purchase and bring the items to their own site. Therefore, my friend has a policy of shipping finished goods to any destination in California although shipping charges are required. The point here is that even though the location may not be ideal, it has to be balanced with the measures that enable delivery inconvenience. My friend took all these measures because he wanted to cut manufacturing costs.

How to obtain raw materials, if applicable; In all normal circumstances it is advisable to locate a manufacturing company as near to the source of raw material as possible, especially if the raw materials are bulky, difficult to transport, and located on inaccessible roads with other difficult accesses. The finished manufacturing product may be lighter, more compact, and can be shipped in safety to the customers, and even more so if the products are selling well. In many cases, the costs of finished products are passed onto the consumers, but there are circumstances where that cannot occur because competition is particularly fierce. If other competitors sell at 40 percent less, the company is in trouble; the company with the higher prices is lost in price competition. That means the company spends more to make the products.

In this case, the game changes because the losing competitor now makes better products than his competition and a better product will sell easier than an inferior one. This game changer will now make the former losing company make better profits and still gain by cutting costs. Much of the profits may be reinvested in the company because of changing technology. Before the competitor can catch up to the product quality, the company must have completed research on another phase of product quality. Unless some unforeseen circumstances occur in the economy, it may be impossible for Company "A" and Company "B" to end up as rivals again.

One must remember that Company "B" grabbed the advantage in the price competition from Company "A" in the niche it developed. If Company "B" refuses to work harder, the situation could be reversed.

This means that no company is secure; every business must work harder all the time, must not be complacent about doing better than its competitors, with the knowledge that most companies fail because they have become contented with the level they have attained in either price of product or quality competition.

How Decisions Could Be Made

Decisions are made in many ways, but in my analysis, I think there are three different ways of decision-making that are popular in any country. These are political decision-making, business decision-making, and participative decision-making.

Political decision-making involves political parties, the vision and mission of the party based on the promises the politicians made to the electorate. Politicians will always state what their party represents. What they believe and what the party believes may be different, but one will never know until the politician is elected. That is where the game begins. The politicians who wants a decision on his/her concern to take place must first prepare a bill; the bill must be read before either the appropriate committee of the House or the Senate. If the bill passes the committee, it then goes before the full House or Senate where it will be debated and a vote taken. If it passes, then it must go to the other legislative chamber for passage or modification, and then to the president for signing if it is passed by both houses.

Political decision-making sometimes may be complicated; it usually follows party lines, and at times, it may affect only the area of which the author of the bill represents—his district or state. In most cases, the majority makes political decisions, and it does not matter if the support for the bill comes from both or either party. In a democratic republic, political decisions are frequently viewed as victories for the party that sponsored the original bill because no one person can overturn it. It may be tested in court to assure the people of its constitutionality and its viability in the law. For example, Obamacare has passed both houses of Congress, and even though the House of Representatives was held by the Republicans and the Senate (at that time) by the Democrats, it has become difficult, if not impossible, for the Obamacare law to be overturned or reversed by the Republican Party once the law was passed. Even then, the law as contested before the Supreme Court, where it was again upheld by the court.

Business decision making, however, is one simply an individual making decisions, tantamount to a dictatorship. The CEO by himself or with a few other company officials may dictate to the company what is to be done. The decision-makers may never be aware of everything about the company, but they may override every suggestion made by people who do their work on a daily basis, and in the end, the end never justifies the means, and he CEO could have a second chance or be removed by the board of directors. I remember Mr. Iacocca, the former CEO of Ford Motor Company, a very successful chief executive officer. However, what many people do not know is that the CEO had very capable lieutenants to whom he listened, and they contributed their knowledge very effectively. Since they wanted to keep their positions, it was a situation where everybody had to be the best he or she could be for the success of the company. The old adage stipulates that two heads are better than one.

Heads. When we talk about heads, we are truly talking about those who have the academic knowhow in the field and can come up with ideas at a moment's notice. I mean remembering when he or she encountered similar things in the university or somewhere and could readily come up with some creative ideas for solving problems, which, in turn, got others to remembering other situations that might lead to a solution to the problem they were facing currently. Academic achievements might not be the only criteria to solving a business problem. Some people are very good at defying the odds, never believing that they cannot solve a problem until one day they arrive at the answer. Two heads are fantastic, but a combination of academics and situation can make a great difference.

Situation. My own life is full of situations. I remember when I was completing my coursework in my doctoral program, and I was seriously confronted with serious financial problems. I could pay my rent, but I could not afford my school fees, which quickly grew to over $25,000. At that point, the Dean of Student Affairs called me into his office and carefully went through with me my record of payments, even though payment arrangements had been made for me. Well, I couldn't argue with that. The Dean asked me if I had a few thousands to keep the situation at bay. The truth was that at that time I was unable to buy a cup of coffee and a doughnut, let alone $1,000 for school. The Dean looked at me sympathetically and told me the rules of the school were that I had to leave school until I had a reasonable amount to pay for the school fees, but he never defined what was *reasonable*. Well, I thanked him for being sympathetic about my financial situation, but I promised him to be back in a couple of months. I looked for a few low-interest paying loans, told them about my situation and asked one company to give me two and a half days to make up 40 hours, while I asked the other one straight five days, 40 hours, and over time, both accepted.

A few months later, I came up with over $10,000, and I was asked to return to school. However, since I was no longer in a hurry because I had nine units to complete my coursework, I hesitated a bit before registering the next semester. However, I went back and paid off what was due. I completed my degree. My whole life has been full of situational issues, but I have kept defying the odds. In high school, just a few years after the British handed over administration of Nigeria to Nigerians, there was no one who could pay my school fees that were about 80 British pounds a year. As a young man, I dreamed frequently of being a medical doctor. I told my mother. She believed me because before I was 21 years old I was already teaching in primary school with the Church of Scotland Mission. A few of my so-called friends heard about it and began making fun of me or my dream or both by singing a song which went "Cut your coat according to size." I confronted them and laughed as I always do and then asked, "If I cut my coat according to my size, who then will wear the other half of my coat?" They could say nothing. I left teaching and began trading in foodstuffs during the holidays. However, the Nigerian Civil War began about that time, and young men like me were severely at risk. However, the dream was still alive, and now I have my Ph.D. instead of an MD. In the United States, there are countless stories of people who have defied the odds.

There are many countries, groups, and individuals who have been confronted with difficult situations and are always very hard working, very creative, and overachieving. However, they do not ask "Why us?", "Why me?". The only thing to say at that point is "Why not?" Situational things are never the end; they are the beginning of new ideas, a new era, and a new understanding. I saw firsthand. Think about great men and women whom you have known or read about from your own country or state. They did not become great overnight; they worked all day and sometimes all night looking for a breakthrough, Without the "why us?" or "why me?". Over the years, I learned a phrase that says, "There has to be a better way!"

Participative Decision-Making. This is as old as human existence. In the early years, paternal family members of a village gathered in the village square and arranged for where in the bush the next hunting party would take place, but usually the most powerful ones would talk the loudest because then people respected power, and intelligence always took the back seat. However, in the end, the family or villagers would feel happy that they consummated a better arrangement. Then, the paramount chief or the village elder would take credit. The village chief's council would then meet. The paramount chief would invite other chiefs, tell them about the recent meetings with the villagers and intimate to them what needed to be done. Of course, there was no opposition. Thereafter, the town crier would be sent to make the announcements around the village including details of the hunt, date, age grade, and punishment for not attending. Group hunting was popular then and a source of hides and skins that enhanced trade.

So, early men knew the usefulness of making decisions as a group. It was also through the use of group decision-making that they were able to fight intertribal wars successfully. Actually, tribal group decision-making is as old as early man. There is much confusion in writing about group decision-making. Sometimes, authors will discuss task work and mistake that for teamwork or talk about business management with some elements of a group that they also called teamwork. In fact, my dissertation was on teamwork in business organization. Throughout my research, most of the things said were very good for business or management studies. They talked about task work, as in the case of President Carter and specialization as practiced by the Post Office where one person sold stamps while another stamped the mail. Having the job done is management, a vital method a company uses and comes from decisions made; therefore, the decision-making method is the nucleus of management. If a company makes poor decisions, it simply implements poorly; that is "garbage in, garbage out."

Therefore, I decided to work harder on participative decision-making. The success of a company depends on its ability to analyze effectively and make great decisions. It could be loss of money due to poor products or not being able to compete in the marketplace. In each case, the strategy for solving the problems differs, sometimes to a very great extent and sometimes only slightly. Sometimes you remind yourself what you think you should be in five years' time. Participative decision-making has proven over time a useful tool for effective decision-making. Overall, decision-making largely depends on situations. If you are losing money, you may not have the necessary resources for expansion. First, ask yourself why you are losing money. Write down some cardinal points to represent elements responsible for the organization losing money. Perhaps this is a turning point for you to invite others to participate in the decision-making. It may not be an issue to invite others to participate in analyzing your viewpoint and their own viewpoints, but there could be a big issue if your company fails due to poor decision-making. Sometimes managers or the CEO fails in business because of their egos; they want to be leaders and be known as leaders. Others are not knowledgeable enough to participate in the decision-making, but before the cock crows, they fumble three times and fail miserably. Then, the board of directors will be all over the CEO and even demand his resignation.

Participative decision-making in the face of competition in this era of a global economy is not a luxury but a necessity. The CEO might be an economist but not a micro manager; he or she knows why the economy, domestic or international, is behaving the way it is and what can be done to combat inflation but with little idea why "Mr. Tom" looks down on women in the workplace, even though both graduated from the same university at the same time, where a woman was a valedictorian. That CEO may not want employees to report about problems; if one does, that person might be considered a *troublemaker*. Even a CEO with an MBA is never all rounded. What do you think about a CEO who appoints Ph.D., MBA, M.A., B.S. degree holders and just high school graduates into the decision-making process?

As a business owner, I know that birds of the same feather usually flock together; that means that the high school graduate communicates more with his or her counterparts. The CEO may discourage that, but eventually the high school graduate may feel shy arguing things with people who hold higher degree. This is a phenomena ingrained in the human psyche. Sometimes it gets better, but in most cases, that is the way it is. Where everyone is represented, the viewpoints arise very clearly. Sometimes, the viewpoints represent the individuals' academic levels and experience, experiences, exposure to varying circumstances, companies they have associated with and economic standards. However, academic degrees may not be a yardstick for some of the participants because they are naturally intelligent.

<u>What is the Product?</u> The product in this case is decision-making, but we do not simply start decision-making. We must understand some prerequisites such as dialogue. I have defined dialogue several times in

this book and in my book on strategic management, but let us go over dialogue again.

Dialogue is a discipline of collective learning and inquiry. Dialogue is exploring the roots of the many crises that face humanity today. It enables inquiry into, and understanding of, the parts of processes that fragment and interfere with real communication between individuals, nations, and even in different parts of the same organization. In our modern culture, men and women are able to interact with one another in many ways. They can sing, dance, or play together with little difficulty, but their ability to talk together about subjects that matter deeply to them seems invariably to lead to disputes, division, and often to violence. In my view, this condition points to a deep and pervasive defect in the process of human thought (Bohm, Factor, & Garrett, 1991).

David Bohm, et al., (1991) stated that in dialogue a group of people could explore the individual and c collective presuppositions, ideas, beliefs, and feelings that subtly control their interactions. Dialogue provides an opportunity for individuals to participate in a process that displays their successes and failures of communication, and it can reveal the often-puzzling patterns of incoherence and often leads them to avoid certain issues. On the other hand, it may lead them to insist, against all reason, on standing and defending their opinions.

Why Dialogue. Dialogue is concerned with providing a space within which such attention can be given. It allows a display of thought and meaning that makes possible a kind of collective preconceptions or immediate mirroring back of both the content of thought and the less apparent, dynamic structures that govern it. In dialogue, this experienced both individually and collectively. Each listener is able to reflect back to each speaker and the rest of the group a view of some of the assumptions and unspoken implications of what is being expressed along with that which is being avoided. It creates an opportunity for each participant to examine the preconceptions, prejudices, and characteristic patterns that lie behind his or her thoughts, opinions, beliefs, and feelings along with the roles he or she tends to play habitually. It also offers an opportunity to share these insights (Bohm, et al., 1991).

David Bohm, et al., (1991) also states that dialogue works best between twenty and forty people seated facing one another in a circle. A group of this size allows for the emergence and observation of different subgroups or subcultures that can help to reveal some of the ways in which thought operates collectively. This is important because the differences between such subcultures are often an unrecognized cause of failed communications and conflict in smaller groups. On the other hand, lack of the requisite diversity needed to reveal these tendencies would generally emphasize more familiar personal and family roles and relationships.

Purpose and Meaning. Bohn, et al., (1991) further stated that usually people gather either to accomplish a task or to be entertained, both of which can be described as predetermined purposes. However, by its very nature, dialogue is not consistent with any such purposes beyond the interest of the participants in the unfolding revelation of the deeper collective meanings that may be disclosed. These may frequently be entertaining, enlightening, lead to new insights, or address existing problems. However, surprisingly, the early stages of dialogue will often lead to the experience of frustration.

What Dialogue Is Not. Bohm, et al. (1999) contended that dialogue is not discussion, a word that shares its root meaning with *percussion* and *concussion*, both of which involve breaking things up. Dialogue is not debate either. These forms of conversation contain an implicit tendency to point toward a goal, to hammer out an agreement, to try to solve a problem, or have one's opinion prevail. Dialogue is also not a *salon*, which is a kind of gathering that is both informal and most often characterized by an intention to entertain, exchange friendships, gossip, and other information. Although the word *dialogue* has been used frequently in similar ways, its deeper root meaning implies that it is not primarily interested in any of these.

Further in their discussion, Bohm, et al. (1999) state that dialogue is not a new game for T-groups or sensitivity training, although it is superficially similar to these and other related forms of group work. Its consequences may be therapeutic, but dialogue does not attempt to focus on removing emotional blocks of any participant nor to teach, train, or analyze. Nevertheless, dialogue is an arena in which learning and dissolution of blocs can and often do take place. It is not a technique for problem solving or conflict resolution, although problems may well be resolved during the course of dialogue or perhaps later because of the increased understanding and fellowship that occurs among the participants. Dialogue is new from other group activities, but I believe that it is an activity that might well prove vital in business or organizational decision-making.

As a business owner, I have seen many changes in business and organizational decision-making based on group work, especially based on dialogue. The act of keeping every one listening, asking questions when questions are necessary, and making a statement when that is required are all very fascinating. These are based on the fact that everyone on the team or every participant wans a solution or solutions to occur sooner rather than later. Technology advances have made that possible. Dialogue as a discipline of collective learning and inquiry requires every input necessary to bring about solutions to the problems. We may think that every group work is the same, but they differ from the rules guiding the organization, the level of problems before the participants, and experts meant to tackle the problems and rewards meant for all levels of the solutions. It must be noted that in most group work there is the feeling as in <u>Animal Farm</u> by George Orwell that "some of the members are more equal than others," but in dialogue it is completely the opposite because all individuals are equal. Otherwise, some participants could maintain dominance and influence more than anyone else, which could also have influence on the decisions being made.

<u>How to Start a Dialogue</u>. Suspension of thoughts, impulses, judgments, etc. lies at the very heart of dialogue. It is one of its most

important new aspects, and it is not easily grasped because the activity is both unfamiliar and subtle. Suspension involves attention, listening, and looking. It is essential for exploration. Speaking is necessary, of course, for without it, there would be little in the dialogue to explore. However, the actual process of exploration takes place during listening—not only to others—but also to oneself. Suspension involves exposing your reactions, impulses, feelings, and opinions in such a way that these can be seen and felt within your own psyche and also be reflected back by others in the group. It does not mean repressing or suppressing, or even postponing them. It means simply giving them your serious attention so that their structures can be observed while they are actually taking place (Bohm, et al., 1991).

Numbers. Between twenty and forty people may be the ideal numbers for dialogue to work optimally, but if we are to see the emergence and observations of subgroups or subcultures, the magic numbers should be between thirty and sixty. This size will enable the people of any subculture to operate freely without knowing that they are being observed. This might not be because of an unrecognized cause of failed communication, but as an unrecognized cause of human nature. Of course, even birds of the same species flock together, as do human beings. However, for an unrecognized cause of failed communication and conflict to occur, the following must not present problems:

1. Educational levels;
2. Language difficulties;
3. Neglect of minority concerns;
4. Cultural insensitivity; and
5. Unresolved problems.

1. Educational Levels. Some of the world's communities today re class-oriented; they want to know who you are academically, and your monetary worth, of course. "All animals are equal, but some are more equal than others," as George Orwell puts it in *Animal Farm*. When we have more people that are unequal in a

community, we begin to realize that a failure in communication has occurred. Recently, I moved from Bayview/Hunter's Point to an exclusive neighborhood in the East Bay where most of the people have college degrees, are well mannered, and, of course, have good jobs. When I was in Bayview/Hunters Point, I realized that the low academic standards there was a problem. I think that in the neighborhood, education was a fully recognized cause of failed communications and conflict, but they were unable to remedy the situation. Of course, they didn't know how, in which case everyone was always right. Therefore, if you disagreed with anyone there, you had to be ready for the consequences, whatever they might be. In fact, Bayview/Hunters Point is not alone in this respect; all areas with low income or no income at all resent the situation, and instead of asking themselves what they can do to get out of the situation, they blame the politicians for not doing their work. Many great politicians from the United States have said many things regarding this attitude; President Kennedy said, "Ask not what your country can do for you, but what can you do for your country." This generation has many causes of failed communication and conflict. The news on television is full of voices that emanate from cases of unrecognized failures in communication and the resulting conflict.

2. Language Difficulties. I think this could describe me; I was asked what language I would use in writing my dissertation, and I said nothing. In the end, I wrote one of the best dissertations that year. I have seen many foreign students who were unable to speak English, and at the end of their term, they did very well. In my observations since my academic and business careers have been in the Bay Area, I have never been a determined immigrant who could not accomplish his ambition because of language. In the beginning, language might have been an obstacle, but never a barrier. I am now a believer that nothing is a barrier to a mind who is determined. Therefore, I think that language is really not an issue.

Cultural Insensitivity. Being insensitive regarding culture is in itself an invitation to conflict, and, of course, failed communication. Without question, an example is that of the Native Americans; they want to keep their ancestral beliefs. They feel happy knowing that they are recognized and respected the same as other people.

There was a man from Southeast Asia who was employed right after he arrived in the United States because his new employer believed he was a refugee. His boss was always playful and friendly with the employee. One day, the boss passed by the Southeast Asian man and playfully cocked his fingers like a pistol pointing at the man and laughed. However, this was not a laughing matter for the Southeast Asian. As soon as he got home, he went shopping for a gun because the boss had cocked his fingers pistol-like directly at him. In his view, this meant his boss wanted to kill him, so he had to be prepared for that eventuality. Fortunately, a co-worker was searching for something, looked into the Southeast Asian man's locker, and discovered the gun. Although quite fearful, he did not raise the alarm but went quietly to the boss and told him about the gun in the man's locker. The boss hesitated believing the information because the Southeast Asian man was so quiet and humble. In any case, he went to the locker quietly and discovered that what the co-worker had said was true. The boss then met with the Southeast Asian and asked him if he knew it was against the law in the United States to bring a gun to the workplace. The Asian man responded that the boss had caused him to bring the gun because he had cocked his fingers at him like a pistol, meaning in his Asian culture that the boss wanted to kill him. The boss said, "No, I don't want to kill you. It is a joke in the United States. You are my employee, and besides, you are a good man."

The Asian employee approached his boss and embraced him; the boss reciprocated; both of them then began laughing. Because of this incident, the boss called for an emergency meeting of the employees and told them about the incident that had occurred. Some employees told the boss that the refugee always stayed by himself, a *loner*. Even though he spoke English very little, he could have tried to communicate with gestures and actively learn the language of the United States, or else he would remain the way he is. However, the boss told the employees that culture is a significant aspect of the story, and that it took two to have a conflict. In addition, inasmuch as they wanted the Asian to learn English and the American culture, they should also try to learn about the Asian's culture and background. After that, at the end of each day, 30 minutes was set aside for cultural training and understanding.

This example is a sample of the problems that can occur, and if not dealt with properly as it was in this case, it could be very troubling. The boss, fortunately, was an intelligent man. While some of the employees thought the Southeast Asian was the problem and that even though he could not speak English well, that he could have actively tried to learn how to speak English and about the American culture. I know it is easy to say these things because in all my courses and classes at the universities I have attended, I have always sat with American-born students, and from my experience, I have never found the English language and the American culture a *piece of cake*. Therefore, insensitivity about culture should be treated seriously as a matter of failed communication and source of conflict.

Neglect of Minority Concerns. In the sixties in the United States, blacks and other minorities had issues with the American laws and courts because they addressed whites only and were silent about the needs and concerns of the minorities. This led to the passing of civil rights legislation. Whatever the concerns may be today, they are not addressed, there is bound to be conflict, sometimes in the form of protests or demonstrations, as well as lawsuits. The fact is that today's ideas of liberty and understanding are far different from in the era of our early philosophers like David Bohm and Associates.

Unresolved Problems. In the workplace, if two employees have a disagreement to the point of exchanging violent words and threats that reveal some bitter thoughts and ideas, this kind of altercation is usually reported to the supervisor. This kind of report must be taken seriously and dealt with promptly. Even if the altercation was reported by a third party, the supervisor should invite the participants who were fighting (verbally or physically) and get them to talk about what occurred. The incident should be addressed with no fear or favor but should be dealt with equitably so that the person(s) found liable may be judged accordingly.

If the dispute is not resolved promptly, eventually the problem will ferment and gather more importance than it should. In other words, if the problem is allowed to continue, rumors will begin and carry the issue to a very ugly situation in the workplace and even beyond. At that point, it might be difficult to resolve the issues quietly and peaceably. The resulting scandal will quickly become a distraction, which, in turn, affects productivity of the company. Of course, rules of the workplace no longer are the norm. At this point, for me the situation is a case of failed communication at some point, no matter where the breakdown occurred.

Countries go to war, regional wars occur, and other types of conflict happen with the participants knowing exactly that it is a case of weapons of mass destruction and that may be a course of unrecognized failure of communication and conflict. For example, the conflict between Iraq and the United States was a clear case of failed communication. Iraq had told the United Nations that it had no weapons of mass destruction. The Secretary of State then told the United Nations that Iraq did have weapons of mass destruction, but the United States sounded more credible, and for that *reason* the U.S. invaded Iraq and overthrew its government. In the end, there were no weapons of mass destruction found anywhere in Iraq. Now, that was a clear case of failed communications that cost many lives and resources and contributed to the U.S. going heavily into debt.

Another example concerns a co-worker who had been asked to work overtime, which he thought would interfere with his plans that he had made for that time. Therefore, instead of explaining the situation to his boss, he simply told his boss that he wouldn't do it. The reason for the overtime was that one of the women became ill and needed surgery; in order to cover her work, every employee was asked to volunteer to work extra hours in her place. The boss was very unhappy with this worker because he thought the employee had no reason for saying no to working overtime. When I talked to the boss, I was told that the employee had recently taken three weeks off while the other employees rallied to cover for the employee who had refused to work overtime to cover for the sick woman. However, this employee said that he wasn't sure why the boss was offended since he was not going to be paid if he didn't work.

The situation between the boss and the employee became a wildfire in that it became the subject of many conversations in the department. Some employees believed that the worker should be left alone since he was getting paid if he didn't work. Other employees were commenting that other employees had covered for this person when he had taken off for three weeks. The division in the department appeared to me to be nothing more than comparing apples and oranges. The boss was concerned because he was held accountable for the work being done, while the employee was not concerned so much about the work as the money he was not going to receive if he didn't work the overtime. For me, it appeared that the employee was insensitive to the needs of his employer.

Participative Decision-Making in Business

It is a characteristic of organizational decision-making that emphasizes equality and social change using dialogue as a mediating variable. It is relevant to businesses of all sizes and in all sectors. Participative decision-making involves everyone working together and making use of individual strengths within a group to achieve the common goal. Being a participant in decision-making does not necessarily mean that one has to have a college degree in participative decision-making in order to qualify as a participant. However, the participant must have an idea about what he or she is discussing, and as such, the participant either must be working for the company making the decisions or must have worked for a similar type of company or have some academic equivalent of such experiences. The fact is that what the participants may be discussing is given to them by the decision-making company, or the *host company*. This company has the problem and writes clearly in detail what the problems are so that anyone who read and understand English can have a grasp of the issues. What really needs to be understood is the situation or the problems facing the company for the participants to discuss. If the participants know the facts but have failed to grasp the issues before them, that is tantamount to being of no help at all.

Participative decision-making could be based around a particular product or service. This style often cuts across structural and functional divisions, and that is to the advantage of employees and management because each individual knows where the others are coming from when they have something to say. The ability of each individual to listen to the other not minding the other person's standing in the company or educational background is a win-win situation for all.

Participative decision-making has many benefits, including the following:

1. Problem-Solving Skills
2. Contributory Autonomy in Decision-Making
3. The Pride of Being a Decision-Maker
4. Accountability to each other and the decisions reached;
5. Valuable feedback by knowledgeable participants;
6. Social contacts and an opportunity to interact with colleagues;
7. Participatory decision-making shows balanced ideas as each member contributes to the pool;
8. Clarity on the process of decision-making in a participative format;

9. A sense of achievement and satisfaction on a job well done;
10. Development opportunities such as improving international or leadership skills; and
11. Exposure to a variety of problems using various skills.

Participative decision-making involves solutions for problems. At this point, we are used to knowing how participative decision-making functions; it has two components—the upper and lower levels. Participants on both levels must know the situation very well. This does not mean that a participant must be an expert or a lawyer. However, it does require knowing the situation and having a basic common sense. The lower level is not the lower level because the requirements are different from the upper level. Even though the CEO and the president of the company belong to the upper level, they have the same requirements. The lower level has a lot specialized knowledge such as that of the engineers, accountants, etc. So, both levels have intellectual specialists.

The differences between the two levels are not due to academic standards either, but understanding of the subject matter and what I call analytical dream; that is, having an in-depth analysis of the subject matter and being able to visualize what one thinks the analysis will mean to the solution of the problem. What I have just said might seem too academic, but that might not be the case for some people because if a participant is devoted to the service, he or she will see how other knowledgeable and experienced participants manoeuver at many points that exposure over time might result in an outstanding skill. At the same time, that procedure may be very overwhelming to some people and such participants may feel that the whole process is too academic.

The principles of exposure have a long history in the old and modern age. An example of this is Nigeria. Even before the British ruled Nigeria, the people in Ikun and Biase in the Cross River State had a system of administration similar to that of the British, as in the following:

1. The Prime Minister (or chief) was Onun Ikun;
2. The Secretary of State was Ufiem;
3. The Secretary of Defense was Onun Imani;
4. The Secretary of Agriculture was Onun Ethok;
5. The Secretary of Internal Affairs was Onun Ekpor Ojoi;
6. Okun; Okwe 1
7. Okwe 2.

The fact is was that each ruler must attend meetings with his son or a close relative who must also be a man or a young man. The purpose of this was for these young people to learn from their elders because the belief was that young people learned faster by observing what their elders did. There was also the belief that, all things being equal, people learn faster if they are exposed to what they want to learn. Therefore, decision-making participants needed a clear understanding of the subject. In fact, those who followed their fathers (the Onuns) to these meetings who did not become Onuns in their lifetime became experts in different fields and even became consultants in native affairs. Many of the Onuns (chiefs) today have university degrees, but one still has to listen and understand the subject matter before doing what is expected. Participative decision-making involves understanding a subject and analyzing it the way one understands it. An individual may not be right all of the time, but whatever point one makes may open another area of discussion.

Business policies and Participative decision-making are similar to that of presidents, prime ministers and their cabinet members operate, because the cabinet members are almost like the employees in a company. Participative decision-makers are asked to participate occasionally or may even participate in making decisions in a lifetime. Businesses are made aware of the fact that making decisions by a few top executives is not a very good practice for the bottom line of the company (profitability). The old adage that two heads are better than one applies here.

Contributory Autonomy. The ability to speak your mind during deliberations without fear of reprisal helps a participant feel powerful and with some sense of autonomy. When a participant has such a sense of achievement and autonomy and he or she is a worker, this may translate into greater productivity. I have always believed that a happier mind is a creative one and a more productive mind as well. A worker who has participated and contributed to discussions and deliberations about decision-making may think that he or she is an employee who deserves more pay because he or she has a more developed mind than their counterparts do. However, that can lead to unwarranted pride and arrogance. The pride of accomplishment in contributing to any kind of development should always overshadow pride or arrogance.

A contribution, whether in kind or in cash, that is meant for solving problems is a positive idea, especially for any worker who contributes in a decision that later becomes the company's policy that may be capitalized in the future and may be sought by other organizations. Even if the individual has no other opportunity of being a participant in other decision-making processes, it is really a great event in being a participant, especially in a major corporation in which the deliberation proposal has become company policy. Its value truly has no price tag, and the activity is always in the curriculum vitae of the participants, whether or not they contributed to the discussion or not. This is true whether the individual was appointed to the participative decision making group or volunteered, and if it contributes to the well-being of the company, it is still a chance of a lifetime for those individuals. Therefore, the decision-making process of a company, large or small, should be taken seriously.

Autonomy in the decision-making process is because the participants know that whatever he or she says or does in the meeting there will be no repercussions or punishment. This is absolute freedom, but we have to understand that in some cases a participant may be asked to leave or be excused from the meeting because of behavior that incites fighting or makes derogatory and abusive comments about other participants or their families. Of course, the victim may institute a private lawsuit against the person who makes such comments, and such actions have nothing to do with the decision-making process. This is a sort of checks-and-balances type because anyone who wants to be disruptive and abusive must understand the law will take its course. Everyone should know that the decision-making process and the final decision belong to the people of proven ability.

Disruptive behavior cannot be acceptable where decisions need to be made or are actually being made. It is obvious that in order to avoid having people who use disruptive behavior the people who select the participants need to review the backgrounds of those chosen to participate so that their personal styles can be known and anticipated. Since human behavior is often unpredictable, disruptions may not be avoided, but the background checks have been done and anything out of the ordinary has been noted. We have talked so much about dialogue and that it is a discipline of collective learning and inquiry. Therefore, from the very beginning the participants need to be aware that participative decision-making is highly disciplined. If the participants with poor deliberations are due to discipline issues, the people selecting the participants should be replaced while the whole process begins again.

In order to avert beginning again, the officer in charge of the program must have the two levels address, informing them of the vital part that their decisions will make for the company and informing them that poor recommendations will affect the company's profitability and may even lead to it going out of business. The speaker should let them know that the only way this program can be successful is to adhere strictly to the principles of dialogue, which is an ability to collectively learn and inquire into facts. The speaker should also emphasize the fact that the company is relying on these participants, and he should encourage the participants to be able to disagree and then examine repeatedly the areas of disagreement. The participants need to be aware of their own personal mindsets, and excellent analysis and facts should be able to take its course.

The Pride of Being a Decision-Maker. For the junior staff, decision-makers appear to be *super human*, and when the junior staff has the opportunity to be part of the decision-making, they are happy and feel that they have actually seen salvation much as I did when my first book, Managerial Handbook, was published. I felt like that because I had bought many of my doctoral thesis books from Stacy Books, and so when I saw my book being sold there, I thought I had really accomplished something. When I began work on this material, I imagined how some of the participants might have felt and what they must have said during the *selection period*.

Taking part in the decision-making process might not mean that you are the most intelligent person that has not ever been. Even within one's workplace, some of the counterparts or co-workers may be smarter, but for whatever reason, that individual was not chosen to participate. Some who are religious might give thanks to their God for the opportunity. If the recommendations the team made were accepted and actually became company policy, then, of course, there is a sense of pride of accomplishment on the part of the participant and he or she may be regarded as a smart fellow because they helped form the policies of the company. However, that may be a stepping stone for a higher responsibility, but the participants must not rest on past glories of accomplishment and live in the past. Participants who have been successful in these circumstance have to be working harder to further their accomplishment. In fact, the participants' future work will enable co-workers to ask, "Who is that hard worker? He is as smart as he works." At that point, of course, respect is a given.

An example is the case about the concerns of a young man in a large company who seemed to have it all—three times manager of the year, delegated to representing the company several times in national meetings. His expertise seemed to be in global economy; yet, he had several awards and recognition as a manager. However, there were times he moved from department to department. If he was told you were in the bathroom, he would call your name over the intercom, and so employees called him the harass*ing man*. Not all the good things he had been doing were remembered; every employee knew him by his harassing behavior. What I am saying here is that in many cases, humility surpasses our individual achievements, and without psychological and spiritual attachment to your material success, you may be hoping against hope. What you thought was important to your existence may have fallen into the cracks where no one can see or even remember. Not all deficits are momentary; some are behavioral deficits, communication deficits, and so forth; so the question is where do you belong? Find your niche and remedy your situation before you have a derogatory reputation. Your image may be different from what you believe.

After a person has been a decision-maker for the first time and having the reputation for being a good decision-maker, an individual has to keep abreast of current events in the company, what is happening on Wall Street and news from radio and TV, as well as business journals and friends In the end, one may have an improved image of business analysis and consequently be an improved decision-maker. I am writing about a person who participated in a successful decision-making process and became very proud of it. There is nothing wrong about being proud of an accomplishment; however, the point here is one's pride may be repugnant to other people. Are you aware of what you are doing to others or do you simply not care?

Being proud of an accomplishment is not a crime, particularly if you do not harm anyone; however, what we need to understand is that many things we say or act upon don't constitute a crime, but may be very unethical. One may think that only criminal behavior is to be avoided, but I tell you that unethical behavior is punished in some way either by the state or other authorities. An unethical person is not trustworthy and may find it difficult to have good relations with others, including a wife, because everyone knows about your behavior. An unethical person may find it difficult to have a business associate (unless someone else who is unethical) because of the image of being unethical.

In the past, record keeping was difficult because filing was the recommended means of record keeping. Today, technology has improved greatly and computer files can be extracted easily and saved easily. In today's world, an untrustworthy person may run but can never hide because most information is available about them and their activities. These activities may be seen in credit reports, and the individual may be denied credit. Having said all this, pride in an accomplishment is a good thing but should be limited to what people around you can endure. The world is full of achievements, and pride must never be allowed to cause you to fail. We should be happy for what we do that may prompt us to do further exploration in a bid to finding what we think is right.

Responsibility to Each Other and Decisions Reached. In participative decision-making, as in any business policy, decisions are never made alone and individually but are made collectively. In most companies in the Western Hemisphere and in many other countries, two-thirds forms an absolute majority for decision-making even if one's vote differs from the other participants. The law of participative decision-making stipulates that once a vote is taken and a clear two-thirds vote is obtained or even a slim majority, then this is to be respected by the company, and any member who goes against such norms is subject to stipulated punishment. The law also stipulates that if you disagree with the majority, you have the option of stepping down or keep your disagreement to yourself and function as a team member.\

The business policy clearly bars all participants from going to the media and stating who said what and who is for against what. When such things happen, the responsible person must only be terminated, but may be liable to a lawsuit. If the person responsible has already been terminated, then a lawsuit might be brought against that person. After a vote has been taken, a majority recognized, and a policy is upheld or ceases functioning, the failure or success of such a company is that of everyone and not just the success or failure of those who made the rules.

The principle of accountability is actually the life of any company because for a company to exist and prosper, commitment is required by the majority in order for the company to succeed. The rules of any company are binding on each employee, even if an employee or group of employees disagrees with the majority. In many companies, there are opinion boxes where the rules that have been made can be reviewed if the minority opinion is very convincing. The principle of accountability also requires democratic principles; otherwise, any major disagreement in decision-making could render the whole process useless. This is, of course, a waste of the company's resources and could push the company into a downward spiral. The principle of accountability in participative decision-making requires togetherness based on mutual understanding of the problem or problems.

The principle of accountability stipulates that anyone who makes decisions that affect a family set-up, company, or organization must own the decision that he or she made. In other words, *if you break it, you must own it* (Colin Powell, 2008). A family custodian of a family's funds decided to invest what the family kept in his custody because the investment seemed very lucrative. He invested the funds; however, the market reacted poorly and the investment lost all of its value. He later denied doing anything wrong. He then refused to tell his extended family what he had done with their money; the family members found out the hard way when they tried to use some of their money and found that they had no money. The custodian of the money told his relatives that he had invested the money because he thought his investment was going to be as promised on the radio. Yet, the custodian thought he did nothing wrong. He told his relatives that he could have put back part of the profits he had made. The custodian, as known by his relatives, said that he never meant harm for the family at all and that looking at the disappearance of the entire fund, it was due to his own inability to invest intelligently. One of his relatives jumped into the conversation and called him by his real name. "Mr. Paul, look, we are not here to prove the motive of doing what you did. If you told the owners of the money that you were going to invest their money for them, probably some would have said "No," while others would have said "Yes." Then, it would have become the issue for the relatives to decide not just you. However, as it is, the entire responsibility is on your shoulders."

On that note, the custodian hired an attorney to represent him because he still believed that he was not accountable for the missing money. Again, his intent was not to embezzle the relatives' money in his custody. One of the money owners shouted loudly, "Boy, I told you, now we have to spend money for an attorney. When I told you that money belonged to the bank, every one of you pretended not to understand me. Now, Paul turn custodian has hired an attorney. You don't even know if he used your money in hiring the attorney against you;"

"What I am saying once again is to make peace with Mr. Paul's attorney. Talking with Paul from now until next year, Paul will simply understand his own thinking, not yours. To tell you the truth, I thought Mr. Paul was a smart man, but now is he playing some kind of a game? I am very confused about our relative. Mr. Paul, let's stop all of this. We may be spending more than we saved. The extended family invited Mr. Paul for talks, but Mr. Paul preferred that his relatives talk with his attorney." Paul's relatives then made an appointment with Paul's attorney, and after prolonged talks with Paul including calls to his attorney on the phone and his attorney, Paul agreed to pay the relatives two-thirds of the money he had spent. The relatives accepted Paul's offer.

Therefore, finally the custodian of the extended family who had refused to be accountable for the investment he had made with the family's funds suddenly changed his mind from wanting to do good for his relatives to making a mistake by not telling his relatives before making the risky investment. This was tantamount to treating the family fund as his own personal account, and for that, he knows that he is responsible for returning the money to the fund where he got it in the first place. The attorney made Paul tell his way of thinking to his relatives. Upon hearing Paul say that he was sorry for not telling them about making the investment before doing so, the relatives were happy to hear Paul's apology. They were also relieved by not having the case drag on. Paul further told his relatives that he lost one-third of the money that was entrusted to his care. The relatives asked Paul to let them have the two-thirds remaining funds. As soon as Paul handed over the funds, the family went to the bank and invested the money themselves. They wrote up a short document stating that withdrawals could only be done by all the executives, with five signatures by members before funds could be withdrawn.

The relatives thanked Paul and his attorney for his courage in recognizing that it was his fault and be willing to be the trustworthy Paul they knew in their family They told Mr. Paul not to worry about the one third of the funds that were lost and these things happen. One of the family members said that he could now think that Mr. Paul's motive for making the investment was meant to increase the value by making profits and putting the profits into the family's account that was already in his custody.

Mr. Paul again stood up and thanked his relatives, his attorney, and everyone. He urged everyone to live up to expectations by developing a spirit of accountability. He thanked his relatives again for being a forgiving family.

Accountability

1. You have just heard a brief story about accountability. Do you think that Paul finally regretted his actions? Explain.
2. Paul and the custodian—are they two different people.
3. Accountability and dishonesty—how are they different?
4. What part do you think Paul's attorney played in the whole issue? What, in your judgment, made the custodian's family accept a settlement?

At the same time, if Paul's relatives made decisions about the money they contributed, Mr. Paul would have to abide by the decisions; otherwise, he would be regarded as someone who refused to be accountable for the decisions that were made when he was present and yet refused to adhere to the details of those very decisions. The same applies to a larger company. If a participant was present during a deliberation, then he or she must abide by the decisions reached, even if they objected to them during the deliberations because they were in the minority. Otherwise, he or she could not have signed off on the deliberations. The participant, after all is said and done, must never criticize or give out information that is meant to be privileged. If the participant does, the company may well punish the participant in one way or another, especially if the participant is an employee of that company.

CHAPTER 8
VALUABLE FEEDBACK BY KNOWLEDGEABLE PARTICIPANTS

1. Valuable Feedback by Knowledgeable Participants
2. Social Contacts and an Opportunity to Interact With Colleagues
3. Decision-Making Chambers
4. Participative Decision-Making as a Contributory Database of Ideas
5. Upper and Lower Level Chambers
6. Clarity to Decision-Making
7. Clarity to Workplace
8. Clarity in Decision-Making
9. Achievement and Satisfaction With a Job Well Done
10. International Business and Opportunities
11. Employment opportunities

CHAPTER 8

VALUABLE FEEDBACK BY KNOWLEDGEABLE PARTICIPANTS

In George Orwell's book, *Animal Farm*, the view is expressed by Napoleon the Pig that all animals are created equal, but some are more equal than others are. This view is often held about humans as well. In this case, it depends on what individual participants studied in college or the type of experience an individual had before being selected as a participant. In a decision-making process, some participants may be business experts, economists, engineers, sales experts, political scientists, or even simply hold a high school diploma. Each has their own way of looking at things and interpreting the world as he or she sees it. The business scientist looks at things the way he or she taught, what has proven to be true in experience, and the individual's personal application of common sense. An engineer will look at the hardware and software of the tools used for operations and the tools used by the company in general.

Psychologically speaking, humans behave, think, talk, and analyze problems before us mostly based on how we were raised in our families and educational experiences. Different backgrounds bring different ways of looking at the same thing. Mr. Simpson, the CEO of the largest clothing company in the state of New York deals with revenue and productivity because he wants to follow in the footsteps of his uncle, Mr. Thomas, who retired 25 years ago when technology was very different from today, when the constitution was very different, and when needs and wants were entirely different. In fact, life itself as we know it today is radically different including the expectations for life generally.

Let us talk about information technology, as we know it today. Supposing you were to go to your competitor, search for job openings, and see a job posting for which you are qualified. You then forward your resume (by either e-mail or regular mail) and may even follow that up with a phone call. You may have the results quickly and may be invited for an interview, be hired for the position, get married, and become an outstanding middle-class citizen and buy one of the best homes in your area. What you have just done in less than three months' time is to better your lifestyle could have taken five years to accomplish and still may not be up to what you desired because everyone is seeing what you are seeing. In the past before our advanced technology, one could be poor without knowing one was poor because people around you were like you. Unless one is homeless, you may find it difficult to define poverty. So information technology is here to stay and will be even more advanced in the future.

E-mail. Look at what e-mail technology is doing to the Post Office. If you want your friend in Nigeria to hear from you in California in the next five minutes, just send your message, and it will be received almost instantly. If your friend wants to hear your voice or see your image, then he or she can call you with the e-phone technology within two minutes in the United States. Now, what I am talking about is that Mr. Simpson who manages a clothing store as it operated 25 years ago and hopes to reap today's rewards; I think a miracle might be needed at this point, as I know in our complicated world of global business today, much needs to be done to make a profit.

Information technology and the e-mail systems are just two of the technologies that have changed business, and so if the team dialogue deliberations mentioned previously you would find that a few people would be different because they are experts in those disciplines. Many of the participants will be very attentive to what these people say because the participants want to learn. What the experts have said will make the overall analysis much easier to conduct, understand, and include in the following discussions. If no one is an expert, the participants will be jumping from topic to topic without managing any topic successfully and without making a great deal of sense in what they are saying. I am not saying that to be a qualified participant one has to be an expert in any discussion, but fortunately, if one is found to be an expert in any area of the discussions, then it is an advantage to all the participants. The most important thing for a participant in the decision-making process is to understand the problem and to be able to put that understanding into a sensible context during the discussions, as well as to be able to ask logical and pertinent narrative questions.

If one asks narrative questions in outline, for example, "Could you tell us why this is so and not this way, then, of course, if that person is an expert or semi-expert, he or she will discuss the question in a convincing way? This may not only be to the liking of the listener, but also to everyone on the panel. Sometimes the answers given may not be very satisfactory to everyone. In that case, a few participants may try to contribute more enlightenment in answering the questions. However, the participants in the decision-making process are never to know the answers to the problems before attending the meeting. Many participants may try to know the answers before a second or even a third meeting because at that point, all the participants have known the issues. As is frequently the case, some participants will be more serious than others will, and that is when some participants become "more equal" than others in a different manner than what Orwell had in mind in <u>Animal Farm</u>. Some participants are said to be more knowledgeable than others are because work so hard in reading, analyzing, and applying their thoughts in working. Still others are experienced in their positions; whatever the case may be, all of them have one thing in common and that is *hard work*.

In as much as we can, categorize our contributions in all we do, in participative decision making if we dogmatize our contributions into *valuable* and non-valuable, we will be driving down contributions, always refusing to say something, thinking it might not make sense. The actual aim of the process is for everyone to contribute something, whether a lot a or a little, in order for the participants to know what the other participants think about the subject being discussed and not so much about the size of individual contributions. We have to remember collective accountability in business where the participants deliberate in private, the results are always public material. Radio and television commentators will talk about them, and the results will contribute examples for either the same company or other companies, or for training purposes. In collective accountability, whether you agree with the deliberations or not, whatever the majority decides is what forms a quorum.

In many companies, breaking the rules and regulations of collective accountability is punishable by the company. The punishment could include being fired, not allowed to participate in the decision-making process again, or relieved of your duties if you work for the same company. There may also be other hidden punishments that may fit the punishment for a whistleblower. When one leaves the company, the testimonial may be less than the stellar one that the individual had desired. Of course, in some cases, retirement may be an option and the individual may want to start his or her own business. In the first place, every participant in the decision-making process is considered *knowledgeable*. No business will go out and simply find someone in the street and ask that person to be a participant in the decision-making process. The participants have to know where he or she has worked or has been working, have an appropriate educational background, and what they have done, including publishing articles and/or books. More often than not, most people selected to serve in the participative decision-making process are smart; some of them are employees of that company. The executives know them very well; they are usually high achievers, very hard workers, and contribute during the decision-making process. Having said all of this about participants and their contributions to the process, some of the participants may offer selections to participate in the decision-making process, but may be lazy, don't work hard, and simply accept the proposals or the contributions of the knowledgeable participants. Because of the law of collective accountability, the contributions made individually will never be acknowledged; collectively, they do great jobs.

Social Contacts and an Opportunity to Interact With Colleagues

In normal circumstances, birds of the same feather flock together. Today, I think that human beings are growing beyond color and nationality divisions, but we are moving very rapidly towards class differentiation. What is his or her level of education? How much does he or she earn per month or annually? What kind of a car does he or she drive? Where does he or she live? With what people does he or she associate? What is her or his title at work? Truly, our world today is a world of class-consciousness and not so much concern about color or ethnicity. A clear example is in the United States where the president's father is an African, while his mother is white. A few years back, this would have been considered a restriction to the highest office in the country, but Mr. Obama has broken the racial barrier simply because he achieved greatness through academics and financial standing through which he became a U.S. Senator and consequently president of the United States. Astonishingly enough, Mr. Obama was elected president. Some people appear to be *born* leaders, while others achieve leadership positions, but leadership by achievement may never be successful without social contact.

Human beings are social animals; most of our politician's careers originated with social gatherings, and from there the people have to know each other. The first group of friends became the inner circle in most of the things we do in life, while some will betray us from the first day that we met them. In any case, social contact brings about either positive or negative relations.

Positive contact is said to be a friend who is there when needed; this is part of the trite phrase, "a friend in need is a friend indeed," but there is truth in that even it is a cliché. This is true in both discussing topics together and agreeing or disagreeing, but disagreements are infrequent. Friendship like this can extend to family members and some friends may be called *family friends*. Family friendships are better than negative extended family relationships. This type of friendship may extend to business partnerships, political associations, and other valuable and productive friendships that were not anticipated when the friendship was first formed.

When I began this discussion of the participative decision-making process, I intimated that dialogue was the centerpiece of participative decision-making and that dialogue is a "discipline of collective learning and inquiry." This should be true to obtain better results, and for that reason, class ideology has no room in the decision-making process. All participants must regard themselves as having equal share and responsibility in the decision-making process. This is clearly stated by systems thinkers such as William Isaacs (1993). An example of this discussion on class is a situation where I have two friends. All of us have our Ph.D.'s; one of my friends gave me a call saying that he had found a girl he wanted to marry. I asked if he was in love with her, and replied, "Yes." I then told him to go for it; then he called the other friend and told him the news, but the other friend wanted to know about her educational background and type of work she did and her title. Then this friend advised the boyfriend to marry a woman with a B.A. because communications at home might be a nightmare and that would put their marriage in jeopardy. The young man who wanted to marry merely hung up on him and cut him off, and I have not heard from since the incident. Sometimes I believe what this tells us is that love (or even sexual attraction) is stronger than class considerations. In some cases, there are jobs that do not pay very much but have a strong appeal to well-educated people because the media makes it known to the public and this could have political appeal should the individuals want to run for political office.

In a situation involving the decision-making process, every participant wants to learn from the others. Academic background notwithstanding, every person's exposure and interest may be different. Some may already be well known in society and whatever he or she says may focus attention on what they say, and many participants may feel privileged to be participants and have the opportunity to meet and interact with their idols or respected personalities. Respect, anyway, is reciprocal, meaning that respect is give and take, but ultimate respect occurs when both parties respect each other. Respecting someone may be due to that individual's contributions to the admirer's field of interest or could be that the man or woman is very attractive physically, which creates another kind of interest. However, the decision-making process requires intellect and that becomes the motivator for interest in another participant.

Some people might think that they are not experienced enough or knowledgeable enough to contribute or comment to a discussion with more famous people or so-called *experts* about a company's issues and finances. Fortunately, any person can enter the room and make a contribution at a very high level that he or she may be a force with which to reckon. The person may be invited on occasion for a contribution to solutions to problems. We do not really know what the future has in store for us. We may be working hard but in the wrong place, and after having done this and that without knowing exactly where we are going. However, some day something may come up where we have either to say or do even less than we do now, and our lives are changed forever.

My life is an example of that; I thought I was going to retire as a district court registrar, but one day I applied to study in California. I thought I wouldn't get the visa anyway, but I heard about the study and applied to the school. I was asked questions and asked to explain my purposes for studying in California, and I answered very carefully and accurately. I was granted a visa after less than 40 minutes of interviewing; I went home and arranged everything with my family. We were very happy even though I knew what I was going after; yet, I made some empirical research with a few friends who had studied in the United States and had returned to Nigeria. They did not intend to go back for further studies as they were now gainfully employed.

Well, to make the story short, I now have a Ph.D., have taught in a university, have published academic books, and have sponsored my children in the universities. One must remember that my few questions and answers at the American Embassy in Lagos changed everything for me and my family, and, indeed, my village and beyond.

Participative decision-making is a big eye-opener. First, one has to read about what is being proposed or discussed. On the floor, one will hear testimonies or comments from people. One might think one is in court, and in some situations, you may think you are in business school. One will never hear comments that sound like a pep rally because the participants have been trained in how to use dialogue in conversations. They listen, they ask questions, and they disagree constructively with a review of ambiguous or unclear sentences. Everything that is accomplished, explained, and analyzed in the name of the decision-making process must be very clear and understandable to the participants. The aim is to let everyone understand what is being said in the meeting in case the media and others may ask them about the process they went through to come up with their decision, which may have changed the way business is done in the community.

Many companies have tried hard to enable their employees to participate in the decision-making process; they have a group, sometimes chaired by the CEO, but you better know what you are saying. There may be a clause depicting that you are free to say what you want and that no participant can be punished for being honest in speaking about what is on his or her mind. That is good on paper; retribution may come in different forms, so you must mind what you are saying. In my version of decision-making, the CEO and his fellow executives are in the upper level, while the lower level is made up of professional, highly experienced individuals who have years of service. Also included here are workers, sales representatives, engineers, and other lower level workers as well as professionals from other companies. In most cases, their recommendations are entirely accepted with few modifications. Their recommendations are as good as the case presented to them for analysis.

My version of decision-making involves the Board of Directors; the CEO cannot decide singlehandedly on what the company must do. Both lower level and upper level recommendations must be presented to the Board of Directors. If the upper level modifies the recommendations made by the lower level, all documents must be presented to the Board. Then, the board has to study all the documents and put aside those that are the most sensible and then summons both lower and upper levels to their chambers and discuss the documents that were given back to them by the Board. Each of the respective chambers takes a vote. The lower chamber then sends their final recommendations to the upper level. Both levels then jointly summarize the findings of both chambers as a document and present it to the Board for review and signing.

If the Board of Directors still finds discrepancies or other problems with the documents (spelling, incomplete sentences, or inaccuracies) that may in due course cause problems in the company, the corrections need to be made by the lower and upper chambers with the Board of Directors. Then, of course, the Board signs off and the CEO countersigns with the Director of Finance. The fact is that if anything goes wrong or if the company fails to improve its financial position or is unable to compete in the marketplace, then the general assembly must meet under the leadership of the deputy CEO, the Board of Directors, the CEO, and the CFO (Chief Financial Officer) are voted on by the Board of Directors. Those that have received a vote of "no confidence" must resign. Again, in that case, the Deputy CEO and three or five of the senior officials, including seven shareholders, must appoint a new Board of Directors within 30 days, and then the new Board must begin looking for a new CEO. In the meantime, the Deputy CEO, the CEO, and the CFO are acting temporarily until they are confirmed by the new Board of Directors.

DECISION-MAKING CHAMBERS

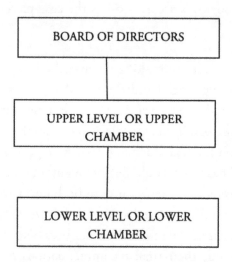

The Board of Directors consists of appointed members, both within and without the company. The upper chamber consists of the CEO, the CFO, General Manager, Chief Sales Officer, Chief Engineer, and about five or ten other executives. The lower chamber consists of engineers, sales executives, business professionals, accountants, tax professionals, financial officers, workers, and five or more other professionals.

One can see why the lower chamber is so highly respected by both the Board of Directors and the upper chamber because of the manpower, both in experience and in academic backgrounds, in which the lower chamber really overpowers the upper chamber. In most cases, the recommendations made by the lower chamber simply need modest modifications and review, which may be then accepted by the lower chamber. Any disagreement must be presented to the Board of Directors for review and comment. The next step is to present both the recommendations of each chamber together with the modified versions to the Board of Directors for approval and signature, which is then countersigned by the CEO and the CFO before becoming company policy.

Participative Decision-Making as a Contributory Database of Ideas

In this book and in most of my other business books, I have talked about the power of collective thinking, which in one word is known as *dialogue*. "There is a beginning to dialogue, but I do not think there is an end," said one president of a local steelworkers union. Dialogue is a discipline of collective learning and inquiry (Isaacs, 1993). That is why it is a contributory database of ideas because it can serve as a cornerstone for organizational learning by providing an environment in which people can reflect together and transform the ground from which their thinking and actions emerge (Isaacs, 1993).

Contributory Database of Ideas. These are the contributions that are made by members during their deliberations. In my dissertation about *teamwork in business organizations*, I noted that our early philosophers and great thinkers believed in shared understanding. What I did in ignorance in my Metro Loans Company was to employ people and then put them into districts in San Francisco and asked all of the district heads to meet in my office in the San Francisco Financial District every Monday because I know that business cases are generally unique, and such situations should be known by other leaders also. I also wanted them to be acquainted with each other and to be able to call upon one another when they desired assistance. I did not know that shared understanding, which I now call *contributory database of ideas*, is a great asset in business, particularly in decision-making. However, just like a team, people must work together to accomplish anything, even though you may have different styles of working. Decision-making entails a clear understanding of the subject, quite unlike building a house as a team where specialization is used. Someone must know how to hang doors, someone else does roofing, another supplies nails and other building supplies, etc.

In decision-making, some specialization such as mathematics, financing, sales, and engineering may be used but not required.

Decision-making requires knowledge of the subject one is dealing with, not so much knowledge of the industry but an understanding of the case study the team was given and a simple research on the unclear areas of the case. This may give the team a good picture of the areas of analysis.

Participative decision-making means simply that one has to say something during the deliberations in the decision-making process, but one has to say what one thinks that makes sense to you,. You should remember that in the deliberations no comment or question is nonsense. It is left to the participants to vote a question up or down as being good enough or not for discussion. If one says nothing, whether you know it or not, it means you are making a vote of no confidence in the meeting. If very many participants do this, it means a few participants will dominate the deliberations in the meeting, and this may mean a waste of time and money for the company supporting the meeting. An individual must participate in the decision-making process so that when things go wrong, no particular individual is blamed.

Another thing to remember is that if the lower chamber fails to perform its duties, the upper chamber may dominate the discussions with the Board of Directors. In most cases, the poor performance of the lower chamber is blamed on the managers or on officials meant to supervise them, but it is rare to have the lower chamber mess up big time like that. However, for the purposes of this discussion, the lower chamber is full of very active professionals who are eager to say something, ask questions, and do research on the problems at hand.

When we speak about contributory database of ideas, we also mean the participant deliberations that are taped and may be used for future sessions or to be referenced in future discussions. It is expensive to conduct a full-scale decision-making process, so if simple processes are forgotten in order to make the system work, the managers may turn to how the last decision-making process worked, including both the long and short lists of deliberations. Sometimes they go back into the system very quickly, but in some cases, they have to do a bit more adjusting to have things corrected. The lower chamber has a reputation of being perfect, if not exactly perfect because of its composition. They are also the pride of the Board of Directors and that is why when the lower and upper chambers agree on something, the Board feels obligated to sign off on what is presented to them. It should be understood that when I talk about *contributory database of ideas*, I am specifically referring to the lower chamber because most of its members are professionals and are either still working for themselves or for other companies. Some of the lower level participants also take classes to acquaint themselves with changes in technology. Of course, changes in technology may directly or indirectly affect business transactions. We have to understand that the upper level is made up of the CEO and other higher management officers who may be looking to retire.

UPPER LEVEL/CHAMGER

- CEO/President
- CFO
- Chief Engineer
- General Manager

LOWER LEVEL/CHAMER

- CPA
- Sales Professionals
- Economists
- Engineers
- Workers

However, it should be noted that the upper level is not composed of a bunch of deadwood or old and ineffective executives. They have done their job for many years and have kept abreast of events and changes technologically and otherwise. We should understand that most of the participants in the lower level may still want to serve in the upper echelon some day. As such, the motivation to work hard differs greatly from those who have "been there, done this, and done that." Workers must be the employees of the company conducting the decision-making process because they are mostly required to talk about their work, and, if possible give the lower level a brief history of their department in the company. All information helps in diagnosing the actual problem the company faces. In most cases, what the managers may call *problems* may be symptoms of a larger systemic problem or indicate the scope of the company's overall problems. In short, every contribution helps in defining what is required to getting the job completed. Most of the workers pay greater attention to what goes on in their jobs and they can point out the trouble spots they notice in the company. They can identify supervisors who are serious about their work and those who are not. I am sure everyone still remembers the story told in one of my books about a worker who discovered the slow pace of productivity in his company. This was a worker who loved his job and felt very lucky to have the job, So, when the company's productivity lessened to below its average, the company began laying off personnel, and he became worried because he wanted his children to be able to go to the university, and he felt his job was his best hope to accomplish this. So, he began paying attention to details in the department and elsewhere. Fortunately, for him, he stumbled upon the plant's engine when it was sounding right, but the operations had ceased. He saw that nothing was moving; unfortunately, he was just a junior member of the staff and no one wanted to hear him.

He heard that his company was going to make a decision on what should happen to the company—either buying new equipment or sell the company entirely. The employee became restless and did not know what to do because he was so junior that no one would think he could contribute to the discussions. In the middle of the discussions, he surprised everyone by entering the room and saying, "This company is my only hope." His supervisor asked him to leave, but he insisted that he had something to say. The owners and executives asked him what he had to say. The employee first greeted the executives and owners of the company and told them he was going directly to what he found out. He stated that from where he worked he saw that the engine had shut down. He also was there when the engine came back on line about two hours later, and he had observed the situation for over two months and saw the same results. The owners and executives went with the employee, and he showed them what he had observed. On the following day, all of them were there before time and witnessed the drama. As a result, the executives changed most break times and lunch periods to suit the system of the engine; more importantly, the employee was promoted. The employee practically single-handedly saved the company from being sold or from unnecessary expenditures, which could have been used in other areas of the company.

In fact, some companies have suggestion boxes or complain boxes. The employee of this company thought that business is better done when there is *interest* and motivation to succeed. The employee wanted the company to succeed; therefore, he was interested in working hours to make his dream come true. He observed intelligently and finally he was able to uncover the fault that was eating up the company's profits and reducing productivity.

One drawback to the contribution of ideas through the Suggestion Box system is that the supervisor or manager has control of whose ideas/complaints are brought forward for discussion. The employee in our story cited above may not have followed the proper procedures but what he did was give information to the executives and owners that saved them from spending a lot of money, and he did it for nothing, although he did get a reward in that he was promoted to a higher position. This employee promised to sponsor his son in college, since he himself was not a college graduate and has known the utility of a college education in the workplace. Of course, the executives have control in the workplace while others are to be seen and not heard. In fact, while the contributing factor of the employee who did not have a college degree has become doctoral research material.

Clarity in Decision-Making

Decision made in business and in organizations must be written in simple, clear language, with correct spelling, clear intentions, and easy to interpret in any language. If decisions are all of the above, so will the work force be less complicated. Decisions will bring about a complicated work force, and poor job implementation because decisions given were poorly made, poorly assigned, incomplete, and scheduling may not be clearly understood. As such, many employees may not show up for work because they failed to understand what was said.

Let me give an example: a husband and wife left home for work in the morning; the husband takes their child at school, but asks the wife to pick up the boy after school since the husband had a lot to do at the office. However, before then he was going to call his wife and let her know the situation. When the school was over, the wife, having not heard from the husband, then thinks that maybe he didn't have as much to do as he had thought. However, no sooner had she stopped thinking about the situation, than a phone call from the teacher at her boy's school informed her that the son was still at the school, She fancied thinking something might have happened to her husband judging from the love her husband had for the son. So, the wife first drove to her husband's office with a lot of difficulties because she even crossed over double yellow lines. When he was busy working, he asked, "Why are you here now and where is our son?" She said, "Let me go for the boy first of all, before I tell you what you caused." The husband said, "Okay." When the wife came back with their son, the father gave his son a big kiss and asked his wife to tell him what had happened. The wife hesitated because she was still very emotional about the situation, but she then went on anyway. She said that he had told her that if he was not too busy he would pick up the boy, but if he was very busy, he would call her and ask her to pick up the son. However, he did not call and did not pick up the boy. The husband then replied, "Dear, I completely forgot what I told you." He then told her he was very sorry because she thought something might have happened to her husband. She said,

"You are right about that because I even crossed over the double line while driving on a busy street, at San Pablo and Grand Avenues."

He told his wife and his son that they were going to where they could have the finest food for dinner. When they got home, the husband prepared a schedule for taking the boy to school and for picking him up from school. The wife approved of the schedule. The husband then concluded by saying that his home did not belong to a family of unclear instructions. He told his wife that in a big company unclear instructions are devastating to the company's productivity.

One can see the effect of unclear instructions at the family level. We shall now talk about small and large businesses, and, of course, the workplace.

Clarity in the Workplace

A friend of mine has a manager who has no system of filing letters or any documents. One would be lucky to find two similar documents in the same drawer, let alone the same folder. The filing cabinet is a jungle in that letters and documents are usually lumped together. Nothing is done systematically. Things are very slow; it takes over two hours to find a document meant for an assignment that was given and was due in an hour. When the manager asks for a new assignment, of course, it will not be ready; The manager will get angry and blame the officers who were to process the document, and sometimes the manager and his employee will have a heated exchange of words. There is a lot of instability in the office. The office supervisor would request an employee to handle the filing, but the manager would disagree, and the unstable situation continues unabated.

Productivity, naturally, suffers a decline; actually nothing is being done or done properly. This is a manufacturing company that relies heavily on information from the office including orders from private and public organization. Orders may be weeks past their due date. The report will be made to the general manager, but the general manager is an uncle of the manager, At the same time the CEO thought the general manager was doing a fantastic job, even though revenue was decreasing faster than anyone knew. This is all because the general manager was falsifying the accounts before the CEO could realize what was happening. The company was at the point of bankruptcy, but that was not unexpected to those who worked in the office because they knew that which happened in the office would spread to the plant. No officer worker said anything, but rather prepared their resume for the inevitable attempt to find employment elsewhere.

The CEO was more surprised than anyone was because he believed that the revenue charts presented to him was the real picture of the company's financial status. The CEO invited each of the employees to hear what they had to say. They told the CEO the same story that actually the company had problems, and the uncle of the general manager tried very hard to bring problems into the company by complicating the filing system because the manager would be the only person to do the filing and that it took almost half a day to find documents and thereby kept delaying what needed to be done. Every one of the employees told the CEO virtually the same thing. The CEO then invited the manager to his office, but the manager had virtually nothing to say other than he did the filing and in some cases there were disagreement. The general manager accepted that the manager falsified the revenue outlook, hoping that business would rebound, and then nobody would know what happened. The CEO fired both the general manager and his nephew.

The CEO then appointed a new general manager and manager, and the manager hired someone to revise the filing system to make it useful, and those working with the computers made the system more accessible. The work went faster, the new manager knows the usefulness of dialogue, and has told his employees that dialogue is a discipline of collective learning and inquiry. The employees put away their resumes they had prepared in order to search for new positions.

Business improved dramatically, and good times came back to an unusual extent of the previous mess. The general manager came up with good news, promotions, and the workers were happy and became more creative with their work. As a result, the Board of Directors and the shareholders loved what was happening and refused to get involved in their management style because the system was now working in everyone's favor.

We have talked about the workplace in small business, although things we have mentioned are applicable to large businesses as well. In a large business, the workplace is the same as in a small business but on a larger scale. They are all very law-abiding, and as such, they are subject to penalties and punishments under the law. Large companies can afford participative decision making with both levels presents (both upper and lower levels) with the lower level understanding how to conduct meetings in a dialogue manner and how to handle disagreements when they occur. The Board of Directors may be needed to hear the disagreements and work with the disputants to resolve the disagreement by analyzing again the subject matter and then voting. The majority opinion will then be brought back to the Board where it will simply read through and sign off on the matter, and that becomes the company policy. If the minority resists and the company problem continues, then both parties are required to go back to the drawing board to make necessary modifications. A small business may not have enough money to spend on this, but whether small or large, all businesses and organizations need clear, concise decisions to enable them accomplish their goals.

Clarity in decision-making in an organization is like putting in information in your computer, and therefore if you put in the wrong information, then, of course, you have downloaded the wrong answers and that is tantamount to garbage in, garbage out. If products are produced without targeting a particular segment of the population, they might sell but not to the people who would want them the most. As a result, the company could lose in many ways, particularly financially.

It is clear that clarity in decision-making in a company is the mainstay of a product that also keeps a company in business.

Clarity in Decision-Making Enhances the Following:

1. Good quality products;
2. Well-informed workers;
3. Happier workers;
4. Customer dependency and loyalty; and
5. Competitive work force.

Good Quality Products. Product quality essentially means producing products you like but also producing products your target likes and will buy frequently—the taste, the durability, and sustainability are essential characteristics by which customers judge products. There is no way all people will like the same thing but when your product has sold more than expected because of the limited area that was targeted or because of the publicity the product generated. In any case, the product must be of high quality.

Well-Informed Work Force. A well-informed work force is a more productive work force because workers know what is required of them. Resources used for productivity are always right for producing the product. Equipment that is meant for the products is always ready for the job; otherwise, employees would complain and management would see to it immediately that the required equipment was made available. Information will also enable shipment of the products to customers be done on time. That, of course, creates efficiency, reliability, and profitability.

Happier Work Force. A happy work force is a highly productive work force because the workers listen to instructions and are always on time to work, and such a work force is always a healthy work environment because early to bed is early to rise" and that is the primary source of knowledge, good health, and wealth for a worker at any level. The point here is that charity begins at home, but you have to know what you did to cause the happiness of your child, whether he or she gets their favorite food, toy, clothes, play time, or whatever. So it is with the adults in the work force; management has to create the work force environment.

The same applies to employees; they need a raise in their pay, vacation time, inclusive pay raises, vacation time, and a workload that is not excessive. A happier work force is a package, an employer must not disregard some employees; otherwise, the employees may not work harder and have higher productivity. They are not bad employees, but this is human nature.

Customer Dependency and Loyalty. If information about a certain product is written out clearly and the product does exactly what it was intended to do, a great deal of advertisement is not required because word of mouth—telling friends, relatives, and neighbors may well be enough to get the word out. However, if mass production is used, then advertising may well be needed to sell the product more widely. Sometimes product efficiency may not be the only reason to depend on a product; some products are culturally based. Whether the product is great or not, people of that particular culture may keep buying it. For example, Chinese food products may be greasy to some people who want to lose weight, or Indian attire may appear to be a little odd by those who are not of Indian background. The African clothing has a lot to do with the weather conditions in Africa and are never monopolized by Africans (black or white), since many other people have come to live in Africa permanently. At the same time, if a product is well made, well understood, and has usefulness in many different lifestyles or for other purposes, then people may well buy it, but depending on the buying because it is "new" may well be a stretch. In this time of global economy, countries produce what may appeal to other people in other countries for an economic advantage.

Competitive Work Force. Recently, President Obama announced to the nation that the United States now sells more products to many countries including the followoing countries: China, South Korea, Panama, and nations of the European Union than before Obama came into office. By saying that he was appealing to the nation's work force to work harder and produce great products. Competition is the actual lifeblood of a capitalist economy. Employees in the United States understand that if they can no longer compete, then, of course, their jobs are on the lines. This could mean firing, layoffs, bankruptcy and/ or liquidation of their company. The work force must be competitive with other companies in the same industry. A competitive work force is a productive company and is innovative because they have the revenue to research and discover different ways of lowering costs while maintaining product quality. In order to have product quality and a competitive work force, internal problems amongst employees must be settled satisfactorily and quickly. Anyone found guilty or liable must be addressed and punished without bias. The pay, retirement pensions, and insurance benefits need to be competitive with other companies in the same industry

Achievement and Satisfaction with a Job Well Done

After all is said and done about participative decision-making, the decisions made by both upper and lower levels in the company and signed off by the Board of Directors and by the CEO, which finally become the rules of the company. The participants who are also employees of the same company may be wearing their badges, and other employees will notice them and inquire about the decisions that were reached. They may also be admired by many employees. This may go on for some time, and when the new rules kick in and try to achieve what was intended, then the participants' deliberations may intensify, even to the extent of demands for better pay, while some may ask for written testimonials so that they can apply for any new openings in their company. Other individuals may apply for a new position outside the company. Therefore, in many instances there are struggles in being a participant in the decision-making process. It is a big eye-opener for those participants who have never been in the process.

The less experienced participants learn from the more experienced ones; they study how to conduct dialogue and the meaning of dialogue. Those persons without a degree and little experience benefit the most intellectually and in experience. It does not mean that only the junior level participants benefit when everything is fantastic. Those in the upper level will, at least, keep their positions and may have some financial incentives, as well as including their achievements in their resumés. Some less experienced participants may not receive credit for their contributions simply because of what is perceived in the deliberations. Outside of the meeting, some of those who know these inexperienced individuals may think those people do not have anything to contribute and may not even take their achievements very seriously.

Whatever the case may be, all of those participants feel the same sense of accomplishment, and whatever outsiders may think or say will not matter so much. One thing about me—I think the same as most human beings. Achievement does not bring closure; rather, it opens up many ways of doing the same work and frequently much better ways. When I wrote my first book, <u>Managerial Handbook,</u> I received many phone calls congratulating me for a job well done. Right there, I was speechless, and I decided to write again. I began by researching for my second book, but most of the materials were mine. Now, my fourth book is in progress. I do not know if the fifth book will come along, but I need to find a marketplace for the ones I have written, although they are not doing badly in the United States. They could have done much better if I had the funds for advertising. This was not my first choice of a career. After I earned my MBA, I thought I was going to work on a book, but water seeks its own level. Now, my career is research development and, of course, lecturing.

It is true that those who participated in the decision-making process will some day advance to more lucrative positions with or without a serious plan for the profession. Sometimes one achievement may lead to another, and before you know it, even people you do not know will be asking you to do this or that for them and these are a combination of your achievements.

I call myself a *business scientists* and not a psychologist, but it is sometimes difficult to figure out why many people hope for one thing or one profession in life, and before they know it, something else comes along and occupies or takes away the space of the former intent and all of a sudden, the person is doing something he or she never dreamed of doing or was not of primary concern. I sometimes feel that the competitive advantage we have in a global economy emanates from our individual competitive advantages that we have over others. Therefore, the total individual advantages in any given country on a particular product is the advantage that country has over another country. In other words, the total individual advantages of a given country's product is the competitive advantage [of or over] another country's product that is less competitive. I recall Mr. Tip O'Neill who said, "all politics are local." I don't want to go deeply into competitive advantages at this point, but the point I am making is that a combination of individual factors constitutes one competitive advantage that an individual has over his or her competitors. Therefore, the individual will resort to working harder on what he or she thinks they can do better than their competition. Consequently, if someone has done one, two, or three things better than his competition, the one who has done those things better will certainly claim an advantage over others. For many people this will make them think that they now have a profession because they can do something better than other people.

Therefore, it is very rare that people simply walk away from their achievements without trying to work on their achievements or replicas of those achievements. When I wrote my dissertation in partial fulfillment of my Ph.D., many people bought copies of my dissertation. I then wrote <u>Managerial Handbook</u>, and many people bought copies, and universities wrote to tell me that military has been trying to pass on the information for good administration, and last but not the least, <u>Strategic</u>

<u>Management</u>, and so on means that I have not been able to walk away from what gives me pleasure to do.

International Business and Opportunities

Recently, the President of the United States intimated to the nation that more goods and services are being sold to more countries than ever before, and this is creating more jobs than in years past. International business involves business transactions between one nation and another or business among all nations and could be called *global business*. Trade between nations is as old as civilization itself when it was known as *trade by barter*. There was no medium of exchange; that is, if you were looking for meat that I owned and had corn that I needed and we agreed to exchange meat for corn, then the trade by barter was completed. It takes time to do trade this way, however; finding someone who wants your product and has something you want in exchange. This type of trade continued until civilization grew broader and more complicated, and other mediums of exchange were developed.

Of course, the problem with this exchange was the trust factor was too low. After different forms of mediums of exchange were tried, the world finally settled on paper money; yet, we still have problems with foreign exchange transactions. However, what we have today is still better than what we have seen previously in use for transactions. Our medium of exchange is infinitely better than trade by barter on the large scale. We now have economies; we count on, calculate, divide, and predict what we now call forecasting. People are now employed. Business is now a developed course of study, and trade within and without nations is a large part of business studies in today's economy.

International business has created many opportunities in every country in the world today. In the beginning of paper money, many countries thought that their country would lose control of their economy. Therefore, protectionism became a popular style in many countries, and some said they were protecting their infant industries from the developed economies. However, what the protectionist nations failed to realize was that progress in business transactions comes along with civilization and improvements in transportation and communication. The protectionist movement also failed to understand that if they were deficient in any or all of the above, it would mean they simply would have nothing to protect. International business has therefore opened up the following avenues in international relations.

1. Employment opportunities,
2. Global understanding,
3. Competition,
4. Cultural exchange,
5. Ability to work in teams,
6. Access to raw materials,
7. Elimination of basic distrust,
8. Increase in communications and dialogue; and
9. Increase in imports and exports.

Employment Opportunities. The aim of participative decision-making is to create solvency for the company; in other words, the company that has not been doing well financially begins to increase its finances. In order for any company to stay in business, its financial outlook must improve or at least break even. The old adage stipulates that two heads are better than one. Therefore, participants, no matter how many there are, are looked at as hopeful signs for good decision-making and consequent increase in productivity and profitability that also increases employment opportunities. The dialogue style we have been talking about enables each member to listen, ask questions intelligently, follow what is being discussed, reflect on what he or she thinks is the actual problem, and then possibly come up with a solution to the complicated problem.

At the end of the meeting, hopefully both levels have accepted a solution as the right thing to do for the company to save it from multiple problems. We have to understand that whatever education and experience the members may have had prior to this meeting, they are still human beings, and they are not immune from making mistakes. However, that is usually infrequent, unless, of course, the right case was not given to the participants. What I mean by *right case* is that if profits were made, it should be stated, and if not, the company should not *cook the books* or misrepresent their financial status in the case study. The phrase, *garbage in, garbage out*, is used in computer studies to describe that whatever case the company has presented before the participants is the case these individuals have to analyze and deliberate. Therefore, the results the company receives from the participants will come from the case that the company presented to the participants for deliberation.

The participants may work harder to turn the company's outlook around because the participants have been committed to doing so, all things being equal. This may mean that the right information given to the participants and the environment is right for everyone to participate. Participative decision-making is one of the best methods in the process of making decisions, and this process enables a company to do the following:

1. Hire and train new workers;
2. Maintain and keep current employers for a longer period;
3. The turnover rate for employees is lower;
4. The company assists in helping more people attain middle class status; and
5. It promotes friendliness between the participants and other employees.

Hiring and Training. A company with a successful participative decision-making process may employ more people in order to increase productivity to meet the increased demand. Participative decision-making is my brainchild, and as such, it is new and very promising for business. Therefore, before a company embarks on creating the participative decision-making panel, it must have been preparing to meet with a positive outcome of the decisions to be made by both the upper and lower levels. Some implementation of the decisions made by the participants may be overwhelming in such a way that if the participants had never previously prepared for such an outcome, events could turn into a disaster in that if the demand created cannot be met. This unpreparedness may include having enough qualified workers as well as enough raw materials to meet the increased demand for the products. Therefore, it is advisable for companies who have the means to conduct such decision-making programs to be prepared for the implementation of the decisions that will be made. "All animals are equal, but some animals are more equal than others,' (Orwell, *Animal Farm)*. This means that some implementation decisions are rather minor with no great demand for the product, but one does not know until the company begins implementation of the decisions what the results will be. If the company gets ready with the right materials or equipment necessary for implementation of its decisions, it means that the company may not be surprised about what to do and what not to do when time becomes a major factor.

Manpower is always one of the largest factors in preparing for these results; however, the fact that this is an existing company may mean there will be little difficulty if the increased demand requires more workers. Training, of course, the new employees will take time, but acquiring new employees ready and willing to work is the key there. In most cases, business is about taking advantage of the opportunities presented. Fortunately or unfortunately, depending on whether the company is prepared or not, the company may be at the *right place at the right time*. This could be of great advantage to the company's financial position for years to come; however, if the company falls short and is not prepared, the opportunity could be lost as well as the potential for increased income. Therefore, preparing for the opportunity with what the company needs to work each day is good business in itself. Compounding the need for readiness is if the company has a program for participative decision-making.

Frequently, it may be difficult to hire the right people for a particular job. Degrees on some jobs are not the answers but it is necessary to have a college degree even in some cases experience may count very minimally because experience may vary from company to company. Even though all roads lead to Rome, the Romans may prefer some roads more than others. Therefore it is advisable for a company to hire its own workers, whether experienced, college educated or not, and train them in the way the company operates and wants the work accomplished. Let the new employees know the company's policies about such continual tardiness with no tangible reason. This needs to be enforced by appropriate punishment such as sending the employee home for that day or suspending him or her for up to a week without pay if repeated. Trained employees must be required to stay with the company for at least six months or longer. It might be a good idea to do background checks on the would-be employees' credit and possible criminal background.

<u>Maintain And Keep Current Employees For A Longer Period</u>. Since manpower is such a large factor in a company training new employees is expensive, the company, particularly if it is profitable, needs to inform the employees about the financial position of the company so they can understand if pay raises may or may not be forthcoming as soon as they would like. This may complicate the way the workers do their jobs because they may feel that the company for its own selfish ends is using them, and they may try to undermine the company's efforts to strengthen its business position. Even though the company may call these employees every name in the book that may project the employees as unproductive and people of bad character, the fact is that the company should ask itself what has gone wrong. The employer must engage in dialogue with its employees at least by letting the employees know the state of the company's financial position currently. Obviously, the company should not make promises it cannot keep, but needs to inform employees that when conditions improve, such as by selling more products, their paychecks will also increase. Employees need to be encouraged, but one has to be careful; otherwise, what you have said

and cannot supply will come back to haunt you. The employees will always talk about what you were unable to implement, even though you have implemented many of the things that was promised them.

<u>Managerial Promises and Conversations with Employees.</u> If you promised the employees anything, add an attachment as I call it. For instance, I will make sure a few of you are promoted, and all the rest of you will have pay raises if productivities will meet the demanded products. All of you know that for the past six months our productivities have fallen below the demanded products because many employees called off from work, lateness to work has risen 50%, employee disagreements with supervisors is at an all-time high. Employee complaints about other employees is at an all-time high, too. If all of you could bring peace to your workplaces that could settle most of what your disagreements are all about. You know that I don't visit your workplaces as I have been doing because I spend all day in my office settling disputes. This is not helping us or, do you think these ae helping to us. Almost all the participants shouted, "not helping." One employee stood up and told the general manager that the problem is that the supervisors discriminate so much, a lot of favoritism. You have to be who they like, the job you do are always perfect or no one should mention the employee's name; otherwise, you may be in trouble. The employee went on telling the general manager that one would hope that a supervisor or all the supervisors would be peacemakers or uniters and not dividers. Apparently, your supervisors are practicing the system of divide and rule. Sir, that system is killing our company. I love this company. I have worked here for about 21 years. I want to retire here, but it frightens me to see what is going on. Please, sir, help us. I have two boys in college; all my hopes are in this company. People like our products. We cannot even produce enough for our customers because we are always against each other while the supervisors fan the flames.

"My friend, what is your name? the general manager asked. "Sir, my name is John Vincent. The general manager continued, "Mr. Vincent,

I will talk to the supervisors, and I will report my findings to this same audience."

Another employee told the general manager that he would like the manager to visit with the employees from time to time, but the general manager told the audience that he loves meeting with the employees from time to time at least trying to know their names and some of their problems. But he no longer knows if he will be your general manager any more, he joked, or judge, of the company because he said he treats individual and group cases from morning until evening, some days with no time left to do my job as a general manager. This company must get itself together so that we may move forward. But I tell all of you this," said the general manager. "I am going to divide my time so that I can have time to meet with all of you from time to time because I sense that all of you want me to visit with you from time to time or that I know you have updated our company." No sooner had the general manager ceased speaking than the employees gave him a long round of applause and wished the general manager a long life.

The general manager then understood the employees were willing to work, but they needed a leader, and that, too, made the general manager realize that another manager to assist in looking after other matters and advice where possible. The general manager clearly saw the case on the day he met with the employees and the blame was squarely on the leaders he employed to take care of the employees. Instead, the supervisors and managers were after their own interests. The general manager also was convinced that if he didn't do something dramatic like suspending most of the managers and supervisors, the problems in the company might get out of hand and out of control.

The general manager also understood that in order to get the company moving forward it was not just a question of money, although money was important. However, human-to-human interaction in good faith was more important. Therefore, the general manager decided to show examples. If reforms about misunderstanding between employees were brought to him, he would not mind hearing both parties. That was to tell supervisors and manager that one has to tell it as it is and not to let themselves be a part of the dispute by keeping the case overnight. If the manager does not have to do more research on the dispute, the justice delayed is justice denied. The general manager was nearly doing the job of a motivational speaker and even most of the employees took strength from what he said. The employees were very often sent out for training, and nearly all of the employees stayed with the company. Their pay might not have been the best in the industry, but the general manager made some timely promises about pay and pay adjustments, as well as other bonuses, which he delivered. Thereafter, the general manager became highly trusted and the hope of most employees.

The Turnover Rate For Employees Is Lower. This is the rate at which the employees leave a company for positions at other companies, frequently in the same industry or a similar one. The rate of turnover can vary from low to severe. When a company's employee turnover rate is negative or even severely high, the causes may include low pay, fewer benefits or no benefits at all, when compared to another company. If the company has trained these employees, then it has lost its investment when they demand higher pay or benefits or for other reasons.

A serious example is that of the San Jose Police Department. Recently the city had a serious cutback in funds. The police department suffered a setback in terms of keeping officers because several police offices defected to other cities that could pay more and/or had better benefits. The city began running helter-skelter trying to see where they could find money to enable the city to pay their officers competitive wages. It is more difficult in businesses because the competition will be happy to have a company's former employees, who will be able to give competitive information about their old company while in training at their new company. Of course, the new company will be happy to have them, while their former employer will be losing valuable employees.

Another example involves me when I was operating a maintenance business. I went to EDD (Employment Development Department) at City Hall in San Francisco. My employees couldn't stay more than three months because they had formed a ring for stealing from my customers. I had to fire most of them; I did this as soon as they were caught, but firing them didn't make them stop stealing. They felt more "manly" and stole for fun. In the end, I discovered that most of them just came back from jail. They had no moral discipline whatever; they tried to harm one another there. I began selling my businesses. I thought that after the sale of Wilson Maintenance Company. I would gain a great deal of peace of mind and would be happy to concentrate on my studies in the doctoral program at the time. The speedy sale of my maintenance company enabled me to complete my studies on time because I had no serious distractions any more. However, the victims of the theft by my employees asked me to pay for some of the items not recovered when the thieves were my employees. Therefore, at this point, I knew employee rate of turnover could come either from the employees themselves or from the employer. The employees may feel they need more pay or benefits such as vacations, health insurance, overtime pay, and if uniforms are involved, who pays for cleaning the uniform.

It is always about money and time, which is also money. Sometimes the employee's point of view comes from their union who views the annual report of the company from when they realized what the company has made profits in the past year or past fiscal year. At this point, they generally feel that the employees should also benefit from the profits. Recently, we saw what happened between BART and its employees; actually it was between the BART officials and the unions when it had taken them so long to come to an agreement while transportation in the city was going badly, and then the governor had to come and stabilize the situation by asking both sides, the union and management, to settle for a more sustainable settlement.

One particular company that could give them more pay in another company in the same industry may simply leave and seek employment elsewhere and discover very quickly that they were better off at the first company and then try to return to the original company.

Sometimes moving from one company to another needs some research to find out whether the employee is better off financially at his or her original company than the new one. If it makes sense, the employee may only leave after having been given the job. A bird in the hand is worth two in the bush—this old adage means what you presently own is more valuable than what you may anticipate owning. Incidentally, many people do not understand that you don't have to quit your job to seek another job. One should simply look for another job while still gainfully employed. In some cases, one has to settle for a job you may not really love to do so, but you have to have a job because one has to eat and pay the bills.

Leaving a job should be a thought out proposition. If you just leave a job because you have parents who love you and you think they may care for you as they did when you were younger. You may be dreaming; your parents may think they did not do a good job of raising you because they may feel that you are not successful in life. However, in many cases parents are proven wrong in that type of thinking because young men and women grow up differently. Some may have instant recognition of what to do as adults, while others may have a long time on what they have to do as adults and may have several jobs before they settle upon one job.

All young people may or may not be college educated, but personal lives may be quite different from academic life. Personal lives generally involve parents, and that may be tricky because parents may well be really nice people all around; Yet, they have children who are completely different from the norm. In that case, also, people may say that the parents spoiled the children because those parents did not give them discipline but simply allowed the children to do what they wanted. That is similar to a garden without a gardener, where the flowers, of course, will simply grow wild.

As I was leaving home, I heard on the radio that a drunk driver who was a member of a well-to-do family who didn't think that their son could do any wrong, let alone try to discipline him killed four people. Sometimes our neighbors know what we do in our homes. It may not be their problems, but we cannot leave them alone in our society. The accumulation of bad behavior in the workplace may come from upbringing. In most cases, behavior is a studied phenomenon though an insignificant portion of it may be inherited, but if recognized by the affected person, the situation can be remedied.

I lived for many years in San Francisco, and most of the yeas I lived in the Bayview District because rent there was cheap. I was then working on my doctoral dissertation; money was very tight for me. Even when I finally graduated, I decided to stay and write books because many people had bought my dissertation, and many of them commented that writing books might well be my true calling. So, to return to Bayview, I am not here to tell you the bad, ugly, and worst of Bayview, nor am I trying to describe lawlessness in Bayview, San Francisco or wound somebody else's feelings. That was why I decided to call the whole scenario *accumulated behavior* because I know the situation could be remedied through hard work. We should all refrain from behavior with incremental catastrophe—that is the more you behave in a certain way the more bad things come your way.

CHAPTER 9
ACCUMULATIVE BEHAVIOR

1. Accumulative Behavior
2. Incremental Catastrophic Behavior
3. The Company Produces More Middle Class
4. Hard Work
5. Global Understanding
6. Language
7. Making the Producer Better
8. Mass Production to Lower Costs
9. Nearness to the Raw Materials
10. Ability to Locate Where Price is Lowest and Where to Sell Highest
11. Cultural Exchange
12. Ability to Work in Teams
13. Expansion of International Business
14. Complexities Management
15. Access to Raw Materials
16. Elimination of Basic Distrust

CHAPTER 9

ACCUMULATIVE BEHAVIOR

People With Accumulative Behavior And Incremental Catastrophic Behavior

Remember that people with accumulative behavior are people whom you can hardly trace one thing as the cause of their behavior. Their parents themselves have zero good behavior; they cannot advise themselves let alone advise their children. As such, their children find it difficult to hold onto a job. They may not necessarily act unlawfully in everything they do, but they are not peaceful in themselves; they are not insane and not violent, but it is difficult for them to listen to advice. As such, they cannot hold a job; they move from job to job, not that they have viable information to transmit from company to company. Some people may think they are stubborn; however, I define stubbornness as taking a position and refusing to listen to other points even though there is no basis for that viewpoint. However, sometimes such people may be right because they are experts in their field; sometimes they are not experts and have no legitimate viewpoint and nothing to offer to any issue, but are just stubborn in their beliefs.

Incremental Catastrophic Behavior

I am not a behavioral scientist, but as a business scientist, I believe there is a lot of common ground here. Incremental catastrophic behavior

(ICB), as I call it, ordinarily refers to people who are normal human beings. They make sense in all that they say and are very logical. However, they are always in trouble, and as such, they go to jail frequently. They do the wrong things, say the wrong things, and are always involved in one form of trouble or another. Like the accumulative behavior (AB) person, the ICB cannot hold a job for a long period. They sound sensible when you first meet with them, but as time passes, one realizes that their viewpoints are all very radical. Usually, if the employer disagrees with them, they simply work out. However, in all normal circumstances, no employer is likely to keep them on the payroll for long because of their radical behaviors. The AB individual understands much better than the ICB person does. The ICB individual thinks that they understand better than anyone else does. They attribute the constant misunderstandings to jealousy or envy on the part of others because other people feel threatened by the ICB's subjective behaviors, though they feel they have the best behavior. However, to be candid about the AB an ICB people, they are equal opportunity employees in today's generation, which means that AB and ICB could come from any background, rich or poor.

The Company Produces More Middle Class

As I have said regarding the AB and ICB individuals, nothing can hold them back from moving from job to job because they have behavioral problems, whereas other employees who may take advantage of their in-service training could move up the ranks to the level of being known as the middle class. The middle class could come from the following:

1. In-service training;
2. Formal education;
3. Fault-finding about the company he or she works for; and
4. Always ready to work harder.

In-Service Training. This type could be organized departmentally where the training is based on a specific area of the company's business. All those in the particular area are asked to come for training on how to handle the specific area of the business. Of course, some employees may be more serious than others may, and those are the employees who may devote their own time in mastering the particular work and may understand that work so clearly that they become qualified for promotion and could be promoted to supervisory positions. Instead of moving from one company to another, they tend to stay put and enjoy more promotions. More employees like that eventually become executives in the company. Working for a particular company for a long time pays a larger dividend in terms of promotions and other rewards such as money, vacation time, and stock options. We have a saying that goes like, "a patient dog eats the fattest bone." This is the center of success, I suppose, because some people think that success should come quickly and sooner, and when that does not happen, they quit and begin another thing from the beginning and work on that for a long time. Perhaps they succeed on this new work this time around or else they're back to square one. So, whatever we do in any endeavor, we need patience and endurance; however, we have to understand that endurance by itself will not solve problems. Patience and endurance must always go with hard work and intellectual discipline.

Formal Education. Formal education can be described in many ways including the studying of subjects of reading, writing, and arithmetic or attending lectures in a classroom with the goal of passing specific examinations, a certificate examination, or a degree examination, and it could be trades such as mechanics, tailoring, cooking, and so forth, all with the hope of higher future rewards. You may receive the training and possibly a degree in what you want to do that will certainly curtail the amount of in-service training that you would have to undergo in order to attain a higher level. A formal education can assist an employee to skip an entry-level position to a higher qualified level. It frequently takes a person without a degree or certificate of training years longer to attain the entry point that a holder of a degree has. An example of this is a friend of mine who applied for a lower California auto insurance. He was a college graduate, but even though he was qualified in some areas, he was told by the government that his income was higher than 250% of the federal poverty level, which is higher than the Enhanced Silver Plan limits, and his income was above the MediCal limit, whereas most of his friends who applied were qualified in nearly all categories, but they had no college or university degree. This is to show how difficult it is for those with a formal education such as a college degree to qualify easily for basic government assistance due to their higher income level. The same is true in the workplace; there are assignments that are given to those without a degree, and there are other assignments that require college degrees. Having said all that, all things being equal that may be business entities, but in an ever-changing world economy, it is easier said than done. In some cases, a college graduate is observed doing odd jobs to make ends meet.

Again, situational business transactions are never reliable as absolute guides, so always be prepared for economic changes so that you can take advantage of any opportunity. When the economy goes down, of course, you are still in good shape. My point here is to tell everyone who can not skip attending college in the interest of our local, national, and the world economy to do so. Economies rely on analysis and creativity that are the basic strengths of a college education. The irony is the interpretation of a college education for many means more pay or wealth. It is not necessarily either one of the two, but it is not impossible to be either one. However, it is problematic to base hopes on either pay or wealth; education is to enable one to help others with your skills. If, for some reason, this generates higher pay or wealth, then that becomes a *lucky situation;* otherwise, usually in business if your aim is to make a lot of money, then you may or may not do so. Your aim in running a business should always be to produce the best product for the services of the consumers. You should have the consumer's best interest at heart when designing your products. It is bad business to aim too much for great profits. The aim of just making money may lead you to lose focus and leave the track of your best business goal in designing your products because all of your ideas may focus not on the consumer's needs but on what will make money. This then defines your failure because you may not break even or be profitable.

A formal education may be able to expose those areas of intricacies or hidden exposures to the owner of the business or an employee of the business. After four or six years of business school, a business owner or a manager should be able to uncover most of the hidden exposures in his business transactions. Hidden exposures are points that are not easily understood by the manager or analyzed easily.

In some cases, those without a formal education regard owning a business a challenge and even being a manager with no formal education but with promotion through the ranks as a challenge, and for that they have to work very hard for perfection. In some cases, those with no formal education get ahead by being very careful and working very hard on improving product quality. These same people who become managers then care so much about what other people say or think about them or their work for the company perhaps think that the slightest decline in their management may bring back talk about their lack of formal education. No one is able to predict how far some companies may go. Some companies may hold off promotions for those without a formal education to a managerial position no matter how intelligent the individual may be.

Fact Finding About the Company. It is always good to know things about your company without necessarily becoming the FBI (Federal Bureau of Investigation). One should try to know those things about the company that interests you. Of course, you cannot know everything about your company; one should ask questions and find out from your friendly superiors. One should not allow fact-finding become obvious to other employees so that they may not wonder if you are doing so to see how long you can stay with the company or if the company's financial position is secure. In short, do not make your fact finding obvious. If the purpose of your fact-finding is based on your suspicions about the company's well-being, then you must investigate carefully and subtly. If you rush it, your suspicions may get ahead of you, and then, of course, you are bound to fail in your investigations because you are not discovering the findings you want. Finally, you move to another company where you have no idea what is going on there, and eventually the other company may prove unbearable. This supports the idea of a bird in the hand is worth two in the bush, meaning in this case that if you were unable to find out why you should change companies but you moved anyway, your efforts are in vain and can only end in failure.

Usually, fact-finding must be motivated by something. Unless one is aware of your motivation for the fact-finding, you may be working for no reason. For example, a handicraft teacher reported to the principal of the school for which he worked that most of his woven baskets, cane chairs, and woven doors were no longer found in the school's store. He began his fact-finding by asking any student he met the following questions: 1) Did you enter the store yesterday? If yes, how many people did you see there? Do you know any one of them by name? The handcraft teacher was very frustrated; he thought that the *stolen* materials might be linked to one of the officials so that he might use that as an excuse for leaving the school for another. If he left, he himself might be suspected, especially if he told his present school that he was finding his way out anyway. Then, of course, he might be the number one suspect.

One may not find anything from one's co-workers because they have already become suspicious by the questions one has asked, which many of them may be too hypocritical to answer. The fact is that if you have no reason for your fact-finding, simply refrain from doing that because your aim may be revealed and misinterpreted. Then, one might be in double jeopardy. Whatever motive one has for fact-finding it should be consistent with the rules and procedures of the company. Remember that another company for whom you may work will require recommendations from your current company. Remember that fact-finding is tedious and complicated, and sometimes may boomerang on you in that the recommendations from the current workplace may not match your ambition or your dream job. Again, remember what you have in hand may be greater than what you anticipate having. In business, patience, understanding, discipline, and hard work are responsible for the level you want to be.

Hard Work. Hard work, if done intelligently, pays great dividends. Before hard work, a business owner has to know the meaning of hard work and why hard work is necessary. It depends on the type of business one is running, but all businesses have one thing in common, and that is hard work. Working without knowing exactly why hard work is required and the meaning of hard work for your business is tantamount to working blindfolded. Many people work to enable them to produce more of their products, because of keen competition, or to produce more durable goods and better products. Producers have different reasons for working hard, but all reasons they have must be positive for their business. Look at the Microsoft or Facebook companies, as well as others. They have worked very hard to be where they are today. They did not work hard just for the sake of working. A student reads and practices for long hours; that is called hard work because he or she wants good grades or an excellent performance. A farmer plants good seeds and weeds the crop because he wants a good harvest. The point is that we work hard for a reason; in some cases, business owners who want to sell their businesses make sure the business is in the best possible condition before selling, which enables them to make the best possible profit.

One thing we also have to understand is that in some cases we may work so hard and apply every ability we have, and yet the possibility of making a profit may prove unsuccessful. The reasons for this may be that the workers do not have the knowhow, meaning they don't have the technical expertise to get the work accomplished. The raw materials may also be insufficient or be the wrong material for the products. In more extreme cases, there may be no clear answers for failures. The only things one can ask are "Why?", "What?", and "How" in some cases.

Overconfidence may account for a failure. Instead of researching and developing studies, the individual ignored all that because he or she thought that the company and management were the experts in the discipline. So, one thinks one has no need of rehearsing. Of course, in competitive world of today, before one knows it, a company may not even be number ten on the list.

Although this may be hard work, I call it a given in business because one must always be ready to compete or risk being run over by competitors. We also laud what we do in our businesses or in the companies for whom we work. Actually, those are the things that we are bound to be doing for the success of our livelihood. Of course, if we do not take care of them, our livelihood will slip away from us. We now know that most businesses need hard work, although some may need it more than others, depending on what is meant by *hard work*. Some work is mental, while much is very physical. The mental aspects usually come first, and this includes planning, sketching or map drawing, analysis, developments on paper, and then the financial aspects follow. Whenever that starts taking shape. When the shape is formed, in some businesses that is when more workers are needed, but the expansion of the work force could start from the beginning if the owner or the entrepreneur knows exactly what he or she is doing.

The physical work might be what we call the *blue-collar jobs*, even though they wear blue shirts and blue shorts. They have one most important thing in common with the *white-collar* workers, and that is *common sense*. No one can simply begin fixing anything without first knowing where each bolt should go; otherwise, one may be constructing what was not intended. My advice is that management should not allow any project to be divided simply by thinking about what you think you are or belong in a company. Do not think a *white-collar* job is better than a *blue-collar* one, especially if you cannot be a carpenter or a draftsman at the same time. If you cannot do both, what makes you think one is better than the other is? Even if one is paid more than the other job that could be based on subjective evaluations, which are very questionable at best.

Global Understanding

In the past, international businesses were for textbooks, primarily for teaching. This revealed what could have been, the results we might have had, and the results that could have been all we could have and not what we really had at hand. Today's international business study is really with what we are engaged. It has become what I call *generational reality* because international business is living up to its name, right before our eyes. We understand more about things and others, and others understand more about us. The sporadic understanding of fewer countries mostly based on war allies and country-to-country proximity has given us what we now call a *global village*. In the past, even countries as large as the United States or Russia found it difficult doing business with itself because of transportation distances and communication difficulties. Today, I write books; my professional word processor lives in West Sacramento, next door to the capital of California, which is also the most populous state in the United States. My editorial staff and publishers are in Indiana hundreds of miles away from California. Even though we do not see each other, the business is being done the way it should be. Some other companies established offices in China and India; yet, everything is running very smoothly. At the same time, consumers are residing all over the world. The following items constitute some of the global understandings in international business:

1. Culture;
2. Language;
3. Food;
4. How Some Raw Materials Are Obtained; and
5. Transportation.

Culture. Culture is the fabric of our existence. It is what we do daily, following our ancestors. We don't have to learn these traits; we use them at will. Culture is a learned behavior, and in most cases as I have seen in my experience, if your parents are academicians, the children will tend to prefer academic activities. In fact, that was one of the things that motivated me to going back to school after my children were born. I thought of showing them my example. It worked for me because almost all of them said they were going to be "like Dad." Before they started high school, I was already a year into my Ph.D. program. Some of my five boys completed their high school programs just when I received my Ph.D. The mistake I made was that I began giving them more money than they required, thereby creating a different lifestyle for them. than was for, but I don't really know if that was a generational gap, but all of them graduated. Even then, getting to my heights was not a piece of cake for them. Even as I am writing, some are still battling to get there. I always wish them luck. I brought in my story to show how parents could be happy when their children follow their footsteps.

I remember my late uncle, Chief C.O. Ikunengwang, who was my role model, even as I am, I feel his presence; yet when he was still over here, he was a Roman Catholic, but I am still a Presbyterian. I called him *Chief,* although he was not a chief; he was a principal executive officer when I left home. I cannot tell for sure if he was promoted to chief before he died or not. Sometimes I wonder what actually creates motivation. May his soul rest in perfect peace. If culture is a learned behavior, so culture is like studying business, economics, mathematics or any subject or discipline, but I will always advise anyone against attending any violent church or organization. Otherwise, in my family we do not have a culture-based religion. In most cases, culture is merely what your parents have been and have told you what they have learned from their parents. We have learned that earlier many people lived in caves; the fact is in today's world how many people around the world would like to go back to cave dwelling? Probably none, but that was a long-standing culture. Why would we change it? Some people would say it is primitive. How many primitive changes do we need? In many countries, young men are brutally murdered by parents for having children out of wedlock in cases where you have to be married before you may have children. No one will listen to why it happened the way it did. They call it culture and many others. Sometimes, culture provides a shield for us, especially for what we do not like, but for anything one likes there must be a way of getting around it because there is a will to proving the culture wrong. Cultural sensitivities are those things you will like about someone, a foreigner or a stranger before they enter your office. Sometimes bending down a little bit or saying *Good Morning* or *Afternoon* or so. Otherwise, the person you are visiting with might conclude that you are rude and may not like doing business with you, especially if he or she is going to pay you, but if you are going to make the payment, cultural sensitivities may be minimal or nonexistent.

Children born in the United States whose parents originated in China or Nigeria have different ways of doing things than when they were visiting with their parents' original homes. Their exposure in the United States, including schools they attended and not being frequent visitors to their parents' homeland could stop them from knowing their original culture. The totality of all of these things makes them virtually non-natives in their parents' homeland. In addition, the language is a big enticement to their place of birth. I came here in my thirties, and about 30 years later I still speak with an accent, although somewhat diminished, but any American born person will still ask where I came from originally. Chinese or Mexican people often come to the United States or were born in the United States and still speak their parents' native languages; this makes them bilingual, but the primary language of business in the United States is English. In the case of Nigeria, because the country was ruled by Britain, English has been a required language for high school completion. Therefore, before a Nigerian decides to study in the United States, he or she must read and write well in English. Before a Nigerian comes to the United States to study, he or she has already overcome the language barrier. That has always been a great advantage for Nigerian students, as Nigerians do not have to learn English as a foreign language.

In prosperous economic periods, the United States has no large barriers in trading with the people of Nigeria, I mean in terms of the language. Even on the African continent, Western ideas have been with us for a long time. I thought South Africa and Zimbabwe would drive most of the South African countries to different ruling ideologies, but former first Black South African President, Barrister Nelson Mandela articulately led South Africa back to Western ideology and much more. I have always remembered Dr. Kwame Nkrumah as the *Father* of modern Africa, but today, in my opinion, Mr. Mandela has taken that title, *Father of Africa* from Dr. Nkrumah. However, Dr. Nkrumah is one of the founding fathers of modern Africa.

Understanding the world today is the brainchild of technology— mostly, the Wright Brothers with the airplane, Alexander Bell with the telephone, and, of course, Alan Turing with the computer. Therefore, communications and transportation have taken the lead in the global economy and understanding all the other discoveries that have kept us prosperous over the years contribute greatly to the longevity and understanding of other parts of the world. Having said the foregoing about culture and our global understanding, we can now see that culture and global understanding today is based mostly on our technologies. Let us take a look at China, which nobody thought anyone could penetrate economically; today, China is a marketplace for American companies because of the great technological advances. The Chinese now have more millionaires than quite a few other countries. Culture is important in peoples' lives, as recognition of the past has done much to settle the present. We now live in the world of needs and wants. Until culture, needs and wants come to equilibrium. Culture will continue to lose its value as much of it will never be at equilibrium with needs and wants. Does culture mean conservatism? If not, in today's era, what is culture. Needs include food, clothing, and shelter. Wants are luxury items such as luxury cars like Mercedes Benz and swimming pools.

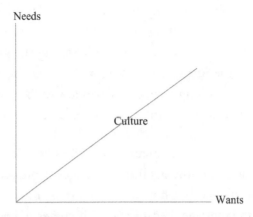

Needs and wants are economic activities and are very well understood around the world by all cultures. The global economy is controlled by economic culture and not by an individual country's culture.

Economic cultures are economic activities such as buying low, selling high; high quality products; high quality raw materials; efficient delivery systems, and efficient communication systems. A country's culture includes recognition of its ancestral behaviors and beliefs, peasant farming, non-academic activities, preparing for conflict with primitive implements, inefficient food production, and poor communication technology. Almost every country's culture is based on beliefs that have nothing to do with science. For example, the *medicine man* or *shaman* believes it would rain because of his activities as opposed to the scientific technology of weather forecasting (even though it is often wrong also). Therefore, an economic culture and a country's culture entirely two different things, but we are talking about culture that enhances our global understanding, and that is pure economic culture.

As we have seen, in economic culture it is very difficult to alter its existence. Let us think about the Wright Brothers—no matter how we alter the structure of an airplane, we cannot change the fact that the Wright Brothers thought about transportation, and likewise, we cannot alter the fact that Alexander Bell thought about communicating when he came up with the idea of the telephone. Those two inventions are

185

truly central to global economy that we have today, and Mr. Turing's computer wizardry changed the world of business and economics with the new computer world we see today. Changing the global economy means changing the ideas of the Wright Brothers and Mr. Bell. The computer has come a long way, but it will always be a support system to transportation and communications for efficiency and durability.

Language. Although language and tribes may differ in various economic activities we understand, languages expressed in economic activity may be spoken but not necessarily most of the time. There is written and sign language, because when it comes to needs and wants, everybody wants to be a part of the prosperity. Language is difficult when it does not address what we need or what we want.

For example, in my neighborhood, there is an elderly woman from India, who is so good as to prepare tea Indian style for me, and she speaks in Hindi about the tea. The fact is I do not understand Hindi, but she talks and holds a cup of tea with her hand extended to me. I know she is giving me a cup of tea. When I said, "Thank you," she said, "Welcome." Then, I knew we were truly communicating. So, one can see how a mere cup of tea can bring people from different parts of the world together even though understanding the language of each is very difficult.

I also remember when I was a young boy growing up in Eastern Nigeria that I saw Asian students studying how to plant palm trees. People said that these students could not understand English and that training them in Nigeria, especially in Eastern Nigeria, was a real waste of time and money. Well, guess what? Today, those students have been back to Nigeria as managers; they now speak English well and work as managers, assistant managers, and supervisors.

In some cases, people attribute language as a larger part of culture, but if language is learned, then that also means that culture is also learned. If everything is learned and people become very good at them, what then do we call culture? Also, who owns any culture? I guess this still comes down to the same hypothesis that we now have a global village and therefore a global economy. In many countries, we have different dialects in neighboring villages, and if the people have to get together to find a common dialect, and yes they can. In Africa, we have Ghana as an example, and in Asia, there is the Philippines. My friend, Dr. Maduekwe, and I went to a supermarket to do some shopping; just as we were entering the mall, two women were speaking in Hansa. My friend joined them and began speaking in Hansa with them because he could understand Hansa. He told me that he had lived there as a boy. The two women jumped on him because they had found a person from their village. They became good friends, and I realized that language is a powerful tool for communication and friendliness. Today, they are still very good friends.

In San Francisco, neighborhoods have frequently been based on a language those who write and speak fluently a particular language. Those who live in and around the Mission District are primarily Latin Americans, although it used to be an Italian neighborhood. People who live and work in Chinatown are primarily Chinese or from Asian countries. The city is made up of such divisions, although it has changed somehow over the years. There has been no rule creating the divisions; it just happened as people moved into neighborhoods in which they heard familiar languages. It might be they listened to the old adage that says like birds of the same feather flock together. Eventually San Francisco, Chicago, New York, and other large cities were populated that way; they are always together for major events like the election of mayors, supervisors, and elections to Sacramento and Washington, D.C. and ultimately the election of the president. The primary language for voting in the United States is English.

Food. Of course, every country has its own dishes and special foods, but with new technologies and better understanding, each country has improved its food production. In recent years, many farmers have advertised concerning organic food, because organic foods are in high demand. I can testify to that because since my birth I have never been to the dentist office as a patient because I have never had problems with my teeth because I was brought up with organic foods. In fact, over 75% of the people of the Cross River State of Nigeria do not visit the dentist office frequently. Occasionally, fewer people visit the dentist in the hospital maybe because of car accidents or other types of accidents. But as the population grows, chemicals may be used to grow more food and that may change the way Nigerians think about food and dentists. At present, Nigerians know what dentists do, but their usefulness is not as well-known as doctors treating malaria patients. Farmers overwhelmingly produce organic food items and sell them cheaply to restaurant owners who prepare the dishes very palatably. This also enabled foreigners to visit repeatedly especially Western businessmen and women. The federal government also lowered the value of the naira (Nigerian currency) and made food very affordable with foreign currencies, particularly the US dollar and British pound sterling.

My grandfather was a businessman trading in palm products— palm oil, palm nuts, cashews, and coconuts. He made many friends and ate many different foods. Every time he visited home, he would tell stories about food from other countries or cities and gave them high credit for food production from Ikun and the entire community we now call Cross River State or *Canan Cities*. Before this, we only recognized Calabar as the Canan City. Today, Canan City stretches to Calabar, Ikun, Ojoja, and Obudu, including Uyanga, Biase, Bahuiumono, Itigidi areas, and the entire Cross River State. Because of food production, all feeder roads are tarred, health facilities provided, much cheaper food and hotel rooms yet fewer medical doctors would call such areas home because they are very congestive, slow, as opposed to the city life, which is very fast and sometimes considered dangerous.

Before airplanes and telecommunications brought us much closer together, countries were very far apart (not just geographically), and each country considered others as less productive than they were and less capable of preparing good food. However, with the arrival of the *global village* of today, we have been able to uncover the types of food each country specializes in, how they prepare their primary dishes, and consequently their contributions to the world food production capability. The results are that the countries can no longer regard other countries as "never do wells" simply because that country is unknown to most of their own citizens. Trading blocs have been in existence since humankind began doing business. Today, food products are not just for satisfaction; it stands for love; most importantly, food is for the rich, healthy, and the poor.

How Some Raw Materials Are Obtained. Raw materials are found in all parts of the world, and sometimes one country arranges with another country for extracting raw materials such as gold and silver from Mexico, and so forth. Sometimes a company from a country with sophisticated expertise may help in the extractions under specific conditions. There are qualified humans and sophisticated equipment necessary for the extraction of the raw materials. I do not mean the technicalities of actually extracting the material from the earth, but one has to be either the oil-drilling engineer or gold-mining engineer in order to have the expertise for drilling and mining.

In most countries, the central government owns mineral deposits, and as such, any foreign or domestic company that wants to extract these deposits must work with the country's government of the area where the raw material is discovered. If both the company and the government agree on terms and procedure for the business, then an agreement is drawn up whereby the company pays a deposit to the host country. If either party violates any part of the agreement, then the terms violated must be corrected, and if there are any penalties, the party that broke the agreement must pay the penalty or the whole agreement is nullified. If necessary, a new agreement may be drawn up or possibly the whole scheme is abandoned.

If everything is managed successfully, the mineral is successfully extracted, and the raw material is transported to the company's refineries at the company's expense. Finished materials could then be re-shipped back to the host country for consumption and/or to other parts of the world. One example is here in Nigeria, the oil industry is well known to many people, and the different oil companies that represent some countries in Nigeria include Chevron, Shell, and Standard Oil. Most of us, who are unaware of the documentation and the process for getting these *concessions*, as they are called, may be aware to some extent about how the oil revenue is distributed to each state within the Republic of Nigeria. The oil producing states are given a larger share of the profits than the others are. The federal government stipulated this distribution in 1973 when the Udoji Commission was established and Nigeria had so much money and even distributed some to the civil servants. Scholarships were given to students and would-be students. Most countries have similar or different ways of equitable distribution of their mineral revenues.

The activities of the ambassadors and consul generals are equally very important in global understanding of each country around the globe. Embassy and consulate intelligence attaches of every nation in the world provide useful intelligence and information to their home countries, and their dealings with the host country may then be adjusted. The ambassadors and consul-generals play the role of liaison in bringing friendly relations between the various countries seeking the raw material. In the *good old days*, the Nigerian consulate in San Francisco celebrated Nigerian independence while promoting investments in Nigeria and the United States.

Transportation. With the advent of the airplane and its many improvements, the world became a *global village*. The time to traverse the distance from San Francisco to New York City was shortened dramatically. This same occurrence changed the world and its view of how to communicate and transport people and products. Before and after the *jackpot*, as I call it, in transportation, besides the airplane, we had improvements in other forms of transportation that includes ships, trains, cargo trucks, and a host of other modes of transportation. Most of these improvements are still in use today and being modified to be even more efficient. An example of what we had long ago, which is still very important, is shipping. The port of Oakland would not be as important as it is without the improved shipping. Of course, trains traverse the country to the big hubs of Chicago and Sacramento 24 hours a day now and load and unload cargo in Oakland. Of course, trucks connect with this and are still very important (i.e. cargo containers). Recently, truck drivers held up work to take actions at the port of Oakland, and this brought the port to a standstill. Transportation, no matter how insignificant you may think it is, makes a great difference in our lives and in the business, we own and conduct. For example, my son called me from the Cross River State in Nigeria informing me that all of the feeder roads into Ikun had been repaved and new bridges built and all connected with lighting_ because cities have food shortages, which makes food expensive in the cities. However, with good roads linking the cities with the countryside, some sort of balance can be achieved and food prices can be brought down.

Transportation not only makes commerce faster, efficient, and timely, but it also helps us understand the true meaning of *transportation* and good roads, airports, and seaports.

Transportation	
Roads	Trucks, cars, cycles
Airports	Airplanes, helicopters, etc.
Seaports	Ships, barges, tugs, etc.
Rivers	Boats

Many cultures have different means of moving people and produce from point A to point B. Chief Uno Egim of Ikun in Biase of the Cross River State in Nigeria was one of the most powerful men there once said that a new era was approaching where trading by bicycle or carrying goods on one's head would not be enough to feed a family of just a husband and a wife. Older people who were boys and girls then now remember Chief Uno Egim, as someone of the past who was predicting the future. The future is now. To support the prediction of Chief Egim, all feeder roads in Ikun have been repaved, and there is an explosion of millionaires in Cross River State. Today, schools and hospitals are no longer luxuries. Business done over there is today done here by use of good, paved roads, shipping, and airplanes.

In the United States, the capital of the capitalist countries, as I call it, understands that if one wants to go to Point C, you have to have more than five different ways of getting there for commercial reasons. Of course, that is one of the reasons everyone I ever met adores this nation. I know that there are many other countries trying hard to reach this same status.

Competition. Competition in international business is like visiting the worldwide web. Some people compete by making the products better. The following items are some of the elements in competition:

1. Making the products better;
2. Mass production to lower costs and sell items cheaper;
3. Proximity to the raw materials; and
4. Ability to locate where the price is lowest and where to sell highest.

Making the products better. In the 1980s, the Japanese were roaring across many continents as the world's automobile lion. Every carmaker in the world tried to see what the Japanese were doing differently. When Prime Minister Nakasoni of Japan visited President Reagan of the United States, he jokingly said that the United States problem, citing the car industry specifically, might have been brought about by the high population of Blacks and Hispanics. The comment sparked quite a turmoil among civil rights leaders, led by Jesse Jackson, until Prime Minister Nakasoni gave up and apologized for his insensitive remarks. The whole incident stemmed from the high quality of Japanese cars, but years later, Japan and the United States have changed positions. The

United States has regained its leadership in the automobile industry. At the time, I was working on my MBA, and I sat down on my couch, watching the Nightly News with Tom Brokaw. Economic news was on top of the agenda. Mr. Brokaw came out swinging. I overheard him say that the Japanese economy is fighting for its life, while American carmakers are booming. Mr. Brokaw followed that with, "Are blacks and Hispanics now living in Japan?" I laughed and said, "Competition in practice."

However, I also remembered that it is difficult to hold a competitive edge for a long time in a global economy, and it may be that Mr. Nakasoni was dabbling in American politics or maybe he was simply making a political statement. In any case, that was an expensive joke. Therefore, one needs to remember when competition encourages people to make products better, it is the best competition because it elevates quality and standards.

There is an adage that states, "The better product sells itself." This means one doesn't have to spend a lot of money on advertising the product; the best advertising is done by word of mouth of the consumer. That is the best kept secret.

The worse aspect of competition being or having an edge over the competition is that no sooner do you stop researching for more ideas to stay ahead, than the competitors overtake your business. Then confusion starts, you get in a hurry to lead again; however, leading takes more than that. It takes dedication, research, and development, and that takes time. The fact is that any time you begin leading, do not slow down until you have achieved a sizable gap over your competition. Even then, the research and development division of your business must continue as if your company was in trouble. Remember that if you lead decisively in business, all eyes will be on you including governments and the media.

Mass Production to Lower Costs and Sell Items Cheaper. The problem with mass production is that often quality is seriously compromised. Even if the quality is not compromised, there must be a psychological barrier where the customers ask questions about why the product is so cheap and may think that the product must be an imitation. Many stories may be told about imitation products, and often very scary stories about product imitation may be told and no one can know how many customers may be turned away. Recovering lost customers who have been turned away on this issue is hard work and getting them back may include heavy expenditures. Therefore, the end may not justify the means, which means that the aim of profit making is fruitless.

If there is someone to convince customers that selling the product cheaply has nothing to do with product quality but rather that it is a sales strategy. That may be sales well done, but that way still is trial and error. The better way with such competition is to make the products much better and reduce the price but no more than 25% or a negligible amount, which also has a psychological maneuvering with the customer thinking that the product is great and yet economical. The first move is to make the product better; all other pricing strategies will evidently follow and look believable. Do not tell the customers that the price has nothing to do with the product. Remember that your competition wants to see or hear about any misleading statements from your business. You don't want to give your competitors an opportunity to expose your company to something that they will surely blow out of proportion.

When your company's misleading statements are taken over by the media, then it will make your business appear terrible. Eventually, a government agency (state or federal) may want to know what is occurring in your company. Of course, at this point your company is simply defending itself. Your company may now have notoriety, positive or negative. Whatever it is, the company may be known as *terrible*, misleading, and much more. However, that may not be the end of your company, though it may lower your expectations.

<u>Nearness to the Raw Materials</u>. Sometimes bulky raw materials make it very expensive to transport them to the site of manufacturing. Therefore, proximity of raw materials to the factory brings down the cost of production and helps the company have competitive pricing in the marketplace. Price competition and production efficiency simply creates classes of customers, those who have money to buy high quality products to satisfy their wants and those who barely have money to satisfy their needs. Proximity to raw materials can enable a company to take care of both wants and needs because they can manufacture high quality products and yet have lower prices. Therefore, in this case, any customer can afford high quality products because of the low cost of production.

High quality products coupled with the low cost or production enables a company to do more research and development that may enable the company to discover what other uses the original products may have, or if a product may be made from the original product, or if there more raw material available, the company can create a different product.

<u>Ability to Locate Where Price Is Lowest and Where to Sell Highest.</u> Buying low and selling high is the goal of most salespeople. In fact, Wall Street is alive today because of people who think like that. Locating where to sell is tantamount to targeting your audience. When your audience is targeted clearly, then, of course, the salesperson has the confidence to buy more of the same product in hopes of making a profit because he or she knows how soon the product will be sold out. In the past, it was easier to find a market or audience to whom you could sell your products at higher prices because of lack of access roads to the same place. However, what if you are doing business in the United States where development is common and the infrastructure (roads, communication, etc.) is well developed. Take a moment and think of the billionaire, Mr. Murffett, who made his fortune in the United States. You may think that Mr. Murffett must have made extensive research to locate his company where he did for people to buy his

products and where he has to sell. It is probably not so much about extensive research as it is about making use of his intelligence—listening and being attentive in hearing news on the radio or television. However, Mr. Murffett is just a great businessman; most of his purchases are done on Wall Street. He buys from a great company that has proved to its investors that its useful days may be over. Then, of course, Mr. Murffett knows that the dying company needs a great activator to revive it from its death spiral, which he does very well and not even thinking he has done something great. We need niches and much more; one doesn't have to rely on one strategy. This is management; remember that management is an artistic work, meaning that what you called an original idea in the morning may be of no use at all in the evening because of all the changes that have occurred. The changes have affected your way of thinking, analyses, and probably your conclusion on a subject. Mr. Murffett knows that many companies lack flexibility and hold onto what they call *company policy*.

Buying low and selling high is what Wall Street does best, but individual investors cannot simply give way to an investment company and then forget about the investments. Keep calling your investment company; ask questions—no question is irrelevant. Many investors do not put all of your money in one place. At one time. I had an investment company in Los Angeles, and I was interested in gold. I sat down in my apartment in San Francisco and thought about diversifying my portfolio. As I ended my analysis, my investor called from Los Angeles enumerating all the advantages of investing big in gold because since he had started investing in gold he had never sustained any losses. I tried several times to discover what investment school he had attended. Sometimes he sounded like a politician; sometimes he sounded like a psychologist, and other times he sounded like a brilliant investor. I called my friend who had referred me to this investor and complained that this investor was a man of multiple personalities. I asked my friend again what he knew about this investor. What I was doing was tantamount to taking medicine after one has died. I lost everything I had invested with that individual. Worse still, I was told he no longer worked for the company.

Cultural Exchange

International business has many opportunities including materials and human-to-human interaction. Usually, when we intend to travel, no one will predict what the outcome may be. Sometimes getting along with your fellows is the hardest job we have to do before we get the proper perspective. Sometimes our phone calls to one another and the letters that we write to our companies are misinterpreted and that can be because of language difficulties. Even if we could understand one another perfectly, we would still harbor suspicions of one another based on nothing more than our own past history of interactions with our grandparents or simply based on ignorance, thereby making our world a much harder place to live.

Sometimes we bring in the younger generations of various countries to stay with us as exchange students, but that may only solve the young person's problem of trust in his or her parent country. The friction remains because older people who make the decisions are still dogmatic and caught up with ancestral traditions that have nothing to do with the present way of thinking. I think even in advanced countries today, some men still think of women as second class citizens even if most of the women are better educated than the men, and all of them from the same country. I do not know if we should now have cultural synergy education between men and women from the same country.

If culture is the world's problems concerning respect for one another regarding gender, religion, race, and/or nationality, how about a brother and sister situation where the brother feels superior to his sister, even though he is much younger. I think the problem with the world has is believe much like the Bible, the developed nations believing that they are superior to anyone in the developing world. It appears that everything the world does is based on belief. Cultural exchange is a great idea, but it works for those who already have accepted the premise and therefore are committed to making it work well for all people. Usually, we think of young boys and girls who simply come to the new found land and make themselves acceptable to whatever we call culture, which may have no effect on their country of origin should they return there.

Ability to Work in Teams

An ability to work in teams does not exactly mean teamwork because this is on an international level. The foreign country with which you are doing business may believe that you have come to impose your style of management on them. From then on, the level of distrust may be higher unless the company overseas is a branch of your company. All those who do business will know their management style and will not mistake teamwork for imperialism of administration. However, working as a team in international business means respect for one another. No country is absolutely wrong in every discussion, suggestions are made, not commands. If you know the people with whom you are dealing have very limited knowledge concerning the business both of you are conducting, do not try to be a teacher, but tell your business partner how you conducted the same business in another country known to you both. Also, let him or her know the outcome of your business venture, especially if everyone profited from the venture, and particularly if your *foreign* partner made more money than you did.

One does not need a degree in psychology to recognize when someone is uncomfortable with you or your style, unless you are not interested in the business in the first place. This would mean a total waste of time and effort for both parties, and that would probably reflect on future business transactions with you and your country. Do your homework before you travel abroad. Be polite and truthful, and remember that your first business in another country is tantamount to letting the foreigner know who and what you are, an ambassador of your own country and its values. To work in international business, one has to be patient and tolerant. We are not all the same, even if we are of the same nationality, and a brother and sister are never the same. Traveling hundreds of miles to a different nation, one has to listen, be patient, and obey. When necessary, bring up your sense of humor if you feel they would appreciate it; humor varies from culture to culture, so what is funny in one country may well be an insult somewhere else.

Therefore, do not begin criticizing any mistake your partners may make, but remember you are not perfect either. Introducing yourself as a perfectionist may well be a way to alienate potential business partners and clients. You need to remember that your mission is to work in a team with your partners. One has to do everything one can to avoid mistrust, as first impressions in international business are very important and may be lasting.

Expansion of International Business

As part of the rapidly expanding international business environment, corporations are increasing exports and imports, establishing foreign subsidiaries, and creating international departments. Industries around the globe must compete in world markets with industrial concerns of other nations. In recent years, this worldwide competition has been growing more and more and the relative competitive strengths of most of the world have grown. The energy crisis with increased oil prices has contributed to the problem of slow productivity in some parts of the world (Longnecker & Pringle, 1995).

Just as I was writing the above, a friend of mine from the United States called and informed me that many people he had talked to about President Obama's economic activities almost all said that the economy has taken the worst turn and the U.S. economy was getting worse by the day and concluded that it was the president's policies that were to blame. I told him that he was still living in the past because in the past, when you talk about America, you are simply talking about the United States, but today, Brazil is not far behind the United States economically. Other countries in South and Central America are not too far behind also.

That is not including China, the Europeans, and former developing nations like South Korea, South Africa, and Nigeria, which had lagged behind due to trading disparities. However, in today's global economy, which is almost like the worldwide web, you can sell your commodities to any country that offers to pay you a higher price, which does not make any difference if you bought the manufacturing equipment from the country that offered to pay you or your country less. I told him that because of all the developments in the global economy, many nations, if not all, are not far behind economically any more. Today's economic activities are on a competitive basis and self-determination, which is very good for the United States and its economy, and, of course, the world economy at large. Because of self-determination, many countries do a lot of research to come up with answers on many topics that may have monetary and other rewards to the host country and benefits to different countries. Therefore, the global economy is global competition, and global competition means new products in the global marketplace. Therefore, thinking about how things were in the past and feeling that things are not running well is tantamount to ignorance of the global economic benefits, although some areas may benefit more than others, and some areas may be giving more benefits than they are receiving.

Complexities of Management

My friend's idea about the United States economy should be as it was years ago made me think that many people do not think about the complexities of managing global businesses. Let's look at complexities in managing global businesses.

'Company Size. As companies become more international in nature, there is the idea of expanding the company and even to create foreign subsidiaries. Then, there are difficulties of managing such a conglomeration because the number of employees has increased; instead of a few thousand, the company may now have over 100,000 worldwide. In addition, we should understand that all of the countries to which the company has expanded have their own legal entities and laws, as well as cultural understandings. Leadership now becomes very complex and complicated because of the many factors involved in production.

Labor. Labor laws and their cultural components are different from country to country; likewise level of technological advancement Most of the employees from the developed and developing nations who have no advance degrees in areas required of their work and which must be trained and promoted to enable them to know that they have more responsibilities and not just the responsibilities of the expatriates. All of these take money and time to accomplish. We could see what the Japanese did in the eighties for acquisition of market share. Sometimes some business executives branded the Japanese as not knowing what they were doing because sometimes they remained in a particular country and amassed losses. I realized then that the Japanese were selling their country and their products more than anyone would think. At the time, I was in MBA program. Before I graduated, the most common words in management were *market share.*

Those two words, *market share* dominated management philosophy for a long time while other nations began the game of catching up economically. I do not know how or what the Japanese thought about what they were doing, but the scenario that I come up with is that both the Western Europeans and the Americans (U.S. and Canada) are old names in management as opposed to the Japanese. The Japanese perceived that they were newcomers, and as such, they had to let other countries know about their products and how they were comparable with Western Europe and America. It was a gamble in my opinion, but it paid off big time and became a model for management philosophy worldwide. The market share scenario had taught business executives how to be patient in doing business, which explains why a patient dog eats the fattest bone. The patient people had been able to encourage companies to send employees to school, knowing that all hands must be on deck if the company was to grow and prosper. Today, government regulations help a lot, and, of course, the union representations with all the regulations included OSHA (Occupational Safety and Health

Administration), the EPA (Environmental Protection Agency), the FDA (Food and Drug Administration, and so on—all of these were the products of the United States.

Remember, "All work and no play makes Jack a very dull boy"; this means that social life must never be ignored. Employees must feel that they have another life other than in the workplace. It is true that all work and no play does make Jack very dull, which is based on the decisions we make. The executives sometimes may think that social life or giving the employees an opportunity to socialize with others may be tantamount to adding compensation to the employees' benefits and thereby less rewards for the company. If the company is able to conduct a research on giving at least a limited time for socialization to some employees and for other employees no chance at all for this limited socialization, the results will be clear that human beings are social animals. They like to compare notes; they talk and understand each other, as well as laugh and play. I always like to remind managers, chief executives, and other executives that management is an artistic work. There is no one answer in management, which means that what works for you today may not be what will work for you tomorrow. What I am pointing out here is that there are many answers in management, but one has to be careful to choose the one answer that will suit the company based on what they want to achieve. Repeating one method daily may not get you to your destination—profit making.

I was passing through a certain department where I worked before, and one of the employees was being reprimanded for an offense his supervisor alleged he had committed. I was so inquisitive that I asked the employee what was it that he did; he told me that someone from outside the company had confronted him, and he had done nothing about it. The case had been resolved and no one was hurt. His supervisor had stated that once one of the employees was confronted by someone from outside the workplace and was very loud, but the employee took charge, asked the perpetrator for his phone number, the man was contacted and punished. The alleged victim told me that his supervisor had fabricated a story that had no basis in fact. However, the issue here was that the supervisor said the perpetrator was contacted and punished, but the employee called that a fabrication because no one was caught, contacted, or punished. The supervisor at this point became offended, thinking that the problem could have been solved in the same manner. Thinking that the supervisor's ideas was tantamount to *cooking the books* or misrepresentation of the facts.

Many supervisors or managers that I have been in contact with or heard from thought that management is like 2+2 = 4. Management is not a mathematics equation; management has its roots in analysis, which needs ordinary basic intelligence. You have to be a little elevated academically. I truly believe that attending a college or a university makes a great difference in our likes and productivities in whatever we do. Some intelligent people with years of service may also make some difference, but only in a limited way. In years past, high school could be of great value, but in today's world, a college education is very necessary, especially as we now deal with global competition.

Access to Raw Materials

Acquiring raw materials from another country may be risky and complicated, especially if the other country is undergoing instability politically. One case is an example—in the 1960s, a mostly military takeover was simply a joke. So were the raw materials, no respect for the rule of law, the raw materials were simply given away because very few people benefited, while most of the population existed in abject poverty. The program *Sixty Minutes*, from CBS News, reported every Sunday evening that the Nigerian military reported that there was a provision in the crude oil trade from Nigeria, which simply encouraged crude oil buyers to buy one ship of crude and get another shipload of crude oil for free. That is what happens when a country is politically unstable. The country's raw materials were simply treated as if the country was up for auction. However, Nigeria was the same country that General Yakubu Gowon told the world that Nigeria's problem was not money, but what to use the money already in the bank for. A few years later Nigeria became indebted to the International Monetary Fund (IMF).

In normal circumstances, it is a big political runaround to have another country enter and extract oil, gold, or any other raw material without signing an agreement. At the same time, both countries should be political allies. Having access to raw materials in a different country must be rewarding for both countries, financially, politically, and otherwise. Now, the Raw Material Research and Development Council (RMRDC) is an agency of the federal government of Nigeria and is vested with the power to promote development and utilization of Nigeria's industrial raw materials. This originated from the recommendations of a workshop on industrial matters organized by the manufacturers Association of Nigeria (MAN) and the Nigeria Institute of Social and Economic Research (NISER) in July 1983. It was established by decree #39 of 1987), but commenced operation on February 10, 1988. It is today Nigeria's focal point for the development and utilization of the nation's vast industrial raw materials (RMRDC, 1988).

The RMRDC was established at a time when dwindling foreign exchange earnings from petroleum was expanded to import raw materials and products which were available or could be competitively produced in Nigeria (RMRDC, 1988).

It is important to see that after years of economic destruction, Nigeria is getting her house back in order under the leadership of the civilian administrations and the critical evaluations of the world body. The RMRDC under President Johnathan is truly conscious, about food production to feed Nigeria's population, but the country still has a long way to go. Nigeria must know many Africans are depending on the naira and the development that Nigeria is providing, especially in education, economy, and agriculture.

Elimination of Basic Distrust

Trust is the central point of business transactions, besides doing business with a foreign entity. For one, you may not be able to pronounce the businessperson's name. The United States legal tender reads "In God We Trust;" the point here is *trust*. Years ago, the mail order business dominated the foreign or international markets but since the invention of the airplane and telephone, the world has become closer than ever; hence, the growth of international business. Having said that, we still have a long way to go before we can declare that the world has no trouble with *trust*. Some people have problems trusting while others only trust what they see and touch; whatever you may be, trust is necessary in order to move our world forward and not backwards.

Back home in Nigeria, the Canan City as we call the Calabar, the capital of the Cross River State of Nigeria and the first capital of the Republic of Nigeria, it is a popular thing to say that *nsu enem ke iko mbakara*, meaning that *telling of lies is great in the English language*. I don't know whether that is a belief or trust or is said just to make people laugh. However, up until today, some people still think that telling of lies is fine in the English language. Look at the investments we make, the stock markets, our bank accounts, and so on—all are made on trust. The world is getting there, but it is a very expensive commodity for some. After the world had made the Russians feel good by having the Winter Olympics in Russia (Sochi), the Russians moved quickly to annex part of its neighbor the Ukraine and is trying harder to make the Ukraine part and parcel of Russia. This is happening in 2014.

It is also true that the global economy is for small countries. Will the attempted partition of the Ukraine be to the overall interest of the people of the Ukraine or simply in the interest of Mr. Putin and the Russians financially, politically, and economically? What then do we call trust? The world is still a dangerous place. Look at China and its neighbor Tibet; the Tibetans want independence while Chinese think that independence will be granted *over their dead bodies* as the expression goes. If political trust is so far-fetched, how can economic trust be possible? The world as a whole is still struggling with political trust because political trust is full of different ideologies. Some country's president wants to rule with an iron fist, meaning whatever the president says is law, no challenges allowed. Any person who says anything contrary to what the president or prime minister says must be punished.

Just as I was writing this, an employee of the post office passed by me and was singing, "There's gonna be bloodshed tonight." I asked the maintenance personnel manager if he knew the man who was singing, and he told me that he knew him but didn't know his name. We were gripped by fear, but until we left for the night shift, nothing happened. That tells one also how little trust we have in each other, but in most cases, it is a lot easier engaging in international business than the local unstable individual. Most international business people are very intelligent, college-educated, and non-violent people, but there are no guarantees to that assessment.

However, in a democratic capitalist nation, those engaging in international business know very well what it takes to be an international businessperson, but sometimes we have white-collar crime that involves stealing from a customer or cheating in other ways. For all I know, international business transactions are safer and more trustworthy than ever because of technology and education in general, meaning that one doesn't have to study physics, mathematics, and chemistry. Any course you take is relevant in the international business arena. It is true that everyone wants the *good life*, no matter what political ideology you may hold. With all the technological advances, one might think that the world would no longer have things to feel distrust about, but this is not true that we ever will have a time when we can feel secure and not have a feeling of distrust. Russia and the Ukraine, China and Tibet, intertribal wars in Africa, Southeast Asia, China and Japan with their dispute over the Spratly Islands (a raw materials argument), and, of course, India and Pakistan.

If your company or you are doing business with a nation that is always in political turmoil, please do not assume that what is happening in that country might spill over to you or your company. It is easier for your business partners to recognize your attitude toward their nation than for you to know much about them. Remember that the people with whom you are doing business will need the same results you need from them; if they were profiting from trade with your business, believe me they would like to keep the business going. If you see unusual events happening two or three times, talk to the management. However, from then on, do not do textbook business with them, use common sense, and do not leave a lot of money in their hands. Always pretend to trust them so much, but do not try to defraud people, but always watch what you say. What you say may be the beginning of a confrontation. If you have a handout for them to read, please let them read them, but don't pretend to be a very intelligent business partner; lie low and succeed. International business is a highly artistic endeavor. If one does it right, the business may be very rewarding.

Be sure of your facts before you talk to the management areas that are doing poorly, and keep your complaints/comments short and simple. Do not complain about every little item or minor problem; otherwise, you create a name for yourself that would make it possible for another country to identify you. Sometimes, easy identification makes you appear less serious and may be asking to talk to your boss. Always respect yourself and the people with whom you are doing business. Respect will be accorded you because respect is a commodity of give and take. If you are honest, intelligent, and have a sense of humor, then, of course, you belong in the new economy we call the global economy. International business (or the global economy, whichever you prefer) is given less credit than it deserves because so many good companies and good people that the world might never have known until the new economy, yet political wrangling has still spoiled what the world should know and what the world should not know. Many aspiring international people end up not taking the challenge without knowing that their actions are big disappointments in the world because of distrust, and they ended up doing local business.

Speaking of local transactions, just as I was writing the above, I happened to tune in to Channel Two at 5 o'clock, California time, and the news was about matching the prices of supermarket shelves with the clerk checking out customers because the prices on the goods on the shelf did not always match the prices paid as the customer checked out at the check stand. That could be a mistake on the part of the company (mispricing items), but what it does is affects the level of trust of the customer for the business. So, whether you dislike doing business abroad or not, distrust is an equal opportunity issue, meaning that it affects everyone abroad or at home. Today, the world is known as the global village in business communications, technology, and other disciplines.

CHAPTER 10
DIALOGUE AND COMMUNICATION

1. Dialogue and Communication
2. Exporting
3. International Franchising
4. Joint Ventures
5. Direct Investment
6. Culture
7. Political and Legal Structure
8. Quotas
9. Exchange Control
10. Trade Agreements
11. Market Groupings
12. Demography

CHAPTER 10

DIALOGUE AND COMMUNICATION

DIALOGUE	DISCUSSION/DEBATE
1. Seeing the whole among the parts.	Breaking issues and problems into parts.
2. Seeing the connections between the parts	Seeing distinctions between the parts.
3. Inquiring into assumptions.	Justifying/defending assumptions.
4. Learning through inquiry and disclosure.	Persuading, selling, telling.
5. Creating shared meaning among many	Gaining agreement on one meaning.

(Ellinor & Gerard, 1988, p. 21).

In dialogue, people gradually learn to suspend their defensive exchanges and probe further into the underlying reasons why these exchanges exist. However, this probing into defenses is not the central purpose of a dialogue session. The central purpose is simply to establish a field of genuine meeting and inquiry (which we call a container), a setting in which people can allow a free flow of meaning and vigorous exploration of the collective background of their thoughts, shared attention, and rigid features of their individual and collective assumptions. Dialogue can be initially defined as a sustained collective inquiry into the processes, assumptions, and certainties that encompass everyday experience (Ellinor & Gerard, 1988).

Dialogue Versus Consensus

In consensus building, according to Isaacs (1993), people seek some rational means to limit options and focus on the ones that are logically acceptable to the most people. Often, the purpose of the consensus approach (the root of the word means to feel together) is to find a view that reflects what most people in a group can *live with for now.*

This assumes that shared action will arise out of a shared position, an assumption that is highly questionable. Although consensus approaches may create some measure of agreement, they do not alter the fundamental patterns that led people to disagree at the outset. Consensus approaches generally do not have the ambition of exploring or altering underlying patterns of meaning (Ellinor & Gerard, 1988).

Let us recap the case we had about the Erei Farm Settlement, the land leased to the Eastern Nigerian government by the people of Erei and Ikun, both in Biase of today's Cross River State in Nigeria. The union was fairly strong, but management was stronger because in Nigerian culture the general manager or the entire team of management could never be told what to do especially by farm settlement unions whose members and leader might never have seen the four walls of a college. Therefore, more than anything, it was a class issue, but the camel's back was broken when management and the union talked. They realized that they had discovered something, but they did not know exactly what that was. They were happier, trusting each other, listening to the other side, and more civilized in dealing with the public. This increased productivity and the farm settlement was able to sell its produce at reasonable prices to countries with which they were doing business. In other words, they competed fairly and effectively with other producers from other countries.

When the governor did visit, both the union and management of Erei Farm Settlement were declared by the governor to be role model management. It was a big deal then, and, of course, even now it can be seen as a major change. One sad aspect is that many of those who took part in this event, including the governor, have gone to their graves not knowing that they discovered how to conduct a dialogue. The union and management learned from each other through inquiry and disclosure, something nobody thought could ever happen because both parties lived in different realities with no connection with each other, meaning that they had different understandings of each other until the day they began really talking with one another.

Even though Dr. M. I. Okpara knew that the management of the Erei/Ikun Farm Settlement was a model and good for the economy of Eastern Nigeria and Nigeria at large, Dr. Okpara, as premier of Eastern Nigeria, had nothing in writing about good management. Of course, no one had an idea about what the farm management and the union did that brought about the excellent management other than talking with each other.

From the consensus standpoint, the situation could have been disastrous in the end, even for the farm settlement to be known as a model for others because they could have reverted to their old system of management by shouting at the union instead of talking and listening to one another. Consensus in agreeing to support what they can live with for now does not solve the underlying reasons for the problems. Interestingly enough until Premier Okpara could have concluded his visit with the Erei/Ikun Farm Settlement, no one could have understood the extent of the progress that the farm had made. Consensus management style is a short-term style of management; a kind of solution that is good for the present only—tomorrow will take care of itself. The consensus style of management is not a very good way of dealing with international business because it is not stable enough to deal with foreigners and their transactions. Dialogue is far more suitable for both local and foreign business dealings because the root causes of any mistake or misunderstanding are uncovered as soon as possible and remedied. That is what the customers, investors, and business interests prefer because the process is quick and stable.

Let us look at the following table.

DIALOGUE, COMMUNICATION, AND CONCENSUS

1. The whole story	Dialogue		
2. Fact Finding	Dialogue		
3. Limited Options			Consensus
4. Inconsistency		Communication	
5. Disclosure	Dialogue		
6. Viewpoint		Communication	
7. Debate		Communication	
8. Creating Understanding	Dialogue		
9. What's for Now.			Consensus
10. Defending		Communication	
11. Short Term			Consensus
12. Does not Alter the Fundamental Patterns			Consensus

When one looks at the above table, one can understand that dialogue, communication, and consensus are all means of transferring information to one another although with different outcomes. Dialogue is concerned with fact finding for great decision-making. Communication is much more concerned with debate, and, of course, someone must win while the other party loses. In politics, one party must win while the other becomes the loser. However, consensus is concerned primarily with what everyone can tolerate for the moment.

All of the above elements are great especially in international business because of cultural differences. Some countries prefer debating in the decision-making because they feel everyone should be heard, and facts rather than logic should be responsible for the decisions being made. Therefore, such countries prepare communications for both domestic and international business. Some other countries will raise no objections to debating facts and/or logic for their decision-making and international transactions if their immediate problems can be solved. Therefore, these countries prefer consensus for domestic and international business transactions.

Some advanced economies prefer a discipline of collective learning and inquiry because they have tried other methods and found them unsatisfactory because they only partially worked or did not work at all, as consensus is about what works for now. Therefore the options are limited, while in communications, winning is important not the solution. In multinational corporations, dialogue has become a way of problem solving.

In business, as in other disciplines, the element the company chooses is their own decision. It is possible the company could choose a combination such as dialogue and consensus or consensus and communication or communication and dialogue, or all of them. However, it is better to choose just one style in order to enable people to know where they have gone wrong. This is management, and I always ask the reader to understand that management is an artistic work. One should not use dialogue because it is popular; use it because it works for you. In business, whatever works for you in the morning may not work hours later in the evening. Assessing what you do in your business is important, and you may be surprised to see the profits you made during the week but may be a loss doing the same thing in the following week. So, one needs to evaluate the stock market as it goes up and down, and so does human life. However, do not feel Wilson Essien has asked you to be conscientious about artistic work in business, and for reasons unknown you misplaced your figures just in the interest of art. Please do not fix something that is not broken. There may be times that you feel you are due for a larger payoff from your business partner, but if you try to buy new materials to replace the existing ones that are still good from someone else, then, unfortunately, the new parts may not fit and may not work with the old material well. Well, your business partner is at the door, and you are not prepared to do business. Eventually, you lose, and then, of course, your business partner at that point may not regard you as a reliable partner, and you may have some explaining to do.

1. In international business, you always need to prepare for the coming of your business partner.
2. Let your business partner know why the price has gone up or has decreased.
3. Do not allow your partner to create an opinion about you and your company.
4. Avoid concentrating on the negative aspects of your business.
5. Do not let your business partner feel that you look down on him or how she or he does business with you.
6. Always use diplomacy in dealing with your business partner, if you know that your business partner is getting fed up with your diplomacy. Supplement what you were saying with humor.
7. Ask for permission before taking anything from him or her so they will think that you are well mannered and considerate. He or she will be more likely to want to continue doing business with you without further analysis of your behavior.
8. Ask your business partner to tell you how he or she feels about the transactions you both are performing because you feel if both of you are transacting fairly with one another, it is more likely that you will have more business transactions. Let him or her say whether they think it is fair or not.
9. Try to know about your partner's family and background while informing him of your own. Listen to what he or she says;

project your family the way your partner does his or her own family.

10. Do not sell yourself short for the sake of respect.

HOW TO START A DIALOGUE

Suspension of anything that will keep you from paying attention is vital because doing two things at the same time is very difficult, since dialogue is at the core of your business decision-making. Anyone participating in dialogue must learn to listen, and listening also means participating in the conversation and asking pertinent questions where possible. Otherwise, listening only may keep you sleepy, drowsy, and inattentive. The following should be present when starting a dialogue:

1. Listening by both parties.
2. Suspension of thoughts, impulses, judgments, and doubts.
3. Participation in the discussion where necessary and asking questions when appropriate.
4. Inquiry and disclosure are very important for the process to develop.

Listening. This is a very important element in a dialogue because if you do not listen you may not understand what is being said, and if you do not understand, some of your responses may be off topic and unrelated to what the other party is saying. In addition, your questions may not be relevant to the discussion. Eventually, everyone will start knowing your name, not because you are very intelligent, but because you sound funny and are entertaining in the worst sense of the word, *funny*. Listening is very important because every person or organization would like to have you as a participant for having the ability to listen and participate in their endeavor. Most importantly, your supervisor at work will allow you to take charge because he or she knows you understand. It is fantastic that you are a good listener, but don't simply pretend to be listening while you may be sleepy or distracted, and don't say anything because you are a smart pretender.

Remember that you may pretend for only so long because eventually your team members will know who you are and may describe you as such. Remember that your team members may not always remember you as a viable contributor during a group meeting, but they will remember you as the person who was always sleeping during meetings. Before you know it, your name may not be on the list for major discussions about decision-making in the company's issues that are important. Dialogue has been proven by major corporations as being very effective in decision-making, and listening is the effective element.

Suspension of thoughts, impulses, judgments, and doubts. The actual process of exploration takes place during listening not only to others but also to you. Suspension involves exposing one's reactions, impulses, feelings, and opinions in such a way that they can be seen and felt within one's own psyche and be reflected back by others in the group. It does not mean repressing, suppressing, or even postponing them. It means simply giving them serious attention so that their structure can be noticed while they are actually taking place (Bohm, Factor, & Garrett, 1991).

If you were to be invited to participate in a dialogue for decision-making, evidently the setting is not that of a student and a professor. All participants are regarded as equals just within the meeting place. As such, every participant must grow up fast to meet expectations. Listening is so important if you must participate in the discussions. That is also evidence that you know what has been going on in the discussions. Participation could be in the form of asking pertinent questions or if there is any point of clarification that one knows very well and would like to share with the group, this could be given also. However, participation in a dialogue formation by itself does not compel you to say anything just to say something, but it is clear that if you have been actively listening to the discussions, something might come up in your mind that requires clarification or you may want to ask a question or say something in response to what others have been saying. This may help others in different ways, so do not feel shy about participating in a dialogue. Remember that everyone is regarded as equals in the eye of a dialogue.

If you listen actively, you may observe some nonverbal expressions from most of the participants such as body language, facial expressions, and eye contact. As you listen actively, you will be hearing verbal expressions. In this case, you listen to the content of the message. First, one has to know the message the speaker is sending, then analyze the contents of that message, and then come up with what your conclusions are regarding the message.

Second, one must listen to the feelings that lie behind the message. If the message was to remove the plant manager or for the company to train more workers to know how the plant works, through your observations you want to know how the speaker was feeling. Any time you want to ask questions, do not ask close-ended questions such as "is the plant broken," but rather ask open-ended questions such as what is the condition of the plant now.

Close Ended Questions	Open-Ended Questions
Is	Where
Can	How
Will	Why
Are	Explain
Could	Tell me
Should	Describe

Close-ended questions can be answered by "Yes" or "No" while open-ended questions require answers with explanations of whatever the question is asking. If you really want to hear more on a subject, an open-ended question is encouraged because the speaker will feel that what he is talking about is being heard and may be his topic makes a lot of sense to the questioner. Therefore, with that encouragement, the speaker is motivated to speak more and more until another question is asked that may divert the speaker's attention to another aspect of the question.

As we said earlier, different types of questions may help expose one's listening ability, but having said that, nothing should deter any participant from asking a question. Do not feel you may disappoint yourself and anyone listening to your question and let this affect your self-esteem that may not let you be what you want to be. Low self-esteem makes you forget even what you know or the question you intended to ask until you hear it from someone else. Speak when you are asked to do so or ask questions when asked to do so. Remember that this is not a pep rally; there is no penalty for asking questions that may not be relevant to someone else. However, being the man who asks the wrong questions all the time is not a good recommendation either. Try to remember that dialogue is a discipline of collective learning and inquiry. I am not telling you to be disciplined, but I am suggesting that a dialogical forum is an avenue where the participants are assumed to be highly disciplined and is a place where everybody wants to learn and inquire, even though it is not a research group.

Inquiry and Disclosure. Remember that we are all equal in the eye of a dialogue; therefore, we have the same assignment and we are a group. The group meets from time to time. In a mortgage loan business, we say *every package has a story*, and at the end of the package, you say what you have done with all the information you have from the package. A brief story may shed more light on inquiry and disclosure.

I have told this story several times since I began writing, even in some of my other books, but it is a fine business story to tell. In the 1990s, I owned and managed a mortgage loan company that I called Metro Loans in San Francisco, the city by the bay. I am originally from Western Biase, Nigeria and other cities by the bay, including Erei and Ikun. Nigerians, as a group, in the Bay Area of California were very few in number, and most of them were students. Therefore, they were renting apartments. In the mortgage-loan business, I believe you must begin with the known and move towards the unknown, meaning that you have to start dealing with the people you know to the people you do not know. So, friends from Nigeria were laughing at me for having no base to start with, but I refused to give up. I began brainstorming, meaning thinking hard and making choices until I decided to have a group of telemarketers, bought a copy of the homeowners' booklet that was meant for cold calling, and it was rather rewarding. I employed loan agents who worked in their own neighborhoods in San Francisco. Every Monday they came to my office in downtown San Francisco where we all sat around a table. Usually, I began by telling them the number of loans I had for the week, the number of loan packages I had placed with banks and private lenders, and the loan packages that were still in process of being made.

I also told the group of the problems I had encountered on each loan package and how I solved each problem and proceeded. The loan packages were funded within the week. Then, they all clapped their hands and did the same type of presentation. Questions were asked of each presenter or comments were offered. Afterwards, we gave ourselves a round of applause. I always bought pizza or some kind of food for the meeting. Everybody would then go back to his or her station with what they had learned that week and try harder to embody those lessons into their own daily activities. Then, the following Monday the group could have some positive stories to tell or presentations to make that might assist other participants in learning.

Actually, I was not working this way because I knew what I was doing, but I was motivated to performing this way because I wanted my agents to stay with the company. All of them were paid a base pay plus a commission. In the beginning, I thought I had made a mistake in doing all of that, but I remembered the writings of Dr. E. N. Amakus from Calabar, Nigeria who said, "Whenever you are confronted with difficulties, do not form the habit of telling everyone; just be patient and work harder." I found this piece of advice very much in line with what I was going through. I also remembered Pope John Paul who always said, "Be courageous." In fact, with the advice of these two great men, I summoned the courage, and within a month, I began making profits from my agents and within their ideas, my ideas began taking hold.

After eleven years, I decided to go back to school for Ph.D., and I thought I could have time still to run my mortgage loan company, but that was merely wishful thinking. My employees in the office no longer worked harder and were no longer making money; my agents then joined other companies and, of course, spread my ideas. I came back to my office one day, closed the office, and paid off my employees.

While I was in school, I discovered what I was doing. The meetings and talking with the participants listening, asking questions, and making comments were all elements of dialogue. I lost my mortgage loan business, but I learned more about teamwork, and my dissertation topic was *Teamwork in Business Organization*. One of the cardinal points of the dissertation was dialogue. Since receiving my Ph.D., I have written several books and taught courses at a university in which dialogue was the important element. Since receiving my degree about 15 years ago, I have heard about authors who depicted dialogue as the central point of business decision-making. I also discovered that teamwork or the team approach without the procedure of dialogue is almost a task force or simple management by division of labor.

One can see what former President Carter is doing today by mobilizing people for an assigned area and building houses. Soon after the buildings are completed, the people disband the organization and move to another area, mobilize people, and build more houses there. That is the principle of task force. Other types of management styles are management by objective (MBO), hierarchical management, dictatorial management, and so on and should never be confused with teamwork and with dialogue component. This is also a management style, but, again, you must remember, "Dialogue is a discipline of collective learning and inquiry." Remember how my agents came to my office each Monday, sat around a table while one person at a time talked

221

and others listened, but then a participant would raise his or her hand and ask a question or make a comment on what the speaker had said. After everyone had spoken, there was a recap of what had been stated by the clerk of the team, and each of them had to be voted on by the participants while each individual returned to his or her station with a copy of the decisions that were made.

For this discussion, you should notice that dialogue could not have progressed but for inquiry and disclosure. The speaker finished his or her story, others asked questions to find out what had happened and how the situation was remedied, and the result of the actions with the potential leader. The procedure for creating the solution, what the leader said, and future advice, if any, were to be disclosed. No information should be left undisclosed, for without the disclosure of necessary information, any decisions reached might fall well short of addressing the problem or problems.

Many companies do not realize the benefits of inquiry and disclosure. This not only applies to local business, but it also is even more important in international business. If you just accept everything your international business partner tells you about what you are going to pay for, then, you may not be serious with the transactions you are running. Most of the time the money you are using is borrowed, and if you are not very careful with your transactions, that could be the beginning of hardship. If your international business partner refuses to cooperate with your fact finding and refuses to disclose what you are concerned about, please move on with your money to another company or individual who will want the best for both of you. However, sometimes the business partner abroad may refused to cooperate with you and your company because of cultural differences or simply because he or his company is aware of what that might mean to them in case of their bottom line.

You do not have to be a business psychologist to do international business, but ask your questions and listen to what the others have to say, observe their body language, and note the eye contacts. You may not always be correct, but you may not be too far from the truth. Remember that both of you do not know each other very well, but your inquiry and expected disclosure from the foreign business partner will get you as close to the facts about the person or people with whom you want to do business. If you have time and money to travel, you should do so in order to meet with your would-be business partner or partners, see where the raw material is generated over there, and check the processes out for yourself. Visit other places in the same city or country. Your would-be partners will understand that you are serious about business and that you may not settle for less than quality products. You may not be regarded as a businessperson who does not know his way in the city or who can be taken for granted. Your proposed business partners may even disclose information before you ask.

Be sure that you are taken seriously. I am not saying that you should always be hard-nosed conservative in every case. They may well think at that point you are looking down on them because of the money you possess or because you think are more civilized than they are. Remember that your most valuable asset is a good name, and this is even more true abroad because a *good name* generates trust in you and your business. It is difficult to buy trust anywhere; therefore, do not think that trust is everything in your business. In some cases, do all you can; do not think that their minds have been made up already about you and your business. In that case, you have to move on, doing your best with them, unless they have created deficits for you. Then, of course, you have to leave them with your business. If they then look for you, most of the dealings must be on your terms. However, always do business with companies that will benefit from you while you are benefitting from them. This brings about a longer relationship.

CHAPTER 11
IMPORT AND EXPORT

1. Import and Export
2. Export
3. Licensing
4. International Franchising
5. Joint Ventures
6. Direct Investment
7. Culture
8. Political and Legal Structure
9. Quotas
10. Exchange Control
11. Trade Agreements
12. Market Groupings
13. Demography

CHAPTER 11

IMPORT AND EXPORT

It is difficult for a modern country to produce everything that it needs for it diverse population. In the ancient days where transportation and communication were almost nonexistent, human beings restricted themselves to their own countries, and for a long time, countries were very suspicious of each other. In Africa, the suspicions were so great that a village was often unable to deal fairly with another village because of the devastation of the slave trade. No country or village could know exactly who would deliver them to slave traders. Even trade by barter was accomplished at the sole dictation of the village ruler. Trade by barter existed because trust did not exist. The medium of exchange if you wanted a chicken, but if you had yams, you had to look for a chicken owner who wanted yams. If you found one, then both of you could exchange chickens for yams; that was trade by barter.

That was just within a continent! Imagine Europeans trading fairly with Africans with all of the suspicion floating around the world. I remember even when Dr. Kwame Nkrumah was speaking about the imagination of West Africa as a nation, most people were saying that Ghana wasn't enough for him to rule and that he wanted to rule all of West Africa. By then, gold was the peak of the Ghanaian foreign exchange earnings, and Ghana was regarded as a rich nation.

The exploitation of international trade or the progress in international trade became the do-or-die of every country or very necessary for almost every nation. The nations of Mr. Bell's telephone and the Wright Brothers' airplane created a broadened world trade because of fast communication and the time conscious business world. In my own mind, these inventions as well as many others helped project the United States of America as one of the nations with which to do business if not the best nation with which to do business. But invention after invention by this great country have actually defined what this great nation is all about. Today, the United States is the primary destination of imports and exports of all commodities around the world.

Due to global transactions, the world of the G-8 has been increased to the G-20 and more members of the wealthy nations "club" may be added because the International Monetary Fund (IMF) will be releasing its biannual world economic outlook soon. Just as I was writing this, a friend of mine from Los Angeles called me and informed me that his uncle from Nigeria had called him and told him that Nigeria is now the largest economy in Africa. I was also told that Nigeria is now the largest African exporter to the United States. By the way, Nigeria is the most populous nation in Africa and is the largest African producer of oil and gas.

I remember when a president of the United States visited Nigeria and openly intimated that he would like Nigeria to diversify its portfolio. In fact, I gave Mr. William Jefferson Clinton a standing ovation, Guess what? Diversification has made the Nigerian economy the power of Africa, and the most interest part of it all is that oil and gas production make up less than 15% of the country's GDP as opposed to what was suggested by many international economists that oil and gas would probably be 50% of the Nigerian economy. What those economists did not understand was that the Nigerian local economies were working harder in diversifying the Nigerian portfolio of industries. Many countries were surprised at the economic progress of Nigeria, including many people on Wall Street, which had shown signs of uncertainty because many investors invested in South African gold. Eventually, Nigeria became the largest trading partner of the United States in Africa. Today, Nigeria has three prominent export trading partners— the United States at 51.6%, Brazil at 8.9%, and Spain at 7.7% (World Fact Boo, 2009).

Export commodities include petroleum, petroleum products, cotton, and rubber. The diversification has been expanded to include the industrial products meant for export. These include, among others, crude oil, oil, tin, columbite, palm oil, peanuts, cotton, wood, hides and skins, textiles, cement and other construction materials, other food products, footwear, chemicals, fertilizers, printing, ceramics, steel, small commercial ships—construction and repair—and other agricultural commodities. The Nigerian local economies worked so hard diversifying the economy, and this has paid off big time. The great difference between Nigeria and most African nations is the human resources that were one of the good things the British implanted in southern Nigeria—every family believes in academics. However, the fact was that Nigerians did not give themselves opportunities to compete with the rest of the world. The atom of opportunity the country now has we have seen that Nigeria ultimately is the largest economy in Africa. Without being told, I know that Nigeria has the strongest military in Africa—I mean the Air Force, Navy, and land forces. The country has been called the "Policeman and Woman of Africa," a name that most Nigerians have rejected and even demonstrated against such a responsibility. However, that has paid off because Mr. Charles Taylor and dictators like him have been arrested and convicted of crimes against their people, which has brought a great sigh of relief to the citizens of those countries.

A case in point is Liberia in West Africa. Today, Liberia is exporting rubber and many other commodities, and for now, at least, the country can employ itself. I am happy that Nigeria is the largest economy in Africa because Nigeria is the most populous country in Africa, the largest oil producer on the continent with the most educated population. If they are not the largest economy in Africa, then there must be something wrong other than the fact that they deserve what they've gotten. I do not really mean that because Africans have suffered so much for so long that Africans deserve any atom of good news they can get. After all, the achievement in Africa is for the Africans.

Nigeria imports machinery, chemicals, transportation equipment, and manufactured goods (World Facebook, 2007). However, as economic conditions have improved, more imports became necessary and mostly from the United States. Diversification is not an easy task; the entity taking this action or doing the diversification must cut its expenditures because the conditions must be developed to capacity or to its appropriate level comparable to the international level. Sometimes, developing the commodities must take special tools. Therefore, Nigeria from now on must spend more money in perfecting its products to compete internationally and maintain her own standards as the largest economy on the continent of Africa.

An issue for me here is about projecting Nigeria as the only competitor on the face of the earth may be the aim of every media. Projecting Nigeria as the leader may make South Africa look bad or ultimately may make the ruling part of South Africa, the ANC (African National Congress) look bad or to promote dirty competition between the two great African nations. After all, there are other African countries not far behind these two, such as Ghana, Egypt, and Botswana. I really want African nations to work harder but have friendly competition, because friendly competition promotes great mutual understanding and also means the Africans have a stake in one another's tomorrows, a continental free trade association, and encouragement for a worldwide free trade with an open exchange of goods, services, communications, dialogue, and ideas. These may promote world peace. All I am stating is that if Africans can promote mutual friendship amongst themselves, the same understanding can be extended worldwide.

The United States is a full participant in world trade; yet, it is less dependent on foreign trade, but things keep changing because of the size of the economy. Having the largest economy in the world, more raw materials may be needed to feed the industries. According to the U.S. Department of Commerce (IPSOS, p.16o), exports and imports average only seven percent of the GDP compared to 20 percent for Germany and the United Kingdom'. But today's Germany and Great Britain have also changed greatly. Most notably, over the years exports have exceeded imports incrementally over the years, and this shows a trade deficit, but the deficit is largely due to the size of the military and other expenditures abroad by the federal government. The United States' exports consist primarily of agricultural products and manufactured goods and component parts (Cal McDaniel, 1982).

Exporting

Exporting is usually the least complicated of those opportunities. A buyer for exports is usually treated as a domestic consumer and is served by the domestic sales force. The buyer for export is essentially a middleman who assumes all the risks and sells internationally for its own account. Direct exporting is the preferred alternative for a firm that wants to maintain control over its export activities and also to avoid middlemen fees. The producer deals directly with foreign customers by using traveling salespeople or by appointing foreign firms as representatives. Sometimes, foreign sales offices are established if there is sufficient demand for its products to justify the expenditure. Sometimes, a company decides that a foreign sales agent/distributor is the most economical method for obtaining direct international sales. The United States Department of Commerce has an agent/ distributor service that helps annually about 5,000 U.S. companies find agents or distributors in every country in the world (Carl McDaniel, 1982).

Licensing

A more aggressive move into the international markets without direct manufacturing is licensing. The licensor agrees to let another firm use its manufacturing processes, trademark patents, and trade secrets, and. in turn, the licensee pays the licensor a royalty or a fee agreed upon by both parties. Licensing is sometimes used to test the international waters before a company engages in manufacturing or in a joint venture. Care must be taken by the licensor to make certain that it can exercise control over the licensee's activities necessary to ensure proper quality levels, pricing structure, adequacy of distribution, and so forth. Licensing may create a new competitor in the long run if the licensee decides to void the license agreement. International law agreement is often ineffective in prohibiting such actions.

One common way of maintaining effective control is to ship one or more critical components from the United States. If the licensee does not possess the technology or facilities to produce these parts, control will be maintained. A second control technique is local registration of patents and trademarks by a U.S. firm and not by the licensee. Some companies add a provision in the licensing agreement for renegotiating contracts to cover new products and improvements in technology (Hopp, 1999).

International Franchising

Hopp (1999) contended that international franchising is a form of licensing. Franchising has been most successful in developed countries that have full-fledged service economies. In addition to the traditional product franchises. such as fast food (i.e. McDonald's), restaurants, and automotive products, service franchising has been growing rapidly including accounting services, credit and collection agencies, employment services, printing services, hotels, laundries and cleaning establishments, and vehicle rental agencies (Hertz, Avis, Thrifty, etc.).

Despite the growth of international franchising, a number of formidable problems have had to be overcome. Official limitations on royalty payments or licensing and trademark contracts and brand names are taxable and payable by the franchisor, whether it is domiciled in o rout of that particular country. Problems may exist in the protection of trademarks as no facility exists for registration. In some cases, franchising arrangements remain solely the concern of the contracting parties, and there are no regulations to safeguard franchising agreements. Tie-in arrangements are discouraged and sometimes forbidden. In some countries, a significant percentage of ownership share of the business activity is required of the national entity; in others, aliens may not own real estate property and in others they cannot own retail businesses.

Joint Venture

These are quite similar to licensing agreements except that the domestic firm assumes an equity position in a foreign company. Naturally, this is more risky than the options just discussed. It does, however, give management a voice in company affairs that it might not have under a licensing agreement. The key to a successful joint venture is selecting the right foreign company and then maintaining effective communications. Attitudes toward marketing, production, financial and growth policies must be clearly delineated. Governmental restrictions should be fully explored before the joint venture agreement is drawn up and finalized. A number of countries require that the local firm maintain at least 51% ownership in any joint venture arrangement (McDaniel, 1982).

Direct Investment

Direct investment in wholly-owned manufacturing and marketing subsidiaries offers the greatest potential rewards. Naturally, the possibility of substantial reward means greater risk. Firms may make direct investments because no suitable local partner can be found. Other companies may form wholly owned operations in order to maintain control (Hopp, 1999).

Hopp (1999) maintained that countries that lack strong nationalistic policies may offer foreign companies substantial tax concessions and/or make long-term loans at favorable interest rates and even construct the plant for the investor and assist in recruiting local managerial personnel as well as a work force. Direct investment may be discourage or prohibited in some countries such as Japan or Chile. In other countries the firm may have difficulty repatriating profits. Argentina and Brazil allow a maximum of 12% profits to be repatriated to the home country. Multinational corporations sometimes develop ingenious schemes to extract a much greater level of profits from their foreign operations. For example, Volkswagen sent $100 million back to Germany as payment for its parent's technical advice and expertise over a ten-year period. The greatest threat to direct investment is expropriation of assets by a government; as nationalistic feelings arise throughout the world, the possibility of expropriation increases. Cartels such as OPEC (Oil and Petroleum Exporting Countries) continue to develop in terms of basic commodities and raw materials. As these grow, these organizations often expropriate the assets of multinational companies operating in their territory (McDaniel, 1982).

Culture

N. K. Denzin and Y. S. Lincoln (1994) has also stated that central to any country is a common set of values shared by its members that determine what is socially acceptable. Culture also forms the basis for the family, the educational system or the social class system. The network of social organizations generates different overlapping roles and status positions. The Swiss housewife, for example, considers the performance of household chores such as washing dishes or cleaning the house central to the housewife's role. She finds it difficult to accept the idea of labor-saving machines or commercial products, and she rejects commercial appeals emphasizing time and effort saved in performing household chores. Special instructions also develop conventions, rituals, and practices governing behavior at different times, such as when entertaining family or friends, or during holidays. In the United States, bringing a bottle of wine for the host at a dinner party is likely to please, while in France, such a gift would be considered an insult to the host's choice of wine, and bouquet of flowers is concerned more appropriate. Without understanding a country's culture, a firm has little chance of effectively penetrating the market.

Political and Legal Structure

Another important, uncontrollable variable facing the international market is political considerations. Government policies run the gamut from no private ownership or individual freedom to little control by the government and maximum personal freedom. As rights or private property increase, government-owned industries and centralized planning tend to decrease. Rarely will a political environment be at one extreme or the other. India, for example, is a republic, but it has shades of socialism, monopoly capitalism, and competitive capitalism in its political ideology. In countries such as Greece and Spain, individual freedoms are highly restricted but private enterprise is allowed to flourish almost unhindered. Failure to understand foreign governments and their modes of operations can lead to marketing failure (Tjosvold & Tjosvold, 1995).

Tjosvold and Tjosvold (1995) further contended that a major pharmaceutical manufacturer a number of years ago developed a process for coating rice with Vitamin A that could withstand cooking. The company believed, with considerable justification, that a serious public health problem endemic to the Far East could be alleviated and went to the extent of enacting legislation to compel all rice millers to incorporate the process. When the rice millers refused en masse to go along with the new government regulations, it was learned that the Philippine authorities had really intended that the Vitamin A program provide a means of determining quantities of rice that were milled, thereby enabling the government to collect its taxes, which the millers had evaded successfully for years.

McDaniel (1982) explained that failure to appreciate emerging nationalist feelings can ultimately result in expropriation. Such problems can be avoided by allowing citizens of the host country equity participation in the operation. In other situations, industries are nationalized to infuse more capital into their development such as airlines in Italy and Volvo in Sweden. They are also nationalized to assist domestic corporations by selling goods and services below cost. For example, Nigeria was supplying coal to users at a loss.

McDaniel (1982) said that closely related and often intertwined with political factors are legal considerations. Legal structures are designed to encourage or to limit trade.

Tariffs. The most common means of limiting trade is through tariffs, a tax levied on goods entering a country. It may be a specific tariff assessed per unit of import such as $300.00 on an imported automobile. In other cases, it could be an ad valorem tariff based upon the value of the import. The effect of any tariff is to make the imported merchandise more expensive, thereby discouraging consumption. In recent years, progress has been made in reducing tariffs throughout the western world. The General Agreement on Tariffs and Trade (GATT) has provided a forum for negotiating multilateral tariff reductions among the member nations. Although GATT has met with success, nationalistic tendencies have prevented many tariffs from being eliminated or lowered.

Quotas. This is a way of restricting trade by imposing import quotas on the amount of a specific product that can be imported into a country. The quota usually has an absolute limit so that importations on the goods stop when the quota is filled. A second common form of quota is combined with a tariff. When the quota limit is reached, the tariff increases substantially. A more severe form of trade barrier is the boycott. This measure excludes all products from certain countries or companies. Some Arab countries have boycotted American firms for their dealings with Israel. In 1980 Iran boycotted all American products and also refused to sell petroleum to the United States.

Exchange Control. Another means of regulating foreign trade is exchange control, a government monopoly on all dealings in foreign exchange. It works as follows. A national company earning foreign exchange from its exports must sell this foreign exchange to the control agency, usually the central bank. A company wishing to buy goods from abroad must buy its foreign exchange from the control agency rather than in the free market. Exchange control always means that foreign exchange is in scarce supply, and therefore the government is rationing it according to its own priorities rather than letting higher prices ration it.

Firms producing within the country have to be on the government's favored list to get exchange for imported supplies, or, alternatively, they may try to develop local suppliers, running the risk of higher costs and indifferent quality control. The firms exporting to that nation must also be on the government's favored company list or otherwise they will lose their market if importers cannot get foreign exchange to pay them. Generally, exchange control countries favor the import of capital goods and necessary consumer goods but avoid luxuries.

Trade Agreements

Not all government efforts are meant to stifle imports or investment by foreign corporations. The GATT (General Agreement on Taraiffs and Trade) is a good example of an organization whose objective is to increase international trade. GATT has been most successful in fostering trade between industrialized and industrializing nations. Developing nations encouraged the formation of the United Nations Conference on Trade and Development (UNCTAD) in `1969. The objective of UNCTAD is to further the growth of developing nations through trade. UNCTAD seeks to improve the prices of primary goods exports through commodity agreements. The idea is to control supply, which, in turn, means higher prices. UNCTAD has not been overly successful; about the only commodity agreement that has achieved its goal is that for international coffee (McDaniel, 1982).

Market Groupings

Trade is also encouraged through market groupings—countries creating common trade alliances. Integrating several markets into a common unit has several advantages:

1. Increased growth for the region;
2. Growth in income within the region can lead to increased exports for both member and non-member countries;
3. Trade creation and diversion possibilities may lead international businesses to invest in production and marketing facilities within the region in order to get behind the tariff wall and to minimize non-tariff barriers.

The best known market grouping is the European Common Market or European Economic Community(EEC) called simply the Common Market. Its members are as follows:

Austria	Finland	Latvia	Romania
Belgium	France	Lithuania	Slovakia
Bulgaria	Germany	Luxembourg	Slovenia
Cyprus	Greece	Malta	Spain
Czech Republic	Hungary	Netherlands	Sweden
Denmark	Ireland	Poland	United Kingdom
Estonia	Italy	Portugal	

Wikipedia, 2015

See map below

The EEC has as its goal the gradual reduction of tariffs among member nations until free trade is achieved. It also has the goal of ultimately creating a single external tariff for the EEC., Another important marketing grouping is the European Free Trade Association (EFTA) which represents over 40 million people and contains several countries (Norway, Switzerland, Iceland. and Liechenstein) that have some of the highest per capita incomes in the world.

Dark green represens current states; light green represents former members.

The LAIA or Latin America Integration Association is another marketing group that is made up of the following nations: with the date the country joined and its population.

COUNTRY	JOINING DATE	POPULATON
Argentina	Founder	40,117,096
Bolivia	Founder	10,426,160
Brazil	Founder	190,732,634
Chile	Founder	17,094,275
Colombia	Founder	45,656,937
Cuba	1999	11,242,621
Ecuador	Founder	14,306,876
Meico	Founder	112,322,757
Panama	2011	3,405,813
Paraguay	Founder	7,030,917
Peru	Founder	29,885,340
Uruguay	Founder	3,424,595
Venzuela	Founder	30,102,382
Total Population		521,213,583

Wikipedia (2014)

Another important market grouping is the West African Economic Community (WAEC) or the Economic Community of West Africa (ECOWAS) or simply the West African Common Market (WACM). The goal is to gradually remove tariffs until free trade is achieved. This economic community is making significant progress. The following countries are members:

Benin	Gambia	Mali	Sierra Leone
Burkina Faso	Guinea	Niger	Togo
Cape Verde	Guinea Bissau	Nigeria	
Cote d'Ivoire	Liberia	Senegal	

Demography

McDaniel (1982) stated that the four most populous nations in the world were China, India, the United States, and Indonesia; yet, population is often a poor indicator of market potential. Density of population is also an important consideration. Oceania has only 5 people per square mile. Egypt has about 94 persons per square mile, and the United States has 57 persons per square mile (not now it isn't—U.S. is 84 and Egypt is 97—GET UP-TO-DATE INFO!!] However, virtually all Egyptians live along the Nile River. The remainder of Egypt is desert. Thus, average population density figures can be misleading unless the population is rather equally distributed throughout the land mass.

Just as important as population is the amount and distribution of incomes in a country. The wealthiest countries in the world include the United States, Switzerland, Sweden, Canada, Germany, and several of the Arab and African oil-producing countries like Nigeria and Angola. At the other extreme are countries like Kenya and India with 6 and 7% respectively of the per capita purchasing power of the American consumer. Even in countries with low per capita incomes, wealth is often not evenly distributed. There are pockets of upper and middle class consumers in just about every country of the world. The demand for luxury goods is present, but often limited by the number of affluent buyers. However, in some cases, affluent people are never the answer for expensive goods. In the first place, some of the people have become affluent because they save more and buy items based on need and only some few middle class people buy things based on wants.

In some countries wants are based on traditional title. On this premise, if a company bases its export decisions on where most affluent people are mostly located, that be tantamount to making a big mistake because some affluent people prefer cheaper commodities. Usually, buying power is a mix where different people buy for various reasons. We hypothesize every economic outlook, per capita purchasing power, income distribution, and so on, but some of these theories have little or no practical results. A case in point is income distribution.

I remember after the Nigerian civil war of 1970 that I saw a group of well-dressed and armed men drive to Ikun Presbyterian School and called out names, but I did not know where they had and handed over bundles of money to almost everybody, all in British £20 notes, but in a month's time, everybody was back to where they had been before they received the money. Years later, I began thinking about income distribution and that what I saw was a very physical income distribution; yet, whether it founds its level shortly, meaning some of those who received the money were not affluent for a long time. The, of course, what is the aim of income distribution? Should that mean short term purchasing power? Or, should that mean men being paid more than women or the majority being paid more than the minority? The only income distribution that makes sense to me is someone being paid according to his or her level of education. By education, I mean an academic standard, mechanical work studied, or practical work studied. Education should not mean experience because only a few people may be given the opportunity to obtain experience before receiving an education. However, many candidates have to receive an education before being employed in their particular discipline.

I am very interested in the income distribution in Nigeria. Employees are paid on certain levels and a level represents an academic standard or its equivalent. Level 2 represents primary school certifiicate; level

3 represents high school incompletion; level 4 represents high school graduation; level 8 represents a B.A. or B.S. degree; level 10 represents a MA or MS degree, and level 12 or more represents a PhD degree. Most people are always between a BA/BS and a MA/MS level, and some people make more or less for being in business for themselves.

Poor income distribution is not a popular subject in Nigeria, but lack of employment opportunities could be more popular. If a woman has an MA or MS degree in a discipline that portrays the job that she is applying for, then, of course, the job is hers unless it is a very physical job that she declines to take such as a job with an oil company and many other jobs like that. Not long ago in May 2014, Pope Francis of the Roman Catholic Church intimated that income distribution is necessary and should be taken ery seriously. Income distribution is by no means a better thing to do, but what is the aim of doing that? And, how many times can income be distributed in a year? Are we talking about full employment? Income distribution is a truly tricky subject.

CHAPTER 12
HOW AMERICAN ENERGY INDEPENDENCE COULD CHANGE THE WORLD

a. Less Than American Energy Independence
b. Oil Exporters
c. Geopolitics in the Middle East
d. Employment
e. The Environment
f. Asian Crude Oil
g. Strict Market Regulations in Africa
h. Export Earnings
i. Commentary: Kasapreko's Expansion Drive
j. Kasapreko's Expansion Drive
k. Dumping Ground
l. Kasapreko's Ambition
m. Kasapreko as an Award-Winning Exporter
n. Kasapreko's and Market Survey of South Africa
o. Measures Taken by Nigeria, South Africa and other African Countries
p. Kasapreko's Earnings in 2013 Were Twice as Much as 2012. What Does that Say to the Company?

CHAPTER 12

HOW AMERICAN ENERGY INDEPENDENCE

Could Change the World?

Less than a decade ago, both the United States and Western Europe as well as Japan were almost spending the same amount of money on oil and gas, but today, the United States spends far less than Western Europe and Japan spend. Energy independence was never a dream masterminded and almost accomplished by President Obama. This was a dream held by most American presidents from President Nixon to President Obama. However, lucky President Obama on his watch the rays of accomplishment have begun appearing, which will be credited to his administration and the Democratic Party. Of course, the winner is the American people whose time for economic rule of the world has come because the American competitors, Western European countries and Japan, are rather planning to invest more in the United States. This is truly a new era for the United States. In fact, all of us who contributed to the growth of this democracy are overjoyed for the success of this nation.

I remember one State of the Union address by President Obama with Mr. Obama sitting and facing the television cameras and someone saying, "The President of the United States." As the State of the Union address continued, the president said, "After years of talking about it, we are finally poised to control our own energy future" (Obama, 2013). I was so happy that I clapped my hands, but after a few minutes, I realized that the United States is the largest trading partner to Nigeria, my birth country, and much of the trade is in crude oil. However, I again came to the realization that no country lives alone and as such, compromises must be made. I also thought that my immediate responses were a microcosm of what most of the world was thinking because the United States is said to be the last hope for stability in the world. In fact, I was thinking about the abundant oil and gas production in the United States could bring down oil and gas prices while the United States' former customers would be selling their crude oil and goods to primarily the industrialized countries of Western Europe and Japan, which would keep up the balance of production and trade.

I predict that productivity, especially manufacturing products, will be more in the United States because manufacturing companies that took refuge in many countries because of costs will come back to their original base and take advantage of low costs in the United States as production and the efficiency of their employees and plants that the world loved before the outsourcing. Many countries such as Canada and those in Western Europe may invest directly in the United States in the hopes of taking the same advantage with the United States. Of course, the winner in all of this will be the consumers. Manufactured goods will be cheaper, while productivity will be high quality. Any person who wanted a job must get one in the United State. Intertribal conflicts, which are often caused by poverty, may no longer occur frequently. Even the religious fanatics may find it hard to convince followers to join them for whatever course they felt was compelling them to do whatever they thought was necessary. I think that good times are yet on the way as a result of energy independence. In fact, the cost benefits analysis could give implications around the world.

In 2013, the United States spent $300 billion (£180 billion) on importing oil, which represented about two-thirds of the country's annual trade deficit. The oil importation also represented 2% of the country's growth. Therefore, if the United States' annual economic growth is 2%, while the oil importation is also 2%, the future growth rate will be free. Comparing now with energy independence, the boost to the United States' economy will certainly be significant (BBC News, 2013).

For a country to have energy independence, it means that the country would be spending less on oil, and even less on domestically generated power. Energy independence will come about only through cheap and abundant shale oil and gas, which could help spark a golden era for manufacturing in the United States (BBC News, 2013).

The International Energy Agency (IEA) and oil giant British Petroleum (BP) certainly believe that the United States will be energy independent by 2035. The agency warned that a persistent trade deficit can act as a drag on economic growth, manufacturing, and employment. Let's talk about these three areas: economic growth, manufacturing, and employment.

1. <u>Economic Growth</u>. We have mentioned earlier the economic growth rate of the United States that stands currently at about 2%. We have also mentioned that in the last year, 2013, the United States spent about $300 billion on oil and gas, which is also about 2%. That means that the 22% growth rate is equal to the trade deficit. The trade deficit must be eliminated, which then means annual growth minus the trade deficit or 2% - 0% = 2% growth rate. No we have the persistent growth rate, which I call real growth, and that is also what I call money in the bank that could also serve as a solution to the country's problems.

2, Manufacturing. Years ago, the United States was the base for manufacturing of goods, high costs of production, wages, and energy became all too familiar to most large manufacturers. Soon, that dreaded word, outsourcing, where manufacturers moved to places where wages and energy were more manageable (i.e., cheaper). Many economists and business scientists were saying that the United States' economy had passed the industrial age of the manufacturing of goods and now had moved to the information age. The observation never sat well with me and to some other people who conversed with me. Outsourcing is a business or economic decision that has to do only with the bottom line. I also came to the realization that any economy without a manufacturing base, whatever growth the economy has, is not deeply rooted, and for that I call such growth temporary growth. Temporary growth does not last very long in any economy. I think that the United States' President and its business team are vividly aware of the differences between deeply rooted economic growth and temporary business or economic growth and that may be why they are fighting for oil independence so as to get back to our manufacturing base. Even as I write, a number of U.S. firms are looking to bring industry back home. Several companies including Dow Chemical, General Electric, BASF, Ford Motor Company, and Caterpillar have announced hundreds of millions of dollars in investing either in new plants or in reopening closed facilities. Even Apple has announced a new factory in Arizona more than a decade after closing its last plant in the United States (BBC News, 2013).

In fact, between 2010 and the end of March, 2013, almost 100 chemical industry projects, valued at nearly $72 billion, were announced according to the American Chemical Council. Indeed, a study by an accounting firm, Price Waterhouse Cooper, estimates that one million manufacturing jobs could be created by 2025 tanks to low energy prices and the demand from the shale/gas industry. Further analysis by the Boston Consulting Group, points to a surge in United States' exports of manufactured goods (BBC News, 2013).

Any boost in production in U.S. manufacturing would obviously lift overall economic growth even further. In fact, the benefits are already being felt. Many economists point to cheaper energy as one reason the United States has outperformed in recent years. Only four years ago, Europe's gas prices were roughly the same as those in the U.S. Now, they are three times higher, and the International Energy Agency (IEA) forecast they will be twice as high by the year 2035. By 2015,

Boston Consulting expects the U.S. to have an export cost advantage of between 5 and 25 percent over Germany, Italy, France, the United Kingdom, and Japan in a range of industries including plastics and rubber, machinery, computers, and electronics. (BBC News, 2013).

As a matter of fact, a number of European companies are already looking to invest heavily in the United States. Royal Dutch Shell has announced a new chemical plant in gas-rich Appalachia. French industrial giant Vallouree recently invested more than $1 billion in a new plant in Ohio, while the Austrian steel group, Vox Stalpine, is investing $750 million in a new factory in Texas (BBC, 2013).

BBC News (2013) also stated that European Council President Herman von Rompuy announced that all leaders are aware that sustainable and affordable energy is key to keeping factories and jobs in Europe. Industries find it hard to compete with foreign firms who pay half the price for electricity like the United States.

Oil Exporters

A number of countries export a large amount of oil to the United States, exports that would all but disappear if the United States achieved energy independence. The impact on these economies, particularly in South America, Africa, and the Middle East would be significant. For example, in 2011 Ecuador's oil exports to the United States were worth about $6.5 billion or 8 percent of the country's GDP. In Colombia, the figures stood at 7% of that country's GDP. Even Canada, one of the world's economic powerhouses and a member of the G8, would be hit hard. Again, the loss would be felt overnight. However, it is not just direct exports to the United States that would be affected. America is currently the world's largest importer of oil; so, if it was no longer buying, the price of oil would inevitably drop. This would hurt all oil producers and compound the problem for big oil exporters to the United States (BBC News 2013).

Geopolitics and the Middle East

With energy independence secured, United States' interests in oil in the Middle East would wane inevitably and affect views around the world on how we objectively or subjectively think of the importance of oil in U.S. foreign policy. However, some commentators have countered that the United States' policy in Syria, a relatively minor oil producer compared to Iraq, one of the largest producers of oil in the world, may not be paid serious attenton beccause of a lack of interest.

In my view, oil has some consideration by oil-producing countries, but oil is not the entire package. In the case of Syria, we should consider its nearness to Israel. If the United States does serious harm to Syria, we would expect retaliation would be taken on Israel. Israel might defeat Syria in a war between the two nations, but at what cost? Remember that the United States is a friend of Israel and would like to see Israel prosper. Where will this prosperity come from if we allow Israel to fight and destroy all of its neighbors. So, I see vividly the concerns of the United States. Again, remember what Russia will do to protect its friend, Syria. Iraq was usually a no man's land because during the Iran-Iraqi war, the United States was on the side of Iraq. People in the United States may not think that broadening regional conflict in the Middle East is to anyone's interest. Whatever the commentators are saying about what and what not the United States is doing in Syria is just comparing apples and oranges—it has nothing to do with one another.

I am not going to defend any group, whether it's Western Europe, the United States, Russia, Japan, or any commentator, but I do think that it is too early in the game to predict the United States' interests in world affairs because if the United States is a super power, her world interest must never be divided and must never be based on something so material as oil. We should also notice that there are many other commodities for import and export apart from oil, defense materials, and just friendliness based on a non-religious ideology. I think that the United States as a super power may look for a positive niche that may still keep her as a role model for the world to emulate. Energy independence should not be regarded as everything by anybody.

Even though oil may be currently a very important aspect of U.S. interests, it is worth noting that the United States is always concerned with the stability of any region and more so with the Middle East, especially as the region borders Russia and China. The United States also has strong historical ties with Saudi Arabia, including lucrative defense contracts (BBC News, 2013).

If the ideological wars have been started by the United States, I do not think that there is any reason why the super power should retreat into isolationism instead of using the opportunity to do more for the world. Just as I was writing, the president of the United States, Mr. Obama, addressed the graduating class of students at West Point Military Academy where he mentioned helping our allies wherever terrorism appears. He commented that he was unhappy with the way the Syrian War is being fought. We also have to remember that American troops were sent to Chad in order to find out where the Nigeria girls who were kidnapped were located. We were also told that armed forced were also dispatched to Chad, which borders the Maiduguri region in Northern Nigerian. I think that this was the next assignment of the super power, the United States of America.

However, as I said earlier, it is too early to predict what the United States will do after it has completely achieved energy independence. Having heard from President Obama recently, I did not hear anything that sounded like a retreat, rather I heard more about helping and much more like good guys versus bad guys speech. Most likely, the United States will lead the *good guys*. This is an enormous assignment.

Employment. We have talked earlier about achieving energy independence by the United States, including the fact that energy will be cheaper here, factories and firms that were outsourced will come back home because they left the United States in the first place because of the high costs of doing business. More firms and factories will be built and some will be renovated, all of which will need work and permanent employees, strictly based on qualifications and experience. Then, of course, many European and other friendly countries are willing and have announced the fact that they will be investing in the United States. Even Apple that left its own country a long time ago is coming back to invest in Ohio. Factories and firms will need employees, more schools, teachers, professors at universities, and so forth. It will be a compete rebirth of the United States, not to mention the need for more hospitals, doctors, nurses, and other health care professionals, other personal private companies, law enforcement officers, courts, and lawyers. Many workers will need to be retrained to enable them to help their companies compete effectively. Silicon Valley companies, which are already short-handed, will be even more so and more workers from abroad will be required. If energy costs are high in Western Europe and Japan and workers are demanding higher wages in China and with high energy costs, the United States will be able, therefore, to afford acceptable wages. Employment opportunities will be high. Right now, housing is a problem, but politicians will fight hard to meet this demand in areas such as the Bay Area, and there are areas where people could spread out the housing and enable companies to be in the countryside to shorten commute distances to work.

The Environment

Overall water (CO_2) emissions in the United States have been falling since about 2008, except for a small increase in 2010, and are now back to levels seen in the mid-1990s. The reason for this is the huge rise in the use of shale fracking, which accounts for one-third of all U.S. gas production, at the expense of most shale, which is generally considered to be more polluting. This may be good for the United States, but not for Europe, which has increased imports of the cheap U.S. coal ousted by shale. However, environmentalists have a more fundamental reason for being wary of the rise of shale—it may be less polluting than coal, but it is far more polluting than renewal energy sources such as wind and solar. If the American reliance on shale continues to grow, and if investment in renewable energy is diverted as a result, then, long-term emissions will be higher than they might otherwise have been (BBC News, 2013).

It is also important to remember that shale oil and gas are finite fossil fuels. If the United States is to achieve energy independence in perpetuity, it will need to do so using renewable energy sources.

Asian Crude Oil

Asian refineries import crude oil mostly from the Middle East, more than twice the volume of crude oil produced regionally, and have been taking more shipments from West Africa since 2003. Now, with regional producers struggling to hold supplies steady as mature fields decline. Kazakhstan, Nigeria, and Mexico are looking to ship more crude to Asia as the United States shale oil boom slashes the need for import there. The United States imports are down and what they are importing is mostly light sweet oil from Africa because crude produced in the U.S. is also light, sweet oil. Asia will require an additional 300,000 barrels of oil per day (bpd) of low sulfur or sweet crudes in 2014 compared with the previous year (2013) to meet demand from Asian refineries and for blending with cheaper, low quality oil according to an oil company analyst. The Asian-Pacific, which produces mainly sweet crudes had been expecting a boost in 2014 from higher output in Indonesia and Malaysia. However, expectations in the Southeast Asia –Pacific Area oil demand overall is forecast to grow by 500,000bpd or 1.5 percent to 30.6 million bpd in 2014 with China's oil use rising 3.7 percent and India's by 2.4 percent, according to the IEA. That is measured against Asian oil output that is expected to rise just 110,000 bpd or 1 percent to reach 35 million bpd in 2014, according to consultant Wood Mackenzie.

To wring the most oil out of decades-old oilfields such as DUN in Indonesia and TAP in Malaysia, Exxon-Mobil, Chevron Corporation, and Royal Dutch Shell, along with Petroilas and Pertaminino, are spending billions of dollars on oil recovery projects to boost output, which is well down from national peaks.

Earlier in this chapter we talked at length about energy independence of the United States. We have been told that Asian crude oil comes mainly from the Middle East, but that a few years ago, Asian refineries began buying sweet crude from West Africa, primarily from Nigeria. However, we also understand that the American crude oil is also sweet crude. We understand that last year, 2013, the United States spent $300 billion on imported oil, which represented two-thirds of the country's annual trade deficit, which also meant that the United States was the world's largest importer of oil. Eventually, if the largest importer is no longer importing oil, even though Asia and India would need more oil imports, the fact is that the two areas may not make up that $300 billion lost by the decline of U.S. importing of oil.

What I am getting at is that there may be surplus oil in the marketplace, but even if the oil is not surplus, oil prices will come down somewhat due to lack of demand. I am not entirely sure that the world has ever experienced a country that has become entirely energy independent. I think that the United States may be spending a lot less on oil because oil production is going to be higher, but then most U.S. companies that left the country to take advantage of low costs of production of manufacturing abroad may be coming back home to take advantage of the new low costs of production in the United States like the following companies that have announced reinvestment at home in the United States:

1. Dow Chemical
2. General Electric
3. Ford Corporation
4. B A S E
5. Caterpillar
6. Apple, Inc. – Apple had announced a new factory in Arizona more than a decade after closing its last U.S. plant.

All of these companies have announced investments of hundreds of millions of dollars either in new plant construction or in re-opening plants that had been shut down (BBC News, 2013). So, if all the companies or most of the companies that are coming back, plus the Western European companies that can't wait to invest in the United States, that will make the saturated solution at all unless limited oil importation is carried out. That makes the independence of any commodity in any country virtually impossible because all trees cannot be one tree, let alone in today's global economy. That being the case, I wish the United States good luck. Perhaps, we may rewrite history of global economy and more so, the world will learn a lot from the United States, and President Obama's administration. If the oil independence exists, we may also know how long that it will last for any country.

I think the case for oil independence in the United States is over because ever since I arrived in the United States from Nigeria, which is a country of 32 states and maybe more, I saw and heard from the citizens of one of my favorite states of the union rejecting the drilling for oil off the coast of the state of California. Instead the state prefers spending huge sums of money on drilling for oil in another country, citing environmental considerations. Today, the oil importing giant, the United States, is drilling for sweet crude in the ocean. The energy independence is not yet half way to completion, but the world is very nervous about what may be coming from OPEC, European Union, and consumers, though today the level of oil production is currently having excellent impact on the economy of the United States. I feel the world should not panic because I know the united States can handle any progress that comes her way, knowing that capitalism progresses when competition exists, and the United States knows that competing against herself is tantamount to less than global competition.

Strict Market Regulations in Africa

High import duties and strict market regulations in some African countries are inhibiting plans by Kasapreko Company, Ltd (KCL), an indigenous alcoholic beverage producer, to expand into other markets across the African continent apart from their own subregion. The Deputy Managing Director of Kasapreko said that some neighboring countries had created artificial banks that sometimes made Kasapreko's products less competitive. The Deputy Director also said that these practices had been adopted by three African countries, primarily Nigeria and South Africa. The Deputy Director continued by saying that these measures that had been taken were done simply to protect local manufacturing companies that created necessary employment and revenue for their citizens (BBC News, 2013).

The Deputy Director continued by saying that the measures taken by Nigeria and South Africa were also intended to limit the volume of exports local currencies from major foreign currencies, including the American dollar. He added that although this is against the World Trade Organization (WTO rule, these have been violated for a long time, and instead of Ghana doing something to protect their industries, the government has sat on the sidelines while industries in Ghana are faced with major challenges and unfair trade treatment. This is so much so that today many of these industries are being crippled, and the entire country is feeling the effects. The free fall of the cedi in recent years is a typical example, Kasapreko's DMD and his colleagues of the management staff undertook a market survey in South Africa in 2014. Their fact-finding revealed that the South African government was overzealous about its alcohol market, much to the detriment of imports, including those from Kasapreko (Management Bachelor's, 2013).

Kasapreko's DMD (2013) said that it is clear that the more Ghanaians consumed alcoholic beverages, the more the industries producing those beverages would expand to employ more people, while the local industry would collapse for lack of patronage. Mr. Nunno, the Kasapreko DMD, said that South Africa charges 115 percent import duty while Ghana charges a maximum of 50 percent, and that is the inconvenience. Kasapreko is planning on adding some two production lines, each with a production capacity of 26,000 packs, to enable it to satisfy the growing demand in the country, while expanding to outside markets. Mr. Nunno also said that what worried him was the unfair trade practices and protectionism that he claims are also rife in Liberia and Nigeria, among other West African countries, and this could hurt their expansion drive should the government continue to pledge action without doing anything (Management Bachelor's, 2013).

Mr. Nunno thinks that these are some of the things that our government and the trade agencies will have to examine to ensure that there is fair trade between Ghana and Nigeria. Mr. Nunno also explained that the company was looking to review its trade relations with countries closing their markets to Ghanaian imports (Management Bachelor's, 2013).

Export Earnings

Kasapreko, which is a closely held family business, currently exports large quantities of their products, including the flagship Alamo Bitters, to neighboring countries such as Nigeria, Togo, Liberia, Cote d'Ivoire, and a couple of European and American companies. In 2012, the company received some US$19.46 million in export receipts and that earned it the enviable Exporter of the Year Award at the 23rd National Export Awards held late last year. Although Mr. Nunno did not disclose the precise amount the company earned in 2013, he stated that indications were that 2013's earnings could be twice as much as the previous year's earnings (Management Bachelor's, 2013).

Commentary: Kasapreko's Expansion Drive

1. Kasapreko's ambition;
2. Kasapreko as an award-winning exporter;
3. Kasapreko and market survey of South Africa;
4. Measures taken by Nigeria and South Africa and other West African countries;

5. Kasapreko's earnings in 2013 are twice as much as 2012—what does this say about the company?

Kasapreko's Expansion Drive

I am very proud of Kasapreko and its management team, as well as its innate ambition. Kasapreko manufacturers a product with a worldwide appeal that is fantastic, and it deserves to be expanded. The fact is their *hotcake item* is an alcoholic beverage that is restricted to adults. If it included children, why would an alcoholic beverage be distributed so easily in Africa? I have more questions than answers. I think that I could have given Kasapreko my own award if they had chosen another line of product that was not alcoholic and intoxicating. Africans need such a successful drink, if only African children were allowed to go to school and make academic reasoning, but I think Kasapreko is mature enough to write "for adults only" on the bottle.

I can believe that Kasapreko pays taxes on its product to the Ghanaian Government, but I think that the Ghanaian Government is not very proud about alcoholic beverages. Call it by any other name one wishes, it is still alcoholic. The aggressive marketing of Kasapreko makes the product even less acceptable to many consumers

Dumping Ground

Mr. Nunno, the DMD of Kasapreko, said that some neighboring countries created artificial barriers and so that its products would not compete effectively in the marketplace, but said nothing about trade agreements between Ghana and any of the neighboring countries of West Africa. Kasapreko and its management team are so driven that they have forgotten what is important to other neighboring countries. Mr. Nunno and his company have felt that any African country that does not accept Kasapreko's export or could be delivered is simply creating a barrier and taking a protectionist attitude.

The DMD of Kasapreko has failed to understand that sending products to another country against the will of that country is called dumping. Let us see; Kasapreko's product is alcoholic in nature but why not also make a soft drink beverage in the interest of African children? The DMD should understand that the product that they have chosen to produce in Africa which has no educational significance for Africa and particularly with African children, cannot be accepted easily and therefore accusations of trade barriers are called for.

Kasapreko's DMD said that the practice adopted by Nigeria and South Africa, including other African nations, are measures taken to ensure that their local manufacturing companies thrived in order to create necessary employment for their citizens. This is also true, but the human components are more important than starting industrialization from the standpoint of producing a lot of alcohol in Africa to keep the people intoxicated for a while and keeping them from doing what they should be doing to compete in a very competitive world today.

Africa has been a dumping ground for a long time. It is, therefore, uncalled for that Africans themselves create dumping grounds for unwanted products. I think that Ghanaian lawmakers know better and should be congratulated for not paying attention to Kasapreko's greedy and aggressive marketing strategy in Africa. My candid advice is that Ghana is an integral part of Africa, and this means that Kasapreko and its aggressive advertising should be turned down even in Ghana to enable the citizens to understand that they have to do more in our competitive world. The leaders of DMD and Kasapreko should understand that promoting alcoholism in Ghana is not the best way of serving the country.

An expansion drive is the most aggressive business style that I have ever dealt with since receiving my Ph.D. A drive to create an Internet business in Africa may be very acceptable by many people on the continent. I think that Kasapreko's drive is an uphill battle in Africa. Kasapreko should understand that just a few months ago Nigeria became the largest economy in Africa, a position held by South Africa since the Apartheid government fell. Kasapreko should understand that every country in the world wants to be the largest economy in its region because the economy is global and truly Africa is never left out.

Kasapreko's Ambition

Kasapreko is an indigenous alcoholic beverage producer in Ghana whose ambition is to expand into other African markets across the continent. Kasapreko currently exports large quantities of its products, including the flagship Alamo Bitters to neighboring countries such as Nigeria, Togo, Liberia, Cote d'Ivoire, and some European and American companies. Kasapreko received some US$19.46 million in revenues in 2012 and that earned them the Exporter of the Year award at the 23rd National Export Awards Meeting held in 2013 (Management Bachelor's 2013).

Psychologically, the success that the company has had have made it aim high for the future, but we are talking about alcoholic beverages. If the Ghanaian company had chosen another line of products and aimed at expanding to all African countries, I would have prayed for the company's success. Today, young people graduating from college or universities are not too sure of employment. Rather, some of them may fall back on what they think will give them comfort and that may be alcohol., and before one knows it, alcoholism becomes Africa's sickness. Remember that Kasapreko's customers are our children who are also the future of Africa. I do not know if Kasapreko has the future of the African continent in Mind. Before Kasapreko continues with its drive, the company should consider diversifying its portfolio to include soft drink beverages and other valuable products that may help rather than destroy our children. Kasapreko should ask why Ghanaian lawmakers pay little or no attention to what Kasapreko calls protectionism. If Africans are protecting anything, they are protecting the well-being of their citizens.

Kasapreko should understand that Africans cannot let themselves get so loose because of alcohol. If Kasapreko's management knows how an alcoholic looks like, they should withdraw any criticism they may have for Africa. When you see a black person becoming unnecessarily white or a white person becoming unnecessarily black, you have to understand that here is a serious medical problem at hand. Kasapreko's ambition to expand and make more money is an enviable ambition if the product were to be equally enviable. I am saying that the ambition is great, but the product is not so great to many people, especially the young.

Kasapreko as an Award Winning Exporter

Kasapreko earned USR19.46 million in export revenues in 2012, and also earned an award at the 23rd National Awards Meeting in 2013 (Management Bachelor's, 2013). It is therefore very clear that Kasapreko has a psychological problem. On examining it closer, the company received an international award and therefore has to feel like international product and would like a forceful marketing or aggressive marketing to get Africans to comply and probably have alcoholic beverages for breakfast and dinner. I think that Kasapreko deserves the award, but they should understand that what it received was a different culture from most African cultures. I know that Ghana's Kasapreko has become so carried away after the award and wanted Africans to make Kasapreko products their favorite. However, they should know that taste and usefulness of the product are also important. Let's look at taste.

Taste: People are different even in the consuming country in accepting a product for political reasons or otherwise. By taste, I mean sensitivities based on every analysis made on the educational, economic, and what the product may mean to the younger generation. If the acceptability of an alcoholic beverage is politically motivated, especially in Nigeria and South Africa, many people will demonstrate and oppose the product to the country's lawmakers. Kasapreko must know that lawmakers of any country feel a lot of pressure from the citizens who elected them in the first place. Of course, if the benefits in buying Kasapreko's products outweighs the ills of the products, then the products could sell well. Kasapreko has earned enough money over the years to enable it to diversify its portfolio. The company is a family-owned company and may not want to hire professionals to plan the diversification of their portfolio instead of developing another product line in a bid to producing more alcoholic beverages. Kasapreko should research what foods Africans, Europeans, and Americans, as well as the rest of the world, like better and develop such a product and may be put on such an aggressive marketing campaign or come up with a new brand of technology. The world today is different; everybody wants where his or her salvation will come from without thinking twice if they will go for it.

Usefulness: I continue to talk about what the Kasapreko product will do for someone rather than what someone will do for Kasapreko's products. Kasapreko's DMD, Mr. Kojo Nunno, said, "the practice adopted by Nigeria and South Africa is among measures taken to ensure that their local manufacturing companies thrived to create the necessary employment for their citizens, and that if it is intended to limit the volume of imports to protect their local currency against the major foreign currencies, including the American dollar" (Management Bachelor's, 2013). It is surprising to see that the DMD knows all of that and continues to aggressively market the company's products to the country he knows they know from a product whether it is useful to them based on what they need or plant.

Kasapreko and Market Survey of South Africa

The market survey by Kasapreko of South Africa is how aggressive in marketing they can go. The fact is that South Africa knows exactly what it wants, no matter how aggressive Kasapreko may be in trying harder for South Africa to import Kasapreko's alcoholic beverages. Africa has several cultures especially African countries which are not entirely homogeneous such as South Africa and Nigeria, even if they were homogenous tribal differences exist. Kasapreko deserve to give Africans their due respect. The United States, which has so much to export, from time to time the country engages in trade talks with its neighbors and that spells out how much duties will be involved in the trade transactions and how much of the commodities will be allowed to be imported on either side to the countries involved. This is a very civilized way of importing and exporting.

For a very aggressive company with an aggressive marketing strategy to start accusing another company or country for what it did or did not do and accusing the other country of protectionism while both countries do not have mutual trade agreements does not make sense. Any trade agreement must be aimed at what the World Trade Organization (WTO) allows. However, Kasapreko's DMD said, "Although this is against the World Trade Organization's (WTO) rules, these have been violated for long and instead of Ghana doing the same to protect its industries, the government sits aloof on the fringe while the industry is face with major challenges and unfair trade treatment." (Management Bachelor's, 2013).

What the DMD has just said about a violation of WTO rules, whet rules is he talking about? What Kasapreko's DMD should understand is that rules or laws are never made with absolute authority. There has to be some leeway where countries can say what is in their best interest. I am not sure whether or not Kasapreko is mistaking WTO rules for trade agreements between nations. The main function of the WTO is see that trade flows smoothly between or amongst nations. Other important WTO functions include:

1. Streamlining customs procedures globally;
2. Advancing discipline and communicate on some agricultural issues globally.
3. Providing support mechanisms and generating opportunities for the poorer members (Yahoo, 2013).

However, the most recent report before the G20 published December 2013, found that trade measures are on the rise.

I am not sure exactly what the DMD of Kasapreko wants the WTO to do for his company. Does he want it to discipline countries who are opposed to flooding their markets with alcoholic beverages and thereby contaminating the young with alcoholism? As I have said earlier about contracts between or among nations, if a contract is drawn up and a breach of that contract occurs in one way or another, then the party affected by the breach of contract agreement could submit a grievance to the WTO, who is one of the powers to discipline or settle such breaches of agreement and bring both nations to a smooth free trade. However, I still think that peace maintained by two high school or university students lasts longer than peace maintained for students by a principal or a dean because one party may think that he (or she) was unduly asked to maintain peace with the aggressor whom he or she did nothing to offend in the first place and may even accuse the principal or dean of taking sides in the dispute. Such a case never ends. However, if the aggressor is able to come forward and meet with the other party, there is a possibility he may say "I am sorry" and that goes a long way. The ego of the offender is very diminished while both will try harder to maintain the new relationship.

Unless Kasapreko's DMD wants some support mechanisms that are meant for the poorest members of the organization, Kasapreko may be fighting a loosing battle. What I have read so far about Kasapreko and its alcoholic beverages it does not appear that Kasapreko is having monetary problems even if the company is not doing business with Nigeria and South Africa. However, as of now, Kasapreko is doing limited business with both of those countries and is still doing well around the world. Kasapreko will be one of the richest companies if it could diversify its portfolio because it has enough money to do just that. Smooth flow of trade between or among nations sounds much like oversimplification of trade because this is about competitive advantages as Kasapreko produces a good alcoholic beverage and wants to take advantage all over Africa without balancing that with what the other countries produce better than in Ghana. Of course, this is the work of Ghana as a country and not for Kasapreko as a private company in Ghana.

One major reason why firms have their assets expropriated or are not successful in the international marketplace is a failure to understand the external environments. The same factors operate internationally as in the domestic marketplace. These include culture, level of economic development, political and legal structures, technological levels, demographic make-up, and natural resource shortages. Another major factor in the external environment is the level of economic development (McDaniel, 1982).

Measures Taken by Nigeria and South Africa and Other African Countries

I think that if Kasapreko and its alcoholic beverage are important to Ghana, the DMD of Kasapreko should campaign for a hearing with the Ghanaian lawmakers in order to see if the lawmakers will vote for amending or redrawing trade contracts with all or a number of African countries. It is Ghana that must draw up a trade contract with another country and it is not the responsibility of a private company to do that. I am sure there must have been a contract agreement on the books which might have some loopholes and which these African countries are taking advantage or simply those African countries may have been so frustrated with the dumping of alcoholic beverages in their countries without any evidence of competitive advantage amongst the countries.

Kasapreko's DMD had already told the world media that these African countries must have diverted their attention to protectionism because they wanted to protect their own infant industries and enable the country to create jobs for their citizens, as well as protect the currencies from the advanced economies. Kasapreko's DMD sounds more like he knows why protectionism occurred, which now means that Kasapreko's

DMD knows exactly that his aggressive marketing in African is against individual countries' ability to create jobs for their own citizens. If that is true, does that mean a conspiracy to control African economies or just aggressive marketing?

Kasapreko's DMD knows that every country that he has mentioned in Africa or elsewhere has alcoholic beverages. Are other competitors complaining also? If not, why not? I should think that Kasapreko should take a peaceful approach to solving trade disputes instead of jumping into any media and accusing countries of protectionism and passing judgment from the standpoint of the World Trade Organization, without seeking any redress from the WTO.

I think that Nigeria and South Africa ar3 truly working very hard to make sure that their citizens are employed because these two nations have very strong democratic systems. Their citizens demonstrate frequently for what they think is not right. However, some other African countries may do the same thing. Although a few others are afraid of their leaders and may not demonstrate for fear of punishment. Therefore, politics is a big part of doing anything that may not jeopardize their citizens' employment opportunities. Otherwise, the politicians' chances of being reelected may be very slim. In this case, the country's president and his or her economic team must do a lot of analyses before yes or no of such dumping.

Kasapreko's Earnings in 2013 Were Twice As Much As 2012—What Does That Say to the Company?

Kasapreko is an aggressive marketing company, privately owned. Its marketing approach is dumping, and the company does not believe very much in contract agreements. The company has been very successful in bullying countries that have refused to accept their products as exports. Kasapreko's earnings were twice as much in 2013 as they were in 2012. This really means that that in 2013 the company made so much in earnings, and if in 2014, the company uses the same aggressive marketing for the sale of its products, then, of course, one can conclude that the company is greedy and wants more money at all costs. The behavior of dumping its products on another country's markets is truly found and may be Kasapreko's behavior is very well known to its neighbors, and the neighboring West African countries can never act in the same way at the same time just for one company.

West Africans have a deep love for themselves. Since the period of the slave trade, they know they have been victims for a long time. After the colonial period, West Africans created the West African School Certificate. Ever student in West Africa must take the same exam on the same date. The individual must pass at a higher grade to be able to take the Joint Admission and Matriculation Examination (JAME) for admission to a university. These countries also created the West African Common Market and the Bank of West Africa. The 15 member nations of the Economic Community of West Africa (ECOWAS) recently met in the Senegalese capital city of Dakar and agreed to a common market with a single currency by the year 2020. With all of the development in West Africa, the possibility of trade restrictions may be due to serious violations of an individual country's trade rules or may be Kasapreko's get-rich quick practices. What Kasapreko calls trade restrictions could be that Kasapreko has failed to diversify its portfolio. Alcohol is a drug, and distributing drugs in Africa is unacceptable, Kasapreko should know the West African countries in ECOWAS and what they will tolerate {See earlier map of ECOWAS). There were 16 nations in the West African Community, but in 1999 Mauritania opted out for reasons best known only to Mauritania.

The Importance of Trade With the United States

The United States is a full participant in world trade; yet, it is less dependent on external trade than any other industrialized nation. Its imports and exports average only 7 percent of the U.S. GDP, as compared to over 20% for Germany and the United Kingdom. Even though exports have exceeded imports every years except 1980, the

United States' balance of payments typically reveals a deficit. This is due to military and other expenditures abroad by the government. American exports consist primarily of agricultural products, as well as component parts and intermediate products used in manufacturing (Carl McDonald, 1982).

Firms that are heavily engaged in international trade are called multinational corporations. These firms move resources, goods, services, and skills across national borders without regard to the country in which the company is headquartered. The multinational corporation is among other things a private "government" often richer in assets and population of stockholders and employees than many of the countries in which they operate (McDonald, 1982).

CHAPTER 13
HUMAN RESOURCES MANAGEMENT

a. Human Resource Management
b. Human Relations Movement
c. Relationship Between Personnel and Line Management
d. The Advisory Counseling Role in the Advisory or Counseling Role
e. Staffing
f. Performance Evaluation
g. Compensation
h. Training Department
i. Employee Relations
j. Safety and Health
k. Case Study
l. Kinkona Study
m. Chart
n. Questions and Answers
o. Comparison of Need Theories
p. Training Versus Education
q. Summary
r. Grievance and Discipline
s. Causes of Grievance
t. Approach to Discipline
u. Negative Approach
v. Positive Approach
w. Diagnosing Disciplinary Problems
x. Case Study of Disciplinary Action
y. Questions and Answers
z. Choosing an Arbitrator, issues, and Process

CHAPTER 13

HUMAN RESOURCES MANAGEMENT

The personnel that work for a company represent the organization's business resources. Therefore, personnel management and human resources management are interchangeable terms and refer to the same processes. An individual who fills the positon of personnel manager has the primary responsibility for coordinating the organization's personnel activities (David J. Cherrington, 1984),

Personnel activities should not be created unless they also contribute to the accomplishment of organizational goals and to the successful execution of organizational strategies. Therefore, personnel activities should be evaluated to determine whether these activities are simply proliferating programs and reports or whether they are making a positive contribution to the economic success and survival of the organization (Cherrington, 1984)

Human Relations Movement

From 1924 to 1933 in the United States under the direction of Elton May of Harvard University, a series of studies were conducted at the Hawthorne Works of the Western Electric Company. These studies examined the effects of working conditions and group influences on production and provided the foundation for the human relations movement that was to extend over the next three decades in the field of management (Cherrington, 1984).

Cherrington (1984) states that the first studies were illumination experiments in which the intensity of lighting was varied to examine its influence on worker productivity. The results of these studies indicated that performance improved when lighting was changed, regardless of whether the lighting was increased or decreased. Therefore, the experimenters concluded that productivity had accelerated because the employees had known that their performance was being measured. This phenomenon in which performance is influenced by the process of observation is referred to today as the Hawthorne Effect.

Another series of studies, called the Relax Assembly Test Room Experiments, examined the effects of rest pauses, hours of work, and financial incentives on worker productivity. From these studies it was concluded that rest periods, changes in the design of the work, and financial incentives had virtually no effect on worker productivity. The variables that significantly influenced productivity were claimed to be friendly supervision and the influence of the informal work group. A later study, called the Bank Writing Room Experiment, examined the influence of group norms. Although the men participating in the study were paid at a piece rate incentive and the experiment was conducted during the Depression when an intense motive to earn money existed, none of the participants produced more than the standard set by the group. This study illustrated the effects of group norms and demonstrated how powerful such norms could be in establishing artificially low levels of performance (Cherrington, 1984).

Cherrington (1984) also said that another segment of the Hawthorne Studies consisted of an interviewing program in which employees were questioned about their attitudes toward their jobs and the company. Several thousand employees participated in these interviews that represented the beginning of non-directive interviewing and counseling. Although the methodology, the results, and the conclusions of the

Hawthorne Studies have been severely criticized in recent years, their enormous influence on management literature and on the development of personnel policies cannot be overlooked. For many years the results of the Hawthorne Studies were used to convince managers that friendly supervision and good human relations had more impact on increasing employee performance than did financial incentives and job design (Cherrington, 1984).

Relationship Between Personnel and Line Management

Personnel managers are required to interact constantly with other managers in an organization. These interactions may produce conflicts unless these managers have a clear understanding of their relationships. To avoid such conflicts, the managers need to create a set of shared experiences regarding their responsibilities and authority (Cherrington, 1984).

Cherrington (1984) stated that a critical issue in the relationship between line managers and staff is whether the line managers are required to follow the recommendations of the stuff. Traditionally, line managers have had the authority to accept staff advice, modify it, or reject it. In recent years, however, greater authority for certain areas of management has been delegated to staff units. In those areas, accepting staff advice is compulsory for line managers subject only to appeal to a higher authority.

Three roles that staff personnel typically perform in in organizations have been identified as follows:

1. The advisory or counseling role;
2. The service role; and
3. The control role.

The Advisory or Counseling Role. In the advisory or counseling role, staff personnel are seen as internal consultants who gather information, diagnose problems, prescribe solutions, and offer assistance and guidance for human resource problems. This relationship between line managers and staff personnel is similar to that which exists between a professional consultant and a client. An example of this role is the responsibility of the personnel specialists to give advice regarding staffing, performance evaluation, training programs, and on redesign. In these situations the Personnel Department provides input that assists line manages in making decisions.

The Service Role. In this role, staff personnel perform those activities that ca more effectively controlled through a centralized staff rather than through the independent attempts of several different units within an organization. These activities are performed as a direct service to the line management and other staff departments. An example of this role is the recruiting and organization training that the Personnel Department provides as a service to the other units within the organization. The record keeping and reporting duties of the Personnel Department are also considered service activities (Cherrington, 1984).

The Control Role. The Personnel Department is required to control certain important policies and functions within the organization. This staff function is sometimes called functional authority. In performing this role, the Personnel Department is expected to establish policies and procedures and to monitor compliance with them. In exercising this role, the personnel staff members are seen as representatives or agents of the management. Because of legislation, the central role has become increasingly important in the areas of safety, equal employment opportunities, labor relations, and compensation. When the Personnel Department place hiring quotas on another department to achieve affirmative action goals, it is exercising its control role. (Cherrington, 1984).

Cherrington also states that a poor working relationship can develop between personnel and the line managers if both sides do not share expectations. Line managers tend to believe that the conflict is created because staff personnel:

1. Tend to assume line authority;
2. Do not keep line managers informed;
3. Steal credit for success;
4. Do not give sound advice; and
5. Do not see the whole picture.

In essence, line managers may see the personnel; staff as being guilty of overstepping their bounds, as non-communicating, as overrated in terms of potential contribution, as incapable of giving good advice, and as narrow in scope. On the other hand, staff personnel believe that conflict is created because line managers:

1. Do not make proper use of staff personnel;
2. Resist new ideas; and
3. Do not give staff personnel enough authority to overcome any disagreements.

Both parties must strive to emphasize the objectives of the organization and to openly discuss their perceptions of a situation in an attempt to create shared expectations.

Cherrington (1984) states that the major functions of a Personnel Department include:

1. Staffing;
2. Performance evaluations;
3. Compensation and benefits;
4. Training and development;
5. Employee relations;
6. Safety and health; and
7. Personnel research.

These functions are necessary for every organization regardless of size and organizational structure even though they may not be assigned as responsibilities of the Personnel Department. For example, a large organization may have a separate safety department, while a small organization may delegate safety responsibilities to line managers. Nevertheless, safety programs and compliance with the Occupational Safety and Health Act are important to every organization and in most organizations, the personnel department is involved in safety activities (Cherrington, 1984).

Staffing

Staffing involves three major activities—human resource planning, recruiting, and selection. Typically, anticipating human resource needs is the responsibility of line managers. As organizations grow in terms of size and complexity, lower management becomes more dependent upon the Personnel Department to gather information regarding the composition of the work force and the skills of present employees. Some Personnel Departments have developed sophisticated human resources planning systems that assist the organization in coordinating the strategic business plan with its human resource needs. More, over time, use of computers has become extremely popular for the storage of personnel information and for the development of projections regarding human resource needs (Cherrington, 1984).

Further, Cherrington (1984) points out that although recruiting is performed primarily by the personnel department, other departments may be involved in providing job descriptions and job specifications to assist the recruiting efforts. Also, line managers may be asked to make recruiting visits to college campuses. In the selection of new employees, the Personnel Department typically is responsible for screening applicants through interviews, tests, and background investigations. Three or four eligible applicants are then referred by the Personnel Department to the manager or supervisor for a final hiring decision. In the United States, because of equal employment opportunity laws and affirmative action requirements, the responsibility of most Personnel Departments for staffing activities has increased significantly (Cherrington, 1984).

Performance Evaluations,

Evaluating the performance of both managers and non-managers is generally a shared responsibility between the Personnel Department and other managers. Department managers and supervisors assume the primary responsibility for evaluating subordinates since they observe the job performance and are best able to make accurate assessments. However, the Personnel Department is generally responsible for developing effective performance appraisal forms and assessment procedures and for ensuring that performance evaluations are conducted. To maintain an effective performance evaluation program, the Personnel Department may need to train supervisors how to establish performance standards, make accurate assessments, and conduct performance interviews (Cherrington, 1984).\

Compensation.

An effective compensation system is an important factor in avoiding excessive turnover and job dissatisfaction. The management of compensation involves the coordinated efforts of the Personnel Department and operating managers. Typically, line managers are responsible for recommending wage increases and the Personnel Department is responsible for developing and maintaining a wage and salary structure. An effective compensation system requires a careful balance between pay and benefits. Pay includes the wages, bonuses, incentives, and profit sharing received by an employee. Benefits refers to all non-wage items such as medical insurance, vacations, and other employee services. Personnel Departments try to make certain that employee compensation is adequate with respect to other organizations, fair in terms of internal equity, legal, and motivating (Cherrington, 1984).

Training Department

Most of the training that occurs in an organization is on-the-job training through the coaching and counseling of supervisors. However, the Personnel Department is usually involved in helping such supervisors become better trainers as well as conducting separate training and development sessions. The Personnel Department is frequently involved in the orientation for new employees, supervisory skill training, and various management development activities. The Personnel Department may also be involved in assessing the training needs of the organization and in evaluating the effectiveness of the training programs. A major responsibility that has been assigned to Personnel Departments in recent years is responsibility for job redesign and for organizational development. These activities often result in a major restructuring of the organization or in the resolution of major conflicts within the organization (Cherrington, 1984).

Employee Relations

Cherrington (1984) commented that in union organizations the Personnel Department takes and active role in negotiating and administering the labor agreements. Gathering information and helping prepare the company's bargaining position is normally the responsibility of the Personnel Department prior to negotiations. After an agreement has been negotiated, typically the Personnel Department instructs supervisors about administering the new labor agreement and in avoiding excessive grievances. Avoiding unfair labor practices, especially during an organizing campaign, is a major responsibility of the Personnel Department. When a union is present, these activities are often called labor relations or industrial relations. Personnel Departments in non-union organizations also need to be heavily involved in employee relations. In general, employees do not vote to join a union when their wages are fair and adequate and they believe that management is responsive to their feelings and needs. To maintain a non-union status, Personnel Departments need to make certain that the employees are treated fairly and that there is a well-defined procedure for resolving complaints. Regardless whether an organization is union or non-union, everyone needs a clearly defined discipline procedure for handling problem employees and an effective grievance procedure to protect employees (Cherrington, 1984).

Safety and Health

Every organization is required to have a safety program to eliminate unnecessary accidents and unhealthy conditions. Even though safe working procedures are designed for the benefit of employees, many employees fail to use safe operating procedures and safety equipment. Employees need to be continually reminded about the importance of safety and instructed on How to avoid accidents. An effective safety program can reduce the number of accidents and improve the general health of the work force. Most Personnel Departments have a major responsibility in providing safety training, identifying and correcting unsafe conditions, and in reporting accidents and injuries (Cherrington, 1984).

Following is a case study of a local businessman in a village bounded on the south by the Cross River. People around there were mainly peasant farmers, small-scale fishermen, palm wine producers, large-scale cassava and garri producers, and large-scale kinkana style alcoholic beverage makers who produce their beverages from the raffia palm tree. This village is medium sized with a gigantic high school that is one of the best in the country and that produced thousands of college graduates, including doctors, lawyers, engineers, and other professionals. The village is Ikun in Biase of the Cross River State in Nigeria. The people are very proud and often the envy of their northern neighbors. Yams from this area are often larger than a seven-year old child.

Case Study

On one occasion there was a millionaire who lived about 65 miles from Ikun's main beach. He felt that the Ikun Beach was a better location for him to do business and went to the city to ask for permission to set up his business there. He described his business to the Ikun chiefs and to the Ikun Youth Association Chairman and its executives on either side. The millionaire was asked to go to Biase headquarters at Akpet Central to obtain all the necessary permits and licenses for the business. At Ikun, he told both places but he visited that he was going to buy nets of a different size for his 75 employees and that his employees were more experienced fishermen.

The Ikun people told this millionaire, whose name was Johnson Agbor, that they were more interested in not polluting the river, and the Ikun people told Mr. Agbor that they would prefer that he prepare sanitation facilities first, and these had to be inspected and accepted by the Ikun Youth Association before the permits and licenses could be accepted by the Ikun community. Mr. Agbor was told by the Ikun community that his company would have to pay a yearly fee of $50,000 and that the company would have to find its own accommodations but that the security of the beach would cover their company and there might or might not be any unforeseen security expenses. If that happened, the company would be notified before the end of the year.

Mr. Agbor and his contractors went on to fulfill the sanitation concerns of the Ikun community. Inspection was done and the conditions were approved by the Ikun Youth Association before Mr. Agbor proceeded to Biase headquarters at Akpet Central for the necessary permits and licenses, both to make the district government aware of the proposed work in the district and for the purpose of district revenues, state, and federal taxes.

All the requirements were fulfilled, and one MBA holder, a Mr. Bassey. from Ikun went to the millionaire and tried to discover if the businessman had taken care of his employee recruitment, even though the company was a small one. Mr. Johnson told Mr. Bassey he did not believe in complicated employment procedures, and he further commented that he was in business to make money. Also, even though he was not all that educated, he had a BSc in business administration and he intended to run the business himself because if the business became large and complicated, which would require employees with advanced degrees. Mr. Agbor felt that he would no longer be in control of the business.

Mr. Bassey laughed very hard, but when he looked at Mr. Agbor, he saw the expression on Mr. Agbor's face; he was clearly not amused at all. Mr. Agbor asked Mr. Bassey why he was so amused, but Mr. Bassey said nothing. He had been a business consultant for about 25 years and had met dozens of people who had little or no interest in human resources. Mr. Agbor really wanted to know why Mr. Bassey had laughed so hard. Mr. Bassey then said, "I know you're the kind of businessman that likes to be in control of everything you hear or say in your business, but that attitude is good. However, you should be careful because excessive control may sometimes leave you without any employees."

Mr. Agbor responded, "How is that?"

Mr. Bassey then said, "Here is the thing, Mr. Agbor; employees want freedom. I am not talking about absolute freedom. I don't mean giving them a blank check to do anything they want to do. Of course, you have to know your employees, get involved in what they are doing. Hold on, Mr. Agbor, You have spent a lot of money on your tools; they are your resources, but they can't stand up and work for you. The people you employ will use the tools and accomplish the job for you. The humans you employ are resources as well, but your human resources cannot be planned large and complicated."

Mr. Johnson said, "Mr. Bassey, I am okay with that topic; if needs be, we can talk about further in the future. Goodbye, Mr. Bassey."

Mr. Bassey then said, "Goodbye, Mr. Agbor." Mr. Johnson Agbor left for his recruitment center, and on the first day he recruited ten employees. He thought he had recruited so many in one day. The second day he recruited five employees. He then regretted not having Mr. Ogban Bassey with him. He thought that two heads are better than one and that he could well afford Mr. Bassey's fees at least for a number of days. On the third day, he employed ten more employees, and this continued until he had fulfilled his quota of 75 employees. He also bought a number of boats, and all of the employees were licensed to run the boats. All of them drove safety to Ikun Beach where they moved into the accommodations that had already been arranged for them. That first evening, they enjoyed the dining places, hotels, and clubs.

The following morning the employees took taxis to Ikun Beach where Mr. Agbor himself distributed the tools and equipment they would be using. The group spent two days rearranging their tools for operating the equipment and boats. By the fourth day, they were all out fishing and some of the boats were full of fish, and they were given a place to dry the fish. After the first week, their catch was enormous.

In a month's time, Mr. Agbor arrived and was impressed. After three months of impressive catches, the men discovered where they could buy cheap garri, rice, as well as beans in Ikun. More importantly, they were shown by the Ikun people where to buy a hot drink called Kinkana or Kinkana Beverage. A glass of Kinkana can intoxicate someone for a whole day. On the second day, the effects would be mild, but one cannot go to work simply because the person would be too weak and be somewhat insensible in doing anything. Usually, Kinkana is not for local consumption, but producers ship it to different states or countries.

Many people who have tasted Kinkana once refused to take it again because anyone with no real reason to stop going to work could simply be fired from his or her job. However, since Mr. Agbor has no one in charge of his company while he was away, the Kinkana party took place in his company. Any day the employees had Kinkana available, of course, there would be a party and that was a Kinkana Party.

Kinkana Song

Kinkana can't kill me;
I will kill Kinkana;
Kinkana can't kill me;
I will kill Kinkana.
Yo, Yo, Yo, Yo, Yo, Yo
I will kill Kinkana.

Since the inception of the Kinkana Party, productivity in the fishing company took a serious nosedive. When Mr. Agbor arrived, people told him what had been happening. Mr. Agbor quickly sent for Mr. Bassey and asked him to do what he thought was proper for the company. Mr. Bassey had no employee records to know or have information regarding each employee. Mr. Bassey and his firm created a personnel file on each employee after an extensive interview with the employees. Even as Mr. Bassey was interviewing employees, he found that some of the fishermen were not ready to work in the open river. They needed sufficient rest and hospitalization or some kind of medical treatment. So, the idea that Kinkana was not addictive was reexamined by the Ikun Youth Association. A study was made and discovered that 51% of the voting age population in Ikun wanted Kinkana production ceased immediately because Kinkana was addictive and might sooner or later affect the behavior of the young people, especially in this day and age when people wanted something intoxicating.

In the meantime, many of the fishermen were no longer medically fit to work in the open river, and so Mr. Bassey had to fire them because the long-term ramifications would be financially disastrous for the young fishing company to bear. Mr. Agbor then terminated those who were no longer fit to work in the open river, but he first sent them for treatment with a month's pay for each individual.

After the rehabilitation of those individuals deemed unfit to work in the open river, Mr. Bassey asked Mr. Agbor to employ about five supervisors for a close examination of the employees. Meanwhile, the

Ikun Youth Association executives were preparing for elections and the village was divided about the existence of Kinkana in Ikun. However, 49% of the voting age voters in Ikun were in support of Kinkana production in Ikun. They campaigned that Kinkana did no harm to anyone, but when people abused Kinkana they accused Kinkana for harming them. They cited the same situation in the United States about gun right and those against them and told the Ikun community that up until that date that large and civilized country like the United States had done nothing to solve the argument for the reason that guns do not kill, people kill with guns. The fishing company began improving, but Mr. Bassey went back to Mr. Agbor and asked him to employ a general manager. Even without a general manager, the fishing company had been making a profit and had grown to include 95 employees. They had kept their taxes current, and meanwhile the Kinkana beverage had paid all of their back taxes.

Meanwhile, the election of the executives in the Ikun Youth Association had intensified, and those opposed to the Kinkana beverage had every poll showing them winning. The chairman of the association wanted a debate because he thought the Ikun people were always so busy working and had no time for politics. So, a day was schedule for a debate. During the debate the current chairman made mention of what was going on with the fishing company and told the people of Ikun that people would say that what happened with the fishing company would never happen to them. He told the debate participants that he wanted to remind them about the United States and gun rights. The chairman told the participants it is always the same argument that guns do not kill but people kill with guns and nothing like that could happen to them. He asked then, "Guess what? Today, abuse of guns or whatever you call it, is an equal opportunity employer in the office, the restaurant, private and public transportation companies, in schools, colleges and universities where guns have been used to kill many people. Today, we have Kinkana; it kills when you don't expect it to do so." He then asked his audience if they drove a car, a boat, or a plane. If you have not had anything happen, it's a question of time. He pointed to the benefits that the only high school in the village had done for the village. He commented, "We have doctors, lawyers, engineers, business executives, and teachers of all grades today. How about tomorrow when most of our children will be drunk?"

In the meantime, the fishing company was getting richer and the new general manager had arrived and was briefed seriously by Mr. Bassey, and the general manager appeared ready to go to work. His name was Bassey Onda, and he had a bachelor's degree in business and a master's degree in political science. He had worked in both the public and private sectors and was very well regarded amongst his colleagues. For the next three months, the company made so much profit. The employees gradually ceased using Kinkana but never left it completely because it was addictive.

After the elections, the candidates for Kinkana had won every seat up for election. When Mr. Bassey heard about the results, he cried and sent for the general manager, Mr. Bassey Onda. Mr. Bassey told Mr. Onda that the company now had a serious problem because those who care about the community were no longer in power at the Ikun Youth Association, but only the chief could nullify the election results. Mr. Bassey told Mr. Onda that most of his employees were addicted to Kinkana.

Mr. Onda could not believe what he was hearing. Mr. Ogban Bassey, a native of Ikun, brought up in the Presbyterian school of Ikun and the Ubaghara High School of Ikun and attended the University of Calabar, was a reason of the soil and wanted the best for the Cross River State. Mr. Johnson Agbor arrived on very short notice, and all three— Mr. Agbor, Mr. Onda, and Mr. Bassey—decided to ask the chiefs to nullify the election results, but the chiefs were also divided because the three executives told the chiefs that the Kinkana beverage that Kinkana spent over 50 million naira for such a small election. The chiefs told the three executives that it was a small election for the Kinkana company because the executives wanted Kinkana out of Ikun where they had been making a very good profit. The company had paid their taxes, employed about 30 people, and had caused no concern in the village. Yet, the executives told the chiefs that what they wanted the unforeseen to be avoided before anything did happen. A vote was taken and it was a tie. The consultant and director turned to Mr. Agbor and tried to find out if he still felt the way he had before in saying he never wanted human resources. Mr. Agbor then told Mr. Bassey and Mr. Onda that he had never owned a business before.

The three executives, Mr. Agbor, Mr. Onda, and Mr. Bassey, left for Biase headquarters at Akpet Central and told the whole story to the supervisors and asked them to nullify the election results, but the supervisors, like the chiefs, told the executives that they had to prove criminal wrongdoing in order to do that; otherwise, they would be going against the law of the Cross River State and even federal law. They confirmed with the executives that the supervisors of the Biase local government are guided by the state and federal laws.

The executive came back and angrily printed a circular to all the employees pleading with them to stop using Kinkana products because the products were addictive and intoxicating, which was not good for the work they had to accomplish. Well, a few employees followed their instructions and ceased using Kinkana; others made Kinkana appear to be a contraband product that was against the law of the land, meaning the local government's rules and regulations, as well as the state and federal laws.

The Kinkana Company began mocking them and laughing at the fishing company and asked the fishing company to leave them alone. One day a fisherman drowned as he was removing fish from the nets. A neighbor saw what happened and thought that was done on purpose, but the drowned man remained in the water longer than was necessary. So, the neighbor called another fisherman and told him that a man had drowned. The third fisherman wasted no time and came down where they both dove in and found the man who did was not responsive at all. The victim was carried to where his supervisors were notified, and three of the five supervisors arrived on the scene very quickly. They checked out the victim and found a medium-sized bottle of Kinkana which was almost half-empty. One of the supervisors quickly called the police.

From Ikun, the body was taken to Calabar where more examinations were done by forensic experts. The family was sent for; the victim was survived by a wife and three children, two boys and a girl. The man's body was left to be frozen pending burial arrangements. After the burial near his home, the fishing company contacted both the Ikun Youth Association and the chiefs. The organizations told them that it was a police case and that they had nothing to do with it.

The fishing company then sued the Kinkana Company for knowingly selling a product that kills. The case continued for months; both sides had high-powered attorneys, and in the end the High Court found Kinkana guilty of selling the strongest alcoholic beverage in the world and knew that their product was also addictive. The court also praised the Ikun people for not being involved in drinking Kinkana. On the day of the judgment, the Ikun paramount chief and the chairman of the Ikun Youth Association were asked to be present in court. Upon declaring the verdict, the judge told both leaders from Ikun that he knew that Ikun was a fast-developing village with health facilities, infant industries were springing up, farmers of many categories, and recently a high-powered fishing company with many employees, and yet at the center of it all they had a destructive company called Kinkana. The judge turned to Kinkana and accused them of doing business in Ikun simply to destroy the young and aspiring minds in Ikun who most villages and cites were admiring. The judge required Kinkana to pay a fine of N5.5 million (N5 million, five hundred thousand) to the dead man's family and and N$1.5 million to the fishing company for time wasted and cost of attorneys. Finally, the judge told Kinkana that the court had no power to put them out of business or otherwise he would have done it in about ten minutes.

When everyone of them came back to Ikun, the Kinkana executives met with both the Ikun chiefs and the Youth Association executives and told them that the Kinkana Company would comply with the judge's decision up to the point that they could afford to do so and that their company would be sold because they would have no money to continue. Kinkana finally closed its doors and that was the end of the Kinkana Company in Ikun.

In general, the Ikun people were very happy that the Kinkana Company was gone because they were concerned about what Kinkana would mean to their children in the long run. Meanwhile, the fishing company hired more people; I mean the fishing company employed more fishermen and made better profits. The organizational chart was as follows:

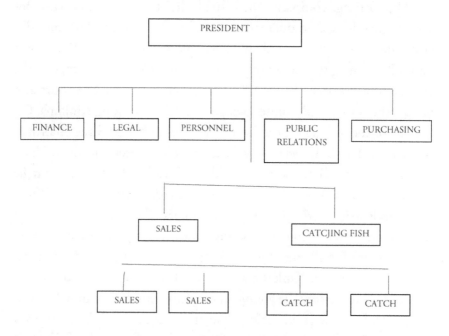

Mr. Agbor, the owner, became the President and Chief Executive Officer, but depended heavily on both the former general manager, who now became the Personnel Manager, and the former consultant and director, who now became the Public Relations Officer. The personnel manager now is Mr. Bassey Onda, and the public relations officer is Mr. Ogban Bassey. The president and CEO had told his director previously that he wanted to control the company. Now, he had a chance to do, if he was not just a figurehead, because all the other company leaders were professionals with years of experience.

Mr. Johnson Agbor	President and CEO millionaire and the founder
(President & CEO)	of the company, with a BSc in business administration.
Mr. Charles Uno (Finance Manager	Worked for the state government and a private company as a Certified Public Accountant (CPA)
Mr. Achibong Okon (Legal Officer)	Worked as a public prosecutor and as a private practitioner in law.
Mr. Bassey Onda (Personnel Manager)	Worked as a manager in public and private companies, and as a general manager in the fishing company. He had a BSc in business administration and a masters in political science.
Mr. Ogban Bassey (Public Relations)	Worked as a consultant and in a public company as a business analyst, had a BSC in business administration and an MBA in business administration.
Mr. Thomas Agboji (Purchasing Manager)	Worked as a purchasing manager for the state and as a sales manager for a private company; had a BSc in sales management and a MSc in political science.

At the second meeting of the executive officers, Mr. Ogban Bassey, the Public Relations Officer, told the group that the Cross River State was very different from most states in Nigeria in that no company could just be staffed with just one gender and that other executive positions should be given to a woman. He said that the new position should not be given to just any woman, but to a qualified woman. Mr. Johnson Agbor told them that he intended to talk to the public relations officer about making sales an executive position, which up until this time had been handled by him directly. He asked the public relations officer to advertise the position and that during the interviews he would sit with the public relations officer and conduct the interview. The CEO then asked the public relations officer to emphasize in the advertising for the position that women should apply;.

Meanwhile, the CEO toured Ubaghara High School and promised them N100 million in about five years. He asked the students to study harder and that Ubaghara High School had a history of success, a tradition that they should continue, and then he thanked the principal, teachers, and non-teaching staff.

The interview date was selected and the press reported that a woman might be the new sales executive. The radio and papers reported that executives of the giant fishing company would no longer be a "men only" club but that a woman might be chosen, while in most companies and even in the government, women were always employed as deputies and then advanced to becoming heads of departments. Well, when "D-Day" arrived, all the candidates were requested to go to the Central Hall with only their resume and that every candidate would have five minutes of interview tune, At 7:30 on Wednesday, Nigerian time, the interviews began with three women and one man. Each candidate was asked to leave after the interview and to expect a letter of notification in the mail about the same time on Monday.

The letters were duly sent out the following day, and one woman was selected for employment, and they awaited her acceptance. This woman was Elizabeth Effiong who was married and had three children, had a B.S. degree in Business Administration and an M.A. in Sales Management. She had worked as a sales manager for the state and as a sales general manager for a private company.

Ms. Effiong was invited to the main office in Ikun, and the press heard about it and invited themselves to be there for the swearing-in ceremony. Ms. Effiong gladly accepted the position, and her husband and children were present. The company gave her a week to prepare to take on her new responsibilities. The president and CEO gave brief addresses and told the press that the era of the oppression of women was over and that a woman who was qualified had every right to a position as a man who was qualified. H asked the press not to tell the world that Ms. Effiong was employed because she is a woman and the company wanted a woman in the position. The CEO emphasized strongly that Ms. Effiong was employed because she is qualified for the position and would earn the same salary as her counterparts, but in his company seniority was highly respected.

The CEO also told the press that what is said about Ms. Effiong is not limited to her but would be applied to all women employees in his company with the same job description, experience, and academic qualifications, and they would earn the same salary and benefits. The CEO continued, "Please, my fellow human beings, understand with me that women are our mothers and men are our fathers, and there should be no distinction between the two in how they are treated.

This is a case of human resource management; it is simply how human beings manage fellow humans. In my writings, I tell stories or cases to enable readers or students understand what a subject is all about. Sometimes, if we go to class and tell students that today our study will be how humans manage other human beings whether at the place of work or during employment procedures, students will have many things to say. However, if you say the study is on human resources management, first of all, the term has to be defined, and you will have a very long today ahead of you.

No sooner had Ms. Effiong assumed her position than she began connecting with various people around the state and Nigeria as a whole and then many parts of the world as well. She was well liked, especially in the media frenzy that followed her interview and consequent employment. She used this to her advantage as her name became more than a typical sales representative. Ms. Effiong not only took advantage of selling the company's product, but also she was allowed to package the product the way she thought would attract customers best. She never just packaged the product, but she packaged herself also. She knew what to say to a new customer and to a long-time customer. Her smile, her quick understanding of a situation in the marketplace, and her immediate responses worked to her advantage. Since Ms. Effiong began working for the company, the warehouse was nearly empty because of the demand from more customers. Even the local communities that were not interested in buying fish from the company because of the prices were convinced by Ms. Effiong that the company's prices fare competitively in the marketplace and were often money saving. The company later became a multinational corporation because it began serving local and international markets.

Questions

1. Where was the fishing company located?
2. Who was the founder of the fishing company?
3. Who is Mr. Ogban Bassey in the multinational corporation?
4. What position did Ms. Elizabeth Effiong hold?
5. Excluding the president, how many executives did the fishing company have?

Answers

1. Ikun Beach.
2. Johnson Agbor.
3. Mr. Ogban Bassey is the Public Relations Officer.
4. Ms. Elizabeth Effiong was the Sales Manager.
5. The fishing company has seven executive officers.

Motivation

Motivation theories are classified in three major categories: Need Theories, Reinforcement Theories, and Expectancy Theories. Need theories focus on the material causes of behavior. People strive to satisfy physical or social needs. Reinforcement theories focus on external causes of behavior—people respond to reinforcing events that occur within their environment. Expectancy theories are goal-oriented and focus on rational thinking and decision-making processes. People decide to behave in ways that provide positive rewards. Although these theories may appear to be quite distinct from one another, recent studies have demonstrated that they actually are highly complementary. In fact, the focus of most of the current research on motivation has not been on the development of any new theory but on the development of an integrative framework for the different theories (Cherrington, 1984).

Cherrington (1984) has stated that several theories of motivation are based on the concept of needs. A need is defined as an internal state of disequilibrium—psychological or physical—which causes an individual to behave in certain ways. Most needs arise because of a physical or psychological deficiency—something that is lacking. To say that individuals have needs is to imply that they have some form of internal stimuli that energizes them or causes them to interact with their environment to satisfy the need. The presence of a need motivates an individual to action to restore a state of equilibrium. Needs theories assume that each individual has a set of needs and that the individual's goal is to satisfy those needs (Cherrington, 1984).

Cherrington (1984) further stated that one of the earliest lists of human needs was developed by Herbert Murray who used a biological/psychological classification in categorizing these needs. Murray first developed a list of 15 needs that were classified as vicerogenic (primary) and psychogenic (secondary). The needs for food, water, sex, urination, defecation, and lactation all associated with physiological functions were examples of Murray's vicerogenic needs. Murray's psychogenic needs classification included abasement, achievement, affiliation, aggression, autonomy, deference, dominance, and power. The initial list of 15 needs was expanded over time by Murray and others until it became quite unwieldy and ambiguous.

Cherrington (1984) also noted that one of the popular needs theory of motivation was developed by Abraham Maslow and is descried in his book, <u>Motivation and Personality</u>. Maslow's theory is historically significant because it served as the foundation for later theories of motivation and job redesign. According to Maslow, individual behavior is directed by the desire to satisfy one or more of five general needs: physiological, safety, social, self-esteem, and self-actualization.

The physiological needs are those associated with biological requirements such as food, water, rest, and sex. The safety needs are those related to protection from danger, threat, and deprivation. Social needs consist of desires for special interactions with others such as friendship, companionship of others, and the expression of love.

Self-esteem needs are those regarding autonomy, dignity, and the respect of others, while self-actualization needs (Maslow's highest general need) refers to needs for self-realization, continuous self-development, and the process of becoming all that an individual is capable of becoming.

These five needs are arranged in a hierarchy of importance called Prepotency. Higher level needs are not important and are not manifest in a person until lower level needs are satisfied, but as the lower level needs are satisfied, needs at the next highest level appear and influence behavior. The levels of the need hierarchy are not rigidly separated but overlap to some extent. Thus, it is possible for a higher level need to emerge before a lower level need is completely satisfied (Cherrington, 1984).

In subsequent research, Cherrington (1984) commented that Maslow's hierarchy has been reduced the needs categories from five to two or three. Alderfer's research only identified three distinctly different needs that he termed the ERG Theory. These were existence, relatedness, and growth needs.

Existence needs consist of Maslow's physiological and safety needs, while relatedness needs includes wants for socialization and social approval. Growth needs refer to the desires for self-development and self-fulfillment, which are similar to Maslow's self-esteem and self-actualization needs. Alderfer found that lower order needs do not need to be filled before higher orders needs emerge. He concluded that all three needs can be simultaneously active.

COMPARISON OF NEEDS THEORIES

Murray	Maslow	Alderfer	Classification Today
Psychogenic	Self-Actualization	Growth	Intrinsic
Abasement			
Achievement			
Affiliation			Social-
Aggression	Esteem	Relatedness	Interaction
Autonomy			
Deference	Social		
Dominance			
Viscerogenic	Safety	Existence	Extrinsic
Food	Physiological		

Water	Physiological
Sex	Physiological
Urination	Physiological
Defecation	Physiological
Lactation	Physiological

Cherrington noted that other studies also have tended to condense individual needs into two or three categories and to eliminate the concept of prepotency. Some models show needs classified in two categories—extrinsic and intrinsic—while other models use three categories—extrinsic, interactive, and intrinsic. Extrinsic needs are normally associated with hunger, thirst, sex, and other biological comforts in addition to pay, status symbols, benefits, and other physical rewards. Interactive needs generally refer to the desires for social approval, affiliation, and companionship. Intrinsic needs concern the yearning for self-development, competency, mastery, and challenge (Cherrington, 1984).

Another contributor to needs theories, according to Cherrington (1984), was the work of David McClelland who studied the needs that he considered had the greatest influence on behavior: achievement, affiliation, and power.

According to McClelland, a high need for achievement is characterized by a strong desire for the following:

1. Personal responsibility for the success or failure of a project;
2. Moderate levels of risk (i.e., a challenging situation); and
3. Accurate and timely feedback on performance.

A high need for affiliation is characterized by the following:

1. A strong desire for interaction with other people;
2. A desire to be accepted by others; and
3. A concern for the quality of interpersonal relationships.

Finally, a high need for power is characterized by the following:

1. A desire to influence and direct someone else;
2. A desire to exercise control over others; and
3. A concern for maintaining leader-follower relationships.

According to McClelland, these needs are acquired through developmental experience and associations with influential adults especially parents. The need for achievement, for example, is determined by the kind of encouragement individuals receive from parents and others who help them set specific, achievable goals, teach them to take moderate risks, and provide them with feedback on their performance. McClelland found that high-need achievers like to take moderate risks that involved responsibility for the success or failure of a project and that they desired immediate feedback on the quality of their performance. Unlike individuals with a high need for affiliation, high-need achievers prefer to work alone or else they choose colleagues with suitable experience and competence. Entrepreneurs tend to be high-need achievers, and McClelland found a relationship between the economic activity of countries and the levels of achievement reported by executives from those countries (Cherrington, 1984).

Training Versus Education

Training development, education, and learning all refer to a similar process. It is the process that enables people to acquire new knowledge, to learn skills, and to perform behaviors differently that previously. The process is largely a private affair. The factors that facilitate learning and training can only be evaluated by examining the conditions under which they occur. Although training and education are quite similar, a distinction usually is made between them. Training refers to the acquisition of specific skills or knowledge. Training programs attempt to teach trainees how to perform particular activities or specific task. Education, on the other hand, is much more general and related to the development of the individual. Education attempts to provide students with general knowledge that can be applied in many different settings (Cherrington, 1984).

Case Study

There were two brothers, Victor Bassey and Uno Bassey, who were leaving for college; both of them were interested in mechanical engineering. They were both admitted to different universities. One early morning, one of the boys went to his parents and told them that he would like to be an automobile or motor mechanic and that he had been researching that dream. He told his parents that he so admired the work that the students were doing. Victor told his parents that he would one day own one of the best mechanic workshops in town in terms of services and prices and that he would also like to sell auto parts. The parents were immediately convinced that this son was an entrepreneur or at least he had the spirit of one. When Uno Bassey heard about his brother's dream, he went to the parents and told them that he was committed to attending the university for mechanical engineering. The parents were also happy for him.

Victor Bassey's parents went with him to see the workshop. First of all, they found that the location was purely a learning environment. All of the students had finished high school with good grades, and more than half of the students had already been admitted to a university, hoping to attend for the theoretical path and, of course, to broaden their ideas or simply to establish themselves on their own. The environment was full of hope. Victor's parents felt love at first sight of the institution's campus full of young and vibrant boys and girls. A careful reading of their faces portrayed that these students were ready to take technology to a new level. The workshop's public relations officer met with the parents, introduced himself to them, and showed them around the campus. Victor's parents quickly told the public relations officer that their son wanted to attend that school. The officer told Victor's parents that it depended on how they defined school and that the institution was simply an automobile workshop where students learned more about trucks, cars, and the like, good and bad sounds, parts, how to dismantle and rebuild vehicles.

The public relations officer told Victor's parents that the students would learn all of these things and much more, but they would receive not a degree but a certificate that was very well recognized by both private and public sectors. Also, theytold Victor's parents that most of the graduates preferred to owning their own businesses and that most of them today were multimillionaires. The PR officer also told Victor's parents that Victor could, upon completion of the workshop, attend any university for about two and a half years or three years to obtain his bachelor's degree in mechanical engineering for the sake of what they call a "business name." then, within a year he would be in the university, and he would certainly learn more things other than the practical aspects of engineering.

Ms. Bassey inquired, "so, does it mean this training awards a certificate?" The PR officer responded, "Yes, but one earns more than a master's degree in engineering." The officer also told the family that when any of their students were hired that they were hired for their practical excellence rather than for theory. The officer added, "Of course, that is one of the differences between training and education. In training, we narrow your focus, while in education, even what one calls a focus or emphasis is very broad touching all one should do as an engineer." The officer told the family that only the smallest aspects of the training is given to how a student can run his or her business. The parents were not very amused at that, and so Victor's father asked, "Will it then not be better to attend business school after this training?" The officer replied, "Well, you will be turning away from being called an engineer, which is your business name."

Victor's father replied, "Oh, yes, everything here is tailored to something else." Victor's mother asked, "Please officer, how do we start? We have another son who will be leaving for his studies soon. We want to go and help him get prepared"

The PR Officer responded, "I know what you are talking about. I have one son here and another is a medical student studying in a different environment. This is a different and difficult period for we parents. Well, there are forms for your son and you to fill out and a few documents that are needed, and then, finally the payment of fees and boarding expenses, if you like. Otherwise, he could be a day student, which would mean renting accommodations for him in town where he would be preparing his own meals."

Victor's father quickly picked up the application, filled it out, and signed it, and his wife co-signed it. They then produced the necessary documents and gently turned to their son and called him by name and told him they were going to pay his school fees, which would include boarding expenses. Victor quickly thanked his parents the three of them moved to the workshop's bookstore where they bought the recommended books for Victor.

Victor and his parents went to the PR officer's office and thanked him for his assistance. Victor told his parents that he had a friend at school whose parents simply asked their son to look for a job or be ready for getting a student loan as they were going to buy a holiday home in another state and also buy another family car. Victor told his parents that they had done all of that for him not because they had too much money but because they had so much love to give out. Victor's parents looked at him and thanked him for his observations and asked him to pass the tradition on to his children.

When the family returned home, Victor's twin Brother, Uno Bassey, was arranging his things for school. He had been admitted to the mechanical engineering program. Victor's father became jeakius of the

PR Officer's children who had one of his children in medical school while the other was in the workshop, hoping to attend a university to become an engineer. Mr. Bassey told his wife that he preferred such a combination for their sons. The wife told him that they could talk Uno Bassey out of engineering school and ask him to wait until the following year where he could enroll in the medical school. Uno Bassey's parents met with him and demanded that he wait until the following year where he could be admitted to medical school.

Uno Bassey kept silent for about three months and then exploded in very loud tones, "Was that what my twin brother asked you to demand? How about himself?" Victor's father jumped in, asking Uno to keep his brother out of this and that his brother had no idea about the discussion they were having with Uno. However, Uno refused and told his parents that physics and mathematics were his best subjects and asked them to allow him to do what he does best. Uno's father declared the discussion over, and Uno Bassey went to school and truly excelled.

Meanwhile, Victor Bassey was doing very well also. Within a semester he was able to dismantle and reassemble a car completely, change the oil, detect faulty materials and keep cars working for long periods of time. He also performed mathematics and a lot of drawings. At the end of the semester, Uno Bassey could not ask his parents for pocket money or major for major expenses. Victor Bassey became a part-time mechanic. When a customer entered, he would ask him to start the car, and the sound alone would indicate to him where the problem was located. So, he was always very quick with his repairs. Many of his classmates were like that also. Victor came home with lots of money. The first thing that occurred was when his parents were arriving home from work and driving the family van, Victor heard the sounds and asked the family to get out of the van and his parents quickly got out of the van, unaware of what was wrong. Victor got the key to the van, opened the hood, replaced certain items, changed the oil, cleaned the parts, and gave his father the car key to start the vehicle. Starting was no longer a problem; the smoke had disappeared. Victor's parents were very happy. Uno, Victor's twin, was astonished at what a difference a semester had made for Victor, but Uno was also very good at analysis and calculations.

Uno's mother shouted, "I know the difference between training and education. In training, focus is so intense and very narrow to the subject, while education is very wide and massive with more subjects to handle than can be delivered in four or five years." Victor responded, "Mom, you aright." Uno called his parents and told them that he would attend his brother's course of study upon completing his education as that would make him all around in his mechanical engineering discipline—cars and trucks. Victor also told his parents that he would certainly attend his brother's engineering school for the sake of a business name as the PR officer had told them and to broaden his ideas about mechanical engineering and its small business aspects. Victor's parents accepted unanimously, as the two boys' parents were happy for their children, but encouraged them to work harder and never think that they had it made.

Before the end of the second semester, Victor was almost a professional, and the brothers were now young men. They jointly owned a workshop on a part-time basis, and upon completion of their initial courses of study, Uno attend the workshop while Victor began attending the university. Upon completion of their training and education, the two brothers worked together for a while and realized that they had too many skills for just one office. So, Uno and Victor were separated with the approval of their parents even though they were earning more than they had expected. The two brothers visited each other often to see how the other was doing. Each of them were training students who paid fees and boarding expenses and enjoyed the training even more than Uno and Victor had done, even though the brothers never really suffered much. The brothers ended up becoming multi-millionaires.

SUMMARY

Training versus Education

A set of twin brothers were preparing for college ; they were Uno and Victor Bassey. Mr. and Ms. Bassey were excited about their twin sons were leaving home for the time to study what they liked best, and that was mechanical engineering at the school of their choice. As arrangements were being moving smoothly, one day Victor Bassey told his parents that he saw a place where young men and women were studying, and it was called a "workshop." Also, the students lived in a dormitory, and Victor convinced his parents to visit the site of the workshop. They loved the training place so much that they made arrangements for Victor to attend that same day.

On the other hand, Uno Bassey was sent to study at the university that had admitted both brothers. After a semester, Victor was adept at repairing cars and making some money. What really broke the camel's back was when Victor repaired the family van. Even Uno, Victor's twin, was impressed by the progress that his twin had made, and even decided to attend the workshop after he had graduated from the university. Of course, that was the advice given by the workshop's public relations officer because even though a student at the workshop might know so much practically, the workshop did not award degrees, and such a graduate of the workshop could not be called an engineer. The public relations officer emphasized attendance at a university because of the business name, "Engineer."

After all was said and done, both brothers graduated and founded a workshop. Uno Bassey was very good at analysis and calculations. Uno finally attended the workshop also to study the practical aspects of mechanical engineering, while at the same time, Victor Bassey attend the university for the theory of mechanical engineering. When both brothers graduated this second time around, they worked for a period of time together, and they decided to split the workshop they had founded because now they had identical skills. The brothers made their family businesses and became millionaires and were truly very wealthy. Uno Bassey's father wanted him to be a medical doctor because the workshop PR officer had told the Bassey parents that one of his sons was in the workshop while his other son was at the university medical school.

Questions

1. What are the differences between training and education?
2. What is the name of the young man who attended training?
3. What is the name of the twin brother who said, "What a difference a semester makes?" and who repaired the family van?
4. Are training and education similar? In what ways? Explain.
5. How did both boys become wealthy? Explain.
6. Uno Bassey's father wanted Uno to become a medical doctor. What circumstance led him to such thinking?
7. Describe in 15 words what you know about Mr. & Ms. Bassey's family?

Grievance and Discipline

Definition of Grievance

A grievance is a work-related complaint or formal dispute that is brought to the attention of management. Union companies use a more limited definition in which grievances only refer to specific disputes concerning the labor management. This definition is quite restricted and ignores many relevant criticisms that ought to be considered even though they are not covered by the union agreement. At the other extreme, grievances are sometimes defined very broadly in non-union companies to encompass any discontent or sense of injustice, even criticisms that are never expressed by employees. Such a definition has little validity because complaints have to be expressed before management can be expected to respond to them. Even so, management needs to be sensitive to unexpressed complaints that are evinced by sullenness, moodiness, criticism, insubordination, tardiness, and declining work performance (Cherrington, 1984).

Causes of Grievances

Most of the behavioral science literature suggests that grievances are caused by seething discontent and unfair management practices. This is partially true. The number of grievances is usually much higher when morale is low and when employees feel frustrated and discontented. Changes in the number of grievances have sometimes been used to measure the effectiveness of management decisions and personnel policies. Although the number of grievances tends to increase when job satisfaction declines, dissatisfaction with the job is not the only source of grievances. Grievances may arise for some of the following reasons:

1. Unclear contractual language that creates differing interpretations of the labor agreement;
2. Violation by management of the labor agreement;
3. Violation of the law, such as the overtime provisions of the Fair Labor Standards Act in the USA;
4. Violation of normal work procedures or other precedents;
5. Perceived unfair treatment of an employee by a supervisor (Cherrington, 1984).

Cherrington stated that even though grievances are related to dissatisfaction with the job, they are not related to any particular kind of job. Grievances do not appear to be more prevalent in one kind of work than in any other work. All jobs can produce grievances particularly if the employees are not well suited for the jobs, if the employees are treated unfairly, or if the employees are expected to do something they believe is wrong (Cherrington, 1984).

Approaches to Discipline

The violation of company rules can be handled in many different ways. At one extreme, a supervisor upon seeing a mistake, may scream at the offender in front of other workers and issue a snap decision aimed at punishing the offender and at deterring others from wrongdoing. At the other extreme, a supervisor, upon seeing a mistake, may respond in a calm and considerate manner with the intent of improving future performance, not of punishing past performance (Cherrington, 1984).

In his work, Cherrington (1984) asked why are there such dramatic differences in the ways in which supervisors respond. The major causes account for the differences. First, supervisors have developed their own characteristic ways of responding to disciplinary problems. How they were disciplined by their parents when they were children and how they were treated by superiors earlier in their own careers have an enormous influence on their styles of discipline. Supervisors tend to model their disciplinary style of other people who have been influential in their lives (Cherrington, 1984).

Cherrington (1984) stated that the disciplinary styles of supervisors also are influenced by the formal discipline procedures prescribed by the company and the dominant style of management of other managers. If the organization has a formal discipline system with a sequence of penalties that supervisors are expected to follow, the supervisors probably will follow the sequence in a calm and rational manner. If the dominant style of management tends to involve concern for the personal growth and development of employees, supervisors usually are inclined to help employees solve problems and improve their performance.

Negative Approach

Cherrington (1984) further found that a negative approach to discipline is sometimes called "punitive" or autocratic discipline. The purpose of punitive discipline is to punish employees for their mistakes. The punishment is usually severe so that it may serve as a stark reminder to others of the consequences of wrongdoing. To produce the desired effect, the punishment is usually administered publicly such as a verbal reprimand in the presence of other employees or firing the employee on the spot. When the mistake is discussed, there may be an emotional outburst. The supervisor may become angry and make irrational decisions. Even though employees may be suspended or discharged only infrequently, the employees may live in constant fear that it could happen at any time. The basic problem with punitive discipline is that it motivates employees to achieve only the minimum acceptable performance. Employees who are motivated by fear are not oriented toward becoming outstanding in their performances. Instead, they are motivated to avoid failure and to produce only the minimum amount of work to avoid punishment.

Another problem with punitive discipline is that severe punishment does not necessarily deter trouble makers. For example, people who break laws usually are thinking about their immediate wants rather than the long-term consequences of their actions. Likewise, employees who repeatedly make errors usually do not think about the consequences of their actions. Severe 0punishments and threats of being terminated are not usually very effective methods of discipline for such employees (Cherrington, 1984).

Positive Approach

The positive approach to discipline is sometimes called constructive discipline. The purposes of constructive discipline are to eliminate future problems and to create effective employees. Employees' mistakes are used to help them learn how to change. The disciplinary discussion is a calm consideration of the problem—what caused it, why it needs to be corrected, and how it can be corrected. The discussion focuses on the problem and how it can be solved rather than who is to blame and why (Cherrington, 1984)).

Cherrington (1984) also found that a necessary prerequisite for the positive approach to discipline is a clear understanding of the rules and expectations. The rules do not need to be an exhaustive list of detailed regulations. In fact, an informal list of individual interpretations are sometimes more useful because they create greater acceptance and commitment among employees than formal rules do. Regardless of the structure of the rules, employees need to know that behavior is unacceptable behavior. The performance standards must be fair and reasonable, and the rules must be administered fairly.

Cherrington (1984) also stated that this positive approach to discipline does not mean that a supervisor should ignore errors or casually disregard problems. It does not mean lax discipline. When an employee arrives late for work, drinks alcohol on the job, willfully damages company property, or commits any other wrongs, supervisors need to act. According to the constructive approach to discipline, supervisors actions should be directed toward the rehabilitation of the employee and the elimination of the problem. The supervisors may need to be very firm and repeated wrongdoing may have to result in suspension and discharge. However, the intent is to help the employee correct problem behavior and to become an outstanding performer.

The positive approach to discipline is closely linked to the development of personal responsibility. When employees are given specific performance expectations, when their performances are evaluated, and when problems are addressed in a constructive environment, the employees tend to develop a strong sense of personal responsibility. These conditions also contribute to the development of self-discipline and a strong work ethic (Cherrington, 1984).

Diagnosing Disciplinary Problems

Disciplinary problems can be caused by a number of reasons that are not equally serious. Understanding the causes of problems is essential because the causes suggest significant different implications for management action. It makes a great difference, for example, to know whether a machine was damaged by willful destructiveness, simple carelessness, or an unwitting error created by lack of training. The cost of fixing the machine will not change in relation to the severity or lightness of the cause, but the appropriate disciplinary action should be different depending on the cause. A careful diagnosis of the nature and cause of each wrongdoing should precede any disciplinary action. Most employee problems can be placed into one of the following categories:

1. Rule violations;
2. Unsatisfactory performances;
3. Personal problems;; and
4. Illegal actions (Cherrington, 1984).

Comparisons Between Positive and Negative Disciplinary Approaches

	Negative Approach	Positive Approach
Motive for Discipline	Retribution Punishment for Errors	To correct behavior and eliminate further errors
Emotional Tone of Meeting	Expression of anger, loss of temper, irrational punishment or threats	Calm explanation of the error and why it is unacceptable
Desired Result of Discipline	Severely punish or terminate the offender serves as an example for others to serve as a deterrent for others	Rehabilitate problem employees and turn them into productive employees
Probable Consequences	Employees will achieve only the minimum acceptable performance	Those who respond will become good employees; those who do not respond will be terminated.

Case Study of Disciplinary Action

During the colonial period in Nigeria, high school education was like someone attending a university, but then, high school education was university education equivalent in many ways. Discipline was almost a prerequisite on campus. The pride in being a student had no price tag; the hope of becoming a member of the future middle class was a joy to think about. High respect was accorded parents who could afford a high school education for their children. Winning a scholarship was nearly like winning the California Lottery., High school at that time was a club for wealthy people.

In the midst of all the financial barriers that affected the majority of the Nigerian people there was a middle-aged lady who refused to succumb to poverty and wanted her only son to be part of the middle class. She was employed in one of the oil palm estates in what is now known as the Cross River State. Her son was actually admitted to one of the high schools. High schools at that time were owned either by the government, run by a Christian denomination, or operated by very wealthy community or individuals. The middle class lady's son was also very hard working. Whenever he was on holiday, he traded on garri, a very stable food in Africa. He also traded on salad, corn, and fish. High school lasted five years, but in the boy's fourth year, his mother began feeling tired most of the time as a laborer. She was unable to finish her task work. Consequently, she was laid off. The supervisor reported the same to the manager who was unable to see the lady and find out what her problem was, but slammed her with punitive discipline.

When the son returned home on holiday, the mother was at home crying and told her son that she was going to kill herself. The son pleaded with her not to think like that because no one in the huge project that she had been involved in should ever think that the road would be smooth, meaning there would be no difficulties in their way. The son then prepared some food and asked his mother to sit at the table and feel comfortable for her lunch. He told his mother that he was going to visit a friend, but instead, he went straight to the general manager's office and asked him how to get ready with his school fees, boarding costs, and other expenses. The general manager responded, "What for, young man?" The young man replied, "You terminated my mother from working; the only person sponsoring me in high school."

The general manager replied, "Your mother works for this estate?"

The young man answered, "Yes."

The general manager then stated, "I don't know how she does it; if so, she does not deserve to be punished. Rather, she is doing what most people in this estate cannot do, and she is doing the best for the country." The general manager then called the supervisors and mentioned the lady's name and asked if they knew her. The manager and supervisor said, "Yes." The general manager responded, "I'm sorry, but I don't think either of you really know her."

The general manager then told the men that they should always try to know their employees and work with them in most cases and that they must make sure that discipline fits the offense committed. The general manager then told them the lady had personal issues and that all of them, including himself, must jointly help her get through them. The general manager went on in telling the manager and supervisor that the lady they had terminated had her only son in high school.

Both men responded, "What? Can this be true?" The general manager told them that the son was in his fourth year of high school and would be taking the West African school certificate examinations the following year. The two men again respond, "What?" The general manager then hinted that whenever they hired a middle-aged person, especially if it was a woman, that they should be careful with her and try to know her intentions in a diplomatic way or otherwise they might be accused of invading her privacy.

The manager said that he never saw this lady in the company of other women or even with a man. She was always by herself. The supervised jumped in by saying, "No, no, no, she has a few lady friends; they speak the same dialect or language. I sometimes got closer to them, but I didn't understand what they said, as it was none of my business. However, I always talked to them in broken English." The general manager then told both men that his own intention with them was not to make them psychologists or even to take courses in psychology, but if they did, they might do better jobs. He added that that he himself had a degree in business and a degree in psychology. "To tell you the truth, "the general manager continued, "my education is responsible for the way I see things and for my decisions."

At that point, the general manager asked the manager to reinstate the terminated, middle-aged lady and pay her for the months she had been terminated. The general manager also asked the manager to send someone over to the lady's home to tell her that she had been given her job back and that she would be paid for the time she had been away from work. The general manager then had a few words of advice for both the manager and supervisor that any time they wanted to discipline an employee they should take the positive approach because that would create self-discipline and a work ethic in the employee.

Questions

1. What type of approach was given to the middle-aged lady?
    a. Positive/constructive approach;
    b. Punitive/autocratic approach; or
    c. Calm/considerate approach.

2. What advice did the General Manager give to the manager and the supervisor?
3. What type of disciplinary approach would you recommend?

Arbitration

Arbitration is the process by which a labor dispute is resolved by an impartial third party who examined information from both sides and renders a judgment. The parties agree beforehand to accept the decision of the impartial judge, called an arbitrator. Arbitration can be used to settle contract issues during collective bargaining. However, arbitration is used most frequently to resolve labor grievances involving the interpretation or application of the labor agreement and discharge and disciplinary actions (Cherrington, 1984).

Cherrington (1984) found that for many years a nagging question challenged the arbitration process—could labor disputes be legally settled by arbitration or should they be settled by the courts as contract issues? The legality of grievance arbitration was questioned because it was viewed as a device to avoid court jurisdiction over contractual matters. Neither side wanted to submit an issue to arbitration if they knew it might later be overturned in federal court. During the 1960s, the situation changed as a result of several U.S. Supreme Court decisions that significantly strengthened the grievance process.

The arbitration proceedings must be fair and regular; the parties must agree to accept an award as final and finding. The award must not be a clear contradiction of the purposes and policies of the Board, and the award must deal with the statutory rights of the parties. The arbitration procedure is usually outlined in the labor agreement's provisions. These provisions generally describe the issues that may be arbitrated, the selection of an arbitrator, the arbitration procedures, and limitations on the authority of the arbitrator. (Cherrington, 1984).

Issues for Arbitration

In Cherrington's work (1984), he stated that although many grievances originate from discourteous or unfair treatment, most of the grievances that reach arbitration involve disputes about specific arbitration or interpretation of a labor agreement. Some of the issues referred to arbitration may frequently include the following:

1. Discharge and disciplinary actions;
2. Seniority and its application;
3. Leaves of absence;
4. Promotions and transfers;
5. Vacations and vacation pay;
6. Holidays and holiday pay;
7. Health and welfare benefits;
8. Management rights;
9. Union rights;
10. Strikes and lockouts;
11. Union security;
12. Wages and hours.

Choosing An Arbitrator

Cherrington (1984) stated that once the parties decide to have a dispute settled by arbitration, the first step is to select an arbitrator or board of arbitration. Occasionally a tripartite board consisting of representatives from management, the union, and an impartial chairperson is appointed. Some companies and unions have an arbitrator that hey all on regularly. Others compile a list of people who are acceptable to both sides and rotate through the list. The names of experienced arbitrators can be obtained from lists compiled in the country's arbitration association. In the United States, it is the American Arbitration Association or the Federal Mediation and Conciliation Service. The choice of an arbitrator may become a serious labor dispute in itself. Sometimes the previous award decisions of prospective arbitrators are carefully scrutinized to determine whether they have made more awards in favor of management or the union. However, since each case is different, this exercise is generally not very useful.

Most arbitrators are lawyers or professors; however, there are no set requirements for qualifying to serve as an arbitrator. Any person who has a reputation for fairness and impartiality might be asked to hear a dispute. An arbitrator is not bound by precedents. His or her job is to render the best judgment possible about the meaning of a particular labor agreement with respect to the specific case at hand. The fact that one arbitrator decides a case in one way does not necessarily mean that another arbitrator will do likewise in a similar case. However, arbitrators usually review the rulings handed down by one another and as a result, a set of general principles has slowly accumulated (Cherrington, 1984).

Arbitration Process

Cherrington (1984) has further elucidated the process by stating that after an arbitrator has been chosen, the arbitration hearing is held. A statement, called the Submission Agreement, is usually prepared; this statement formally outline the issues for arbitration and grants final authority to the arbitrator to settle the issue. The hearing may be as formal as a civil court hearing and involve written testimony, signed statements and affidavits, the swearing in of witnesses, cross-examination, and recorded transcription of the proceedings. However, the hearing also might be very informal involving an opening statement by each side and then questioning by the arbitrator. To save time, most testimony by witnesses is obtained in advance and presented to the arbitrator. Normally, the hearing does not last more than one day. Most arbitrators stipulate that the burden of proof is on the party which initiated the complaint. If the union alleges violation of the agreement, it must provide evidence of what happened and describe how the agreement has been violated. If an employee was discharged or disciplined, the company must provide evidence showing that the action was legitimate.

Cherrington (1984) further described the process by stating that after all of the evidence has been assembled, the hearings are adjourned, The arbitrator reviews the evidence, examines the labor agreement, and usually looks at previous arbitrator decisions. Within thirty days, the arbitration award is usually announced to both parties along with a written review of the case. The written review is important because it contains a rationale for the decision and helps each side understand the decision.

Cherrington (1984) continues by stating that even though grievance arbitration contributes to the peaceful resolution of labor disputes, it has its problems. Grievance arbitration is generally criticized for three reasons: it costs too much; it takes too long; and it has become too formal. The costs of arbitration usually increase each year because arbitrators increase their fees and because their expenses grow larger. The average time involved in processing a grievance through arbitration is so long that it is discouraging to most employees. IN 1970, the average time delay between the initial grievance filing and the final arbitration award was 245 days. The growing costs and increase time delays are partially attributed to what critics call "creeping legalism." The trends in arbitration are toward greater use of lawyers, more formal grievance hearings, longer testimony to examine, and more technical language in the labor agreements.

To overcome delays in arbitration, several companies have developed systems designed to expedite grievance procedures as efficiently as possible. Employees in the steel industry, for example, can obtain an arbitration hearing within ten days of filing an appeal. An arbitrator is selected from a panel of arbitrators, hears the case, which is presented by local plant and union representatives and involves no written transcripts or briefs. Since the award is made within 48 hours of hearing, costs are generally reduced by this method. Moreover, such a speedy hearing appears to promote better employee relations and seems to lose little in legalistic thoroughness (Cherrington, 1984).

An arbitrator hears a case from both parties and renders an impartial judgment. It is an easy thing to say because an impartial judgment to one side is a partial judgment to the other side. Unless the other side unanimously accepted the judgment based on what they perceived was correct and the right thing to do. Some companies may perceive the process to be disgraceful because other chiefs may fear the chief executive (CEO) and other top ranking officers cannot stand the tide of times in their company. In other words, the company's chief executives and top ranking officers are unable to do the right thing or they do not know what is right or wrong in their company. The company may be criticized for spending large amounts of money looking for services of an arbitrator. In some cases, the arbitrator only talks about what the company did not do than what both parties could have done to keep the company stable and profitable. Arbitration in some cases is very educational to employees because the arbitrator makes it clear to the employees the do's and don't's of an employee as well as to the executives, which is positive to both.

I believe that costs and delay are clearly problematic in a company because these two things drain the resources far more than expected, especially in a company where the profit margin is slim. I think that arbitrators should come from impartial employees of the company, unless in extreme cases where outsiders and he media may be interested in the case.

CHAPTER 14
BUSINESS POLICY: UNITED STATES POSTAL SERVICE

CHAPTER 14

BUSINESS POLICY

United States Postal Service

History—19th Century

The postal service played a crucial role in national expansion. It facilitated expansion into the West by creating an inexpensive, fast, convenient communication system. Letters from the early settlers provided information and boosterism to encourage increased migration to the West, helped scattered families stay in contact and provided neutral help, assisted entrepreneurs to find business opportunities, and made possible regular commercial relationships between merchants in the West and wholesalers and factories in the East. The postal service likewise assisted the Army in expanding control over the vast Western territories. The widespread circulation of important newspapers by mail, such as the *New York Weekly Tribune* facilitated coordination among politicians in the different states and territories. The postal service helped integrate established areas with the frontier, creating a spirit of nationalism and providing a necessary infrastructure (Wikipedia, 1970).

The post office in the nineteenth century was a major source of federal patronage. Local postmasterships were rewards for local politicians who were often the editors of party newspaper. About three-fourths of all federal

315

civilian employees worked for the postal service. In 1816, it employed 3,341 men and in 1841, the service employed 14,290 people. The volume of mail expanded much faster than the population, as it carried annually 100 letters and 200 newspapers per 1000 inhabitants, in 1840. The post office department was enlarged during the tenure of President Andrew Jackson. As the post office department was expanded, difficulties were experienced due to a lack of employees and transportation. The postal service's employees at the time were still subject to the so-called "spoils" system, where faithful political supporters of the executive branch were appointed to positions in the post office and other government corporations as a reward for their patronage. These appointees rarely had prior experience in the postal service and delivering mail. The system of political patronage was replaced in 1883 after passage of the Pendleton Civil Service Reform Act (Wikipedia, 1970). According to the on-line Wikipedia, it was ten years before waterways were declared postal roads in 1823. The postal service used steamboats to carry mail between post towns where no roads existed. Once it became clear that the postal system in the United States needed to expand across the continent, the use of the railroads to transport mail was instituted in 1832 on one railroad in Pennsylvania. All railroads were then designated as post pouches. After passage of the Act of July, 1838, mail service by railroads increased rapidly. An act of Congress provided for the issuance of stamps on March 3, 1947, and the postmaster general immediately let a contract to the New York City engraving firm of Rawdon, Wright, Hatch, and Edson to produce postage stamps. The first stamp issue of the United Stamps was offered for sale on July 1, 1847 in New York City, with Boston receiving stamps the following day and other cities thereafter. The 5-cent stamp paid for a letter weighing less than 1 ounce (28 grams) and traveling less than 300 miles; the 10-cent stamp was used for deliveries to locations greater than 300 miles or tice the weight of the 5-cent stamp (Wikipedia, 1970).

Twentieth Century Postal Service

The advent of Rural Free Delivery (RFD) in the United States in 1896 and the inauguration of domestic parcel postal service by

Postmaster General Frank Hitchcock in 1913 greatly increased the volume of mail shipped nationwide, and motivated development of more efficient postal transportation systems. Many rural customers took advantage of the inexpensive parcel post rates to order goods and products from businesses located hundreds of miles away in distant cities for delivery by mail. From 1910 through the 1960s, many college students and others used parcel post to send home dirty laundry as domestic mail was less expensive than washing the clothes themselves. After 4-year old Charlotte May Pierstorff was mailed by her parents to her grandparents in Idaho in 1914, mailing of people by mail was prohibited. In 1917, the pot office imposed a maximum daily mailable limit of two hundred pounds per customer per day after a business entrepreneur, W. H. Colthorp, used the inexpensive parcel post system to ship more than 80,000 masonry bricks some 407 miles via horse-driven wagon and train for the construction of a bank building in Vernal, Utah (Wikipedia, 1970).

TEXAS POST OFFICE, BUILT BETWEEN 1911-1913

The advent of parcel post also led to the growth of mail order businesses that substantially increased rural access to modern goods over what was typically stocked in local general store. In 1912, a carrier service was announced for establishments in towns of second and third class with $100,000 appropriated by Congress. From January 1, 1911 until July 1, 1967, the United States Post Office Department operated the United States postal savings system. An act of Congress of June 25, 1910 established he postal savings system in designated post offices effective January 1, 1911. The legislation aimed to get money out of hiding, attract the savings of immigrants accustomed to the postal savings systems in their native countries, provide safe depositories for people who had lost confidence in banks, and furnish more convenient depositors for working people. The law establishing the system directed the Post Office Department to re-deposit most of the money in the system in local banks, where it carried a 2.5% interest. In `1912, Operation Santa Claus was started at the James Farley Post Office (Wikipedia, 1970).

On March 18, 1970, postal workers in New York City, upset over low wages and poor working conditions were emboldened by the Civil Rights movement and organized a strike. The strike initially involved workers in New York City only, but it eventually gained support of over 210,000 United States Postal Office workers across the nation. While the strike ended without any concessions from the federal government, it did ultimately allow the postal worker unions and the government to negotiate a contract that gave the unions most of what they wanted, as well as the signing of the Postal Reorganization Act by President Nixon in 1970. The act replaced the cabinet level post office department with the independent United States Postal Service and took effect on July 1, 1971 (Wikipedia, 1970).

Current Operations

The United States Postal Service employs some 574,000 people, making it the third largest employer in the United States behind the federal government and Wal-Mart. In a 2006 U.S. Supreme Court decisions, the court noted that each day, according to the government's submission here, the United States Postal Service delivers some 160 million pieces of mail to as many as 142 million delivery points. As of 2011, the USPS operates 31,000 offices and locations in the United States and delivers 177 billion pieces of mail annually. The USPS operates the largest civilian vehicle service in the world with an estimated 218,684 vehicles, the majority of which are easily identifiable Chevrolet/Grumman LLV (Long Life Vehicles_, originally also called the CRV (Carrier Route Vehicle).

1908 Postal Service Delivery Truck

For every penny increase in the national average price of gasoline, the USPS spends an extra $8 million per year to fuel its fleet of vehicles. The number of gallons of fuel used in 2009 was 444 million at a cost of US$1.1 billion. The fleet is notable in that many of its vehicles are right-hand drive, an arrangement intended to give drivers the easiest access to roadside mailboxes as some rural letter carriers use personal vehicles. Standard postal service vehicles do not have license plates.

A Fleet of Post Office Vehicles at the James Griffith
Station, Spring Branch, Houston, Texas

These vehicles are identified by a seven-digit number displayed on the front and rear (Wikipedia, 1970).

Also, the Wikipedia (1970) article states that the Department of Defense and the USPS jointly operate a postal system to deliver mail for the military. This is known as the Army Post Office (for Army and Air Force postal facilities) and the Fleet Post Office (for the Navy, Marine Corps, and Coast Guard postal facilities). In February 2013, the postal service announced that on Saturdays it would deliver only packages, mail-order medicines, priority mail, and express mail effective August 10, 2013. However, this change was reversed by federal law in the Consolidated and Father Continuing Appropriations Act of 2013.

Five –Year Plans

In October 2008, the postal service released Vision 2013, a five-year pan required by law starting in 1993. One planned improvement is the introduction of the intelligent mail bar code, which would allow pieces of mail to be tracked through the delivery system as competitors like UPS and FedEx currently do.

Initiatives

In 2011, various media outlets reported that the USPS was going out of business. The USPS strategy came under fire as new technologies emerged, and the USPS was not finding ways to generate new sources of revenue. On March 15, 2012, MIT held a communications forum called "The Future of the Post Office" with David O. Williams, the Inspector General of the USPS. The forum was organized and moderated by MIT Professor, V. A. Shiva Ayyadurai, who had been openly critical of the USPS. In April 2012, at the Postal Visions 2020 Conference for USPS officials on new directions for the USPS, Ayyadurai presented a paper on why the USPS should embrace e-mail. Ayyadurai's Research Center for Integrative Systems (ICIS) was hired by the USPS-OIG to do a detailed analysis on how e-mail and other initiatives could furnish new revenues for the USPS. The analysis, which is the subject of ongoing research, projected that the USPS could potentially generate servicing over $250 million per year through e-mail servicing (Wikipedia, 1970).

Budget

Revenue Decline and Planned Cuts. In 2012, the USPS had its third straight year of operational losses, which amounted to $4.8 billion.

Declining Mail Volume. First class mail volume peaked in 2001 and has declined 29% from 1998, due to the increasing use of e-mail and the worldwide web for correspondence and business transactions. FedEx and the United Parcel Service (UPS) directly compete with services, making nationwide deliveries of urgent letters and packages. Lower volume means lower revenues to support the fixed commitment to deliver to every address once a day, six days a week. According to an official report on November 15, 2012, the US Postal System lost $15.9 billion in its 2012 fiscal year (Wikipedia, 1970).

Internal Streamlining and Delivery Slowdowns. In response, the USPS has increased productivity each year from 2000 to 2007 through increased automation, route reorganization, and facility consolidations.? Despite these efforts, the organization saw an $8.5 billion budget shortfall in 2010 and was losing at a rate of about $3 billion per quarter in 2011. On December 5, 2011, the USPS announced it would close more than half of its mail processing centers, eliminate 28,000 jobs, and reduce overnight delivery of first-class mail. This would close down 252 of its 961 processing centers. (At peak mail volume in 2006, the USPS operated 673 facilities.) As of May 2012, the plan was to begin the first round of consolidations in the summer of 2012, pause from September to December, and began a second round of consolidations in February 2014. Eighty percent of first class mail would still be delivered over night through the end of 2015 (Wikipedia, 1970).

Post Office Closures

In July 2011, the USPS announced a plan to close about 3700 small post offices, Various representatives in Congress protested, and the Senate passed a bill that would have kept open all post offices further than 10 miles from the next post office. In May 2012, the service announced it had modified its plan. Instead, rural post offices would remain open with reduced retail hours (some as little as 2 hours per day) unless there was a community preference for a different option. In a survey of rural customers, 25% preferred the "village post office" replacement (where a nearby private retail store would provide basic mail services with expanded hours), 15% preferred a merger with another post office, and 11% preferred expanded rural delivery services. Approximately 40% of the postal revenue already comes from on-line purchases or private retail partners including Wal-Mart, Staples, Office Depot, Walgreens, Sam's Club, Costco, and grocery stores. The American postal workers union has argued that these counters should be manned by postal employees who earn far more and have "a generous package of health and retirement benefits" (Wikipedia, 1970).

Elimination of Saturday Delivery Averted

In an update, Wikipedia (1970) claims that on January 28, 2009, Postmaster General John E. Potter testified before the Senate that if the postal service could not readjust its payments toward the contractually funded carried employees retiree health benefits as mandated the Enhancement Act of 2006, the USPS would be forced to consider cutting delivery services to five days a week, particularly during June, July, and August. Bill HR22, addressing this issue, passed the House of Representatives and the Senate and was signed into law on September 30, 2009. However, Postmaster

General Potter continued to advance plans to eliminate Saturday mail delivery. On June 10, 2009, the National Rural Letter Carriers Association (NRLCA) was contracted for its input on the USPS's current study of the impact of five-day delivery service along with developing an implementation plan for a five-day service plan. A team of postal service headquarters executives and staff had been given a timeframe of 60 days to complete the study. The current concept examined the impact of a five day delivery service with no business or collections on Saturday with post offices with current Saturday hours being open (Wikipedia, 1970).

Further information from Wikipedia (1970) includes the information that on Thursday, April 15, 2010, the House Committee on Oversight and Government Reform held a hearing to examine the status of the postal service and the recent reports on short and long-term strategies for the financial viability and stability of the USPS. The title of this hearing was "Continuing to Deliver: An Examination of the Postal Service's Current Financial Crisis and Its Future Viability." At the hearing, Postmaster General Potter testified that by the year 2020, the USPS cumulative losses could exceed $238 billion and that mail volume could drop another 15% from 2009. In February, 2013, the USPS announced that in order to save about $2 billion per year, Saturday delivery service would be discontinued except for packages, mail order medicines, priority mail, express mail, and mail delivered to post office boxes, beginning August 10, 2013. However, the Consolidated and Further Continuing Appropriations Act of 2013, passed in March, reversed the cuts to Saturday delivery (Wikipedia, 1970).

Retirement Funding and Payment Defaults

The Federal Accountability and Enhancement Act of 2006 (PAEA) obligates the USPS to fund the present value of earned retirement obligations (essentially past promises that have not yet come due) within a ten-year time span (to contrast, private businesses in the United States have no legal obligation to pay for retirement costs at promise-time rather than retirement time, but about one-quarter of them do. The Office of Personnel Management (OPM) is the main bureaucracy responsible for the human resources aspect of many federal agencies and their employees. The PAEA created the Postal Service Retiree Health Benefit Fund (PSRHB) after Congress removed the Postal Service contribution to the Civil Service System (CSRS). Most other employees that contribute the CSRS have 7% deducted from their wages. On September 30, 2013, the USPS failed to make a $5.6 billion payment on this debt, the third such defaulted payment (Wikipedia, 1970).

Rate Increases

Congress has limited rate increases for first class mail to the cost of inflation, unless approved by the Postal Regulatory Commission (Wikipedia, 1970).

Reform Packages, Delivery Changes and Alcohol Delivery

Comprehensive reform packages considered in the 113th Congress included S1486 and HR2718. These bills included the efficiency measure supported by Postmaster General Patrick Donahue of ending door-to-door delivery of mail for some or most of the 35 million addresses that currently receive it, replacing that with either curbside boxes or nearby cluster postboxes. This would save $4.5 billion per year out of the $30 billion delivery budget. Door-to-door delivery costs annually, on an average, $3.53 per stop, curbside $2.24, and cluster boxes $1.60 (and for rural delivery, the costs were $2.78, $1.76, and $1.26 respectively). S1486, also with the support of Postmaster Donahue, would also allow the USPS to ship alcohol in compliance with state law from manufacturers to recipients with an I.D. to show they are over 21. This is projected to raise approximately $50 million per year (shipping alcoholic beverages is currently illegal under 18 USC §1716. In 2014, the postal service was requesting reforms to workers' compensation, moving from a pension to a defined contribution retirement savings plan, and paying senior retiree healthcare costs out of Medicare funds, as is done for private sector workers (Wikipedia, 1970).

Government and Organization

The Board of Governors of the United States Postal Service sets policy, procedure, and postal rates for services rendered, and has a similar role to a corporate board of directors. Of the 11 members of the Board, nine are appointed by the President and confirmed by the United States Senate. The nine appointed members select the Postmaster General who serves as the board's tenth member and who oversees the day-to-day operations of the service as CEO. The ten member board then nominates a Deputy Postmaster General who acts as the Chief Operating Officer and becomes the 11th member of the Board, The independent Postal Rate Commission is also controlled by appointment by the President, confirmed by the Senate, and it oversees the postal rates and related concerns, having the authority to approve or reject USPS proposals (Wikipedia, 1970).

The USPS is often mistaken for a government-owned corporation (such as Amtrak) because it opiates much like a business, but as noted above, it is legally defined as an "independent establishment of the executive branch of the Government of the United States," as it is controlled by presidential appointees and he Postmaster General, It is a quasi-governmental agency. It has many special privileges, including sovereign immunity, eminent domain powers, powers to negotiate postal treaties with foreign nations, and an exclusive legal right to deliver fist-class and third-class mail. Indeed, in 2004, the U.S. Supreme Court ruled in a unanimous decision that the USPS was not a government-owned corporation and therefore could not be sued under the Sherman Anti-Trust Act. The Supreme Court has also upheld the USPS' statutory monopoly on access to letterboxes against a First Amendment freedom of speech challenge. It thus remains illegal in the United States for anyone, other than the postal employees and agents of the US Postal Service to deliver mail pieces to letterboxes marked US Mail. The postal service also has a Mailers' Technical Advisory Committee and local postal customer councils that are advisory and primarily involved business customers (Wikipedia, 1970).

Universal Service Obligation and Monopoly Status

Article 1, Section 8, Clause 7 of the United States Constitution grants Congress the power to establish post offices and post roads, which has been interpreted as a de facto congressional monopoly over the delivery of first-class residential mail and is defined as non-urgent, residential letters (not packages). Accordingly, no other system for delivering first-class residential mail, public or private, has been tolerated absent Congress' consent. The mission of the postal service is to provide the American people with a trusted, universal postal service at affordable prices. While not explicitly defined, the postal service's universal service obligation (USO) is broadly outlined in statute and includes multiple dimensions, geographic scope, range of products, access to services and facilities, delivery frequency, affordable and uniform pricing, service quality, and security of the mail. While other carriers may claim to voluntarily provide delivery on a broad basis, the postal service is the only carrier with a legal obligation to provide all the various aspects of universal service at affordable rates (Wikipedia, 1970).

Competitors

FedEx (Federal Express) and United Parcel Service (UPS) directly compete with UPS express mail and package delivery services, making nationwide deliveries of urgent letters and packages. Due to the postal monopoly, they are not allowed to deliver non-urgent letters and may not directly ship to US mailboxes at residential or commercial destinations. However, both companies have transit agreements with the Postal Service in which an item can be dropped off with either FedEx or UPS, who will then provide shipment to the destination post office serving the intended recipient where it will be transferred for delivery to the US mail destination, including post office box destinations. These services also deliver packages that are larger and heavier than USPS will accept. DHL Express was the third major competitor until February 2009, when it ceased domestic delivery operations in the United States. A variety of other transportation companies in the United States move cargo around the country, but either have limited geographic scope for delivery points, or specialize in items too large to be mailed. Many of the thousands of courier companies focus on same-day delivery, for example, by bicycle messenger (Wikipedia, 1970).

Alternative Transmission Methods

The Post Office Department owned and operated the first public telegraph lines in the United States. Beginning in 1844 from Washington to Baltimore and eventually to New York, Boston, Buffalo, and Philadelphia. In 1847, the telegraph system was privatized, except for a period during World War I, when it was used to accelerate delivery of letters arriving at night. Between 1942 and 194t, V-mail (for Victory Mail) Service was available for military mail. Letters were converted into microfilm and reprinted near the destination to save common transport vehicles for military cargo. From 1982-1985 electronic computer originated mail, known as E-com, was accepted for bulk mailing. The text was transmitted electronically to one of 25 post offices nationwide. The postal service printed the mail and put it into special envelopes bearing a blue E-Com logo; delivery was assured within two days (Wikipedia, 1970).

Law Enforcement Agencies – Postal Inspection Service

The United States Postal Inspection Service (USPIS) is one of the oldest law enforcement agencies in the United States. Founded by Benjamin Franklin, its mission is to protect the postal service, its employees, and its customers from crime and protect the nation's mail service system from criminal abuse. Postal inspectors enforce over 200 federal laws providing for the protection of mail in investigations of crimes that may adversely affect or fraudulently use the U.S. Mail, the postal system, or postal employees (Wikipedia, 1970).

The Wikipedia (1970) article also states that the USPIS has the power to enforce the monopoly of the USPS by conducting search and seizure raids on entities they suspect of sending non-urgent mail through overnight delivery competitors. According to the American Enterprise Institute, a private conservative think tank, the USPIS raided Equifax offices in 1993 to ascertain the mail they were sending through Federal Express was truly "extremely urgent." It was found that the mail was not, and Equifax was fined $30,000. Lastly, the USPIS oversees the activities of the postal police force who patrol in and around selected high-risk postal facilities in major metropolitan areas of the United States and its territories.

Office of Inspector General

The United States Postal Service's Office of Inspector General (OIG) was authorized by law in 1996. Prior to the 1996 legislation, the postal inspector service performed the duties of the OIG. The inspector general, who is independent of postal management, is appointed by and reports directly to the nine presidential appointed, Senate-confirmed members of the Board of Governors of the United States Postal Service. The primary purpose of the OIG is to prevent, detect, and report fraud, waste, and program abuse, and promote efficiency in the operations of the postal service (Wikipedia, 1970).

How Delivery Services Work

Elements of Addressing and Preparing Domestic Mail. In their description of the Postal Service, Wikipedia (1970) states that all mailable articles (e.g., letters, flat envelopes, machinable parcels, irregular parcels, etc.) shipped within the United States must comply with an array of standards published in the USPS Domestic Mail Manual (DMM).

Before addressing the mail piece, one must first comply with the various mailability standards relating to attributes of the actual mail piece such as minimum/maximum dimensions and weight, acceptable mailing containers, proper mail piece sealing/closures, utilization of various markings, and restrictions relating to various hazardous (e.g., explosives, flammables, etc.) and restricted (e.g., cigarettes, smokeless tobacco, etc.) materials, as well as other rules articulated in §601 of the DMM.

Key elements when preparing the face of a mail piece are:

1. Proper placement of delivery address (party receiving mail);
2. Proper placement of return address (party sending mail);
3. Postage according to the rates set by the USPS.

Formatting of the address line is usually as follows:

> Line 1: Name of Recipient;
> Line 2: Street Address or PO Box;
> Line 4: City, State, and US Zip Code or APO/FPO codes;
> for example:
> Clifford Clavin
> 789 Beacon Street
> Boston, MA 02186-1234 (Wikipedia, 1970).

Paying Postage

The actual postage can be purchased via:

1. stamps at a post office, from a stamp vending machine, or "authorized postal canters" that can also handle packages or from a third-party (such as a grocery store or drugstore);
2. Pre-cancelled stamps for bulk mailing;
3. Postal meters;

USPS Dodge Caro Van Used for Residential Delivery in Omaha, NB

4. Pre-paid envelopes with correct postage; and
5. Shipping labels purchased on-line and printed by the customer on standard paper (e.g., with "click-n-ship" or via a third party such as PayPal or Amazon Shipping).

Bulk Mail

Discounts are available for large volumes of mail; depending on the postage level, certain conditions might be required or optional for an additional discount:

1. Minimum number of pieces;
2. Weight limits;
3. Ability for the USPS to process by machine;
4. Address formatting standardized;
5. USPS readable bar code;
6. Sorted by three digit Zip Code prefix, five-digit Zip Code, Zip+4 or 11-digit delivery point;
7. Delivered in trays, bundles, or pallets partitioned by destination;
8. Delivered directly to regional bulk mail centers, destination SCF, or destination post office; and
9. Certification of mailing list accuracy and freshness (e.g., correct Zip Codes, purging of stale addresses, processing of change of address notification) (Wikipedia, 1970).

In addition to bulk discounts, discounts on express, priority, and first-class mail, other postage levels that are available for bulk mailing include:

1. Periodicals;
2. Standard Mail (A):
   a. Automation; and
   b. Enhanced carrier route;;
3. Standard Mail (B):
   a. Parcel Post;

b. Bound printed matter (cheaper than media mail, for advertising, catalogues, phonebooks, etc.) up to 15 lbs.;

c. Special Standard Mail; and

d. Nonprofit organization mail.

Extra Services

Depending on the type of mail, additional services are available for an additional fee; these include:

1. Certificate of mailing providing proof of date package was mailed;

2. Certified mail providing proof of mailing, and a delivery record used for serving legal documents and for sending US. Government classified information up to the *Confidential* level;

3. Collect on Delivery (COD) allows merchants to offer customers an option to pay upon delivery of items up to $1,000 valuation, including insurance;

4. USPS Tracking/Delivery Confirmation provides proof of delivery to sorting facilities, local post offices, and destination, but no signature is required;

5. Insurance is shipping insurance against loss or damage for the value of the goods mailed; amount of coverage can be specified up, to $5,000;,

6. Registered mail is used for highly valuable or irreplaceable items and classified information up to the "Secret" level. Registered mail is transported separately from other mail in locked containers. Tracking is included and insurance up to $25,000 is available.

7. Restricted Delivery requires delivery to a specific person or their authorized representative, not just to a mailbox;

8. Return Receipt Requested actively sends signature confirmation back to the sender by postcard or e-mailed PDF (as opposed

to merely putting this information into the on-line tracking system);

9. Signature Confirmation requires a delivery signature, which is kept on file. The on-line tracking system displays the first initial and last name of the signatory.
10. Special Handling is for unusual items like live animals.

International Services

In May 2007, the USPS restructured international services to correspond with domestic shipping options. Formerly, USPS international services were categorized as Airmail (letter post), Economy (surface), Parcel Post, Airmail Parcel Post, Global Priority Mail, Global Express, and Global Express Guaranteed Mail.

The former Airmail (letter post) is now first-class mail international, and it includes small packages weighing up to four pounds (18 kg.). Economy Parcel Post was discontinued for International Service, while Airmail Parcel Post was replaced by Priority Mail International. Priority Mail International flat-rate packaging in various sizes was introduced with the same conditions of service previously used for Global Priority Mail. Global Express is now Express Mail International, while Global Express Guaranteed is unchanged. The international mailing classes with a tracking ability are Express, Express Guaranteed, and Priority (except that tracking is not available for Priority Mail International, Flat Rate Envelopes, or Priority Mail International small flat-rate boxes).

One of the major changes in the new naming and serviced definitions is that USPS supplied mailing boxes for priority and express mail are now allowed for international use. These services are offered to ship letters and packages to almost every country and territory on the globe. The USPS provides much of this service by contracting with a private parcel service—Federal Express (Wikipedia, 1970).

Further in the article, Wikipedia (1970) states that on May 14, 2007, the USPS cancelled all outgoing international mail (sometimes known as "sea mail") from the United States, citing increased costs and reduced demand due to competition from airmail services such as FedEx and UPS. The decision has been criticized by the Peace Corps and military personnel overseas as well as independent booksellers and other small businesses who rely on international deliveries. The USPS provides an M-bag service for international shipment of printed matter previously known as surface M-bag, but with the elimination in 2007 of surface mail, only airmail M-bags remain. The term M-bag is not expanded upon in USPS publications. M-bags are simply defined as "direct sacks of printed matter sent to a single foreign addressee at a single address." However, the term is sometimes referred to informally as "media bag" as the bag can only contain "discs, tapes, and cassettes," in addition to books for which the usual umbrella term is "media." Some also refer to them as "mail bags."

Wikipedia (1970) also stated that military mail is billed at domestic rates when sent from the United States to a military outpost and is free when sent by deployed military personnel. The overseas logistics are handled by the Military Postal Service Agency in the Department of Defense. Outside of forward areas and active operations, military mail first-class takes 7-10 days, priority takes 10-15 days, and parcel post takes about 24 days. Three independent countries with a compact of free location with the United States (Palau, Marshall Islands, and the Federated States of Micronesia) have a special relationship with the United States Postal Service.

1. Each associated state maintains its own government mail service for delivery to and pick up from retail customers.
2. The associated states are integrated into the USPS addressing zip code system.
3. The USPS is responsible for transporting mail between the United States and the associated states, and between the individual states of the Federated States of Micronesia.

4. The associated states synchronize postal services and rates with the USPS.
5. The USPS treats mail to and from the associated states as domestic mail (as of November 19, 2007, after 23-month period of being treated as international mail).
6. Incoming mail does require customs declaration because like some US territories, the associated states are outside the main customs territory of the United State.

Sorting and Delivery Process

Processing of standard-sized envelopes and cards is highly automated, including reading of handwritten addressed mail from individual customers and public post boxes, which is collected by mail carriers inn plastic tubs that are taken to one of approximately 251 mail processing and distribution centers (P&DC) across the United States. Each P&DC sorts mail for a given region (typically within a radius of around 200 miles (320 kilometers) and connects with the national network for international mail. At the P&DC, mail is placed in hampers that are then automatically dumped into a Dual Pass Rough Cull System (DPRCS). As mail travels through the DPRCS, large items such as packages and mail bundles are removed from the stream of mail. As the remaining mail enters the first machine, the Advanced Facer Canceler Systems (AFCS), pieces that passed through the DPRCS but do not conform to physical dimensions for processing in the AFCS (e.g., large envelopes or overstuffed standard envelopes) are automatically diverted from the stream of mail. Mail removed from the DPRCS and AFCS is manually processed and/or sent to parcel sorting machines (Wikipedia, 1970).

Types of Postal Facilities

Although its customer service centers are all called post offices in regular speech, the USPS recognizes several types of postal facilities including the followg:

1. A main post office (formerly known as a general post office) is the primary postal facility in a community.
2. A station or post office station is a postal facility that is not a main post office but is within the corporate limits of the community.

Historic Main Post Office, Tomah, Wisconsin

3. A branch post office is a postal facility that is not the main post office and may be outside the corporate limits of the community.
4. A classified unit, station, or branch operated by USPS employees in a facility owned or leased to the USPS.
5. A contract postal unit (or CPU) is a station or branch operated by a contractor typically in a store or other place of business.
6. A community post office (or CPO) is a contract postal unit providing services in a small community in which other types of post office facilities have been discontinued.
7. A finance unit, station, or branch that provides window services and accepts mail, but does not provide delivery.
8. A village post office (VPO) is a post office concept that began in 2011 and became an integral part of the USPS to close low-volume post offices. Many of these VPOs have replaced many village post offices that filled the role of the post office within a zip code and are located in a local business or government center and is operated by those entities as specified in the contract negotiated between the entity and the USPS.
9.

A Typical Post Office Station in the Spring Branch area, Houston, Texas

10. A processing and distribution center (P&DC or processing and distribution facility, formerly known as a General Mail Facility) is a central mail facility that processes and dispatches incoming and outgoing mail to and from a designated service area (251 centers nationwide).

11. A Sectional Center Facility (SCF) is a P&DC for a designated geographical area defined by one or more three-digit zip code prefixes.

12. An International Service Center (ISC) an international mail processing facility. There are only five such USPS facilities in the United States, located in Chicago, New York, Miami, Los Angeles, and San Francisco.

13. A Network Distribution Center, formerly known as a bulk mail center (BMC) is a central mail facility that processes bulk rate parcels as the hub in a hub and spokes network.

A Combined Post Office, Customs House, and
Federal Court House in Galveston, Texas

14. An Auxiliary Sorting Facility (ASF) is a central mail facility that processes bulk rate parcels as the spokes in a hub and spokes network.

15. A Remote Encoding Center (REC) is a facility at which clerks receive images of problem mail pieces (those with hard-to-read addresses, etc.) via secure Internet-type feeds and manually type the addresses that can decipher using a special encoding protocol. The mail pieces are then sprayed with the correct addresses or are sorted for further handling according to the instructions given via encoding. The total number of RECs is down from 55 in 1998 to just 5 centers in April 2009. In 2010, there were just two remaining RECS open—in Salt Lake City, Utah and Wichita, Kansas. More closured occurred as computer software became more able to read most addresses, but a few centers are still open (Wikipedia, 1970).

A 24-Hour Automated Postal Center Kiosk Inside
the Webster, Texas Post Office.

Evolutionary Network Development

Wikipedia (1970) also commented that while common usage refers to all types of postal facilities "as substations," the USPS Glossary of Postal Terms does not define or even list that word, Post Offices often share facilities with other government agencies located within a city's central business district. In those locations, often the courthouse and federal buildings, the building is owned by the General Services Administration, while the US Postal Service operates as a tenant. The USPS retail system has approximately 36,000 post offices, stations, and branches. Temporary stations are also set up for applying pictorial cancellations.

Automated Post Centers

Further, Wikipedia states that in 2004 the USPS began deploying Automated Postal Centers (APC), which are unattended kiosks that are capable of weighing, franking, and storing packages for later pick up as well as selling domestic and international postal stamps. Since its introduction, APCS do not take cash payments; they only accept credit card or debit payments. Similarly, traditional vending machines are available at many post offices at which customers may purchase stamps, though these are being phased out in many areas due to increasing use of Internet services. As of 2009, no retail post office windows are open 24 hours. Overnight services are limited to those provided by an automated postal center. In February 2006, the USPS announced they planned to replace the nine existing facility-types with five processing facility types:

1. Regional Distribution Center (RDCs), which would process all classes of parcels and bundles and serve as surface transfer centers.
2. Local Processing Centers (LPCs) which would process all single piece letters and flat mail pieces and cancel mail.
3. Destination Processing Centers (OPCs) which would sort the mail for individual mail carriers.

4. Airport Transport Centers (ATCs) which would serve as transfer points only.
5. Remote Encoding Centers.

Over a period of years, these facilities are expected to replace P&DCs, customer service facilities, bulk mail centers, logistics and distribution centers, annexes, the hub and spoke program, air mail centers, and international service centers. The changes are a result of the declining volume of single-piece, first-class mail, population shifts, the increase in drop shipments by advertising mailers at destination postal facilities, advancements in shipments, and technology redundancies in the existing network, and the need for operational flexibility (Wikipedia, 1970).

Airline and Rail Davison

The United States Postal Service does not directly own or operate any aircraft or trains. The mail and packages are flown on airlines with which the postal service has a contractual agreement. The contracts change periodically depending on the contract; aircraft may be printed with the USPS pain scheme. Contract airlines have included UPS, Emery Worldwide, Ryan International Airlines, FedEx Express, American Airlines, United Airlines, and Express One International. The postal service also contracts with Amtrak to carry some mail between certain cities such as Chicago and Minneapolis-Saint Paul. The last air delivery route in the continental United States is to resident in the Frank Churchill River of No Return Wilderness Area was scheduled to end in June 2009. The weekly bush plane route, which was contracted out to an air taxi company, had in its final year an annual cost of $46,000 or $2,400/year per residence, over ten times the average cost of delivering mail to a residence in the United States. This decision has now been reversed by the United States Postmaster General (Wikipedia, 1970.

Wikipedia (1970) stated further that private U.S. parcel forwarding or U.S. mail forwarding companies focusing on personal shopper, relocation, ex-post and mail box services often interface with the United States Postal Service for the transfer of mail and package for their customers.

USPS Contractor-Driven Semi-Trailer Truck near Mendota, California

Delivery Timing – Delivery Days

In 1810, mail had been delivered seven days a week, but in 1828, religious leaders noticed a decline in Sunday morning church attendance because of local post offices doubling as gathering places. These leaders appealed to the government to intervene and close post offices on Sundays. The government, however, declined and mail was delivered seven days a week until 1912.

Wikipedia (1970) notes that today (2015), the mail (with the exception of Express Mail) is not delivered on Sundays, except in a few towns where the local religious leaders have had an effect on the policy, such as in Loma Linda, California, which has a significant Seventh Day Adventist population and where U.S. mail is delivered Sunday through Friday, except on observed federal holidays. Saturday delivery was temporarily suspended in April 1957 because of the lack of

USPS Ford WindStar used for residential deliveries in Olympia, Washington

funds, but quickly restored. Budget problems had prompted consideration of dropping Saturday delivery beginning around 2009. This culminated in 2013 announcement that regular mail services would be cut to five days a week, which was later reversed by Congress before it could take effect.\

Direct Delivery vs. Customer Pick UP

When the Post Office began operations, mail was not delivered to homes and businesses but to post offices. In 1963, city delivery began in urban areas with enough customers to make this economical. This required streets to be named, houses to be numbered, withy sidewalks and lighting provided, and these street addresses were to be added to envelopes. The number of routes served expanded over time. In 1891, the first experiments with Rural Free Delivery began in less densely populated areas. There is currently an effort to reduce direct delivery in favor of mailbox clusters to compensate for high mail volume and slow long-distance transportation, which saw mail arrive at post offices throughout the day. Deliveries were made multiple times a day. This ranged from twice daily for residential areas up to seven times a day for central business districts, such as in Brooklyn, New York. In the late nineteenth century, mailboxes were encouraged, saving carriers the time it took to deliver directly to the addressee in person. In the 1910s and 1920s, they were phased in as requirement for service. In the 1940s, multiple daily deliveries began to be reduced, especially on Saturdays. By 1990, the last twice daily deliveries in New York City were eliminated (Wikipedia, 1970).\

Today, in 2015, mail is delivered once a day on site to most private homes and businesses. The USPS still distinguishes between city deliver (where carriers frequently walk and deliver to mailboxes hung on the exterior of a residence or to commercial reception areas) and rural delivery (where carriers generally have to drive). With "curbside delivery," mailboxes are at the end of driveways on the nearest convenient road. "Central Point Delivery" is used in some operations where several nearby residences share a "cluster" of individual mailboxes in a single housing. Some customers choose to use post office boxes for an additional fee, for privacy or convenience. This provides a locked box at the post office to which mail is addressed and delivered (usually earlier in the day than home delivery). Customers in less densely populated areas where there is no city delivery and who do not qualify for rural delivery may receive mail only through the post office boxes. High volume business customers can also arrange for special pick-ups.

Another option is the old-style general delivery for people who have neither post office boxes nor street addresses, and mail is held at the post office until they present themselves with proper identification and pick up the mail. Some customers receive free post office boxes if the USPS declines to provide door-to-door deliver to their location or a nearby box. People with medical problems can request door-to-door delivery. Homeless people are also eligible for post office boxes at the discretion of the local postmaster or can use general delivery (Wikipedia, 1970).

Special Delivery

Wikipedia (1970) indicates that from 1895 through 1997, a service called Special Delivery was available, and this caused a separate delivery to the final location earlier in the day than the usual daily rounds.

Same-Day Trials

In December 2012, the USPS began a limited one-year trial of same-day delivery directly from retailers or distribution hubs to residential addresses in the same local area, a service it dubbed "Metro Post." The trial was initially limited to San Francisco, and the only retailer to participants in the first few weeks was 1-800-Flowers. In March 2013, the USPS faced new same-day competition for e-commerce deliveries from Google Shopping Express. In November 2013, the postal service began regular package delivery on Sundays for Amazon customers in New York and Los Angeles, which it expanded to 15 cities in May 2014. Other competition in this area includes online grocers such as Amazon Fresh Webvan, and delivery services operated by gr0oceries stores like Peapod and Safeway (Wikipedia, 1970).

Forwarding and Holds

Residential customers can fill out a form to forward mail to a new address and can also send pre-printed forms to any of their frequent correspondents. They can also put their mail "on hold;" for example, while on vacation, the customers can have the Post Office store the mail during the hold instead of letting it overflow in their mailboxes. These services are not available to large buildings and customers of a commercial mail receiving agency where mail is sub sorted by non-postal employees into individual mailboxes (Wikipedia, 1970).

Wilson Essien

Financial Services

Postal money orders provide a safe alternative to sending cash through the mail and are available in any amount up to $1,000. Like a bank check, money orders are cashable only the recipient. Unlike a personal check, they are prepaid and therefore cannot be returned because of insufficient funds in an account. Money orders are a declining business for the USPS as companies like Pay Pal, Paid By Cash, and others are offering electronic replacements. From 1911 to 1967, the postal service operated the United States Postal Savings System, not unlike a saving and loan association with the amount of the deposit unlimited. A January 2014 report by the Inspector General of the USPS suggested that the agency could earn $3.99 billion per year in revenue by providing financial services, especially in areas where there are no local banks, but there is a local post office, and to customers who currently do not have bank accounts (Wikipedia, 1970).

Employment in the United States Postal Service

The postal service is the nation's second-largest civilian employer. As of 2011, it employed 574,000 people, who work in areas divided into offices, processing centers, and actual post offices. The United States Postal Service would rank 29th on the 2010 Fortune 500 Companies List if it were considered a private company. Labor unions representing the USPD employees include The American Postal Workers Union (APWU), which represents postal clerks and maintenance workers, motor vehicle mail equipment shops, material distribution centers, and operating services, and facilities services employees, postal nurses, and IT and accounting. The National Association of Letter Carriers (NALC) which represents rural letter carriers, and the National Postal Mail Handlers Union (HPMHU).

USPS employees are divided into three major crafts, according to the work they are engaged in (Wikipedia, 1970):

A. Mail Carriers, also referred to as mailmen or letter carriers, prepare and deliver mail and parcels. They are divided into two categories: city letter carriers who are represented by the NALC, and Rural Letter Carriers, who are represented by the NRLCA. City carriers are paid hourly wages with automatic overtime paid after 8 hours or 40 hours a week of work. City carriers are required to work in any kind of weather, daylight or darkness and carry three bundles of mail (letters in one hand, magazines in a mailbag) in addition to parcels up to a total of 70 pounds. Mail routes are outfitted with a number of scan points (mailbox bar codes) on random streets every 30 to 40 minutes apart to keep track of the carriers' whereabouts up until the last five minutes of any given work day.

B. Rural carriers are under a form of salary called "evaluated hours" usually with overtime built into their pay. The evaluated hours are created by having all mail counted for a period of two or four weeks, and a formula is used to create the set dollar amount the carrier will be paid for each day worked until the next time the route is counted.

C. Mail Handlers and Processors prepare, separate, load, and unload mail and parcels by delivery zip code and station for the clerks. They work almost exclusively at the plants or larger mail facilities now after having their duties assessed and reassigned to clerks in post offices and station branches.

D. Clerks have a dual function by design where their assignment is either as window clerks, directly handling customer service needs at the counter, sorting box mail, or sorting first-class letters, standard and bulk-rate mail for the carriers on the work floor. Clerks may also work alongside mail handlers in large sorting facilities, outside of the public view, sorting mail; Data conversion operators, who encode address information at Remote Encoding Centers, are also members of the clerk craft.

Mail handlers and clerks are represented by the NPMHU and the APWU respectively.

Other non-managerial positions in the United States Postal Service include:

A. Maintenance and Custodial workers who see to the overall operation and cleaning of mail-sorting machines, work areas, public parking, and general facility operations.
B. Transitional Employees (TEs) who are hired for the terms of 360 days (with the option of appointment to another 360 day term after a five-day break) are given the same hourly base pay as a part=time, flexible carrier, but receive no benefits other than annual leave. Transitional employees may be released by the USPS upon completion of their 360-day term, lack of work, or for "just cause" and can be represented by the NALC.
C. Carrier Part-Time, Flexible and Transitional employees (career, PIF &TE DCOs) at a remote encoding center are still under clerks category but under a different contract than a plant worker or mail carrier, and therefore, are also under a different union (AWU) than the above-mentioned carrier TEs and PTFs. There are several differences between working as a carrier or plant worker versus working at a REC. Even pay is different.

Although the USPS employees many individuals, as more American send information via e-mail, fewer postal workers are need to work the dwindling amount of mail, Post office and mail facilities are currently downsizing, replacing craft positions with the new machines and consolidating mail routes through the MIARAP (Modified Interim Alternate Route Adjustment Process) agreement. A major round of job cuts, early retirements, and a construction freeze were announced on March 20, 2009. (Wikipedia, 1970).

Workplace Violence

In the early 1970s, widely publicized workplace shootings occurring at the postal facilities by disgruntled employees led to a human resources effort to provide care for stressed workers and resources of co-worker conflicts. Due to media coverage, postal employees gained a reputation among the general public as more likely to be mentally ill. The USPS Commission on "A Safe and Secure Workplace" found that "postal workers are only a third as likely as those in the national work force to be victims of homicide at work." In the documentary, *Murder by Proxy: How Americans Went Postal*, the film argued that this number failed to factor out workers killed by external subjects rather than by fellow employees (Wikipedia, 1970).

Wikipedia (1970) stated further that these series of events, in turn, have influenced American culture, as seen in the slang terms "going postal" and the computer game, "Postal." In an episode of *Seinfeld* the character, Newman, who is a mailman, explained in a dramatic monologue that postal workers "go crazy and kill everyone" because the mail never stops, also, the final insult. The series of massacres led the postal service to issue a rule prohibiting the possession of any type of firearm (except for those issued to postal inspectors) in all designated USPS facilities.

Summary

I researched many companies for my development including the United States Postal Service. At first, I resisted writing about the postal service because I thought it was going to be involved with classified and unclassified documents, but I realized that even its founders wanted the United States Post Office to be run as a private company and even show a profit. However, my fascination comes from the fact that the USPS was depicted as a glue that binds the great USA together. Imagine the president of this great nation appointing the Board of Directors who were nine members, the nine members of whom appoints the tenth member who becomes the Postmaster General. I think that the United States Postal Service was not only depicted as a glue of this vast nation, but also united the early arrivals' letter writing and early magazines. Let us look at the analysis of the following topics:

1. Expansion of Mail From 1910-1960 and Beyond;
2. Budget;
3. Governance and Organization;
4. International Services;
5. Employment in the USPS; and
6. Law Enforcement Agencies.

Expansion of Mail From 1910-1960 and Beyond The advent of Rural Free Delivery (RFD) in the United States in 1896 and the inauguration of domestic parcel post service by Postmaster General Frank Hitchcock in 1 913, greatly increased the volume of mail shipped nationwide and motivated the development of more efficient postal transportation systems. Many rural customers took advantage of inexpensive parcel post rates to order goods and products from businesses located hundreds of miles away in distant cities for delivery by mail. From 1910 to the 1960s, many college students and others used the parcel post to mail home dirty laundry as doing so was less expensive than washing the clothes themselves. The postal service imposed a maximum daily mailable limit of 200 pounds per customer per day after a business entrepreneur, W. H. Colthorp, used the inexpensive parcel post rates to ship more than 80,000 masonry bricks some 406 miles via horse-drawn wagon and train for the construction of a bank building in Vernal, Utah (Wikipedia, 1970).

The RFD was a big incentive for those living in rural areas, coupled with the fact that it was very inexpensive to use the mailing system. So, the politicians made the mailing expansion very possible and appealing to the customers and the politicians also made the system difficult to abuse as could be seen with "Mr. H. W. Colthorp" when he used the inexpensive parcel post to ship the more than 80,000 bricks some 400 miles. The mail expansion made it possible for loved ones to locate each other and for students to do research for their papers more conveniently.

Budget. In 2012, the USPS had its third straight year of operational losses, which amounted to $4.8 billion (Wikipedia, 1970).

Declining Mail Volume. First-class mail volume peaked in 2001 and has declined 29% from 1998 to 2008, due to the increasing use of e-mail and the worldwide web for correspondence and business transactions. FedEx and UPS directly compete with the USPS express mail package delivery services, making nationwide deliveries of urgent letters and packages. Lower volume means lower revenues to support the fixed commitment to deliver to every address once a day five days a week. According to an official report on November 5, 2012, the USPS lost $15.9 billion in fiscal year 2012 (Wikipedia, 1970).

In response, the USPS has increased productivity each year since 2000 and 2007 through increased automation, route optimization, and facility consolidation. Despite these efforts, the organization saw an $8.5 billion budget shortfall in 2010 and was losing money at a r ate of about $3 billion per quarter in 2011. On December 5, 2011, the USPS announced it would close more than half of its mail processing centers, eliminate 28,000 jobs, and reduce overnight delivery of first class mail. This would close down 252 of its 461 processing centers. (At peak volume in 2000, the USPS operated 673 facilities.) As of May, 2012, the plan was to start the first round of consolidations in the summer of 2012, pause from September through December, and then begin a second round of closures in February 2014. Eighty percent of first-class mail would still be delivered overnight through the end of 2013 (Wikipedia, 1970).

It is not surprising to see such competition bringing the postal service down as it did and for a company which was founded on the ideology of monopoly, all of a sudden saw the competition taking control of the business and dictating the pace of competition doing the best they could and still losing $3 billion per quarter. Clearly indicated that the USSPS was out of the competition, but the USPS's hands were tied; the post service could not have been that bad without the Congress telling the postal service, "No, you cannot stop Saturday delivery." In fact, the USPS cannot carry out its initiative without first asking its big boss if it will be allowed to do so. Of course, there were always "sorry, you can't do that" whereas Federal Express and UPS will always do what they intended to do with less restrictions.

Wikipedia (1970) states that in July 2011, the USPS announced a plan to close about 3,700 small post offices. Various representatives in Congress protested, and the Senate passed a bill that would have kept open all post offices further than 10 miles from the next post office. In May 2012, the postal service announced it had modified its plan. Instead rural post offices would remain open with reduced retail hours (some as little as 2 house a day) unless there was community preference for a different option. In a survey of rural customers, 20% preferred the "village post office" replacement (where a nearby private retail store would provide basic mail services with expanded hours), 15% preferred a merger with another post office, and 11% preferred expanded rural delivery service. Approximately 90% of postal revenue comes from on-line purchases or private retail partners including Wal-Mart, Staples, Office Depot, Walgreens, Sam's Club, Costco, and grocery stores. The American Postal Workers' Union has argued that these counters should be manned by postal employees who earn far more and have a generous package of health and retirement benefits."

<u>Governance and Organization</u>. The Board of Governors of the USPS sets policy, procedure, and postal rates for services rendered and has a similar role to that of a corporate board of directors. Of the 11 members of the Board, nine are appointed by the President of the U.S. and confirmed by the United States Senate. The nine appointed members then select the US Postmaster General, who serves as the Board's tenth member and who oversees the day-to-day operations of the postal service as its CEO. The ten-member Board then nominates

a Deputy Postmaster General, who acts as chief operating officer and as the eleventh and last open seat on the Board. The independent Post Regulatory Commission (formerly the Postal Rate Commission) is also controlled by appointees of the President, confirmed by the Senate, and it oversees postal rates and related concerns having the authority to approve or reject USPS proposals (Wikipedia, 1970).

International Services. Wikipedia (1970) also explains that in May 2007 the USPS restructured its international service names to correspond with domestic shipping options. Formerly USPS international services were categorized as Airmail (letter post), Economy (Surface), Parcel Post, Airmail Parcel Post, Global Priority, Global Express, and Global Express Guaranteed Mail. Former Airmail (letter post) is now First Class Mail International and includes small packages weighing up to four pounds (1.8 kg.). Economy Parcel Post was discontinued for International Service, while Airmail Parcel Post was replaced by Priority Mail International. Priority Mail Internarial Flat Rate Packaging in various sizes was introduced with the same conditions of services as previously used for Global Priority Mail. Global Express is now Express Mail International, while Global Express Guaranteed is unchanged. The international mailing classes with a tracking ability are Express, Express Guaranteed, and Priority Mail (except that tracking Is not available for Priority Mail International, Flat Rate Envelopes, or Priority Mail International Small Flat Rate Boxes). One of the major changes in the new naming and definitions of services is that USPS supplied mailing boxes for priority and express mail are now allowed for international use. Those services are offered to ship letters and packages to almost every country and territory on the globe. The USPS provides much of this service by contracting with private parcel services such as Federal Express.

Employment in the USPS. Wikipedia (1970) stated that the postal service is the nation's second largest civilian employer. As of 2011, the postal service employed 574,000 people, working in office, processing centers, and actual post offices. The USPS would rank 29th on the

2010 *Fortune 500* list of companies if considered a private company. Labor unions representing USPS employees include the American Postal Workers Union (APWU), which represents postal clerks and maintenance workers, motor vehicle mail equipment shops, material distribution centers, and operating services, and facilities services employees, postal nurses, and its accounting personnel. The National Association of Letter Carriers (NALC) represents city letter carriers, and the National Rural Letter Carriers Association (NRLCA) represents rural letter carriers, and the National Postal Mail Handlers Union (HPMHU).

USPS employees are divided into three major crafts according to the work they perform:

A. Mail Carriers, also referred to as mailmen or letter carriers, prepare and deliver mail and parcels. They are divided into two categories: city letter carriers who are represented by the NALC, and Rural Letter Carriers, who are represented by the NRLCA. City carriers are paid hourly wages with automatic overtime paid after 8 hours or 40 hours a week of work. City carriers are required to work in any kind of weather, daylight or darkness and carry three bundles of mail (letters in one hand, magazines in a mailbag) in addition to parcels up to a total of 70 pounds. Mail routes are outfitted with a number of scan points (mailbox bar codes) on random streets every 30 to 40 minutes apart to keep track of the carriers' whereabouts up until the last five minutes of any given work day.

B. Rural carriers are under a form of salary called "evaluated hours" usually with overtime built into their pay. The evaluated hours are created by having all mail counted for a period of two or four weeks, and a formula is used to create the set dollar amount the carrier will be paid for each day worked until the next time the route is counted.

C. Mail Handlers and Processors prepare, separate, load, and unload mail and parcels by delivery zip code and station for the clerks. They work almost exclusively at the plants or larger mail facilities now after having their duties assessed and reassigned to clerks in post offices and station branches.

D. Clerks have a dual function by design where their assignment is either as window clerks, directly handling customer service needs at the counter, sorting box mail, or sorting first-class letters, standard and bulk-rate mail for the carriers on the work floor. Clerks may also work alongside mail handlers in large sorting facilities, outside of the public view, sorting mail; Data conversion operators, who encode address information at Remote Encoding Centers, are also members of the clerk craft. Mail handlers and clerks are represented by the NPMHU and the APWU respectively.

Law Enforcement Agencies. The United States Postal Inspection Service (USPIS) is one of the oldest law enforcement agencies in the United States. Founded by Benjamin Franklin, its mission is to protect the postal service, its employees, and its customers from crime and protect the nation's mail service system from criminal abuse. Postal inspectors enforce over 200 federal laws providing for the protection of mail in investigations of crimes that may adversely affect or fraudulently use the U.S. Mail, the postal system, or postal employees (Wikipedia, 1970).

The Wikipedia (1970) article also states that the USPIS has the power to enforce the monopoly of the USPS by conducting search and seizure raids on entities they suspect of sending non-urgent mail through overnight delivery competitors. According to the American Enterprise Institute, a private conservative think tank, the USPIS raided Equifax offices in 1993 to ascertain the mail they were sending through Federal Express was truly "extremely urgent." It was found that the mail was not, and Equifax was fined $30,000. Lastly, the USPIS oversees the activities of the postal police force who patrol in and around selected high-risk postal facilities in major metropolitan areas of the United States and its territories.

Questions

1. What do the following abbreviations stand for:
   - a. USPS
   - b. NALC
   - c. RFD
   - d. APWU
   - e. UPS
   - f. NRLCA
   - g. NPMHW
   - h. TE
   - i. PTF
   - j. USPIS

2. Who appoints the Board of Governors and who confirms them:
3. What are the duties of the Board of Governors and the Independent Postal Regulatory Commission?
4. What are the duties of the Postal Service Office of Inspector General?
5. How many people did the postal service employ as of 2011?

Answers

1a. United States Postal Service;

1b. National Association of Letter Carriers;

1c. Rural Free Delivery;

1d. American Postal Workers Union;

1e. United Parcel Service;

1f. National Rural Letter Carriers Association;

1g. National Postal Mail Handlers Union;

1h. Transitional Employees;

1i. Part Time Flexible;

1j. United States Postal Inspection Service

2. The President appoints 9 of them; the U.S. Senate confirms them.
3. The Board of Governors of the U.S. Postal Service sets policy, procedures, and postal rates for services rendered and has a similar role to a corporate board of directors.

The Independent postal Regulatory Commission (formerly the Postal Rate Commission) is also controlled by appointees of the President and confirmed by the Senate. It oversees postal rates and related concerns and has the authority to approve or reject USPS proposals.

1. The Inspector General, who is independent of postal management, is appointed by and reports directly to the nine presidentially appointed, senate-confirmed members of the Board of Governors of the United States Postal Service. The primary purpose of the OIG is to prevent, detect, and report fraud, waste, and program abuse and also to promote efficiency in the operations of the postal service. The OIG has oversight responsibility for all activities of the Postal Inspection Service.
2. The Postal Service is the nation's second largest civilian employer. As of 2011, it employed 574,000 personnel, working in offices, processing centers, and actual post offices. The USPS would rank 29th on the 2010 *Fortune 500* list if considered a private company. Labor unions representing USPS employees include American Postal Workers Union (APWU), which represents postal clerks, maintenance workers, motor vehicle personnel, mail equipment shop workers and operating services and facilities personnel, and postal nurses.

CHAPTER 15
BIASE LUMBER COMPANY

CHAPTER 15

BIASE LUMBER COMPANY

In the early 1960s when Ibiae, Dunlop, Erei-Ikun, Biakpan, and Akamkpa estates were being developed, many trees were cut down and very quickly a lumber company was born by the quick thinking Biase investors who could only afford one sawmill, and two plants. before 1968, this company has grown to three sawmills and five plants; they had a plant and sawmill in Biase, a plant in Calabar, and Ikom and Ejegam, a sawmill in Akamkpa, and Obudu. The company had Biase well covered with their products. They produced softwood lumbers, hardwood lumber, plywood, and veneer. The company has received widespread recognition as a maverick among forest products companies.

The biggest fan of the Biase Lumber Company was the former premier of what was then Eastern Nigeria, Dr. Mll. Okpara, who so heralded the efforts and creativities of the company. They employed quite a few people in both their sawmills and plants and made lumber products so big in Nigeria, mostly in Eastern Nigeria. Dr. Okpara made sure that the company did not spend so much on lumber especially with those from the government land. The irony in this case is that Biase Lumber Company had no known competitors, but there were many logging companies who meant to log and sell it overseas or sell to the Biase Lumber Company (BLC), but never had a sawmill and plant. Even though logging competitors were not well-known business people, they had a significant impact on lumber prices, BLC paid higher per log because they had few or no employees at all, while the company paid for insurance and many other benefits.

Forest products companies may compete in one or both of two basic industry segments; one of which is pulp paper products that is largely restricted to large companies because of the high capital investment required for the mills and plants The other segment. ;lumber products, has varying capital requirements depending on the technology employed, size of the facilities, land level of timberlands self-sufficiency, if any. The size of firms logging in the wood products segment varies from very large to very small (Thompson & Strickland, 1990).

Wood Products and Services

Firms engaging in the wood products business produce one or more of a number of products, including dimension lumber, beams, siding, hardwood for furniture, cabinets and other industrial uses, railroad ties, poles, plywood decorative paneling, and composite panels for construction and industrial uses. Products used in residential and commercial construction are essentially undifferentiated and compete as commodities. Industrial products and special dimension or proprietary products for the construction market are less vulnerable to direct competition and substitutes and can command a premium price. Special services to buyers, even among producers of commodity products, can allow a producer to command a higher price and/or a preferred supplier relationship. Services such as technical assistance on selecting the best type of product for a particular application, rapid order processing assured delivery, shipment of assorted products and split shipments are being offered increasingly especially by larger firms attempting to gain a competitive advantage (Thompson & Strickland, 1990).

We have heard about wood products and services that have occurred in developed countries, but I am primarily writing about Nigeria in the early 1960s, as nation during the able leaderships of Dr. M. L. Okpara who was premier of the former state of Eastern Nigeria when oil, palm, and rubber estates were a large part of the Eastern Nigeria economy. At the beginning of the logging of the forests, people were not sure what to do with the forests. Even individuals who could export timber to foreign markets were hesitant because they thought that the government might not allow them to continue. So, when a few Biase people checked with the government managers about paying something to log the trees that were already there, they were asked by the general manager to put their request in writing and state specifically what use they would make of the lumber. They stated quite clearly what use they would make of the lumber and stated that the uses would include plywood, composite panels for construction, and industrial use products for residential and commercial uses. Also, they stated that the prices would be lower than foreign lumber products. They disclosed that their company would be the Biase Lumber Company and already had money for one sawmill, and if allowed the trees, then money for another sawmill would be readily available and most importantly, the logging, transportation of products, and the operation of the sawmills and much more would afford employment opportunities for many Eastern Nigeria citizens.

When Dr. Okpara understood this, he never minced words; he thought his subjects were truly coming of age, and he accepted, through his general manager, and even gave them a year to harvest the timber free of any taxes or penalties. The general manager invited the executives of the proposed Biase Lumber Company to a meeting where he gave them the good news. Of course, the executives were happy and rushed down to their offices and confirmed the appointment of the president, vice-president, and chief of operations and general manager. Man of the would-be employees were told that the premier of the former Eastern Nigeria had accepted their request and would even like them to use the trees for a year and after about six months, the premier would visit the lumber sawmill and plant and assess the production to see what progress had been made and if any help were needed. A few of these would-be employees were so happy. The following day an announcement was made over the radio asking for drivers of different grades, sawyers, timber specialists, and other workers with varying skills to report for employment. Different people left their current employment and joined the company because they felt that opportunities might arise in the Biase Lumber Company, whether in transportation, sawmill operations, or general skills that even included office workers.

Television and radio began covering the news of the operation and probably worked harder than the Biase Lumber Company's employees because Dr. Okpara was always watching the evening news and was particularly interested in the Biase Lumbee Company, its headquarters plant and sawmill. One morning Dr. M. L. Okpara had his entourage arrived at Biase Lumber Company headquarters greeted the executives, quickly moved to the mill and plant, and wasted more time at the warehouse where he saw plywood, residential, and commercial products. Dr. H. L. Okpara was highly impressed; the prices virtually drove away the high priced foreign products coupled with all the good things about the wood. Many contractors announced in the contractors' union that the wood was especially made for local cement factories in Nigeria.

When Dr. Okpara arrived at his office in Enugu, he held a press conference and told the press that he was giving Biase Lumber Company another free forest for another year and that was not all about it, but that Biase Lumber had qualified for £2.5 million. Biase Lumber already had a surplus of £10 million. Eastern Nigeria was then leading the country with a very healthy economy, and that was where I understood that a healthy economy is a healthier academia. In other words, the good economy of a nation must be a by-product of the high academic standards of that nation.

Factors Affecting the Productivity of Biase Lumber Products

The Biase Lumber Company had no sooner had acquired the raw materials and a promise of future help by the government than the company began formulating policies that could affect efficiency and profitability. Included in these were high quality products, price, and prompt delivery.

The Biase Lumber Company knew that in order for a company to grow they had to compete in terms of quality with foreign-made products. First, the sawmill and the plant had to be up-to-date technologically and, of course, not to employ people simply because they were relatives or because individuals knew them, but because they are qualified to do the work. Biase Lumber knew that all former Eastern Nigerian eyes were on them; their successes or failures would echo through the media. Therefore, they had to work harder and smarter. High quality products entail creation of in-service training, where more skills can be developed. Having seen foreign-made plywood, Biase Lumber needed to brainstorm to come up with different ways of making plywood that was better quality than the competition.

MAP OF FORMER EASTERN NIGERIA

Having competed successfully in high quality products, the price competition became much easier because of combining low prices with high quality plywood would automatically create high demand for the company's products. The demand would be even higher in foreign markets. The demand for the products could be even higher abroad if the contractors found that Biase products were very good for building along with the products' durability the buildings and homes. Product quality is so important for Biase Lumber because the Eastern Nigeria had helped the company and wanted it to succeed. The employees and investors really put their time and creativity into what they thought would make the company grow and prosper. Price can be a major factor in affecting productivity, but the timber was freely given to the company by the government, even though the company was a private enterprise. The major government interest in the company, I think, was the fact that the company was well managed. This curtailed foreign dumping of lumber products in Nigeria, and most importantly, the company created employment opportunities, especially for the people of Eastern Nigeria. This was a big assistance to the government, especially at a time where private companies were not hiring and paid barely livable wages. Surprisingly, seeing a start-up company that pays almost higher than the government, and this created a lot of hope in the minds of many Eastern Nigerians and not only the government.

Even though the quality of Biase Lumber products was graded "A", those individuals who were familiar with foreign products thought that the low prices of the locally produced lumber products were due to poor quality. Therefore, it became something of a belief until the individual used Biase's products before he or she became convinced of the high quality. The turning point for the skeptics of the quality of Biase Lumber products occurred when these products became scarce because he demand for overseas products was higher and they paid more for them. Then, local customers who were skeptical of Biase's quality began patronizing Biase Lumber products, more employe3es were hired, and three more sawmills and three more plants were built.

Free Delivery. Biase Lumber Company kept increasing its market share by introducing free delivery within Eastern Nigeria. The company realized that many people lived in the countryside, or rather in the suburban areas, but when they moved there with their lifestyles, the transportation of products became a problem, as in the case of poor roads, for example. Therefore, when Biase Lumber began free delivery, the demand for Biase Lumber's products exploded. Even then, the government of Eastern Nigeria under the leadership of Dr. Okpara refused to charge the company any fees for the forests for about two years, and then only small amounts. In the meantime, Biase Lumber Company continued their innovations with their products and made its employees and investors happy financially. The company knew that it had to make the customers appear important by attending to them where they lived in Eastern Nigeria.

Factors Affecting Profitability

Thompson and Strickland (1990) stated that production does not decrease proportionately with demand during downturns. Often mills continue in operation as long as variable costs are covered. Independent mill operators tend to continue producing until insolvency forces them to close down. The overcapacity that results during periods of decreased demand intensities price competition. On the other hand, increases in demand are readily matched with increased production through the addition of staff, restarting closed facilities, and the addition of new mills.

Thompson and Strickland (1990) also commented that in addition to price, cost is a major determinant of profit at the individual producing mills. Raw materials, that is lumber, are the largest single cost item. Therefore, the availability of a low-cost source of logs is critical to profitable operations. Some firms buy logs on the open market at a completive price or purchase timber harvesting contracts from the state or federal governments through competitive bidding. Others harvest timber on their own timberlands while open market log prices are high. Companies that harvest their own timberland tend to have a cost advantage because of the typically lower costs of timber assets acquired in the past. On the other hand, when log prices are depressed, buying on the open market can provide an advantage over harvesting timber from owned land.

Thompson and Strickland (1990) further commented that transportation cost is another important factor in the ability to serve markets profitably. Most wood products are bulky and costly to transport. As a result, marketing tends to be limited to the regional markets closest to the mills or plants, especially for commodity products. If there are many competing mills all vying for the same markets, competition tends to reduce prices and profits. An exception to this dependence on immediate regional markets exists for firms with access to bulk ocean shipping. Firms with such access to ocean-going vessels and with production sufficient to fill a ship are able to serve other regions easier. For example, some Oregon and Washington coastal mills are able to compete cost effectively in Southern California and Gulf Coast markets. The availability of substitutes is an additional factor that can impact the profitability of wood products. Lower cost (and price) particle-board has been gaining user acceptance and making competitive inroads against plywood. Non-wood substitutes have also reduced demand for wood; for example, aluminum siding in place of wood siding; steel posts and beams for wood; and asphalt shingles for wooden shingles.

The above discussions are very relevant, but the issue here depends on circumstances. Some may affect one business or another. In this case, the raw materials or logs were given to the Biase Lumber Company free of charge by the Eastern Nigerian government, and so both the analysis and profitability may not be as the situation Thompson, et al. (1990) had suggested because the circumstances are different. I have always mentioned them in most of my management and business writings that management is an art. It is very artistic; one does not even have to take every concept a lecturer demonstrates as the only approach to solving the alleged problems. However, students, business people, and others should always listen to these concepts and learn how to use the concepts at the appropriate circumstances and times. Management is not like two plus two, which is always four. It is a multifaceted endeavor and is not exactly trial and error. One must have seen something work for someone or some business and you have a similar or related case at hand, but finding the differences and similarities between your case and the successful case you've heard about means you should think deeply about what those differences are and what they will mean to you. Of course, the similarities need to be considered as well. The gap between the similarities and the differences is what one is looking for. If a company is a little bit larger or one can afford the participative decision-making, that will be ;much better because both—the lower and upper levels of management—are made up of people who understand the situations and have enjoyed more success than failure.

Mere reading through what Blaise Lumber Company has done and said is almost identical with what the developed lumber companies have said and done. The differences are primarily circumstantial. One of the problems with lumber companies in Nigeria is that they are not well organized. Just like any business, lumber companies are either owned individually or mostly family-owned and operated. They are not well known even within a local governmental area, let alone the country. They employ mostly family members, their tax structures are complicated, some of the family members pay no taxes, and the government does not care much about that. However, today the Nigerian government is trying harder to make oil production less a center of the Nigerian economy, and with that type of thinking, small or family lumber companies must certainly come forward for revenue reasons for the government.

<u>Competition</u>

The Biase Lumber Company has very few competitors in the whole country, but the family-type lumber business is very unpredictable because these companies deal mostly with timber, and they get money from foreigners in advance and sometimes pay more for timber with little overhead. The Nigerian government pays very little attention to what they do, but as I write today, the lumber business is growing greatly, and foreigners have intensified efforts to sending their finished products to Nigeria. Yet, the Wall Street type of mill organizations are yet to come of age in Nigeria. For some reason, cabinet makers in Africa prefer wood from Nigeria. The Biase Lumber Company knows that it has a great advantage when it comes to Africa. The wood is strong and needs no chemicals for growth. The sawmills may be expensive to buy, but all other advantages complement the expensive mill if there is a will to do so. This research and development is about the business policy of the Biase Lumber Company. The company knows that when it comes to the raw materials, logs and durable wood, which are in abundant supply in Nigeria and that is given freely by the Eastern Nigerian government, it has a competitive advantage.

Having realized these advantages, the Biase Lumber Company devised policies that would help the company grow in the face of world competition. The wood must not be cracked, the plant/sawmill must be up to standard for the technological age, and the manpower must be adequately treated, including in-service training and advanced education in universities paid for by the company, and with competitive wages that match the rest of the world. Then, of course, quality should always be a number one priority. With such thinking the Biase Lumber Company rapidly progressed and competed very well with medium companies in North America and Western Europe. Biase Lumber Company is now one of the most viable lumber companies in Africa and other developing nations. The company received several awards in Nigeria for producing excellent and durable products.

Thompson and Strickland (1990) have commented that the wood products industry in the United States is comprised of approximately 15 large and mid-sized companies and a large number of small, localized firms. Many of the large firms have advantages in financial resources, research, engineering capabilities, and in marketing. A mill sees its competition as other local mills, whether operated by a large company or independently owned that compete with it directly for logs, labor, and sales. International competition in the United States comes primarily from Canada, which accounts for nearly 30% of United States' sales. Significant competition in foreign markets comes from Northern Europe, Asian, and Australian firms. Virtually all of the U.S. competition is involved in producing commodity products such as lumber. In addition, all are striving to lower their costs of production. Owning or controlling timberland for self-sufficiency and developing differentiated higher value-added products are other strategies being pursued by a majority of the larger firms. Two of the largest, Georgia-Pacific Corporation and Weyerhauser Company are seeking improved customer services and market penetration through use of extensive multi-product sales and distribution systems.

Market segmentation strategies are being followed by several of the major competitors in an effort to better identify and respond to customer needs and shift production and marketing emphasis to capitalize on profit potential. The major movement has been to de-emphasize the building contractor segment and shift resourcing towards serving the do-it-yourself and industrial segments. The do-it-yourself segment is seen as particularly attractive because it is not directly tied to the housing cycle. The aging of residential structures indicates that repair and remodeling demand will continue to be strong. It even tends to increase during housing down cycles as owners try to make do with other structures by improving them. While the industrial segment demand is dependent on business conditions, it is not as sensitive to interest rates as are the residential and commercial construction segments. Thus, developing do-it-yourself and industrial markets Is seen as ways of stabilizing revenues. Typical major competitors include Boise Cascade Corporation, Georgia Pacific, International Paper Company, Louisiana Pacific Corporation, Pope and Talber, Inc. and Weyerhaeuser. These companies vary considerably with respect to their strategic thrust, but all produce and sell commodity wood products (Thompson & Strickland, 1990).

Operations

Despite Biase Lumber Company's gift of logs from the government, the company began thinking ahead by emphasizing specializing, differentiated wood products and capital investment in technology.

Differentiated Wood Products. Most of the timber given to Biase by the government seemed to be identical wood and in the interest of competition, the company had to have a variety of woods, natural color, and sizes. In that case, owning a specialized timberland became a necessity. In the company's general meeting, it was decided unanimously that the company buy a specialized timberland. Money was then set aside immediately. Within three months, Biase Lumber Company became a specialized timberland owner. Specialized products came out of this timberland. Biase Lumber Company was also able to compete effectively with foreign products. The company became a source of Nigerian pride because from cabinet making to building a whole house became more than a dream for privileged few. Houses and cabinet ownership became a dream for a determined citizen because of the cheaper prices and the availability of jobs and the equitable distribution of income.

The Biase Lumber Company (BLC) produces and sells a variety of wood products primarily in the following categories:

a. Softwood lumber;
b. Hardwood lumber;
c. Softwood veneer; and
d. Plywood and chips.

Softwood lumber is the major product and consists of studs and other dimension lumber in a wide range of widths, lengths, and thicknesses. The predominant species that are converted into softwood lumber are hemlock, white pine, lodge pole pine, red pine, spruce, and larch. Although softwood lumber, along with all other products, is branded with the name of BLC's marketing organization and its logs, these products are basically commodities competing against similar substitute products.

The second largest source for sales was chips, a residual product made from the parts of logs not suitable for conversion into lumber or veneer. Chips are used to make pulp for later conversion into paper products. The plant is now located in Akwo Ibom state in Nigeria. The product with the third largest sales revenue was veneer, a thin layer of wood peeled from logs and used in the lay-up of plywood. Hardwood is the fourth largest revenue producer and is produced in sizes appropriate for cabinet and furniture manufacturers. The major species is older although some maple is also cut. Plywood plants using veneer to produce sheeting, underlayment, sanded and marine plywood in standard sizes were the fifth largest source of sales revenue.

With the minor exception of a few specialty or highly finished products such as marine plywood, some sanded plywood, and special cuts of wood for furniture, the company aims to produce and move commodity-like product sin volume, relying on high per-worker output.

Sales and Marketing

All marketing, sales, and distribution of Biase Lumber products are the responsibility of Abatim, plc., a wholly-owned subsidiary of Biase Lumber., with approximately 65 sales, managerial, and clerical employees. It is located in Atan Onogom, Cross River State, Nigeria. Through this centralized sales and marketing unit, Biase Lumber Company gains economies of scale not available to independent mills. Abatim is able to coordinate production at various mills to satisfy customer orders, arrange lowest production location transportation cost alternatives, and fill orders for an assortment of products beyond the capacity of any single mill. In addition, centralized credit management is responsible for the marketing and sales for one or two of the company's mills, fewer salespeople are needed than if each mill handled its own sales.

Abatim has targeted the construction, industrial and remodeling and replacement (do-it-yourself) segments. Of these, the construction segment is the most active. In some years most sales were to do distributors and wholesalers, industrial users and retailers. Products are sold to approximately 550 distributors and wholesalers. Sales include softwood lumber for the residential construction, commercial construction, and remodeling and replacement segments; hardwood boards for the construction and remodeling and replacement segments; and plywood for both construction and remodeling and replacement segments. Ninety-five percent of Biase Lumber Company's sales have been to buyer sin Nigeria and the remaining five percent has been to other African buyers.

Most sales are arranged through telephone contact between a salesperson and a buyer. Biase Lumber Company offers competitive delivered prices, a variety of products, availability of products, and reliability as competitive advantages. The company has been named by a group of buyers as the major Supplier of the Year for its reliability, cooperation, and quality. The company also offers a 2% discount if an account is paid within 15 days, providing an effective incentive for prompt payment. In addition, Biase Lumber Company attempts to create a name familiarity by identifying all product lots with Abatim's trademark and name of the producing mill after the products are packaged wrapped.

Transportation is the third largest cost component of a delivered product, exceeded only by logs and labor. Abatim arranges for the transportation of products from all Biase Lumber mills, and, as a result, the company is able to secure volume discounts that help Biase Lumber to be profitable and price competitive. Shipments of products are normally made direct from the mill to the buyer's destination via rail, truck, or ship.

Human Resources

Biase Lumber Company considers people to be the most important factor in determining company profitability. The importance is operationalized in the human resources strategy and policies that support objectives of efficiency in the use of the total work force and high levels of individual and work team productivity. High productivity is motivated by programs that highlight the importance of individual contributions to the company through incentives based on these contributions.

Functional Specialization

Activities that benefit or apply to more than one mill are performed at a centralized location in order to gain advantages of functional specialization and scale. Sales, market development, engineering, financial, and legal services are the key activities that are centralized. Log buying specialists are located at the individual mills because of their need to be familiar with and responsive to local conditions, suppliers, and mill needs. With most support functions performed elsewhere by others, local mill managers can concentrate on what is most important to them—effective and efficient production.

Specialization and centralization have enabled Biase Lumber Company to operate with a relatively lean support structure. Out of approximately 1500 employees, fully 82% are directly engaged in mill production. Marketing and sales (Abatim) account for 3% of the employees, while Biase Lumber's corporate management and support involve 3%, and mill management and administrative support account for the remaining 12 percent.

Incentives

Biase Lumber Company is unionized because the company has help from the government, and from its inception, the company policy has been to a role model for other lumber companies. It has a very strong union; however, the union has never had cause to demonstrate or protest because the company believes in the contributions of the employees. The more contributions the employees make to the company the more they enjoy the fruits of their labor. The employees have been enjoying vacations with pay including a flight to their vacation destination with their families and many more benefits for their team contributions in their daily activities and hard work for BLC.

The employees are meant to work eight hours a day, 40 hours a week, and any hours worked after those 40 hours is paid at an overtime rate, which is time and a half. This means that if an employee makes $20 an hour, worked 9 hours for one day, then, of course he earned $20/hour times 8 = $160.00, plus the hour overtime which now would be $20 +$10 = $30, and for the week his or her gross pay for that day would be $160 + $30.00 = $190.00, That, of course, is the gross pay, meaning payment before taxes; then money paid to the employee after taxes are deducted would be net pay. However, if the employee worked 6 hours over the 40 hours, then BLC would pay 40 hours regular pay,

4 hours at time and a half, while 2 hours would be paid double time. This would be calculated as follows:

40 hours	=	$160.00 regular rate of pay
4 hours	-	$60.00 time and a half rate of pay
2 hours	=	$80.00 double time rate of pay.

Bonuses are given at the end of each year to every employee, but some bonuses may be larger than others—for exceptional hard work and dedication, for those who did not call off guide often, real team workers, many times ready to help or cover for someone who is sick or out for other reasons. Bonuses can range from money to vacation time and much more. This period of payment of bonuses is a very proud period for both employees and management. Employees who thought their rewards or bonuses are only in the afterlife because no one on earth acknowledged their hard work here eventually believed that someone on earth has seen their labors and doing the right thing. While the supervisors and managers who successfully advised until the end of the year become proud and happy because they believed that when their employees were happy, they would be happy as well, and the following year would appear much better.

BLC does not discriminate between salaried, hourly, full-time, and part-time employees. Bonuses are given for hard work and dedication. The company takes the health of its employees very seriously. Every employee is given health and safety insurance. In addition to safety insurance, the company has its own clinic where first aid is administered as necessary before sending an employee to an emergency room or a primary hospital.

Biase Lumber Company provides long-term employment for its employees and for their retirement, pension benefits are provided. The company does this to avoid poverty in the employee's old age, and this is a great incentive for many employees. Many employees even say openly that it make sense to work for BLC because it makes someone live happier and longer. BLC also provides loans to employees for purchasing homes or for building a new house if the employee already has land. These home loans make it all the more worthwhile to work harder for BLC. The loans are interest free; the principle is at 5% and deducted from the employee's monthly check. Although paychecks are given twice a month, there is no deduction for home payments the first two weeks, and are tax deductible. The fact is that all the good things done for the employees have a large payoff in the employees reporting for work promptly most of the time and work harder with increased productivity. The employees make reliable and durable products and are well liked by many customers. Customers can receive transportation assistance or discount in lieu of transportation assistance. Customer credits are also available.

Student Loans. The student loan program is mean for BLC workers or their dependents. Fifty percent of the loan is interest free while 50% has a 1% interest rate. The employees' dependents have a 60% chance of working for BLC after they graduate from a college or university provided they have taken 3 units each of log, plywood, and wood management courses. Also, a graduate must have a grade point average of at least 2.00 GPA. BLC is aware of the fact that the stability of a family is very important for the repayment of the mortgage loans and the student loans, so if a family member reports a family conflict, the company very quickly ensures a counselor or counselors are on hand to settle disputes. The counselors also ensures before an employee begins work that minor disputes are settled, while stains are clearly shown on their jeans, meaning that they have smiles on their faces. To know the company well, one has to read the inscription before entering the main office and cafeteria which reads "stable employees constitute a stable work force."

Life insurance is also provided for employees who need it, but families are clearly warned against taking a partner's life in the interest of collecting the insurance money. They are warned that if a partner dies violently, a thorough investigation will be launched, both medically and with law enforcement. In any case, the facts will be disclosed, and nay criminal activity will be dealt with appropriately. Families like the insurance because the job has to do with heavy equipment and timber. Although measures have been taken to prevent accidents, however, sometimes an accident simply happens and such unforeseen circumstances can be remedied with life insurance proceeds. BLC employees may also borrow against their life insurance policies and then arrange to pay it back in installments.

Because the work is so lucrative in pay and incentives, life expectancy is high; so, a housing complex was built for the retirees who cannot live alone. The apartments are rented based on affordability of the retiree. Medical officers stop by daily to check on the retirees, and the very ill ones are taken to the hospital promptly. Their medications are either given to them when the medical officers visit or they can go to a nearby pharmacy to have their prescriptions refilled. The company also provides recreational areas for the retirees to get exercise and other extracurricular activities to keep fit and healthy. A cafeteria is also provided that serves nutritious meals three times a day and with a great variety of food. This housing complex is landscaped with trees to provide shade in the summer or when the sun is intensely hot. Among the recreational activities a dance is held on Saturdays where both employees and retirees can dance together and become happy, and on occasion, the authorities will invite comedians or other entertainers to entertain the retiree.

Growth in Financing

Biase Lumber Company has a two-step process for financial growth—both externally and internally. The capital required to support these two types of growth is primarily from reinvestment of profits.

External Growth. The company's raw materials were given freely to the company so that it can neither assume existing debt nor create a new debt. So, the only option is to reinvest the profits. BLC logs were given to them by the Eastern Nigerian government under the leadership of Dr. Okpara. Of course, as they logged the timbers, they helped clear vast farmland, and ironically, even employed people comparable to farm workers and even paid its workers above a living wage. Whatever that meant, BLC paid higher than the farms. The population or the number of the employees with BLC were even more than the employees employed by the government in the farms because many farm rubber estate workers jumped ship, meaning that some of the rubber estate workers preferred working for BLC because the pay was higher and the benefits such as insurance, vacation pay, overtime pay, and so on. The government warned against punishing employees who left for better pay and benefits.

The reinvestment of profits was interesting to watch because the idea of interest payment was so foreign; therefore, the profits had nowhere to go other than savings and expansion. BLC did not expand foolishly; the management is so competitive; every investment they made was well analyzed while he application of participative decision-making was applied and applied rightfully and correctly. The reinvestment policy was not only a resounding financial success for Biase Lumber company, but also commanded high confidence for a private company in a fast developing Eastern Nigeria, competing for the control of lumber products and local market shares with the giant companies of Western Europe and North America. The idea of participative decision-making is my own element today; then, it was called teamwork because decisions could be overridden by senior officers at any point of the discussion. BLC still managed to compete very effectively with the well-known foreign companies.

This reinvestment policy of BLC has lasted longer than many of the BLC's policies and is fully as popular as ever. The fact is their start-up raw materials were simply given freely to BLC. Even though that will always be said about the company, that is one of the reasons for their financial success. However, the company has other reasons for their success including management based on effective implementation of decision-making, and, of course, with the availability of skilled personnel.

Internal Growth

Acquisition criteria was adopted for greater availability of funds. Even though the Eastern Nigerian government gave them the raw material they would be using, the company was still thinking ahead in case of unforeseen circumstances such as some of the wood decaying or dying in the cool forest land. Therefore, BLC invested in timberland and he purchase of unproductive mills at the lowest possible price while the its engineers used ideas in rebuilding these mills and put them to better use. The fact is that in purchasing a mill plus the cost of rebuilding it may be equal to the cost of purchasing a new mill. Sometimes some of the old rods in the mill may go bad and break down while the equipment is in operation and may require complete replacement with new equipment. However, in some cases, the old mill may need just minor repairs that may outlast a new mill. Some new mills are what I call "economy" mills. They are made to break down in the shortest time possible for the company to come and buy anew mill and spend more money on the same item.

Biase Lumber Company sells most of its trucks to the general public, so the company organizes public sales from time to time to raise funds and keep trucks that do most of the work strong and ready to go when required. Truck repairs and buying of parts are very expensive; therefore using strong and new trucks keeps the jobs going without many breakdowns. The policy saves a lot of money to the company. The company felt that the value of a used truck in such a load-carrying intensive business will enable them to spend more money on trucks than most of the undertakings they have had to face in the company. The whole process and reason for organizing truck sales for some of the trucks are explained to the general public to enable the public to understand that trucks of such nature are not good for heavy loads such as timber and iron to avoid breakdowns and unnecessary expenditures. Therefore, companies that run light businesses and may not use the trucks for long distances are encouraged to buy these vehicles. Such companies may dismantle the trucks and sell the parts in the used parts markets.

For the sake of competition, the company may purchase private logs for color, texture, and durability, but in some circumstances soft wood may be needed for some furniture and other types of home decoration. Such wood may not be in the company's inventory, and the company may be required to purchase it from companies that want to sell. Lumber companies are very artistic businesses. Things change daily, different countries are attracted to different ways in their own country, and for some others, another country may become attracted to such styles, for example, a type of window. Such companies like BLC may enter into those markets and try to compete, but some competitions are very risky. For others, because a window is completely built with foreign materials, there may be a chance of not making any profit at all. If a company continues doing business that way, such a company may not last long in business. Business, in general, is an act that is why knowledge of any business or company is important. Otherwise, artistic expressions may be very hard to undertake. If someone does not understand what goes on in his or her own company, flexibility might be impossible, he or she might be nervous and unable to reason well to the standards required in the business.

Sometimes internal growth may require all the scraps of log that are left behind to be gathered at a particular place or places and offer them to the general public for sale. Sometimes companies that deal in wood may buy these scraps wholesale and retail them to consumers; such accounts are classified under "timber and timber-related assets." Biase Lumber Company never borrowed money from the bank, but sometimes BLC buys rods and nails and some other low-level items on short-term credit, but generally pays this off very quickly within a few days. Wood is not a big money-making item, but wood supply is always constant. Even though wood is not sold in the millions of naira, it adds up at the end of the year, and, of course, they pay taxes on them to both state and federal governments, as well as local taxes.

BLC'S CONSOLIDATED BALANCE SHEET (in Millions)

ASSETS	April 30, 1965	April 30, 1963	April 30, 1962
Current Assets	$ 1,009.50	$ 709.50	$ 185.50
Cash and near cash	380.00	7,705.50	-------
Account Receivables – Net	10,090.50	5,275.00	5,715.50
Inventory	10,550.00	8,672.50	4,119.00
Prepaid Expenses	1,142.50	452.50	190.00
Timber and Timber-related Assets	5,442.50	2,297.50	1,196.00
Total Current Assets	28,235.00	20,235.00	12,206.00
Notes and Accounts Receivable	673.60	132.00	123.60
Timber and Timberlands	6,812.00	1,229.00	?
Property, Plants & Equipment	39,565.00	23,787.00	8,451.00
Less Accumulated Depreciation	(8,374.50)	(5,098.00)	(3,430.50)
	31,191.50	18,691.00	5,020.50
Construction	5,674.50	986.00	326.00
	36,866.00	19,677.00	5,346.50
Other Assets	1,455.00	1,400.00	133.50
Total Assets	73,041.00	51,716.50	17,815.00

BLC'S LIABILITIES AND STOCKHOLDERS' EQUITY (in Millions)

ASSETS	April 30, 1965	April 30, 1963	April 30, 1962
Current Liabilities			
Notes & Acceptances Payable	$ 5,512.50	$ 7,096.50	$ 4,589.50
Accounts Payable	5,481.00	4,793.00	2,895.00
Accrued Expenses	4,258.50	2,709.00	1,506.50
Income Taxes Payable	91.00	487.00	605.00
Timber Contracts Payables	2,566.00	245.00	2,195.50
Current Maturities, Long Term Debt	1,164.50	1,452.00	1,106.00
Total Current Liabilities	19,073.50	17,062.50	12,598.00
Deferred Income Tax Payable	160.60	295.50	221.00
Long-Term Debt, less current Maturities	24,360.50	6,839.50	3,434.00
Senior Subordinated Debentures	3,500.00	15,000.00	83.00
Stockholders' Equity	7,917.50)	7,090.00	7.50
Common Stock Paid-n Capital	7.50	7.50	
Retained Earnings	8,022.00	3,822.00	1,471.10
Total Equity	5,947.00	11,519.50	1,562.00
Total Liabilities & Stockholders' Equity	73,041.00	51,716.50	17,815.00

Management

Biase Lumber Company manages its 9 operating locations which are as follows.

Company	Location
Abatim	Atan Onoyom
Abini	Abini
Erei	Abawan
Egup IPA	Okurike
Ehum	Betem
Umon	Ikot Ana
Utima	Utima
Ubaghara	Ikun
Okurike	Abini

Using a decentralized/centralized structure, individual production units (mills, plants, or operating sales locations) are profit centers under a manager who has overall responsibility for the profitability of the unit. Each production unit is incorporated as a wholly-owned subsidiary under a name that identifies it as a local company as follows:

Abatim is the center located in Atan Onoyom, and all marketing, sales, and distribution of BLC products are the responsibility of Abatim, plc., which is a wholly-owned subsidiary of Biase Lumber Company. Abatim is staffed by sales manages and one senior manager, and clerical employees. BLC practices centralized sales and marketing, and this enables BLC to gain economies of scale by coordinating production at various sites to satisfy customer orders, arrange lowest production location transportation cost alternatives, and fill an assortment of orders for products that is beyond the capacity of any single mill or plant. In addition, centralized credit management creates efficiency, fewer salespeople than if each mill handled its own sales and credit checking. Most of their sales transactions are made through the telephone. Abatim has targeted the construction. Industrial, and remodeling of homes for their markets. The construction segment is very profitable.

The management or the sales managers are employed solely at the headquarters located at Abini. All of the managers must have bachelor's degree, and it would be good to have had experience as well and/or a degree in wood management or technology. Otherwise, it may not be very necessary because in-service training are always available; however, those with degrees move faster along the ladder.

Erei. is a clan in the Biase local government area, which lies between a farmer settlement and the Cross River, and, of course, is bounded on the south by the Ikun Bay. The Biase Lumber Company is located in Abawan where it is accessible both on land and water. The Abawan Mill, plc. Is a wholly-owned subsidiary of the BLC. The mill is staffed with 15 plant managers, one senior plant manager, and 17 clerical employees. The plant manages and the senior plant manager are employed at Abini, the headquarters of BLC, and they are also disciplined or terminated by the management at Abini.

The clerical employees are hired by the senior plant manager sitting with the five plant managers; they also discipline and terminate the clerical staff including janitors and drivers. Logging engineers and technicians are hired and disciplined by management at the headquarters under recommendations of the senior plant manager. The senior plant manager must also be a plant engineer and must have had courses in wood technology or experience in wood technology or worked under a wood engineer who is both a plant and a wood engineer.

Erei Mill receives its raw material from Erei Farm settlement. The raw material was given to Biase Lumber Company, plc. By the Eastern Nigerian government under the leadership of Dr. Okpara, but most of the timber in the Erei Farm Settlement is very similar. Depending on the products the company wants to produce, the mill management may ask for some other type of timber, hardwood for furniture, cabinets, and other industrial uses; railroad ties and composite panels for construction and industrial uses.

Because of competition, the mill must mix production, especially when it comes to foreign competition. Having a variety of products is very important. All wholly-owned subsidiaries of Biase Lumber Company must adhere to the instructions of headquarters. The company's headquarters makes its decision from the mills' monthly returns and mostly from Abatim, which deals with both sales and distribution.

Eguip Ipa is a clan in Biase local government that lies between the Cross River and the Ikom-Calabar highway. The people are primarily business people, teachers, peasant farmers, and fishermen for local consumption. The Biase Lumber mill is located at Okurike and known as Okurike Plywood, plc., a wholly-owned subsidiary of BLC. The mill operates as a private company. It hires and terminates clerical employees, including janitors, security officers, and truck drivers, although the plant managers and the senior plant manager are hired and terminated by the headquarters office at Abini. The wood engineers and technicians are also hired and terminated by the headquarters office at Abini upon the recommendation of the Eguip Ipa senior plant manager.

The Okurike Plywood Mill has 15 plant managers and one senior plant manager, and 17 clerical employees. Five plant managers sitting with the senior plant manager hire and terminate or discipline clerical officers, drivers, janitors, and so on. Titles below plant managers, engineers, and technicians are clearly the responsibility of the senior plant manager and five of his or her most senior managers, but all of them must agree with the punishment/discipline given for any particular offense. Otherwise, the senior plant manager must simply issue a warning and document the incident involving the employee or employees for future reference.

Disciplinary Actions Against Senior Officers

A manager, engineer, or technician who misbehaves or has committed a serious offense that may only be against the rules of the company and not against the law of the land—if it is against the law of the land, the employee must be turned over to the police—otherwise the senior plant manager must write up the offense committed by the senior official and submit the write-up to Abini Headquarters. Ten days after the submission of the report, the headquarters must send a form entitled *Complaint Form* to the suspect (s). After filling out the form and returning it to Headquarters at Abini, after five days of submission of the complaint form, a letter to appear is sent to both the suspect and the complainant to appear on a specified date where both parties would appear before the Discipline Committee. After hearing from both parties, they would be asked to go back to work and wait for a verdict. After approximately one month they could be asked to appear again to face the Discipline Committee for the verdict. The verdict is binding and is not subject to an appeal; instead, anyone who goes against the verdict may be subject to prosecution in a court of law and may also be subject to dismissal.

If improprieties exist between a member of the Discipline Committee and either the suspect or the complainant or both, meaning if a Discipline Committee member is a party to the dispute, then that member has to step down, and a new member is appointed by the chairperson of the board of directors. At that point, the case is heard all over again.

Ehum is a clan in Biase that lies along the Ikom-Calabar Road, bounded on the north by Ibie Palm Estate and on the south by Ehum District Court. Ehum people are business people, teachers and other professionals, hunters, civil servants, and peasant farmers. The Biase lumber mill is located at Betem, and is known as Betem Lumber, plc., a wholly-owned subsidiary of BLC. Betem Lumber operates as a private company; it hires and disciplines clerical personnel, officers, janitors, security officers, drivers, and the like. The senior plant manager must accompany five of his plant managers, selection based on seniority, when hiring or terminating employees; however, the senior plant manager, 15 plant managers, wood engineers, technicians, and mechanics are hired and disciplined by headquarters at Abini and the Discipline Committee there. The clerical staff are always 17 in number, but the senior plant manager and his staff of five plant managers could hire more based on the amount of work available in the mill. As stated earlier, all sales, marketing, and distribution are the responsibility of Abatim, plc., which is also a wholly-owned subsidiary of Biase Lumber Company. Like the Erei Mill, the Betem mill is always busy because of its nearness to the raw material. Because of its busy nature, more employees are hired here, so 25 plant managers are employed with the one senior plant manager and an one senior assistant plant manager. The operations are the same as at the other mills, but more wood engineers and assistants are necessary here.

Betem and Erei mills, as well as a few other mills, are very productive based on less overhead because of their nearness of the raw materials. Heavy trucks are not needed frequently and as are the drivers. Betem is endowed with virgin forest where different kinds of trees are found. BLC, therefore, seizes that advantage or opportunity by buying thousands of trees, which assists the mill in mixing up its products as competition demands. Due to abundant raw material, Betem Lumber is able to come up with different creative productivities.

When the former premier of Eastern Nigerian visited Abini, the Biase Lumber Headquarters, he was taken to Betem by the company's Chairman and CEO Mr. Obu Otim Okoi where Dr. Okpara saw firsthand the great job Betem Lumber had done to generate such outstanding high revenue. The premier also saw firsthand the cleanliness of the environment and the mill that gave no room for rusting and saw that every small and short routes were tarred, and communication links were excellent around the complex. The most important commendation made by the former leader of Eastern Nigeria was that of the teamwork by both the managers, engineers, technicians, clerical staff, janitors, and security offices down to the lowest rank and file. Everyone worked as if they had rehearsed their parts before they were visited, not knowing that is what they do every day of the week.

Umon is a clan in Biase that lies between the Cross River and the Ikom-Calabar highway. Umon people are business people, civil servants, fishermen, professionals, and peasant farmers. The Biase Lumber mill is located at Ikot Ana and known as Ikot Ana Plywood, plc., a wholly owned subsidiary of BLC located at Abini. Ikot Ana Plywood, plc. Operates as a private company, hires and terminates junior staff such as the clerical staff, drivers, and the like.

The senior officers—the senior plan manager, wood engineers, technicians, and the like are hired and terminated by the discipline committee at the headquarters located at Abini. Ikot Ana Plywood is somehow difficult to run because of its distance from raw material; the logs have to be transported tom the Ibia Palm Estate located at Betem. The Ikot Ana mill employs many drivers and has purchased heavy duty trucks and well-trained truck mechanics. They employ about 15 plant managers and one senior plant manager. The Senior Plant Manager oversees the management of the plant, but all hiring and termination of employees involves five plant managers and the senior plant manager. Whatever discipline is meted out must fit the offense; otherwise, although appeals are not allowed, exceptions can be granted if injustice is indicated during the verdict. This could be interpreted to mean lack of convenience on the senior plant manager. If the injustice is proved beyond reasonable doubt that it was done willfully by the senior plant manager, the senior planet manager could be demoted or dismissed for incompetence in using his or her judgment.

The clerical staff are supposed to be 17 in number, but if the volume of work is high, then the senior plant manager and five of his or her senior managers can employ more workers as the work dictates; however, headquarters must be notified of the new hires and acceptance given before additional employees can be added to the payroll, even though lower level employees are paid directly by the mill at which they work. The mill has to account for all money paid out. Ikot Ana has a high overhead because its raw materials are shipped in from neighboring forests and are very expensive because private logging companies compete in the area. The private logging companies are paid in advance from abroad, and these foreign companies pay more than the local companies for trees. The local companies, BLC, and Ikot Ana Plywood have to be so happy because the high cost of logs will make foreign products more expensive and local products less expensive and more sought after.

Local products must have warned against the price competition, that will enable local producers to be very creative in their competition with foreign products. Even in Nigeria, any mill that is close to the raw materials makes greater profits than its counterparts, who are not as close to the raw materials. In business, any small advantage makes a lot of difference monetarily or otherwise. The longevity of a business may be due to an advantage acquired sometime in the past

Utima is a village in Umon of Biase local government area. It is bounded on the north by very hostile neighbors and on the south by the Cross River. Utima looks very lonely in the midst of hostility, but the village itself is very stable. The people of Utima are professionals, civil servants, peasant farmers, and the like. The mill is located at Utima and is known as Utima Furniture, plc., a wholly-owned subsidiary of Biase Lumber Company of Abini. Utima Furniture, plc. Operates as a private company in that it hires and terminates employees such as the clerical staff, security officers, janitors, drivers, and the like. The company is very well cared for by its parent company.

Utima Furniture, plc. was not located in Utima because BLC thought it was going to be very profitable, even though it does little more than break even. The primary aim of having a mill in Utima is to prevent the hostility in the area by creating jobs that employ the people of Utima and its neighbors. BLC researched and discovered that the lack of employment opportunities was the main cause of hostilities in the area. Fortunately, since the establishment of the mill at Utima, both the neighbors and Utima itself have enjoyed peace and tranquility. People come from great distances to witness the artistic work of the mill. Of course, the sales training is the responsibility of Abatim. The people of Utima and its neighbors developed trade seemingly overnight from the wood that they bought from Abatim. Most of the best doors and windows, chairs, couches, and even houses are creatively built because of the availability of the wooden furniture. Foreign furniture is made of expensive wood and therefore unable to compete effectively in Nigeria.

Ultimate Furniture is run by a senior plan manager and 15 other managers, wood engineers, technicians, chemical staff, and, of course, with the support of janitors, security officers, drivers, and some others. The senior plant manager, accompanied by the five senior managers hire and/or terminate employees. The number of engineers and technicians is dictated by the size of the job needing to be accomplished. The senior plant manager has to apply for engineers and technicians from headquarters at Abini, and the head office does the disciplining when required by a report of the senior plant manager.

Having a degree is an advantage for one working here, but if an individual does not have a degree, in-service training is available. In-service training could enable one to be promoted just as a degree may. The fact is that whatever one does in Ultima Furniture and does it efficiently, one is bound to be promoted to a higher level. The senior manager at Utima Furniture felt that it is necessary for one to be efficient at his or her work pace and not necessarily for Mr. Tom to be better than Mr. Johnson because that may be tantamount to competing with other people, which may mean a house divided against itself. The result of this can never be whole, so Utima has what it calls progressive recognition. What happens is that many officials move around the plant, offices and other areas to see the progress of the employees is being made and who has made progress. Every quarter of the year, progress reports are published on information boards where employees can meet with the authorities to correct any errors that might be made in their work and work habits. After this, a final list is posted on the same boards, from which employees are selected to be promoted.

Like the Ikot Ana mill, Utima Furniture employs many drivers, including heavy duty truck drivers, who load and drive the logging trucks to their destinations, sometimes for very long distances because the mill is not near to the raw materials. Close location to the raw materials enables a mill to have more room for development because it reduces overhead, and with the money saved, the mill can reinvest the savings in better equipment or save it for emergencies. The original aim of building furniture was to create a stable situation in the region and was to create jobs for people there, and ultimately in Biase as a whole, it has created stability and wealth and more in the region.

Ubaghara is a clan in Biase local government area; some area is 2—3 miles away from the Cross River. It is bounded on the north by Erei Ikun Farm Settlement and Biakpan Rubber Estate with abundant hard and soft wood. The mill is located in Ikun and known as Ikun Plywood, plc., a wholly owned subsidiary of the Biase Lumber Company, but operates as an independent company. The people of Ubaghara are teachers, civil servants, professionals, business people, peasant farmers, hunters, etc. The Ikun Plywood, plc. Employs janitorial staff, chemical workers, security officers, drives, and clerical staff. The company has one senior plant officer and 15 plant managers, engineers, and technicians. The engineers and technicians are employed based on the volume of work available. The senior plant manager is required to apply to headquarters at Abini for such officers and describe the work volume Ikun Plywood faces at the time. If headquarters is convinced that more employees are needed, then new employees are added within a month of the request and sent to the mill. Otherwise, a senior official comes down from headquarters to inspect the work before something can be done. The same is done with clerical staff if more clerical staff is required.

If the volume of work grows, the senior plant manager applies for one senior and a senior assistant clerical staff member, while he senior plant manager sits with five of his senior managers to hire and terminate other clerical staff. The senior plant manager, his 15 other plant managers, technicians, engineers, and senior clerical staff can only be hired or disciplined by the Discipline Committee at headquarters if the rule broken is not against the state. If it is violation of the law, then the culprit will be sent to the local police for prosecution Otherwise, the senior plant manager must write up a report to the office at Abini. A complaint form is then sent to the suspect(s) after filing and sent to headquarters. Then after about five days, a letter to appear is sent to both the complainant (senior plant manager) and the suspect. Both parties present their case to headquarters, after which both parties are asked to go back to work and wait for the verdict of the Discipline Committee for about a month. At the end of that time, both parties may be asked to appear face to face again for a finding verdict, meaning no appeal is necessary by either party. If a member of the discipline committee is a party to the dispute, the member may be asked to step down while the chairperson of the Board of Directors will appoint a replacement member, and the case begins again with questions and answers and any witnesses.

Raw materials are very important in this business. Ikun, Abandan, and Betem are so important to Biase Lumber Company because they are near the source of raw material. Ikun Plywood obtains its raw materials from Erei Ikun Farm Settlement and from Biakpan Rubber Estate. Both estates contain softwood and hardwood. Ikun Plywood needs no purchases of wood varieties to compete very effectively. Ikun, like its counterpart in Erei, has a lot of customers from the East Central State. Most of Icon's customers prefer wholesale business; they retail their own purchases and use some for home furniture. They prefer buying from Ikun because transportation is easily accessible to any part of the former East Central State. It is only 15 miles from Ikun Plywood Mill to the Cross River. The Cross River is not deep enough for ocean-going vessels, so they use engine boats in transporting plywood and other products to their destinations. Like other BLC mills, sales are perfectly handled by Abatim, which handles all sales of BLC mill products.

Biase Lumber Company practices centralized sales and marketing which enables BLC to gain economies of scale by coordinating production at various mills to satisfy customer orders, arrange lowest production location, transportation, and most importantly, single avenue of credit management. Every business today allows its customers to buy many items on credit. A busy mill such as Ikun Plywood cannot do it all, and special units like Abatim with specialized managers and clerical staff are able to be creative in sales and marketing. Ikun Plywood products are primarily for industrial construction, which is very profitable, though they also produce products for home building and remodeling.

Biase Lumber Company, Plc., Headquarters–Abini

Abini is a rapidly developing area in Biase local government. It is about five miles from Akpet Central, the capital of Biase Local Government. Abini is located on the Ikun-Calabar Road and a tourist attraction all year around. Abini is a rather decent, quiet place where crime is almost nonexistent like the local government itself with beautiful hotels and restaurants. Abini is a business center populated by civil servants, business people, and professionals.

The Abini headquarters of BLC is primarily an administrative center. The campus is about half a mile square, containing seven buildings, most of which are three floors with an in-service training block in the rear adjacent to the playground. The offices are well decorated with a big sounding clock at the western end of the campus. There are directions to offices and parking places, security officers armed with batons rather than guns. There are janitors cleaning the streets, which are well-tended, and there is a general kitchen at the northern end of the complex. The sanitary department ensures that every corner of the campus is as clean as it can be, and any abnormality is treated in a professional manner. The campus is truly beautiful, and any young person who sees the campus can tell his or her parents that when he or she grows up that Biase Lumber Company will be the place they will want to work.

The company is not only beautiful on the outside, but the offices are air-conditioned, handsomely decorated with hard and softwood chairs. Corruption of any time, including paying money for a free service, is enough to get the offender shown the door to leave. I mean any dishonesty by a person of any level at BLC will enable the company to discharge that person, whether it is an executive or a janitor. On one occasion there was a man who attended an in-service training course and had failed his final examination. He could have repeated the training, which was free of charge, however, he preferred to try and bribe an official of the training course. The official wrapped the money with student's results and took it to the appropriate authority on the campus. The student was not prosecuted but was given less than an hour to get his things and leave the campus, never to apply to any of the mills owned by the company. When BLC says there no jobs available, one should believe them that when jobs become available, they will clearly tell you that all who qualify will be able to get a job, but if any criminal activity is indicated, one may be detained or simply asked never to apply at the company again. That person's name will be added to a list of people not to be hired at BLC.

BLC was able to afford updated technology from abroad when many manufacturing companies in Nigeria were struggling to repair their older equipment. The Abini headquarters had a storage facility where equipment was stored, and any of the mills who required heavy equipment for lifting, cutting, and slicing logs would go to get one after inspection by the head office at Abini. The head office gave out trucks to the subsidiaries, but these had to be new ones as older vehicles would not last long and might need constant repair, which would take a lot of resources from the company. Instead, the company sells the older trucks to start-up companies and the general public. The funds raised are reinvested in the parent company or its subsidiaries. The company employs many mechanical engineers who inspect the mills and plants to discover what assistance, if any, that headquarters can give or if any repairs or new supplies are needed.

The headquarters office has felt that since their idea of centralized sales at Abatim has worked out very well, is profitable, and promotes economies of scale in the company, a centralized storage facility might save money allowing specialists decide when to buy and when to sell equipment. This would also allow them to avoid rust and general wear and tear on equipment so that it would be usable and strong.

Even though the Eastern Nigerian government had been very kind to BLC, the fact is that nothing is given for nothing. Dr. Okpara belonged to a political party, and party requires funds to stay in business. BLC has been a great contributor to Dr. Okpara's political party—the National Council of Nigerian Citizens (NCNC). Of course, in exchange for the money BLC paid or invested in the NCNC, the party and the premier made policies favorable to BLC. Most of the employees belong to the NCNC including the CEO Mr. Obu Otum Okoi. The fact is that someone need not be a member of NCNC to qualify for employment at BLC.

Questions

1. What is this case about?
   a. What is the most notable policy you think Biase Lumber Company has made?

2. Who was Dr. M. I. Okpara?
   a. Did Dr. Okpara help BLC?\
   b. In what way did he assist, if any?

3. How did BLC show its appreciation to the NCNC?

4. Write a short essay about Abatim, its duties, and benefits to Biase Lumber Company.
5. Describe the wood products and services of BLC.
6. Describe what happens during employment and dismissal of a junior staff member.

Answers

1. This case is about business policies.
   a. Biase Lumber Company has made many policies, but the most notable one was the creation of mills and Abatim for sales, all as wholly-owned subsidiaries of BLC. All the subsidiaries operate as private companies, but they only hire and discharge junior staff such as clerical staff, janitors, security officers, drivers, and the like.

2. Dr. M. I. Okpara was the premier of former Eastern Nigeria and the leader of the National Council of Nigerian Citizens.
   a. Yes. Dr. M. I. Okpara or Dr. Michael Thurugera Okpara did help the BLC.
   b. Dr. Okpara authorized BLC to use the trees or logs from the government properties for its private use.

3. Biase Lumber Company showed its appreciation by contributing greatly to the NCNC, a political party led by Dr. Okpara in Eastern Nigeria.
4. Abatim is a subsidiary of Biase Lumber Company and operates as an independent company with approximately 65 sales managers and clerical staff. The company is located at Atan Onoyom in Cross River State of Nigeria. All sales, distribution activities, and marketing of Biase Lumber products are the responsibility of Abatim. BLC practices centralized sales through the services of Abatim.
   Abatim's Duties: Abatim coordinates production at the various mills to satisfy customer demand, arranges the lowest transportation

costs to the various mills, and fills orders for an assortment of products beyond the capacity of any single mill. In addition, Abatim's centralized credit management creates efficiency in the many transactions of BLC, and because responsibilities are narrowed and easily dictated, Abatim has targeted the construction, industrial, and the remodel and replace (do-it-yourself) businesses. Of these, the construction industry is the most active.

Benefits: Through marketing, sales, and distribution by Abatim, BLC is able to gain economies of scale not available to independent mills. Through the marketing, sales, and distribution by Abatim, fewer salespeople are needed than if each mill handled its own sales. Economies of scale occur because Abatim is able to coordinate production of the various mills to satisfy customer demand, and increase production and lower production costs.

5. Firms engaging in the wood products industry produce one or more of a number of products including dimension lumber, beams, siding, hardwood products for furniture, cabinets and other individual uses, railroad ties, poles, plywood, decorative paneling, and composite panels for construction and industrial use. Products used in the residential and commercial construction industries are essentially undifferentiated and compete as commodities, industrial products, and special dimension or proprietary products for the construction market are less vulnerable to direct competition from substitutes and can command a premium price.

   Special services to buyers, even among producers, of commodity products can also allow these producers to command a higher price and/or a preferred supplier relationship. Services such as technical assistance on selecting the best type of products for particular applications may be offered Rapid order processing assures delivery, shipments of assorted products and split shipments are being offered increasingly, especially by larger firms attempting to gain a competitive edge.

6. During employment and dismissal of junior staff, the senior plant manager sits down with five of his senior managers and

interviews an employee. Whatever this group comes up with is binding on the employee, but the decision must be unanimous or otherwise the senior plant manager must write the employee up pending further misconduct.

Biase Lumber Company is a fictional story but with some elements of reality. BLC and the characters never existed. The former premier, Dr. Okpara, did not give falling trees or logs to anybody or if anybody asked for the logs. I mentioned Dr. Okpara because he was a visionary; his government of the former state of Eastern Nigeria was able to establish rubber estates, palm estates, and a farm settlement system and almost brought unemployment to a halt in Eastern Nigeria. Today, even the whole of Nigeria cannot maintain the estates Dr. Okpara created and maintained until the Nigerian civil war. The news about the estates today is that a part of the farms are controlled by foreigners, while in the 1960s foreigners sent their students to study how Nigerian specialists ere planting palm and rubber trees. I think the pride of Africa has been sold.

However, this is actually a tale of two cities because today Nigeria is the largest economy in Africa, even though the estates have been left fallow with stylo for a long time, and even though foreigners have come to rescue some of the estates, of course, this may be due to the impact of the global economy. However, the national pride has given way to the pride of acceptable prices.

It seems to me that the forces of the global economy follow very much the focus of competitive advantage, Whatever one thinks of this global economy, I think t he true colors of that economy in Cross River State of Nigeria is that of an equal opportunity employer (EOE). Surprisingly, too, as I follow up on the Nigerian economy, I have found that even the almighty oil and gas industries that many economists thought might be over 50% of the Nigerian economy turned out to be less than 50% of the Nigerian gross domestic product as opposed to suggestions made by international economists that 50% of the Nigerian economy might be oil and gas. This is an indication that Nigeria has truly diversified her portfolio. I remember when former US President William Clinton visited Nigeria, he spoke so much about diversification of the country's portfolio. I think the country heeded this advice. Today, we are all very happy about it, no matter whose advice was followed.

As a young man in high school, I saw Premier Dr. Okpara of Eastern Nigeria and his government were creating estates and farm settlements that employed several thousand people, I became fascinated and visited all of the estates. Some of my friends thought I might be thinking of being an agricultural officer; however, one of my sons is an agricultural officer today with his BSc in Agriculture. However, I wound up studying business and advancing to the Ph.D. level.

To return to my early dreams about the logs in the estates, which were used for nothing, but I thought then they had some salvage value. I even went to the managers and general manager's offices to talk to them about the tree, but every one of them looked hostile and conservative. Therefore, I said nothing to any of them, thinking that they would say I was a troublemaker who did not know anything. None of them asked what I was looking for; I looked so innocent besides which at my age then, no one expected such a young person to do harm. However, as I left, some of them said, "This young man is fascinated by the environment and may become an agricultural officer. You never know." I did as if I never understood what they were saying but kept moving faster away from the environment until I got to the bus stop.

Therefore, when I began writing this case, my mind went straight to my early experience and thinking about the trees in the estates and what I thought about the salvage value of those logs. At the time, carpenters were buying plans for building houses and for making furniture, private persons were buying foreign-made doors, windows and chairs at very high prices, while these logs were lying around wasted. I think that my thinking made sense then and still does today. Then, Nigerians gave unnecessary obedience to their elected officials, but some other people simply refused to take advantage because they might be uncovered for tax reasons. Eventually, no one wins. Whoever wins, the services or disservices are left for the taxpayer to shoulder.

CHAPTER 16
BUSINESS ORGANIZATION STRUCTURE

a. Plan
b. Business Organization Structure
c. Formal Organization
d. Critical Views of Detailed Organization Planning
e. Systems Approach to Organization
f. Technology and Structure
g. Size and Structure
h. Environment and Structure
i. Multicultural Society
j. Strategy and Structure
k. Patterns of Organization
l. Functional Pattern of Organization
m. Function of the Pattern
n. Product as the Pattern
o. The Geographic Pattern
p. Creating Organizational Structure, Human Facilities in Structural Designs, Personal and Organizational Goals
q. Questions and Answers

CHAPTER 16

BUSINESS ORGANIZATION STRUCTURE

Plan

Introduction

I. Importance of Organization
    a. Formal Organization
    b. Benefits of Organization

II. Critical Views of Detailed Organizational Planning
    a. Systems Approach to Organizing

III. Underlying Forces That Shape Organizations
    a. Contingency Theory and Organizational Structure
    b. Technology and Structure
    c. Size and Structure
    d. Strategy and Structure
    e. Underlying Forces and Management Design

IV. Pattern of Organization
   a. Function of the Pattern
   b. Product as the Pattern

   c. Geographic Pattern
   d. Personal and Organizational Goals

V. Achievement of Organizational Purpose
   a. Industrial Growth and Development
   b. Social Satisfaction
   c. Human Factors

Business Organization Structure

The manager's organizing decision involves the formal structuring of relationships among jobs, people, and activities. Given an assortment of jobs, how shall they be related or grouped? This chapter examines structural aspects of organizational life, specifically the process of creating organizations, underlying forces that influence their shape, patterns of grouping jobs, and activities and human factors in structural decisions (Longenecker & Pringle, 1984).

To integrate the contributions of many individuals, a manager must devise some pattern that relates each of them to the others without some such pattern of coordination resulting in chaos.

Formal Organization

Longenecker & Pringle (1984) have stated that social scientists developed a theory of formal organization that stressed the rational nature of this formal organization and applied the name, bureaucracy, to it. According to this theory, the formal organization is visualized as a pyramid of officials who direct and coordinate the work of specialists by use of formal procedures. It is considered important that roles be carefully defined and rules for interaction clearly delineated. The formal organization or bureaucracy therefore consists of the management of specified framework of relationships. This formal organization makes up that skeleton for the social system and is supplemented by informal relationships that develop spontaneously among organization members without explicit definition by management (Longenecker & Pringle, 1984).

Longenecker and Pringle (19840 commented further than the benefits of good organization are those related to what a theorist calls sound organization. Charting an organization, for example, brings to light and helps eliminate weaknesses including gaps in responsibility, overlapping of functions, duplication of efforts, and working at cross purposes. At best, patterns of relationships in large organizations are extremely complex. The organizer attempts to create a logical structure; that is, a structure designed to work efficiently through careful work specialization, well-defined hierarchy, and a set of rules and procedures. In addition, a clearly outlined organization structure provides an incumbent of a position with a clear understanding of management expectations. It also stresses unity of command, thus eliminating confusion and identifying the line of responsibility for each individual. The planned organization also specifies the authority assigned to each position. Therefore, the incumbent will know the scope and limits of authority in the position.

The theorists must have made good arguments on what they called "sound organization," but all along I have made it very clear that business scientists should be very careful about definitions because business or management in general is an artistic work. In management what makes you laugh in the morning may make you think very deeply in the evening. That many not mean you are done in management; it may mean rather that you have been given food for thought or homework, if you will. However convincing your language may be in management, remember that management philosophies are not constant all of the time. Participative decision-making is a way to start. Management is at times historical because you have to remember the best decisions your company made last year and under what circumstances, brainstorming. This means you should think hard even in a participative decision-making situation. Today's problem in management may look identical with last week's problem; the fact is that you may attempt to assign the same solutions to today's problems. However, that is where you begin going wrong. Situations may be different; characters may be different; the structure may look different. Work harder on every problem; come up, with your own definitions for each problem your company faces. If you and your team defines the problem well, the solution may not be out of reach. Do not define your problem simply to give you a solution you can live with for the present. A manager must always listen and use dialogue instead of just communication. Dialogue is a discipline of collective learning and fact finding while communicating justifies and defends assumptions.

Critical Views of Detailed Organization Planning

Administrators and scholars do not agree on the desirability of extensive organization planning. Critics argue that some flexibility in relationships and procedures is desirable. These critics feel that excessive detail in specifying responsibilities is stifling and that efficient operations can be achieved without extensive organization planning and without its paraphernalia including charts and manuals. In general, critics of the carefully planned organization object to rigid chains of command and organization charts that become ends in themselves. Bureaucracy is replaced by bureau pathology in which red tape triumphs and means become ends. These critics condone some leapfrogging over supervisory chains and crossing over organization lines to reach into other departments with ideas, suggestions, and criticism. Both advocates and critics of organization planning have a point. It is desirable to study and structure organizational relationships. At the same time, some flexibility is necessary in practical day-to-day organizational life (Longenecker & Pringle, 1984).

Earlier I stated that management is an artistic work. I think both the administrators and the scholars are making my case for me. I think that extensive planning an organization is somehow out of step with the complex factors affecting the principles of the global economy. The biggest factor is flexibility and not rigidity. Just like any other thing done, too much becomes a hindrance. Organization planning, of course, is needed. Just as we run our families, we have to make plans, but not excessively. In today's economy, you have to find out what your competition at home and abroad is doing. What you want is your own niche or what your company can offer to create some kind of a difference between your products and that of your competition. Excessive planning may be confusing to those who work with you. Participative decision-making is a way to go in today's economy where two heads are better than only one.

Systems Approach to Organizing

In light of systems theory, organizing may be visualized as a design function—creating the structure or framework of the system. Managers establish those relationships among component parts that will provide the most effective system. If a mangers approach organizing without a systems point of view, however, they may adopt organizational rules of thumb or follow conventional practice with little regard for the unique requirements of the particular system. After the key activities provide the basic framework, the organizer uses decision analysis and relations analysis to ask questions about the type of decisions that must be made and at what levels it is most appropriate for them to be made. Can the system functions be more effective by delegating broad decision-making authority to lower levels of management. Relations analysis examines the points of contact among activities and personnel. The structure must facilitate cooperative relationships among people whose functions are intertwined. Once again, the focus is upon the working relationship of the components of the system (Longenecker & Pringle, 1984).

Underlying Forces That Shape Organizations

Contingency Theory and Organizational Structure

The dynamic nature of modern organizations produces repercussions in organizational relationships. For example, business firms that diversify their product line may find it necessary to modify their structure in order to produce and sell the new products efficiently. If he products are drastically different from those in the existing line, completely new departments may be required. Similarly, decentralization may be justified by change in the type. Personnel changes also lead to organizational changes. This is particularly true of replacements of the top management positions. Personal abilities differ among executives and modifications of an organization are made to accommodate the strengths or weaknesses of any particular executives. New executives also have their own ideas of organization, and these frequently differ from those of their predecessors.

Since organizational structures reflect the functions and purposes of an organization, it is not surprising to find that structures differ because of the basic differences among organizations. Contingency theory stresses the unique nature of structures and the impact of situational variables on management and organizational performance. It thus helps to explain variations in structure. We would not expect a church, a business organization, and a college football team to use identical patterns of organization and management. Nor would we expect an organization to retain the same structure over time while it was changing in other ways. No doubt many aspects of organizational situations logically call for variations in structure. Situations are so complex, however, that scholars find it difficult to isolate the most important variables and to understand their implications for design of organizations (Longenecker & Pringle, 1984)

Let us now discuss the following variables: technology and structure, size and structure, environment and structure, and strategy and structure.

Technology and Structure

A few decades ago, writers generally assumed that organizational concepts were universally applicable. Today, however, that assumption is questioned by those who emphasize the drastic differences in industrial technology. (Technology in this case refers to methods of operation including both machinery and related techniques or methods.) Perhaps, the best-known approach in this area was the study that involved about 100 British manufacturing plants and was conducted by a university research team and reported by Joan Woodward. The researchers gathered extensive data about the features of the formal organization of each plant, but they experienced difficulty in discerning a logical pattern. The type of organizational structure did not initially appear to be significant in explaining the differences in degrees of success. Organizational differences became sharper, however, when the plants were grouped according to type of production technology. Eleven classes of technology were established involving variables such as kind of unit, production batch production, mass production, and process production. When the plants were divided into the eleven categories, organizational patterns were immediately apparent. The patterns include such traditional features such as span of control and uses of line and staff (Longenecker & Pringle, 1984).

Size and Structure

In their work, Longenecker and Pringle (1984) point out that the size of an organization also appears to affect its structure. In general, research studies have compared organizations of varying sizes in terms of a number of variables. One such variable is "formalization"– the extent to which rules, procedures, and instructions are written. Another variable is "concentration of authority"—that is the degree of which authority is given, types of decisions of concentrated on higher levels, or delegate to lower levels. One of the early and most famous studies was conducted by the "Aston Group"—a group of scholars associated with the University of Aston in Birmingham, England. They concluded that organization size played an important role in determining structure, especially when compared to technology. The correlation of organization size with specialization, standardization, formalization, and centralization was consistently stronger than the correlation of technology with these same factors.

Other studies have subsequently investigated the relationship of size and structure, and the findings have varied. Although size has been rather consistently related to structure in those studies, the precise nature of the relationship is unclear. Even the Aston Study did not suggest that size was the only variable affecting structure. It appears that organizational size influences its structure, but the precise nature of this influence remains a question.

Environment and Structure

Longenecker and Pringle (1984) stated that organizations exist in different environments. We recognize, for example, that steel production, residential builders, private universities, and public utilities face substantially different external situations. Some environments are described as stable and predictable, whereas others are characterized by shifting conditions, uncertainty, and difficulty in predicting the course of events. Uncertainty in a business environment is created by the existence of many competitors and competitive products, broad price ranges and price instability, and numerous changes in product knowledge. Do such differences in environments affect organizational structure? The answer is yes, although research is only slowly unraveling the nature of the environment-organization relationship (Longenecker & Pringle, 1984). The relationship between the environment and organizations can be complicated om a multicultural society such as the

United States, while in a homogeneous society like Japan and Nigeria, the differences are culturally based.

Multicultural Society

In a multicultural society with places like the city of San Francisco in the United States where I lived for many years, the difference between the downtown business organizations and the Chinatown businesses can be seen in a variety of ways such as the prices for commodities, product quality, and competitors with unstable and violent situations including product quality. In situations like that, prices for commodities are often negotiable because the competition really wants to sell the product instead of the other competitors. These conditions create uncertainty. The interesting point is that what happens in Chinatown business for the buyers does not represent what happens in San Francisco. The market conditions in Chinatown does not mean that the businesses do not know what to do, but rather that what happens there is what I call cultural conditions. Cultural conditions affect only the organizational structure where the business owners of that culture stay and do business. It is difficult for such cultural conditions to be transferred and be represented in the downtown business organization. Even though culture can create a lasting behavior in the people who practice the culture, but could not have overwhelming impact on other organizations in downtown San Francisco.

This type of environment is, in most cases, created. I knew what type of business environment we had, even after the Nigerian independence; it was stable and predictable until the military took over and initiated instability, which stayed for a long time. If at all, we still call them businesses, but I call them anything goes. The instant that was created affected not only business organizations, but also social and political affairs. The uncertainty in Nigeria at that point was not created by many business competitors, but rather by less business competition because businesses were always advised on how they should conduct their business. The environment teemed so much with difficulties and uncertainties that foreign associates became scared about doing business with their Nigerian counterparts. Scarcity of raw materials made most industries non-existent.

I truly believed from my eye-witness account that environment does not exist in isolation of any type of organization, including business, social, and political organizations. I believe that both environment and organizations are created by humans apart from geographic influences, which come from nature. I also believe that organizational structure is always at the mercy of what human beings want to do with the environment.

In my view, in the United States every four years the country holds a presidential election to elect a qualified candidate who can help create an environment for a good economy and keep the country strong and competitive. No matter what culture one is affiliated with, everyone wants an environment where good things are created. Therefore, environment and organization are related, but the leader is a part of the environment that acknowledges or occupies the establishment of an organization. It is difficult for a poor environment to generate a reputable organization, but not impossible, because today Nigeria has the largest economy in Africa, after having one of the poorest economic environments in Africa due to the constant military takeovers, but what a difference a decade makes.

Having said what I have said, I think that it makes sense to say that the environment is one of the important things we need to build our livelihood. Most of the people in China and Cuba may have been entirely different for better or worse due to the environment created by the governments. Sometimes our soldiers go to war, and the environment created is warlike because of the support the environment has from the war—the media and politicians. Social and business environments never come to us by design; they are manmade. The similarities between environment and organization is that both are manmade, while their differences are that any environment is created by the government while an organization is created by a group of people.

Strategy and Structure

Longenecker and Pringle (1984) have stated that as environments change organizations devise new strategies and adapt their structures to pursue those strategies to discover the influence of strategy on organization changes that accompany or follow strategy changes.

It is true that when environment changes organizations also change simply in order to adapt to the situation at least to break even or make more profit. A case in point is the Palm Oil Estate (PAMOLE) established by the British during the colonial era in Calabar, Nigeria. When the British left Nigeria, Nigerians had not been properly introduced to the business of palm oil. Even though most of the employees were Nigerians, the sales of the final product decisions were made by the expatriates. However, the employees neve failed to get their salaries or wages. Therefore, the Eastern Nigerian government that took over from Great Britain thought that the only business was to manage the estate well and sell the products to where prices were the best or even back to the colonial masters without knowing that the British government had to subsidize the earnings so as to enable the employees being paid.

The Eastern Nigerian government realized later that the earnings of PAMOL were subsidized by the government, but that the Nigerians had been doing the job well. For that reason, the Nigerians came to the realization that the environment had truly changed and they would have to do things on their own—thinking and research—in order to make a profit. Therefore, they researched and found that a rubber plantation might be more lucrative, and so, the Nigerian government had to phase out the palm oil trees and planted rubber trees in their place, which they still maintain to this day. Therefore, in putting the environment in perspective, I should say change of environment is the time of reality. The time of fantasy was when wages and salary were paid just in the interest of creating jobs, but reality came up when Eastern Nigerian began making decisions for productivity and sales. The change of environment is the time of dialogue and is the time of deep thinking; it is the time of strategic restructuring. Then, Eastern Nigeria had many issues at stake, if they never happened to look for remedies to the issues left to them by the British, the estate could have been bankrupt.

These types of change in the environment occurred all over Africa as the colonialists were leaving the continent. The worst thing was that most African countries were not given the chance to see what the colonialists were doing in their own countries, even though independence was given to unprepared Africans. Many African countries began running their countries on a trial-and-error basis, because when the environment changed, they were simply left in the cold because they did not know what to do. PAMOLE was obviously one of them but lastly had their priorities in perspective.

A		**B**
More Work Available		Lower Prices
High Interest Rates	Profit Squeeze	Costlier Funds
Inflation		Higher Operating Costs

1. In Column A we see that we have a lot of work to do before we have the final product, which is palm oil; yet, in Column B we realize that prices paid are lower than the work performed.
2. We also realize that interest rates from the bank are high and therefore, funds are costlier.
3. Inflation comes up high as a result of higher operating costs.

The estate managers sensed that dramatic changes were occurring. Therefore, they identified environmental factors that were responsible for the poor productivity and sales.

The environmental profit squeeze have not been so severe with the palm oil estates in a Ibiae, including the farm settlement in Erei and Ikun and the rubber estate in Biakpan because the development of the estate and the sale arrangements have been done by Eastern Nigerians. The feasibility studies were done by them, the productivity and sales arrangements have been done by the people of Eastern Nigeria. Therefore, the level of failure has been minimal as opposed to what it might have if someone else had researched and put up for sales. Environmental constraints are often the cause of many failures in business, but sometimes the failure can be remedied. Today, the world economy is taking a tumble because of factors that include low oil and gas prices that affect countries who depend on oil revenues and companies for whom oil and gas production is their mainstay.

Sometimes environmental constraints are not the first thing to realize in business. Environmental constraints may be considered later on but the environment is the "back burner" of any business feasibility study or analysis. A limitation to accomplish anything one wants to do should never be forgotten when dealing in business. Environmental constrains are much like making a family budget; one may not keep budgeting without knowing exactly what one has in the bank and what one is expected to have in the near future. Making mention of profits and loss is very important when analyzing the outcome of a business.

Again, if we have more jobs to do while wages paid for the jobs are so low, we are now talking about profit squeeze if all profits were made. At the same time, we do understand that interest rates re the cost of funding. Therefore, if the interest rates are high, eventually the cost of funding the business will be high. Higher operating costs may mean more money in circulation, which also may mean more money chasing fewer goods that bring about inflation.

Patterns of Organization

Longenecker and Pringle (1984) stated that this section explains the way in which individual jobs—machine operators, engineers, accountants, sales representatives, and others are grouped for purposes of management. We accept the jobs themselves as given and concentrate upon relationships among them. In choosing a pattern, managers have options in grouping jobs into particular departments. At the top level are two basic structural patterns. Perhaps the best known is the functional pattern in which the type of activity or function serves as the organizing principle. The tax office at city hall or the sales organization of a small manufacturer are examples of functional departments.

FUNCTIONAL PATTERN OF ORGANIZATION

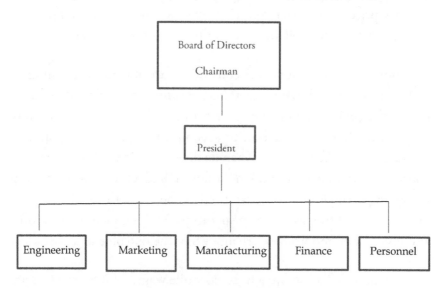

The major alternative to the functional pattern is the divisional organization, and it has two varieties. The most popular form, product divisionalization, brings together activities related to a given product line; for example, manufacturing and sales activities related to refrigerator appliances. Other organizations such as the Federal Reserve banking system, use geography as the basis for divisional grouping.

Divisionalization frequently goes hand-in-hand with decentralization of authority. Major segments of the General Motors Corporation, for example, operate somewhat autonomously under the general direction of the corporation. (Longenecker & Pringle, 1984).

Function as the Pattern

Longenecker and Pringle (1984 commented that small manufacturing enterprises find the functional pattern particularly appropriate. This pattern is not limited to the top level of an organization; however, within the manufacturing department (a functional department) work may be further subdivided on the basis of function. This level may include drilling, grinding, painting, and so forth. Different offic4e units similarly may perform typing, filing, and messenger services.

Efficiency and economy are among the more important advantages of functional organization, especially for relatively small companies. All selling, for example, is concentrated in one department. A potential weakness in the functional pattern is its tendency to encourage narrowness of viewpoints. It is easy for functional executives and personnel to look at problems from the standpoint of selling or manufacturing or some other functional specialty, rather than seeing all of these from the viewpoint of a company as a whole. Growth in an organization may produce strain on the functional organization. Extreme product diversification and widespread territorial expansion, in particular, contribute to the difficulty of successfully operating on a simple functional pattern (Longenecker & Pringle, 1984).

Product as the Pattern

Longenecker & Pringle (1984) stated further than product patterns are used not only at the top level (product divisionalization), but also at lower levels. In a functional sales department, for example, sales personnel may be specialized on the basis of product lines. Similarly, the grouping of college professors into such departments as English,

Philosophy, and Economics provides an example in the field of education. The advantages of product divisionalization are particularly significant in the case of a highly diversified product line. The work of manufacturing or sales personnel in a consumer products division, for example, is drastically different from the work of similar personnel in atomic power division. Product patterns permit specialization in terms of the product or group of products. Executive development is another attractive feature of product divisionalization. In the functional organization, executives are trained in functional areas and imbued with functional viewpoints. Only by rotating positions or service in different areas do the individuals acquire experience outside their own field of specialization. In contrast, the general manager and assistant manager of product development are responsible for dealing with issues in various functional areas including production, sales, research, and development (Longenecker & Pringle, 1984).

The Geographic Pattern

Longenecker & Pringle, (1984) also commented that some organizations use geographic divisions rather than product divisions as their primary pattern. This includes some business corporations, even though most divisionalized business firms follow the product pattern. In the geographic division structure of the Prudential Insurance Company, each of the nine regional home offices is headed by a president who directs operations including the selling and servicing of individual and group insurance in his or her territory. The actuarial staff in each regional office has the freedom to underwrite new business within actuarial standards set by the corporate office. All regional home offices have their own staff and service divisions in public relations, advertising, methods, research, and personnel administration.

Longenecker & Pringle, 1984 also commented that geographic divisionalization has certain advantages in common with the product pattern. Breadth of management experience is secured in the administration of regional areas. Financial control of operations is also facilitated because managers can prepare a separate income statement for each geographic area and determine its contribution to corporate profits.

Creating the Organizational Structure

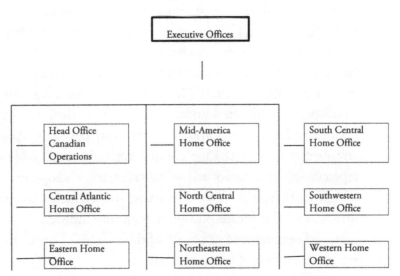

Prudential Insurance Company of America Regional Office Organization

The locational format is also used at lower level in organizing sales activities; for example, adaptation to local situations and knowledge of customer needs peculiar to a given area are facilitated by the locational pattern (Longenecker & Pringle, 1984).

Human Factors in Structural Decisions

Personal and Organizational Goals

Longenecker & Pringle (1984) stated further than as in other phases of business enterprises, decisions about organizational structure affects both the organization and its members. These effects are not necessarily the same for all parties involved. What is good for the organization is not necessarily good for the individuals; hence, the following framework:

1. <u>Achievement of Organizational Purpose</u>. A structural change is typically introduced because of its presumed benefit for the particular organization. Formal evaluation of a proposed change is made almost exclusively in terms of this particular value. Few changes have a chance for adoption if they cannot be shown to have positive advantages in terms of this dimension.

2. <u>Achievement of Self Maintenance and Growth</u>. Members of organizations are also concerned with organizational changes for purely personal reasons. Organizational decisions are made by real managers interested in their own career advancement who operate with the blinders derived from their particular backgrounds, training, and organizational positions. Almost any organizational change could have quick and profound repercussions in terms of an individual's status and opportunity for growth. Jobs may be eliminated, departments trimmed in size, and the future possibilities for any individual greatly curtailed or enhanced as a result of the changes. Threats to the status of existing departments and positions, therefore, may arouse major opposition.

3. <u>Achievement of Social Satisfaction</u>. Employees derive social satisfaction from the work group. They feel themselves a part of a social group and enjoy the contacts and friendships involved in their association with others. A change of organization may disrupt the social group and social relationships of affected employees. It is apparent that the change might be viewed as negative and threatening to existing satisfactory social relationships or the changed situation might be welcomed because of a promised improvement in social relationships.

To illustrate the concept, suppose that production employees worked in small groups with each employee assigned to a part of a closely-integrated team. Then, suppose that for technological reasons, the nature of the work arrangements was changed to break up the work teams that existed. If these employees were removed from their original groups, scattered as individual members along an assembly line, and denied all opportunity for close social relationships with other employees, they might be less satisfied. Measured along this dimension, then, organization change prompted by considerations of organizational efficiency might, at the same time, be damaging to the personal social satisfaction of employees (Longenecker & Pringle, 1984).

Questions

1. What is individual growth and development?
2. Comment on the geographic pattern.
3. Describe strategy and structure in your words and ideas.
4. Discuss the critical view of organizational planning.
5. What is formal organization?
6. What is environment?

Answers

1. Individual growth and development is concerned with organizational change for purely personal reasons by managers who are interested in their own career advancement and who operate with the blinders derived from their particular backgrounds, training, and organizational positions. Almost any organizational change could have quick and profound repercussions in terms of an individual's status and opportunity for growth, jobs may be eliminated, departments trimmed in size, and the future possibilities for any individual greatly curtailed or enhanced as a result of the change. Threats to the status of existing departments and positions, therefore, may arouse major opposition.

2. Some organizations use geographic divisions rather than projects as their primary pattern. This includes some business corporations, even though most divisionalized firms follow the product pattern. In the geographic division structure of Prudential Insurance Company, each of the nine regional home offices is headed by a president who directs operations including

the selling and servicing of individual and group insurance in his or her territory. The actuarial staff in each regional office has the freedom to underwrite new business within actuarial standards set by the corporate office. All regional home offices have their own staff and service divisions in public relations, advertising, methods, research, and personnel administration.

3. As environments change, organizations devise new strategies and adapt their structures to pursue those strategies. There is a saying in Effick that goes "eyeowong etie ukap ukap abooi etie ukap ukap," meaning if a young person is crafty, his or her creditor changes his way of dealing with him or her or if a young person changes his or her dealing with parents, the parents must devise means of combating the changes. In this case, environment could mean government agents while the organization could mean the people they govern.

    Recently, we have seen in the United States that some policemen and women have become impatient in dealing with people. A case in point occurred in California where a boy of 10 years of age was playing with a toy gun and pointed it at a police officer. The officer asked the boy to drop the gun; the boy refused much as boys of his age would do. Without hesitation, the officer shot the boy dead before finding out that the boy was holding only a toy gun. Many stories such as that have sparked a series of demonstrations in the country. Even though two policemen were killed later because the killer did not understand that the series of demonstrations were not meant to get even with the police but for changes in policy. So, the environment has been created that has resulted in unnecessary policing that has also made citizens react with a series of demonstrations simply to change the policies. Even when the police offers are tried and convicted, the policies have not changed that would not mean better policing; subjects and police officers must work together. =By the same token, poor products must enable producers to get ready with high quality products in order to compete in the global marketplace. Of course, if the same productivity persists, the end results may be bankruptcy.

4. Administrators and scholars do not agree on the desirability of expensive organization planning. Critics argue that some flexibility in relationships and procedures is desirable. These critics feel that excessive detail in specifying responsibilities is stifling and that efficient operation can be achieved without extensive organization planning and without its paraphernalia including charts and manuals. In general, critics of the carefully planned organization object to rigid chains of command organization charts that become ends in themselves. Bureaucracy is replaced by bureau pathology in which red tape triumphs and means become the ends. These critics condone some leapfrogging over supervisory echelons and crossing over organization lines to reach into other departments with ideas, suggestions, and criticism. Both advocates and critics of organization planning have a point, and that is it is desirable to study and structure organizational relationships. At the same time, some flexibility is necessary in practical day-to-day organizational life.

5. Formal organization is visualized as a pyramid of officials who direct and coordinate the work of specialists by use of formal procedures. It is considered important that roles be carefully defined and rules for interaction clearly delineated. The formal organization makes up the skeleton for the social system and is supplemented by informal relationships that develop spontaneously among organization members without explicit definition by management.

6. Organizations exist in different environments. We recognize, for example, that steel producers, residential builders, private universities, and public utilities each face substantially different external environments. Some environments are described as stable and predictable, whereas others are characterized by shifting conditions, uncertainty, and difficulty in predicting the course of events. Uncertainty in a business environment is created by the existence of many competitors and competitive

products, broad price ranges, price instability, and numerous changes in product knowledge.

However, the differences in an environment can severely affect the organization structure and more so in a multicultural society such as the United States where organizations can be complicated. In a homogeneous society like Japan or Nigeria, the differences between environment and organization are culturally based. In a multicultural society such as in the city of San Francisco in the United States, where I lived for many years, the differences between the city's downtown business organizations and the Chinatown businesses can be seen in a variety of ways like the prices of products and the product quality. In San Francisco's Chinatown, prices are subject to negotiations, while in the city's financial district, the price you see is the price you pay and so on.

CHAPTER 17
MARKETING

CHAPTER 17

MARKETING

Marketing is one in which economic activities are left to men and women freely responding to the opportunities and discouragements of the marketplace, not to the established routines of tradition or the dictates of someone's commands. A market in capital means that there is a regular flow of wealth into production—a flow of savings and investments organized through banks and other financial institutions where borrowers pay interest as the price for using the wealth of the lenders. There was nothing like this before capitalism, except in the very small and disreputable capital markets personified in the despised money lender (Heilbroner & Thurow, 1998). The services of labor, land, and capital that are hired or fired in a market society are called the factors of production (Heilbroner & Thurow, 1998).

However, let us return to the *market in capital*; growing up in Ikun in my early years with Chief Uno Egim, his impact was felt in and around the jurisdiction of Ikun. He was not just a warrior, but he was a multimillionaire of the time. The Ikun community primary school was to be upgraded from standard five to standard six. The Ministry of Education wanted the community to build a few classrooms more and have a head master's office, including a homework teacher's demonstration facility. To contribute to the development was not an easy task.

The project began in 1954 and was to be ready by 1959 for classes to begin in 1960; yet, half of the job was not done, so Chief Uno Egim applied the principles of *market in capital* where capital could freely flow into the project. So, when the inspectors from the Ministry of Education visited the project, they recommended that the Ikun Community should be given standard six in 1959 instead of 1960. So, Chief Uno Egim was paid back his money with interest by the Ikun Community.

Market in Capital sometimes has a different meaning for the developing nations than in the developed nations. In developing nations, market in capital could be a status symbol. The lender may not have enough money for the project and may borrow from friends and family in order to fund the project. Even if the activities are regarded as a status symbol, yet economic activity has taken place, even though it has only cultural recognition.

In the western world, market in capital has a clear meaning. The money is either borrowed from a bank, a group of investors, or just from a single individual just in the interest of capital flow to implement production on hand. Thus, it is a free flow of capital to accomplish production. Having heard a little about developing and developed nations on market in capital is purely based on business principles while in developing nations, market in capital could be based upon both being a status symbol and business principles because of the dual ways of administration in developing nations (status symbols and business principles).

Marketing is a human activity directed at satisfying need and wants through the exchange process. Exchange occurs when there are at least two parties and each has something of potential value for the other. When the two parties can communicate and have the ability to deliver the desired goods or services, exchange can take place. In the United States, exchange typically involves one party offering money and other a product or service. For example, when you obtained this book, you probably exchanged cash for the text at a bookstore (McDaniel, 1982).

Having become aware of what marketing is all about and then researched and experienced the process, I came up with the functions of marketing:

1) Delivery;
2) Efficiency;
3) Wealth;
4) Competition; and
5) Awareness.

Before continuing, let me give some background information for my marketing functions. Years ago, just after Nigerian independence was gained from Britain in 1960, primary highways and even feeder roads were constructed based on political connections. Economic activities were not even considered, but as time went on, food became scarce commodity in cities, and so salaries were spent on rent and food. Eventually, the feeder roads became essential to connect with the villages in order to reduce the cost of food delivered to stores in cities. Food then became cheaper and more affordable for city dwellers. This illustrates my five principles.

Delivery – inaccessible roads that were impossible to get through became very accessible. Trucks and cars could be seen running to and fro on the feeder rods. A cup of garri that sold for 25 cents a cup in cities could now be bought for 10 cents and even cheaper. For some reason, gasoline prices stabilized; delivery not only affected good roads but also aided the tourism industry and the standard of living. This is what I call practical marketing, which does not need radio or television advertising for awareness. Good roads and delivery systems are not only responsible for our better standard of living, but also created more after marketing strategies for other commodities and thus helped the efficiency of village production.

Efficiency. Marketing is not a "one-way street" because you sell and then, in turn, you buy the area where you sold your commodities. This creates efficiency if the products you bought from one producer are of the same kind but more expensive than what you produced. Then, you have to understand that the products have more value than your own product so that you have to step up to produce a better product or at least of the same quality as the competition. The case here is that if other producers or consumers buy your products and consequently you bought from producers who made your kind of product, the tendency is for both parties to compare quality, and so each may modify any deficiencies in their own product. This, then, creates efficiency if modification was performed the way it should be based on the availability of raw materials, equipment, and manpower. With efficient productivity, employees become more hopeful about the future.

Wealth. This is a large function of marketing; a case in point is my own case where I have written five books, but my revenue is mere "chicken feed" meaning that I make very little revenue because I do not have enough funds for advertising apart from the Internet. In the United States, if you want to make money from your products, then you have to advertise and understand it is not very affordable. In developing countries, highways and feeder roads are the mainstays of sale, and wealth, then, is the scenario with developed nations. Nigeria has stepped up road construction ever since it became the largest economy in Africa, especially in the construction of feeder roads.

Wealth created by either the governments or companies is what I call "community wealth" because such wealth is owned by every citizen. Private roads may not be very private either because delivery vehicles may use them also, but most feeder roads are fairly short in length. Creation of wealth can be done in different ways including being gainfully employed or self-employed, but most wealth is created by proximity and accessibility to locations of businesses. Therefore, roads are necessary for the creation of a better standard of living.

<u>Competition</u>. This is a great function of marketing. Competition can be based on the product itself or its price. If the products have the same raw materials, each producer will see the type of equipment that his competition uses and may try to see where the best equipment can be obtained. The next, and very important, factor is manpower, and then location and access roads. All things being equal, competition will be high if only prices are taken into consideration.

Price competition and product efficiency are closely connected because if the product is efficient, the price may not matter for some consumers. However, if the prices are comparable with other producers' items, but more efficient than that of the competition, then, of course, the producer of the efficient product stands to sell more products. Price competition is a very artistic work and must be done with care by the producer discovering what the competition sells its products for in order to make quick adjustments where necessary. Price competition is tricky and requires current information with a full-time employee managing it. However, product efficiency is the core solution to marketing and more effective than pricing that is backed by nothing.

<u>Awareness</u>. This aspect is closely associated with accomplishment. One has to be aware of what he or she is doing or will be doing in order to be creative. Every company or institution must operate for the present as well as its future projections. The company must be very conscious regarding what it does; its decision-making process must balance with the economic effectiveness of the business. The feasibility studies that were made before the business began must not be forgotten but reassessed. A careful evaluation of any competition must be made before moving into the market. A blind competitive move may produce a negative result that may mean management is unaware of their current market situation that led to price or product competition or both.

It is difficult to do anything well with no awareness at all. Doing things without being aware of the marketplace is tantamount to not knowing what you are doing. We research and develop the facts for a research paper; by that time, the writer has become aware of what he or she intends to write about. Awareness enables a book writer to be capable of defending the book. Even though most of the facts may have come from various sources, the writer has made the facts his or her own through an awareness of what the writing is all about.

Awareness may mean being present, knowing what is going on at the moment, and trying hard to discard distractions. For example, if a competitor has been more profitable in a season than you have been, based on price competition, one does not leave the current research and engage in price competition. However, the company must be aware of what is going on in the industry. Awareness means *being* and not necessarily *doing*. If you are the leader of your company or the manager, one has to be in the state of being and never in the state of doing because *doing* may not give you the chance to listen, observe, and react positively.

Some companies have a shorter life span because they do not understand very well what the industry is all about. They list the information that the company has; they become worried and panic. This leads to lack of concentration on what needs to be done in order to compete effectively. Awareness, like any other factor in business, is also important. Living or managing in the present is an artistic work, and the mainstay of deep thinking. Managing in the present is not just knowing and understanding but includes creative understanding that increases output or productivity.

Market Segmentation

This is the process of dividing a given market into divisions in order to satisfy a given population of consumers. It is a strategy a producer uses to produce more products for consumers and may be based on taste, smell, or beauty meant for satisfaction of any kind. It is a method of dividing sales based on identified targets. For example, a farmer from Ikun in Biase of the Cross River State in Nigeria specialized in planting what Ikun people call Ogboto. This farmer made a good living

425

for his family. One season (one year) the famer decided to attend a red yam meeting, which he did, and discovered that it was more expensive planting white yams but very profitable planting red yams because a local research institution told red yam consumers that red yams contain an antioxidant. People from many parts of Nigeria heard about it through advertising on the Internet and became consumers.

The farmer instantly became interested in having a red yam farm, which Ikun people called Eviang, and he decided to attend a six-month course on how to plant the red yams and when to harvest them, as well as what the target market was for Eviang yam. The farmer had a long discussion with his wife and then proceeded to the business of farming the Eviang yam. After the training, the farmer went home smiling. As soon as he got home, he told his wife that the Eviang farm was not complicated and the procedure was very much like Ogboto farming, except for some variations based on weather conditions and planting locations. The farmer then cleared quite a large portion of land and planted the 2000 Eviang yams they had bought from the local market. The most important duty was to have the farm cleared of weeds much like the Ogboto yam farm. The Ogboto yam was planted between February and March and harvested between December and January, while the red yam was planted between March and April and harvested between February and March. Ogboto and Eviang consumers were in every community, and that made the producer aware that it was necessary to assemble white and red yams side by side or clearly identify the audience and be able to transport each segment directly to its consumer. It was fairly difficult for the first year, but the farmer more than broke even in the second year and afterward. The transactions became so routine and made more profit year after year. The farmer and his wife discovered more consumers in many communities. Consumers even applied for the market mix; these were also yam business people who owned their own transportation and were able to sell their yams in distant places and were able to double their purchasing prices. Market segment is a division that makes it very possible for consumers to buy what they want at a given price or to be informed about they want at a given price.

Segmentation is predicated upon examining a market with one or several criteria and then designing a marketing mix to reach the target segment. It is a market-oriented strategy.

Product Differentiation

Product differentiation has a different conceptual basis from market segmentation. The objective here is to distinguish one finished product from another. The differences can be either real or superficial. The bases for product differentiation are usually brand name, minor ingredients, product features variations, and packaging. Thus, the manufacturers of one aspirin will tell you that "doctors recommend it most "; another one says that their aspirin "gets into the bloodstream faster"; and yet another will state, "it won't upset your stomach." Promotion is the vehicle that makes product differentiation work. It the consumer over and over again that Brand A is different from Brand B (McDaniel, 1982).

Buyer Behavior

Consumers may be motivated by several actors including the following: 1) the type of purchase; 2) resources of the buyer; and 3) the usefulness of the product for the buyer.

I had a friend who viewed a product that a high school friend used, but he was short of money at the time, so he passed the product by for the time being. Then, as a young man he travelled to far western part of Nigeria not far from Lagos where, to his surprise, he came upon the same product but again had no money on him for purchasing it. The young man became very inquisitive and asked the salespeople if the product was always in stock, how much it cost, and about the usefulness of product. Later, when he traveled back home and happened to go to the far eastern part of Nigeria, he brought extra cash with him, and, luckily, he saw the product again. In fact, he simply asked for the product's price, and with no questions he bought it. Many producers usually come up with imitations of the same product. This young man was by no means a rich man, but he was able to buy the product because of its quality and durability. He was able to buy the product because he avoided many other products that he could have bought and save his money for that particular product, which eventually became an opportunity type cost for the young man, meaning that the young man could only afford the product and could not afford any other products or services, or the money he had could only cover the cost of that product and nothing else, meaning he could only buy one thing at a time because of lack of funds.

Resources of the Buyer

This story of the young man who created an opportunity cost for himself by ignoring all he could have purchased just for one product he desired tells us that where there is a desire for something there is usually a way. Another way of viewing buyer behavior is that some buyers prefer saving their money upon first seeing something they desire or need, and when they eventually do buy the product, they prefer the least expensive item, while people with greater resources may prefer the more expensive version. This means buying a product comes down to *preference* on the part of the buyer and not really because of fewer resources. What I am saying here is that occasionally money becomes an issue, but in some cases, a buyer's preference takes center stage—what the buyer perceives as being more valuable to him or her rather than the price of the product. Therefore, the complaint is about a lack of money when product preferences of the product then available are nonexistent.

Earlier I discussed the opportunity costs, which is about having the money for only buying one thing and not enough for buying something else. Some buyers can afford them either by making a down payment or by buying outright on credit. In the case of a down payment, if the price of the commodity is $100.00 or more, then the down payment may require 10% of the price being paid up front, or for $100.00, $10.00. Therefore, the buyer can buy all of the items he wanted to buy by paying 10% or even 20% (or $20 in the case of $100.00) and pay the remainder in installments, either weekly or monthly, until the debt is liquidated. Outright credit means the buyer pays no money down such as in the down payment process, but may pay interest, known as APR, on the amount that is on credit. In either case, the buyer takes the product or products home with him/her that day.

The Usefulness of Product for the Buyer

If a Mr. Johnson has a headache and the only medicine the doctor has prescribed for him was Excedrin to relieve the paid, then the buyer may cease buying expensive breakfasts in order to have enough money to purchase the headache medication. If the consumer were to take an examination but had no pen with which to write, even though he has enough money to buy coffee, which may be the same price as a pen, the consumer has to make a choice. All things being equal, the individual taking the examination may prefer to buy a pen (an opportunity cost) since the money he has can only pay for a pen and not a pen and coffee.

Another example would be on a Christmas day, coming from a Christian home, your daughter desires to go out on an outing with her friends, but she only has a pair of old shoes to war. These shoes are worn and are over three year old. Buying new shoes for your daughter may be as important as buying your lunch because seeing your daughter with her friends on a busy, friendly Christmas Day may increase your life expectancy because of the happiness and pleasure you received from seeing your daughter happy with her friends. You may buy your daughter shoes and anything else, but you cannot buy her pleasure at being with her friends on a specific Christmas Day celebration.

The happiness of parents is quite different from that of a young boy or girl especially having dressed up on a Christmas Day, singing and praising Israeli for successful return from Egypt under slavery. A direct example from any society portraying the usefulness to the buyer is that of a young man who recently graduated from high school and has decided to become a truck driver, but he must have a license for that position. So, he applied to a truck driving school, was accepted, but was informed that the school fees have been increased by 2%. It was $100 a semester and now is $110. The young man calculated all the benefits of even paying higher fees. Again, the obstacle was that he had no money for the school fees. He then started driving a taxi and saving his money for the school fees. He finally passed his test and received his truck driver's license, even though it took him one extra semester to complete the course because he had to work to pay the school's fees. A month later the young man was driving a truck with an experienced truck driver and after three months' probation, he was assigned his own truck to drive. Therefore, the fact that the young man paid more for his license and even took more time to obtain his license did not bother him because he was able to fulfill his dream of being a truck driver. Therefore, a product in need is a product indeed, meaning that one does not care about the cost of what he or she likes best.

Another example is that of a man who was going to an important meeting very well dressed. Unfortunately, he went to catch a bus, as he was no driving, and it began to rain. Luckily, he found a bus stop shelter, and so he moved quickly into the shelter. Behind the shelter, an individual was selling umbrellas of various kinds. He met with the umbrella merchant and asked how much he wanted for a particular umbrella that had caught his attention. The merchant quickly said, "$25.00." The man became very impatient, and without any hesitation, paid the merchant $25.00 and thanked him for his service. Then, he moved quickly to the oncoming bus. This event shows the usefulness of the umbrella for that individual at that point in time.

Dynamics of Change

An example of the dynamics of change occurs in the story of a young girl who grew up seeing most of her friends graduated from colleges as nurses and teachers. She invited both of her parents to her room and told them that she was graduating from high school that year, and they commented that "yes," they knew that. She then went on to tell them that she wanted to be a mechanical engineer, and they said, "What?" Her mother said, "Go, girl," but her father asked if her skills in mathematics was strong enough. She had made a "B" in algebra only a semester previously. So, the girl promised to work harder on her mathematics skills. The mother told her husband that she knew that he thought mechanical engineering was a man's world, but she thought they should give their daughter support she needed. The father quickly said, "Young lady, you have my blessing, and please do not hesitate to ask me for help if you think that I can help you or if I can pay someone to help you in the difficult course you have chosen. Your mother and I will team up, to make sure that your dream comes true for you." The daughter (Mary) was very happy upon hearing that her father would support her in her dream because he had been very critical of himself for having no son.

The wife was a nurse, his older daughter was in her final year of nursing school, and so when Mary was born, he said, "Here we go again; another nursing student has been born." Everyone smiled, but Mary's mother privately wept bitterly because she had not given birth to a son for her husband to cherish. However, Mr. Johnson (Mary's father) and his wife encouraged Mary to work harder. Astonishingly, Mary became the valedictorian of her class. When she was asked to speak, she became very emotional and was unable to talk; her father shouted, "My strong young lady, I am over here, go ahead."

Her father was also emotional because when he had been invited by his friends, each of them said something about their family. Mary's father proudly stood up and told his friends that his daughter would study become a mechanical engineer. Surprising to Mr. Johnson, all his so-called friends laughed, and said "Yeah, right." One of his friends said, "Why doesn't your daughter try to become a medical doctor, who is very womanly, rather than a mechanical engineer." Mr. Johnson stood up and said, "That's it, you are more sexist than I ever thought you would be," and quietly walked out.

Then, he was no longer thinking about gender when his wife, Comfort, had her third pregnancy, and behold another change occurred. She had a baby boy, and Mr. Johnson was drained of emotion. Although he told his wife that no nurse would be good enough for his son except for Comfort and himself. Mr. Johnson said, "My pastor has talked about miracles, but today I found one in my family." Mr. Johnson held his wife and kissed her and thanked God.

Comfort called on God and thanked Him for making the family's dream come true; her daughter had graduated high in her class and was the class valedictorian because of her hard work and discipline and now the couple had their first son. "Lord, I couldn't thank you more," Comfort exclaimed. Both husband and wife became very happy over all the changes that had occurred in their family. They were now the parents of two daughters and newly-born son, who they named Charles. Chelsea, the oldest daughter, had become a nurse like her mother, while Mary became a mechanical engineer. The family had become almost dysfunctional because of the father's unhappiness at not having a son, through no fault of his wife, In any case, all of that was behind the Johnson family, and their hopes for a better future was enhanced. The Johnsons became devoted Christians and very thankful for their blessings. Mr. Johnson learned that the family must always come first.

Nigerian Independence

The flip side of the dynamics of change occurred after Great Britain granted independence to Nigeria. At first, it was a welcome scene; all Africa rejoiced that Nigeria has become an independent country, even though a few individuals in Africa suspected that political anarchy might be coming soon because of the events preceding independence. Independence was to have been granted earlier, but the political disagreements and squabbling became a stumbling block and made it appear that Nigeria was not ready for independence. However, the various leaders made them appear to be united, and in 1960 Nigeria became an independent nation. A marching at the time went, "Nigeria, we hailed thee, but our own dear native land, though tribes and tongues may differ, in brotherhood we stand."

A few years later, a general election was a test for brotherhood, and for what the country represented. In fact, the general election proved Nigeria was no way near brotherhood; anarchy might be the better word for what occurred because human lives became just the price of a bullet. Federal and state governments were the same; no one was able to advise the other. The military stepped in big time and killed many politicians. There was political darkness in the history of Nigeria, but gradually the dynamics of change began taking shape, the Nigeria economy grew stronger than expected, economic activities were diversified. The oil and gas industry, which was expected to be 50% of the Nigerian GDP, actually became only 15% of the GDP. Agriculture, which was almost destroyed by the instability of the country, now made up over 35% of the GDP, and most surprisingly, the industrial sector, which is now 50% of the GDP, has pushed Nigeria into being the largest economy in Africa.

MAP OF AFRICA

Yet, as I am writing this chapter, perfection is far from attainable; someone called me from Nigeria and told me that the atmosphere of unrest is rising in the Eastern states of Nigeria because the newly-elected president, General Buhari, has selected his ministers from the north and western states of Nigeria with no representatives from the East. This is against the representative provision in the Nigerian constitution and thereby is providing a fertile ground for people in Eastern Nigeria to secede from the union and declare itself an independent country. The military, once again, has been asked to quell the unrest, and I do not know how this will end. However, according to the reliable sources this is rumor that voters should make President Buharri a one-term president and vote against him in the next presidential election.

I think that is politics or the law of politics in Effik or Calabar where we say, "Utu ke mbok esin uda yak edim edep," meaning "instead of resting to bring catastrophe, let it rain." Of course, when it rains, outdoor roofing, which is very cultural, stops. This is the same thing with politics; any president who does not perform well in his or her administration then should be voted down in the next election instead of creating unrest or turmoil.

Nigeria today is the largest economy in Africa, and situation where unrest abounds is not good for any economy; therefore, I think that Nigeria should "give to Caesar what belongs to Caesar and to God what belongs to God." I mean by that expression Nigeria should give to politics what belongs in politics and disagree when disagreement is necessary. Nigeria should always aim at a progressive government, not a regressive one. The regressive administration Nigeria had before cause the most suffering to the minority population, and at the end of the Biafra War, there were no discussions about all of the atrocities committed by both sides. Nobody was arrested despite innocent people being killed, banks looted, and villages burned to ashes. Those who witnessed the breakdown of law and order in this time should never think about breaking down law and order again. Even though I was fairly young at the time, I do not know if some 60-year old people have witnessed such events. An elected official needs a political solution not a division or war. I have come to believe that the dynamics of change can be either good or bad.

I know that the Iraq War lead by the United States under the leadership of President George Walker Bush and supported by Great Britain and other countries was carefully thought through, thinking it might be like the Second World War where Germany and Japan were defeated and later became world economic powers. However, the Axis Powers (Germany/Japan) and the U.S./Great Britain alliance and the rest of the world was a much more civilized conflict than the Iraqi-U.S. War. The Iraqi-U.S. War has been a clear case of the dynamics of change, and we have to remember the use of weapons of mass destruction on his people by Saddam Hussein. President Bush thought that enough was enough and, of course, Hussein was warned to leave and go into exile like Philippine ex-President Marcos, but Hussein would not do that. Apparently, Saddam Hussein was killed by his people, and the same thing happened to Gadhafi of Libya. We truly have a lot to learn about the world's new order. The Iraq War reminds me of ant soldiers who protect their young and the weaker ones and anyone who goes against them must cause them to scatter all over the place and attack whoever they come in contact with. The anti's may arrange themselves in groups or semi-groups of a few antis who can also inflict terror. More than any other thing, civilized and uncivilized war must be analyzed and studies before embarking on such wars again. A clear difference between civilized and uncivilized war is that you may know when the war began, but you may have no idea when it will or may end, and—that is uncivilized war. However, in civilized war one party must surrender and the killing must stop immediately.

I am not saying that the Western World has no idea about how uncivilized wars are fought. After all, it was General Powell, former U.S. Secretary of State, who said that, "if you break it, you must own it." That is what is happening today; everybody wants ISIS to be stopped. On November 22, 2015 U.S. Senator Diane Feinstein on the program *Meet the Press* on CBS asked President Barak Obama to stop ISIS from advancing even though all other semi-groups have begun worldwide. However, stopping ISIS might mean keeping the subgroups on the run.

Later, the world leaders and heads of state, including President Obama, met in France to discuss climate change. I know they could not talk about climate change isolated from the war against ISIS. I think some countries might think that France needed help. That is a mistake; rather, the world needs help because what is at stake here is the global economy. Do we know if France and Western Europe have been experiencing poor macroeconomic management? We know that an economy does not grow in unstable economic conditions. The interesting part of the global economy is that whatever effects one country negatively affects all other countries in the world to a greater or lesser degree. Although some countries may be in denial of this, sooner or later they will begin facing the realities of the economic downturn. That is one of the reasons the Paris France conference is commended by both politicians and economists.

The sooner the world economy stabilizes, the better it will be for every country or possibly every country will become economically wealthy. The world today has to remember the Nigerian anthem which should now say, "The world we hailed thee, though countries and tongues may differ, in brotherhood we stand." I think that this is the type of philosophy we need today. We have enough religious beliefs; we have to summarize our beliefs and call it *Love*. I think that God himself is tired of all our clamoring and/or stupid claims. All the unnecessary claims we have introduced are causing us so many problems in every sphere of life, including economic wealth. I hope the dreams and hopes of my children fare better than that of my dreams and hopes because our unrealistic dreams and hopes are making me sick.

The most unusual situation in the quest for Nigerian independence was that Great Britain never resisted granting independence to Nigeria; rather, the country could have had independence earlier but for discrepancies among Nigerians. The only thing I might comment about was the non-inclusive attitude ono the part of the British in their administrative decisions, which were made in London and handed down to Nigerians for strict adherence. That I think was the starting point for the Nigerian disagreement amongst themselves because some political parties wanted Nigerian culture to be in the mix, while other political parties wanted administrative copyright from Britain. The confusion brought about social and political anarchy to the entire country, which was a nightmare for all.

Eventually, one disagreement led to another until a civil war erupted for two years. Nigerian economic development was held to a standstill, 1968-1969, but not the disagreement that led to the civil war that were created by foreign ideology and tribal understanding, and, of course, some religious beliefs. It became virtually impossible for one to listen to anyone; the center couldn't hold anyone or rather social and political anarchy developed faster than the expected economic development. However, when the citizens of Nigeria realized that the destruction of their country was not to anyone's interest, the voices of reason began to take control once again. Nigerians who somehow found it difficult to stay permanently in a different country heard the government's appeal for Nigerians living abroad should return (mostly business owners) because tax incentives and funds were available for them to develop business. On that note, many Nigerians returned.

Even though many promises were not kept immediately, business owners were better served than staying in a foreign country. In the long term, all of the promises made by the Nigerian government were implemented and the news spread like wildfire. People began returning home. Farmers began cultivating the land once again, importation of food ceased, savings in banks increased, and bank loans became more available for qualified borrowers. Life in Nigeria began taking on a different shape for the most populous country in Africa. Without any doubt, today, Nigeria is the largest economy in Africa.

With this fast pace of development in Nigeria, women were still left out, and most politicians and many of the more wealthy people believe that it took two to tango, meaning that it took husband and wife to make a family. However, less than 50% of the Nigerian population believe that way, while a greater portion of the country felt that Nigeria could grow independently, being a capitalist country and a country of law. Some argued that boys and girls should take a look at the Nigerian Senate and House of Representatives where men made up most of the members. If they were worried about playing such hardball, they might do better in business and other professions they could choose. Most men and women in Nigeria intimated that women needed self-awakening to get themselves moving because in universities in Nigeria there were thousands of professors, with M.A.'s, Ph.D.'s, and other degrees. Many of the women made more money than men because in Nigeria an academic degree and experience mattered most in employment, but calculating how many men and women businesses exist becomes much more complicated than when men had a monopoly on positions because today many businesses are owned either by husband wife or brother and sister. In either case, the eight executives lead the company. In Nigeria today, much is also expected of the women because of their education, income, and percent of the population.

Today, the population of women in Nigeria is about two or three women to every man. The sexual population density has to be revised for more accuracy, but the facts are that women outnumber men. Primary school registration is a case in point, and university admissions could also indicate this. The work force and any other human endeavor without women looks so illegitimate or very much not wanted by the electorate, yet the core jobs are held by men and even accepted by women. Jobs such as heavy lifting deep sea diving, and many other physical labor jobs are not very important because of technology. However, men still in politics and education hold core positions because men began earlier than women, although the gap is closing fast. It will still take some generations to close it up.

Another Case in Point: US Elections

There is no clear explanation of the dynamics of change as clear as the American presidential elections between the Democratic Party, the Republican Party, and sometimes an independent third party. My purpose here is not to blame any one of the parties for anything, but to discuss the commonality of all the parties. What I am talking about is what the system needs to modernize in itself or to make sure that the country works competitively with other advanced countries.

First of all, there is campaign debates where everything within the human endeavor may be talked about in order to understand the positions of each candidate on an issue. This reaches from the first president of this great nation—George Washington—to President Lincoln, to President Clinton on up through President Obama. All of these men hold in common the need to make sure they understand what is wrong with the country that they desire to correct and what each individual candidate would do to correct the ills they see. Therefore, every four years, the candidates for president gear up for campaigns and debates and discussions of issues for over 200 years. One would think that most, if not all, of the things needed to be reinvented had all been done, but every four years the candidates have many new things so as to enable voters to rethink the issues and to vote for the dynamics of change. This entails a process that makes change an endless phenomenon or endeavor.

This is an enjoyable process in a democratic country which encourages research and development in an earlier stage. Even though this research and development may be conducted by the private sector, it may have government support financially or private investors may be of viable financial assistance.

We can China today through the changes that the communist government has permitted so that China is now the world's second largest economy. Changes are generally progressive, while no change is regressive. A regressive economy has no room for growth or its growth may be so slow and small and lack momentum for creativity and real growth. Real growth is a sustainable growth. CBS's program *Sixty Minutes* reported that Chinese productivity was based primarily on stealing secrets from other countries, primarily the United States, which explained that Chinese development is not deeply rooted. Of course, my ideas about Chinese development may be from my own biases, but the world today sees the United States as one of the progressive nations. Therefore, researchers prefer to assume and attribute all successes to the United States, since it is the most progressive and better known technologically the world has ever known. It may be ridiculous to think that a great nation such as China has copied its progress from a third world nation. So the United States becomes the nation of choice for this *copying* scenario.

However, the Japanese began by imitating the Americans and any other country that they felt was intelligent enough for the Japanese to forget the copyright laws. I think that capitalist laws or ideologies are the motivators of smart thinking and doing things and expecting big reward. I am also an example of this capitalist ideological research development; the eyewitness account got me to producing readable, interesting books for new ideas. The Western Europeans also came up with original ideas about many things we use today such as the cuneiform writing, the barter trade concept, and some ancient trading activities. The contributions from Asia, Africa, South and Central America—in fact, the entire world— throughout history have been many and great, but history has not been so kind to them in terms of relating accounts of their contributions to the world body. I think that what I am saying here is that every country in the earth has its own usefulness or contribution to its own people and eventually, the world as a whole, no matter how significant that contribution may be.

Another way of viewing dynamics of change is that our world today is polarized with conflicts that has segregated our world into religions, haves and have nots, educational standards, and other inequalities, most of which are simply due to changes in the communities. Religious changes in _____, black life in others in the United States; in both cases people are being killed for reasons best known to organizers. Sometimes, legitimately so and in some others this comes simply out of selfishness. Some people simply like things the way they have been since their grandparents or do not like any changes. The fact is that human beings have different ways of accepting or rejecting change.

The Power of Presentations

Presentations, whether academic or just friendly gatherings must contain or portray some sort of agenda or reasons for what you know about the subject, pros and cons of what you are talking about, economic reasons, political implications, of the subject, business applications, religious factors and so forth.

For some reason, students begin taking presentations seriously because of academic grading. In reality, presentations start at home; most parents do not realize what is happening between them and their children. Some parents may consider their child a good talker. In college, the young man may be a class prefect or something else, but the young man's professor may suggest there the young man should be headed in his life, even though the professor could be wrong. Having said all of that, every person is different and changes from time to time. Even then, the parents could suggest what their children could become in their lifetime, though we are never too certain.

The power of presentation should never be underestimated; for instance, the presidential elections, the CEO talking with his employees, the president of a country presenting his or her fiscal year projections. Let us return to our individual home; for example, the Ogban Family. Mr. Ogban had two boys, Etim and Bassey. Etim Ogban know exactly what he is looking for but does not know how to tell his parents that he may prefer to be a high school principal or in another profession than what his parents prefer. Mr. Ogban, the father, will tell his wife that Etim is just a joke; he is about 18 years of age and must know what he wants. Mr. Ogban continues to be impatient with Etim's indecision on his life, but Mrs. Ogban has told him that people grow differently. However, Etim still does not know how to present what he wants in his life to his parents, and his mother knows that this is becoming a problem. Etim was in his final year in high school and began perceiving that maybe his parents didn't like him, and his attitude began changing for the worse. This also began threatening the Ogban's marriage until a marriage counselor told them that Etim had done nothing wrong and that at his age, he needed directions that his parents had refused to give him. The counselor told the Ogbans that they were confusing young man and that they should give him instruction son how to ask for something from them and when Etim does, they should listen to him and not judge him. Etim's case is actually than presentation parents; it is a case of dialogue with parents.

The parents and Etim need to find ways of improving their thought processes, especially in groups where a solution depends on people reaching at least a common formulation of the problem. It is for this reason that governments, communities, and organizations focus increasing attention on the theory and practice of dialogue. Proponents of dialogue claim that it holds promise of helping groups reach higher levels of consciousness and thus become more creative and possibly more active.

At the same time, the uninitiated may view dialogue as just one more oversold communication technique or nothing more than a new variation of sensitivity training (Schein, 1993). However, sensitivity does not belong to the relationship between parents and children. Again, parents can help their children in any way possible. For instance, Bassey Ogban, Etim's younger brother, once met his parents and told them that he had met his friend's senior brother who was attending a certain university of his choice and that he would like to study mechanical engineering. The most interesting part in the whole story was that after one academic year a god student might be given a certificate to practice his/her profession and earn money, which Bassey thought would help his parents concentrate on his brother Etim. Bassey's father clapped his hands and said, "What a decisive son! He knows what he wants!" However, Bassey's mother was not amused, but this was not anything beyond the family.

I remember I made presentations in my brother's degree program, but much more intensely in my MBH degree program. That was a professional presentation and I did much more in my Ph.D. program. Yet, when I had my mortgage business that was advanced because I was no longer looking for grades but talking to real investors who were to spend money and keep metro loans going. Thus, the suit I was wearing, the gestures I made, my attitude I revealed, and how I answered questions with smiles were all part of my presentation. In business presentations, one must remember that while one is selling the investments to clients one is also selling you to them. Any mistakes one makes may lose the sale. One doesn't rely much on those who attend investment seminars, but relies more on those who would later hear the news from their friends and relatives. These will be the ones who will pay you a surprise visit in your office with deep pocket s and more investments will follow provided one has delivered on the promises made, meaning that if one has invested smartly, and made money for your investors.

Investing is an equal opportunity employer; your nationality and race has nothing do with it; all that matters is your ability to deliver on promises. That means you have to do your research and find large and small businesses that you believe are growing, expanding, and very stable. Then, of course, one must know the history of the investment and have visited the companies yourself.

If one owns a business of about 10 to 15 employees, one does not depend on delegating most of the departments while you stay in the office most of the time, but you talk with your customers and remember that every customer is important. Therefore, even if you delegated an assignment, you follow it by making calls, and introduce yourself by saying, "Hell, Mr. Johnson, my name is Okoken, the CEO of Okoken Paper Manufacturing Company. How are you? How many cartons do you need? One of my employees visited with you three days ago. I am sure that you have used our paper before and that even your word processors use them. Now, I am telling you that I will give your company a discount of $3.00 per carton that you purchase, and you will enjoy free delivery with every visit with us. Me. Johnson, It was nice talking with you. Thank you and goodbye." Do not think that everyone will like what you are doing, but most of your customers will give you credit for following up the employee visit with the customer and being so positive during your conversation with them. Here, we ae talking about presentation, which is not based on dialogue and academic, but is simply based on the transactions the paper company is running with its customers. Dialogue must be used for transactions with a customer trained to use dialogue; otherwise, the transaction will be about apples and oranges, meaning that the two of you may not be talking about the same thing.

We have heard plenty about the young Etim, popularly known as *ET*, a senior brother to Bassey Ogban (or *BA*). Although Bassey is younger, he has a special gift in that whenever he wants to talk to his parents about his future, he will invite them to a quiet place in the early morning or evening. He will greet them with either "Good morning" or "Good evening" and say:

> My parents, I just want you to know that I am very interested in mechanical engineering. You know that last semester I had an *A* in mathematics, an *A* in Physics, an *A* in additional mathematics, an *A* in chemistry, a *B+* in English and Economics, as well as an *A* in Drawing. I know that you have many things to do with your money, and that is why I want to do mechanical engineering because after one year I will be able to do some mechanical engineering jobs on my own or for an established workshop where I will be paid well and that will assist both of you. I love the two of you very much. Thank you.

One might remember the presentation that one made in the business class and the applause that one received from one's classmates and from the instructor, and recall how one felt as a result of that presentation. Of course, that was how Bassey felt because his father was smiling; he must have been thinking, "Yes, that's my son." I am a father, and I know I would have been thinking the same when my son or daughter excelled in any endeavor they did. However, how did Bassey's mother feel? She couldn't smile as such because she wanted both of her sons to excel. So, is it amusing for one son to be better than the other; rather, it is something of a concern.

As I write, people are demonstrating in the street about Donald Trump building a wall separating the United States from Mexico and about the return of undocumented immigrants from many countries. Many people have been injured and some jailed. At this point in time, the 2016 election is yet to come. Presentations as we understand them could generate good, bad, or ugly information; yet, we have to live with the results, understand them, and probably use the information for our own welfare. Mr. Trump's presentation about not letting Muslims visit or come to the United States ignored a firestorm of criticism in Europe. Mr. Trump himself may be denied entry into the United Kingdom if his preference becomes a reality, although at this point, the courts have denied him this. Sometimes, we think that political means anything that lets you succeed in politics without knowing the world is listening to what you are saying. Without knowing it, you may be shooting yourself in the foot or saying things that only cost you votes or damage your message.

Presentations sometimes mean a big step forward in someone's life; for instance, President Obama was a young senator from Illinois and not very well known as he is today, but he was lucky to be a keynote speaker for the former senator and presidential candidate John Kerry. Ironically, Mr. Kerry became the Secretary of State for Mr. Obama in his second term of his presidency. Mr. Obama presented an arousing speech, After Mr. Kerry was nominated by the Democratic Party, he was not elected president; however, in the following presidential election, Mr. Obama became the Democratic Party standard bearer and was elected president and then re-elected.

However, all presentations are not equal; some are better than others. The fact is that political presentations may be different than business presentations, but both have some things in common. They both have audiences and would like their audiences to believe them, and that means they must be convincing or they will lose their audience. Former Senator Obama wanted the Democratic Patty to win the general election, even though he came up short, but Obama's former audiences did not leave him stranded but voted for him and elected him president of the United States.

Mr. Trump, the 2016 Republican presidential candidate, might be very outspoken, but Trump and Obama came from very different backgrounds, and their world views represented their understanding of the world and their different upbringings. Mr. Trump was born into a business family, while Mr. Obama was born in a working class American family, struggling to get a scholarship for college, but neither background makes anyone good or bad. Presidents who are considered very good are judged on the circumstances of the day, especially in today's world where religious fanatics do things without considering the ramifications of what they do or thinking about what they will be doing. Any president of my country may be held responsible for allowing the country's subjects to suffer extremely. In some cases, the president must let his or her country know what is happening or might happen on national television or radio. In any case, the president must do some presentations to his or her nation.

Presentations are vital in business not just in politics. We could ask the late Steve Jobs how he made his business so great—with presentations in introducing his product line, but Steve Job's successor is trying very hard to emulate him.

As a young man in the 60's, I saw Chief Uno Egim and other chiefs, including my grandfather Chief Bassey Essien, gather at the central town square. Usually, it was about how to protect Ikun and even though the boundary lines were already in place, marked by the British administration based on the central owners of the land. Without question, the decision was unanimous, but the chiefs continued bringing up issue to the forefront of their discussions in the central square meetings, and thereby making the issue more alive as the years passed. It was the central town square meetings that authorized the native soldiers to patrol the bush every two weeks. The central town square meeting authorized a few villages around to cross the boundaries and farm a specific amount of land and the amount to be used for environmental cleanup.

Years ago, the Ikun chiefs consisted of only men because every discussion they held was about war and territorial expansion like Eroyima. Women were thought to have less to contribute in such topics, but as time passed, the seven villages that make up Ikun began to realize that the population of women was more than of men, and the men were becoming politically active. So, many men wanted women to begin voting; therefore, women stood tall and wanted bicameral legislation that created women rulers. Therefore, from the 1940s on, any serious issue brought to the central square meeting had to be discussed and agreed upon by both arms of the village government. Some women parliament chiefs were simply orators and very intelligent; men could not tamper with the power already given to women, even though they didn't go to war. However, the young men who did go to war were their children, and because the native army was voluntary and many young men listened to their mothers, there was a large checks and balances. When a woman leader spoke, there was a lot of applause because of the speaker's gender, which has nothing to do with blood ties; men usually fill their presentation with ancient proverbs while the women usually began their presentations with the injustices of previous years or of the past. The contributions of the past were gradually giving way to cooperation and a sense of one Ikun because without this, Ikun could be a divided community that would be difficult to overcome the challenges facing them from other communities.

We may take an example from the United States; the candidate for president, Mr. Trump may not be precisely as bad as people think he will be as a president. Mr. Trump may well be practicing a system of divide and conquer in order to win the election. He has no presented his case to the whole American public. He is presenting his campaign to a section of the American people who may be at odds with Islam as a religion and Hispanics who might be illegal immigrants, thus breaking the law. Look at it this way: if Mr. Trump was presenting his campaign saying he would unite the American people and would address the root causes of illegal immigration in the United States and encourage cooperation in trade and education so as to enable Americans to stand tall in the face of the world and improve the penal system, then Mr. Trump might well be depicted as someone to listen to and might become one of the best presidents the U.S. has ever had. The problems of the Middle East are vast, and that needs America's leadership, but that the government will be committed to bringing about a peaceful accord and that may be done by bringing together all he legitimate leaders and talk to other factions and some illegitimate factions may face what may seem fit by the Middle East. The term Muslim Religion must not be used for the settlement; the crises in the Middle East is unique and must be treated as such and have nothing to do with Islam. It certainly would be first among equals in the eyes of the world.

However, if Mr. Trump entangles himself with the idea of world peace, his political party may reject him as its standard bearer, accusing him of being too liberal and thinking he should be a Democrat with its liberal agenda. Then, Mr. Trump may not be conservative enough to represent the Republican Party, and his political direction may put him at odds with his party but accepted by voters who really matter at this point. So, the power of presentation may not always be regarded as political or as a marketing tool. You may be dealing with some intellectually; you may be believed with no questions asked. Presentations may make everything you say appear believable, prepare people for war, make people more likely to succumb to difficulties, or may make people more determined to accomplish a task.

During the Second World War when Hitler's air force heavily bombed Great Britain, Winston Church, the British Prime Minister, announced that Britain would never surrender to Hitler's army and gave the British soldiers more determination to fight and defeat Hitler's army. Eventually, Britain not only survived the bombing, but was part of the victorious army that saw Hitler defeated and jubilation of the Allies and United States armed forces.

Another example of the power of presentation is that of Rev. Martin Luther King, a Baptist minister, who led Black Americans to a million-man march and where he made his powerful *I Have A Dream* speech which was so powerful that it inspired people to fight for the rights and freedom of King's people. Dr. King told Blacks and Americans that he had seen the Promised Land, but that he might not get there with them. Soon afterwards he was killed, and the world mourned for his ideas. Today, he is the only individual, either Black or White, honored with a public holiday. He is studied in schools; schools and public roads were named in his honor.

A former Pope of the Roman Catholic Church told us never to be afraid of doing the right thing. Some presenters are called motivational speakers. I mention this because presentation is a vital part of business; writing, too, may be important as well, but communication in a dialogical format makes a lot of difference. I mean the presenter talks, while the audience listens and asks further questions where possible and not a *pep rally* or *free for all talk,* as I call them, a situation where no one understands each other.

However, there is a scenario where some people can write better than they can talk, and in that case, everyone should do what she or he can do best. This does not mean that one is better than the other, but it portrays elements of specialization and that makes academics and other disciplines coexist in harmony. The United States is a clear example of differences coexisting in harmony, which makes the country the best or one of the best in research and development and it will remain that way as long as political stability and independent thinking coexist. A recent prime minister of Great Britain was perplexed on what a US presidential candidate said about Muslims and no tolerance for allowing them to even visit the United States. Of course, Mr. Trump may adjust his stand on that (especially in light of recent court rulings against his policies).

Sometimes political campaigns differ from actual ruling; I could see from Mr. Trump that real adjustments may be needed in his administration if that becomes a reality because I do not think that he will go against the wishes of his supporters. In the case of a president's first four years, the president has to be careful in all that he does because that may reflect on his reelection possibilities unless, of course, he just wants one term in office. Even in Russian politics, things are truly changing even as Mr. Putin has found out in his last electoral campaign in 2014. Many young people wanted changes made; for example, a president's term of office, which also reflects other laws that may be too severe for the general public in Russia, as opposed to Mr. Gorbachev's openness that he wanted for the Russian people and the communist world in general.

Presentations made by world leaders always bring out specific language to emulate such as "Gorbachev has to tear down the wall" expressed by a former president of the United States when he visited the former West Germany. Mr. Reagan also heard from Mr. Gorbachev himself about openness. Even though all the leaders made outstanding presentations, what really stood out for President Reagan was to "tear down the wall.

Some years ago, one of the most famous of American presidents, John F. Kennedy, said, "Ask not what your country can do for you; ask what you can do for your country." As a youngster, I fell in love with that creative expression. When I finally heard of a school named after Mr. Kennedy, I determined to attend that school, which is in Orinda, California. My uncle Ukwen Bassey Eko named his son after President Kennedy, which also love so much heavily in my community at Ikun in Biase, Cross River State, Nigeria.

Some of the presentations by any leader could articulate international understanding, which could change human thinking on issues. My grandfather was one of the rulers of Ikun; he always invited me to go to his office, telling me that his father was and how he himself had turned out and why that dynasty should not be disrupted. My grandfather's advice or presentation to me has kept me disciplined up until today. It is one thing to show your children examples, but a presentation of your dreams about them makes a great difference in their daily lives. Once again, an author said, "Lives of great men reached and kept were not attained by sudden flight but kept toiling every day in their day and age," and in years to come we will continue to be seeing the benefits of the presentations in politics, business, and economics.

CHAPTER 18
BUSINESS AND GOVERNMENT

CHAPTER 18

BUSINESS AND GOVERNMENT

When a business organization fails to meet its ethical obligations to satisfy the needs of its various contributors such as customers, employees and investors, then the government through its elected representatives of the society will pass laws to force a business organization to comply. This basic truth in a democratic society is the underlying principle for the passage of laws affecting business organizations.

The federal government derives its authority and responsibility to pass legislation from the people of that country; for instance, in the United States, the basis of this authority is the Constitution, and in the Constitution are two clauses in particular—the *general welfare* clause and the *necessary and proper* clause that give the federal government the authority to enact laws to protect the needs of the various contributors to a business. The *general welfare* clause states, "Congress shall have the power to lay and collect taxes, duties, impose, and excises to pay the debts and to provide for the common defense and general welfare of the United States." The *necessary and proper* clause states that, "to make all laws which shall be necessary and proper for carrying into execution the foregoing powers and all other powers vested by this Constitution in the government of the United States or in any Department or Officer thereof."

A recent example of the application of these clauses is the *truth in packaging* bill. This law ensures that customers of a business organization will have correct and exact labeling on the package or product purchased from the business. It is necessary for the general welfare of people and it is proper to do so because some businesses have not met their obligation to provide truthful information about their products to their customers (Hayd & Gray, 1981).

We have heard so much about laws and clauses in the United States, but that has so much to make business organizations much better and trustworthy in the United States, but today we have global businesses. This does not mean that the world is made up of only one country and one business, but rather we have many countries and many businesses. The question is how will the laws and clauses of the United States affect the rest of the world. The fact is that if a business in the United States is better than those in the rest of the world, then, of course, the rest of the world will want to emulate the American business is doing to get ahead of them. At one time on television, President Putin of Russia commented on the creative modernization of technology in the United States. I am not sure Mr. Putin is alone in that thinking. Now, many people want to come to the United States because they like what they have heard and seen about America, its educational institutions, technology, creativity in the arts, athletics, and much more besides its politics.

All of the above-mentioned good things that bear the name of the United States and which makes the rest of the world want to live here and study or do business here are not the same elsewhere in the world. The stability of the country's politics, let alone its currency, which is easily accepted all over the world with the same quality in Wall Street and Main Street. We, therefore, need no other evidence in declaring the country more successful.

In developing countries, laws are on the books, and then the government transcends the realities of what the laws should represent.

Corruption makes all the difference; there is corruption in the schools where answers to tests are given to students in advance so they can pass the tests easily. The students do not have to work hard to be given certificates. A high official responsible for employment must demand some money; the official responsible for giving out contracts must demand 10% of the contract, so that the contractor is left with 90% of the money for the contract. Eventually, the work is never done or done halfway, and the job contains unfinished work and no one cares about the economic effects of the unfinished contract. Government departments meant to supply services then look the other way because the officials have been given kickbacks, meaning that they have been bribed to keep their mouths shut about the issues and to forget what really happened.

The point here is that no matter what America and a few other countries do, it will be like a grain of rice in a cup of rice, meaning that no one will even notice what the U.S. is doing. However, the world is able to understand this point because the United States has a lot of outlets the world over and export and import commodities from different countries and has a stable currency that is sought by countries all over the world. Therefore, U.S. officials and/or consumers become vocal on what they like or do not like. At this point, the companies who have imported the product may warn the producers of those commodities to produce better and more durable products; otherwise the importing company may no longer purchase their products.

In this case, the United States as a whole is not concerned; it is a company in the United States versus a company in a "B" country that will understand that the United States is not in a trade war with them, but it is a question of quality. From that point of view, the "B" nation may even uncover the fact that the producers in their country are producing substandard products for their own consumption as well, and may even make the same demands that the United States has made. Gradually, the global market may be made up of standard products that brings real wealth to all nations and brings about political stability in most parts of the world.

Country	Standard Products	Substandard Products	Trading Partners	Global Market
TABLE 1 COUNTRY'S STANDARD AND TRADING PARTNERS				
USA	Yes	No	USA	Standard
United Kingdom	Yes	No	United Kingdom	Standard
Germany	Yes	No	Germany	Standard
Nigeria	Yes	No	Nigeria	Standard
Japan	Yes	No	Japan	Standard

1) In the table above, the United States says "yes" to standard products, "no" to substandard products, in trading with the United Kingdom, Germany, Nigeria, and Japan.
2) The United Kingdom says "yes" to standard products, "no" to substandard products, and therefore trading partners with the United States, Germany, Nigeria, and Japan.
3) Germany says "yes" to standard products, "no" to substandard products, and therefore trading partners with the United States, United Kingdom, Nigeria, and Japan.`
4) Nigeria says "yes" to standard products, "no" to substandard products, and therefore trading partners with the United States, United Kingdom, Germany, and Japan.
5) Japan says "yes" to standard products, "no" to substandard products, and therefore trading partners with the United States, Germany, Nigeria, and. the United Kingdom

The above countries in the analysis are just examples of how countries could emulate each other without international regulation of acceptable products or exclusionary methods of elimination of some countries from the global economy for poor quality products. However, as I said earlier, eliminating a company from any country is not solely the duty of an importing country. It is just between the importing company and the exporting company. If the import is made and consumers of the product in the importing country care about the products because of quality, then, of course, the exporter must begin exporting better quality products; otherwise, not many countries will import those products. When the exporter cannot break even in its business, it means that that particular company may well cease producing or even go out of business. Of course, that does not mean that the president, prime minister, or king has asked the exporting company to cease production. In a global economy, no one company can dictate to others, but rather the ones who dictate are the consumers who may or may not like the exporting company's products.

If consumers from the exporting country do not like the products, they may not buy such products even on the grounds of patriotism because the dislike of the product may be based on reasons of health, taste, and other reasons that are not questionable. Being unwilling to spend your money on a particular product is a choice and not a crime, especially in a democratic capitalist nation. The producing nation that is also the exporting nation has at this point has to modify its products by doing more research first on the taste of their native people and hearing their criticisms of their own products from the producing country, and even break even in their own country alone; then, the company or the exporter may be hopeful of trying sell abroad.

An example of this scenario was the Japanese of the 1940s through 1960s were a little far behind; they produced products that were not even good for local consumption. They did not blame other countries for not buying their products, but they contacted American businessmen and technical people about what they had to do to have good products. Producers were asked to do their best on a product and compare this product to what was available outside of Japan, but not to copy exactly what they saw, but they could make it better based on what their culture defined as being better. It was a trial and error process for the Japanese.

Then came the eighties and nineties when even the Japanese Prime Minister Nakasone joked about Blacks and Latinos dragging down the U.S. economically because the United States was producing substandard cars, and that was the time of an economic downturn for the United States. It was no laughing matter. Sooner or later, Mr. Tom Brokaw, the anchorman for NBC *Nightly News* at the time, asked in his newscast why the Japanese] economic downturn was much more severe than the one the United States had because Prime Minister Nakasone told Mr. Reagan, President of the United States at the time, that American economic problems must have been caused by the high population of Blacks and Latinos in the United States. Well, no one could answer Mr. Brokaw's question but many people from the United States suggested that the then Prime Minister of Japan, Nakasone, was mistaken in making such a statement that could not be proven politically or economically.

We have heard so much about the economic powerhouse of the Western European countries even before the United States became a country; yet, from time to time, one or two or even all of the Western European countries may experience an economic downturn. Analyses are made explaining how the economic downturns occurred and how such downturns may be prevented. However, all the analyses maybe to no avail as economic downturns continue to repeat themselves. Even as I am writing, many companies are trying to cross the Atlantic to Italy; yet, the Italian economy is not an example of a good economy.

At the beginning of the Industrial Revolution, the doctrine of *laissez faire* espoused by Adam Smith prevailed. Business people were left free from government interference in conducting their affairs. This doctrine left the doors wide open to the unethical practices that followed. The self-interest principle of Adam Smith prevailed with competition as the only restraining force. Unfortunately, competition did not and has not always existed throughout the American economy (Hayd & Gray, 1981).

Robert D. Haydn and Edmund R. Gray (1981) stated that with the advent of the corporate structure coupled with the rugged individualism of the so-called *robber barons*, the people of the United States became concerned with the unethical practices that were condoned by business managers at the time in their dealings with competitors, customers, creditors, owners, and suppliers. It was felt that some form of restraint had to be placed on business giants who had so much power vis-à-vis an individual customer, employee, supplier, owner, and so forth. Business was considered evil and had to be controlled if the needs of the individual and other contributors were to be satisfied. To see that these needs were satisfied, the government stepped in and began enacting glass to regulate business practices.

Haydn & Gray (1981) also stated that larger and more powerful businesses usually have the resources to force their smaller competitors out of the market. For example, in the late 1800s, Standard Oil Trust used unethical practices by today's standards to drive its competitors out of business, thus destroying one of the basic components of our economic system—freedom of competition. A competitor usually needs at least some type of fair and indiscriminate competition. When competition is threatened, the federal government will enter the scene. Government interference with business practices began with the passage in 1890 with the Sherman Anti-Trust Act, which forbade acts by businesses to restrain competition. Two results of this law was the horizontal breaking up of companies like Standard Oil into smaller, competitive companies (i.e., Standard Oil became Sohio, Socony, Socal, Esso, and others). With the passing of time, these companies grew vertically by creating and acquiring companies that explored for oil, drilled for oil and gas, refined oil, transported oil and gas, transported the resultant products to the ultimate consumers. These oil companies now have been threatened by the government to being broken up vertically by being forced to divest the varied functions of exploration, production, refining, transportation, and marketing. The same rationale is being applied by the government; that is, the huge oil companies are not competitive enough with each other, and thus, the consumers' price needs are not being met (Hayd & Gray, 1981.

Customers' Need For Quality Goods and Services

According to Robert Edmund Gray (1981), in the United States the customers' needs include quality products, sufficient quantities of the product at the right time and place, and sufficient knowledge of the product and the product firm's activities. In addition, customers need to have a product that is safe. Although a business has an obligation to satisfy these needs that has not always been the case. Customers have been subjected to the *caveat emptor* (Let the Buyer Beware) philosophy, and as a result, customers have been left to the mercy of unethical business managers. In 1906, the Pure Food and Drug Act was passed by Congress to protect consumers and ensure quality products. Following its passage, the *caveat emptor* philosophy still prevailed between some businesses and their customers. Consumer regulations followed in the 1930s and early 1970s. The Wheeler Lea Act provided guidelines for proper advertising of products. The Robinson-Patman Act provided price protection as well. Various labeling laws provided guidelines for proper and accurate labeling of product. *Truth in Packaging* and *Truth in Lending* laws were additional laws to aid customer protection against business abuses. The Customer Product Safety Act was also created to ensure some degree of product safety. When a business does not respond to customer needs in an ethical manner, the government will pass laws to force business to do so. Enforcement of these laws, however, is another matter (Hayd & Gray, 1981).

Government Need for Tax Revenue and Information

Robert Hayd and Edmund Gray (1981) have commented that the governmental units that affect a business have certain requirements of their own; one of the first is an adequate source of tax revenues to finance the various programs. It expects a business to pay taxes when on time. One primary source of tax revenue is the corporate income tax. The right of the federal government to impose taxation is derived from the Internal Revenue Act of 1912, which was based on the Sixteenth Amendment to the Constitution of the United States. This act provided for the income tax being the primary source of revenue for the operation of the federal government. It also set forth guidelines for thee collection of income taxes. These guidelines have been interpreted by the courts during the past and have been formulated into the Internal Revenue Tax Code, which stats the rules for determining taxes.

Hayd and Gray (1981) further stated that with the passage of so many laws it became obvious that there was a need for business to supply information to the government for regulatory purposes. When all of the various agencies requested duplicate information, this overlap required additional personnel to supply the information and fill out the forms. Additional personnel in both government agencies and businesses have created a vast bureaucracy in both, creating additional expenses for the government and businesses. Such cases and confusion create frustration for both business and government.

Like the United States, many developed and developing capitalist nations derived their authority to collect income taxes based primarily on their country's constitution. As a former district court registrar in Nigeria, I interviewed many income tax defaulters in order to assess whether they should appear before a judge to interpret the tax laws and possible prosecution. Of course, the judge has to interpret the tax laws and decide on guilt or innocence. Some tax defaulters do not even stay in their business offices. In that case, the Nigerian constitution stipulated that the tax defaulters could be arrested by the employees of the Board of Internal Revenue in company with the police. The income tax defaulters who have the money they owe to the government may be allowed to pay the defaulted taxes on the spot. In that case, internal revenue employees issue a receipt, and the defaulter is let go if the information given is correct.

In Nigeria, as well as in most countries, information is the primary source of income tax revenue. In most businesses, information provided on file or in the computer is scratchy and unclear; income tax is written off as a loss. Sometimes the balance sheet is not even provided or is entirely unclear or maybe government inspectors are given a kickback (bribe) just to overlook what has been going on or not going on, as the case may be. Most of the time in developing nations no one cares about information because most taxpayers don't even believe that they belong in the government. Most taxpayers in Nigeria do not even know for what the tax revenue is used. Well, roads are bad, the railroads too poor, seaports cannot even contain most barges, and airports are too narrow and congested. Most controllers are not well trained and are inattentive to what goes on with flight, but poorly paid income tax revenues collected from taxpayers is not always made known to the public. Some government workers work in their tribal areas and let their tribes get away with irregularities. Many Africans from other countries work for the Nigerian government, and most of their purposes are simply to make money to send home, but most are afraid because they could be made scape goats (meaning the Africans could be accused of defrauding the federal government of Nigeria) and consequently be deported to their home country.

Information is a hard-earned commodity in every part of the world. Dispensing information to another business, another country, or to any unfriendly person may obtain a jail term for the informer. However, information given gladly to a friendly person or country is accompanied by a thank-you. Information and authority is nothing new; today is information, and business years ago, it was information and tribal fighters trying to take over another village or trying to stop another village from defeating them and taking their village, all of which are in dire need of adequate information. Of course, capturing a village may mean taking over the farmland of the captured village, farmland that was the lifeline of the people, and when it is gone, adequate livelihood of a people is gone. So, information, then, even as important as it is new. Today, we even go to school to be informed and to be made aware; yet, information is still a problem. Although villages still fight, but businesses in most instances have taken over from tribe and village warfare. More so, governments are more active and aware of the consequences of not doing anything to stop unnecessary conflicts. In a democratic system, this may mean electing a different government. Even in an autocratic system of government, people no longer keep quiet when the citizens are overly abused.

Employee Needs and Government Laws

Basic employee needs include adequate wages, good and safe working conditions, reasonable hours, fair treatment, equal opportunity, two-way communications, recognition, and so forth. One of the most fundamental employee needs is adequate wages to satisfy the worker's basic physiological needs. These include adequate compensation for services rendered. The federal government in the United States recently a minimum wage law—the Fair Labor Standards Act—in 1938. This law provided a minimum wage to be paid to employees of companies engaged in interstate commerce. Other laws have been passed, beginning in the 1930s, which have required businesses to satisfy basic needs of the employees. One such law was the Wagner Labor Relations Act guaranteeing employees the right to join unions and the right to strike. Further legislation was passed concerning union-management relations in the Taft-Hartley Act, the Landrum Griffin Act and other civil rights laws were passed in the 1960s to provide equal opportunity for minority people. Then, in 1970, the Occupational Safety and Health Act (OSHA) was passed, forcing businesses to provide safe jobs and working conditions for employees. Other labor legislation was passed because of businesses' reluctance to provide for the needs of their employees (Hayd & Gray, 1981).

Community Needs for Safety and Welfare

Hayd and Gray (1981) contend that usually a community in which a business operates has certain needs it desires to satisfy; for example, a community does not want a business to pollute the environment. Due to a general lack of interest in discharging this responsibility, businesses came under intense pressure by environmental groups. These groups persuaded Congress to pass laws forcing businesses to clean up their environment. One such law was the Clean Waters Restoration Act, a precursor of the Environmental Protection Act. The Environmental Protection Agency (EPA) has now set standards for all businesses to follow in all forms of pollution—land, air, water, solid waste, noise, and other forms of pollution. This action was necessary to preserve a quality of life, which businesses were not preserving prior to the passage of various environmental protection laws. Thus, when a business failed to discharge its obligations to its various contributors, the government would step in to pass laws to assure that these needs would be met. The preceding historical overview points out this fundamental reason why legislation was needed (Hayd & Gray, 1981).

Benefits and Burdens of Regulation

Hayd and Gray (1981) commented further that a useful concept in determining the value of any service or any goods is the *benefit minus the burdens equals needs satisfaction* theory. That is the benefits of government regulation should exceed the burdens imposed if the regulation is to have any value or need satisfying ability. Of course, it is difficult to quantify the benefits and the burdens, but it may be useful to at least describe the benefits and burdens of governmental regulation. The benefits of government actions are many, especially for business:

1. Government provides protection to business; for example, national security, police, fire safety, and so on.
2. Government provides political stability that makes it easier for business to plan for the future.
3. Government serves as a customer of many businesses, and for some businesses the government is their biggest customer.
4. Government provides regulations that help equalize efforts to improve the environment; that is, if an individual company

voluntarily makes an effort to improve the environment, employee health or consumer products, it bears the full cost while other companies become freeloader that enjoy the benefits but do not share the burdens. Government sets the rules for fair competition, forcing the other firms to also share in the costs.

5. Government deals with social and economic problems that individual firms cannot solve, such as tariffs, inequitable distribution of income, the right to privacy, and others.

There are certain burdens imposed on businesses through governmental regulation, and these include.

1. The actual dollar costs of employee wages spent on filling out government forms is very expensive. These expensive are gradually passed on to the consumer in the form of higher prices.
2. Regulatory red tape cuts down on the speed of accomplishing activities.
3. Some regulations seem aimed at trivial problems.
4. Excessive taxes dampen innovation.
5. There are conflicts between regulations from various regulatory agencies.
6. Regulatory agencies are selfishly regulated by and for regulated interests rather than for the public interest.

The Interdependency of Big Business and Government

Since the amalgamation of Northern and Southern Nigeria in 1914 by Lord Lurguard, the British administrator, big businesses in Nigeria were owned by the British. While the British had to regulate even infant industries, it was accused by the Free Nigeria movement of excessive control Ironically, today big and infant industries are more regulated than in the British era because Nigerians know now that businesses can abuse its power by treating employees any way they like, and with the emergence of the global economy, politics is at its highest peak, and as such, only the government can handle such high-level politics.

In a capitalist nation, most big businesses are privately owned, but elected officials have a say in how businesses treat their employees in terms of wages, hours worked, and some domestic mishaps, such as not allowing unions to function. One of the most important [governments??] in business is when a foreign country organizes a high-jacking of an airplane or pirating a ship full of goods to be sold in a different country, This could cause a war between the two countries. For example, pirates in Somalia have seized American cargo ships for ransom, but the United States has refused to bargain and instead took up arms and waited for the perpetrators on the high seas. Some were captured and punished, and brought such activities to a halt. American goods owned by American companies were then allowed passage to different countries to deliver their goods.

There was a time when oil and gas were among the hottest commodities in the market, and there was what I call "street sales" of oil and gas in Nigeria. No one then was in control until the oil companies complained, and the culprits were then rounded up, arrested, and detained; their respective governments then came up and pleaded for their release. Individual oil companies could not have had such power and authority over the culprits. Of course, that could have been in international lawsuit, but by the same token, there was a dispute between the oil companies in the 1900s in the Delta area of Nigeria. It was the federal government of Nigeria that strategized its policies by making one of the illustrious sons of the vice president of Nigeria, from where he was finally elected president of Nigeria. That strategy totally brought up what was to be a complete nightmare for the entire country of Nigeria. When I talk about government, I am talking about elected governments. Elected governments think a lot about elections, and that is a big *checks and balances* on politicians, while non-elected governments such as the Communist countries like North Korea and military governments that come to power through coups do not have these check on their activities. The global economy works better when ideology about business transactions are so similar but not necessarily the same because business is most of the time based on culture. However, in order for the global economy to work better, culture must combine with common sense, which I think is a universal language and understanding.

Based on common sense and understanding, various governments are able to prove their case about another country not doing business on a recognized international understanding. A case in point is China's manipulation of its currency. The United States was able to point out that immediately, and that was based on an understanding of international monetary rules. Sometimes, culture might interfere with international understanding of how international marketing works country by country. For example, the Ghanaian alcoholic beverage complained about Nigeria and South Africa not patronizing the sales of Ghana's alcoholic beverages in their countries without considering those countries" viewpoints on their young people's abuse of alcohol. Buying less alcohol from Ghana for South Africa and Nigeria frequently means less alcohol consumption by their youth.

In the United States, the question of *dumping* has conflicted with a domestic understanding of other cultures, and the Ghanaian government has refused to support what the alcoholic beverage companies were trying to instigate in Africa. Both the Nigerian and South African governments have turned deaf ears to the accusations that these governments have blocked the sale of alcoholic beverages contrary to the World Trade Organization/

Anticipated Strategies for Business in Dealing With Governments

The interdependency principle would suggest that business has certain obligations to the government and that government has certain obligations to business. Consequently, it would seem plausible for business to pursue certain strategies in dealing with government; these include the following:

a) Pay all taxes when they are due.
b) Obey the laws that pertain to the type of business involved.
c) Cooperate with government officials who regulate the business.
d) Become actively involved in governmental affairs that affect its specific business interest and society in general.

In return, it would seem plausible that the government discharge certain obligations to the business community as follows:

1. Provide protection for businesses.
2. Provide the necessary services for a business to flourish.\
3. Establish a favorable political, social, and economic environment for the conduct of business.
4. Enforce rules and regulations in providing fair competition among business firms (Hayd & Gray, 1981).

I remember at the peak of the military takeover in Nigeria when businesses in the 1980s would simply go out of business or relocate to a different country because the military government was unable to protect them due to corrupt practices and because companies could not function well in an unstable environment. Then, the military government was unable to develop a kind of interdependency principle that could make business profitable, let alone flourish. But I think the rest of the world, especially the Western world, thought about military rule, but the military rules found out what the rest of the world though about them in s very different way. The military government in Nigeria was unable to borrow money from any country other than the International Monetary Fund, who made the military government understand that they were not supposed to run a civilian administration.

The respect that was due to the most populous country in Africa was treated with disdain and discord. Business people were no longer in the country to bring about creativity, and the worst was the absence of teachers and professors for the schools and universities. High schools were left for poor people; other professionals scattered all over the world; universities were deserted. Those who had an inferior education were lamenting every day they saw the daylight. Life expectancy age was down for the average human in Africa. The military government was not particularly evil, even though I am not in support of their program, but in ways evil things happened because Nigeria was considered a model country for Africa to follow. However, despite all the mineral wealth and much more, Nigeria kept sliding backwards because of the rule of government that ruled the country. The best that I can emphatically say is that the internal disgust was not towards the civilian population but towards the military rulers that operated by decree instead of by a democratic system of government or an elected government.

In Nigeria, then, the relationship between the military and business was either very poor or nonexistent for the few businesses that elected to stay in the country. In today's civilian administration in Nigeria, the relationship between the government and business is still developing. It is a lot easier to destroy the economy of a country than to rebuild one, especially in today's global competition. Years ago any product could be sold below market value, but today, products sold below market value must meet the recommended value or standard. That means spending more money for a product. At this point, there is no amount of encouragement a government could give to a business without monetary help. The Nigerian government is trying to do what it should be doing, but I am happy that the will do that is there; therefore, sometime in the future this will become a reality to avert poverty.

Discrimination and Poverty

The preamble to the U. S. Constitution states that all men are created equal and enjoy certain inalienable rights that are guaranteed in order to enjoy life, liberty, and the pursuit of happiness. This political equality concept, however, has not always been applied to all members of society including women and minorities in the United States. People frequently pride themselves on having the ethical concept of fairness in dealing with others. People expect to be treated fairly; however, when people ae not treated fairly, certain; repercussions occur, especially if such discrimination threatens the needs of people to be treated fairly. Those people will seek assistance from the government to ensure that they are receiving fair treatment as guaranteed by the Constitution. Businesses that do not meet the needs of people to be treated fairly will be forced to do so by government laws passed by elected representatives of the people. In the United States such is the case with the passage of anti-discrimination laws dealing with potential employees of a business (Hayd & Gray, 1981).

All over the world, discrimination and unfair treatment is common or the norm, but some areas are more unfair than others. A case in point is India where some citizens are called *untouchables* and are made to worship others. Even though the unfair treatment of some citizensons, is contained in the constitution of India, I believe that opportunitsts donot care how he less fortunate are treated. The government of India is still trying to bring about equal treatment and less or no discrimination, but it is an uphill battle since it is culturally and religiously ingrained in the society. I hope sometime the Indians themselves will realize what unfair treatment and discrimination is doing to their economy and global competition.

The Peoples Republic of China is the second largest economy in the world today; India could be some day because of their democratic system of government, but because of how they treat themselves, it might take longer than usual, if ever, for Indians to reap the benefits of their population. There was a time when I talked with an Indian in the United States; in our conversation, I asked him if he would go back home someday. He kept quiet for a long time, and then, finally, raised his face and quietly told me, "I will never go back home again. The United States is now my home; thank God, I am now a citizen. No one treats me unfairly like they did in India. I am an American now."

Nigeria, my birth country, is not an exception to the rule of unfair treatment and discrimination. Nigeria is primarily a homogenous country; about 20% of the country is other Africans, Europeans, Asians, Americans and others. Only very few foreigners have voting rights. Unfair treatment in employment is rare because academic qualifications and experience count for a great deal if a candidate has completed the following:

1. Primary school education, one earns level 2.
2. Incomplete high school, one earns level 3.
3. Completed high school, one earns level 4.
4. College education, BS, BSc, or BA, one earns level 8.
5. Master's Degree, MS, MSc, MA, MBA, one earns level 9.
6. Ph.D., PsyD, and others and more depending on what you can do, level 10.
7. Experience may upgrade one to a different level.

These are not just political equalities granted by the Nigerian constitution. It is a real business; many people have been jailed for not adhering to the Constitution. In this case, it is difficult to compare someone's level any other way; otherwise, a court case awaits the employer or a government agency may intervene and force the employer to do the correct thing.

One of the ways unfair treatment and discrimination can occur is if the company wants a cleaner, and the employer comes from the same village as one of the candidates. In this case, academic qualifications mean very little, so the employer is supposed to use his or her intuition for this employment. Therefore, he may choose his or her village person to fill the position, unless another interested person questions why the employer gave the position to his village neighbor and not to another candidate from another village. At that point, the company may require someone with experienced and/or another senior officer may substitute for the first employer. As far as employment goes, it does not matter if you are a man or a woman, from a majority or a minority group. \

Another hurdle in Nigerian employment is bribery and corruption. The employer may ask for money or sex. In this case, the employer does not care if the candidate is from the same family as himself (the employer). The punishment for bribery/corruption is being fired on the spot or being fined and imprisoned. Firing means one leaves one's job. The government of Mr. Buhari does not care about who you are; if you are proved to be corrupt, and then you must be punished according to the law.

The European Union and the British Economy

No Access to Single Market Without Migration

European Union leaders drew a line along the English Channel telling Great Britain that it could not keep valuable business links with its former continental partners in a seamless, single EU market if it didn't also accept European workers. The challenge cuts to the heart of the British vote to leave the bloc after a virulent campaign where migration from poorer EU countries was a key concern of the voters. It also set the scene for the complex departure negotiations facing departing Prime Minister David Cameron's successor for which nominations opened in London. Meeting for the first time without Britain, the 27 other EU nations set out a united strategy to face the next British government that will seek to salvage as many of the EU privileges as possible while reneging on a maximum amount of obligations. The nations emerged from the summit insisting that the *four freedoms* central to unity are indivisible; the free movement of people, services, good, and finances. In Cameron's absence, the most palpable remaining link to Britain at the summit was the English language used. The remaining presidents, chancellors, and prime ministers showed a firm common resolve. Committing to be absolutely determined to "remain united," EU Council President Donald Tuck said the leaders sought to dispel any idea that the referendum results would amount to the EU's Waterloo (*SF Chronicle*, 6/30/2016, A3).

The *SF Chronicle* article further stated that the Prime Minister of Luxembourg, Xavier Bettel, contended that "With a disunited United Kingdom, we need a united Europe more than ever" (2016, A3). There is a widespread sense that the post-war project to foster peace via trade has become too bureaucratic and undemocratic with not enough meaning for its 500 million citizens. The initial EU founding nations in the West were lean toward a tighter, closer union, while newer member nations in the East want to keep more control with the national governments, notably of their borders. France is among the EU countries facing calls for a referendum concerning quitting the EU mainly from the far right (*SF Chronicle, 2016*).

The issue here with Britain is not the pride of Britain ruling the world; it is about what I call political economy, much like what is the type of migration which is similar to South and Central American peoples into the United States. In Europe, is about the poorer, Easter European countries having their people flood Western European countries with more developed economies. The British was afraid of losing their jobs and may be succumbing to minimum wage pay, which would erode their pride, middle-class status, and the British lifestyle. This is all about a fear of the unknown even though the British stock market has rebounded, that is not yet the remedy to the recent British economic downturn that occurred with the worldwide economic depression. The British fear of the unknown continues to climb because no one really knows what the European Union will come up with. As of now, the British stock market index is dominated by multi-nationals that do not reflect the national economy, which the Bank of England's chief economic has would need more monetary stimulus after the vote to remove itself from the European Union. Unfortunately, this vote helped plunge Britain into an existential crisis and opened up new uncertainties for businesses. The economic outlook has deteriorated, and some monetary policy easing will likely be required because the clouds on the economic horizon have been identified by the Bank of England that could mean a cut in interest rates or an injection of billions of pounds more in the financial system at their next meeting. Mark

Carney, the central bank chief, warned further however that the central bank could not protect the country entirely from economic shock, and he stressed it was important for the government to have a plan in how to navigate the country through this uncertainty. This was a thinly-veiled dig at the disarray engulfing Britain primary political parties. Britain's economy is facing a drop in investment among businesses as it remains unclear what trade relationships Britain will have with the rest of the European Union. Some businesses have frozen hiring and issued warnings that their earnings will be less than expected. Other businesses are considering relocating some jobs to mainland Europe. The American stock markets have recovered since plunging for several days following the vote that separated Britain from the EU. The FTSE 100 was up 2-3 percent at 6,504, above the 6,338 level where it stood before the vote (*SF Chronicle*, 2016, 12).

According to the *SF Chronicle* (2016), experts say the FTSE index, however, is a poor indicator for the British economy because many of its listed companies are multi-nationals that do most of their business outside of Great Britain and benefit from the pound's big slide since the vote, including an 11% drop against the dollar. Oil companies BP and Royal Dutch Shell make their money in dollars, the currency in which crude oil is priced internationally. So, when they bring that money back to Britain and translate it into pounds, their revenues will be a higher share; BP stock is up 15% and Shell stock is up 8T since the vote to leave the EU, about as much as the pound has dropped, not coincidentally. Other companies that have global operations will see their earnings made in other countries boosted when repatriated to Great Britain. Fashion powerhouse Burberry, which has become popular in Asia, has also seen its shares rise since the vote was taken. The global presence that Britain's largest companies enjoy is expected to help them through the uncertainty and will help the British economy to a certain degree. Beyond this clutch of companies, there is no question that Britain's companies are taking a hard hit. Those that depend on access to the EU market, particularly financial firms, are down sharply. Barclay's Bank is down almost 30%. The prospect of a looming recession could push house prices down, and that has crushed shares in real estate companies (*SF Chronicle,* 2016).

The *SF Chronicle* (2016 article stated further that a retailer like W. H. Smith Whole Shops sells magazines, books, and snacks is ubiquitous in British town centers and is down 9% on the exchange. Auto Trader is down 17% because people are expected to have less disposable income in case of a recession. Bakery chain Greggs' is down 12%.

<u>London</u>: In a real life political drama mixing Shakespearean tragedy with House of Cards, Britain's victorious anti-European Union campaigner Boris Johnson watched his chances of leading his country evaporate after the defection of a key ally. The former London mayor dropped his campaign to become Conservative Party leader and Prime Minister after Minister of Justice Michael Gove abruptly withdrew his support for Johnson and announced he would run himself. Johnson, a prominent campaigner for Britain's withdrawal from the 28-nation European Union told a news conference where he was expected to announce his candidacy that the next Conservative Party leader would need to unite the party and ensure Britain's standing in the world. He said, "Having consulted colleagues and in view of the circumstances in Parliament, I have concluded that that person cannot be me." He said it was time not to fight the tide of history but to take that tide at the flood and sail on to fortune. It appeared to be a dig at Gove; the reference is to a line spoken by Brutus, the Roman leader's ally turned assassin in Shakespeare's *Julius Caesar.* Johnson's departure made Gove and Home Secretary Theresa May the favorites among the contenders to lead the Conservative Party. The decision by Johnson, 52, was an unexpected twist in a political career that saw him serve as journalist, legislator, and mayor, building a public profile on Latin quips, cycling, and rumpled eccentricity while nurturing a poorly concealed ambition to lead his country as Prime Minister (*SF Chronicle,* 2016).

<u>Newport, Wales</u>: A businessman who owns a painting company in Newport indicated that his leanings in the recent referendum to leave

the European Union would seem obvious. Grants from the European Union have funded many of the projects he has worked on including the former bank branch he was painting. European Union funds help him fund hiring apprentices and that Wales got back far more money from the EU than it paid in. However, many of the poorer places in Britain that received the most from Europe also voted decisively to leave the union. Promises were made by the leaders of the so-called Leave Campaign that exiting the EU would lead to a bonanza of money no longer being sent to Brussels, the seat of the European Union Parliament. After the vote, they almost immediately retreated from those promises, leaving the future of aid programs funded by the EU in peril. Even some in Newport who knew what they stood to lose were in conflict over the vote (*New York Times*, July 6, 2016).

London: The financial strain from Britain's vote to leave the European Union is starting to show as worries continue to ripple through the county's real estate market (*NY Times*, July 6, 2016, B1). The *Times* further stated that in the most prominent sign of the pressure, three major real estate funds have frozen withdrawals in two days to slow the exodus of nervous investors. By doing so, the funds are trying to present a vicious cycle of selling that could force them to dump assets at ultra-low prices, deepen losses, and prompt more investors to rush for the exit doors. The turbulence, after investors rapidly exchanged risky assets for safer haven yields such as American Treasuries, have touched new lows, while the pound is down sharply. Stocks have been shaky and shares in some British real estate companies have shed more than a third of their value. The three real estate funds run by Standard, Life, Aviva investors, and M&G Investments each pointed to heightened levels of stress in the market, prompting investors to sell off. "The reality is we do not really know what the economic impact of the BREXIT is going to be," said Laith Khulaf, a senior advisor at Hargreaves Landdown, a British financial services company. "The concern is it's going to be negative."

The *New York Times* (2016) commented that authorities around the world are paying close attention to the economic, financial, and political fallout of the vote and have plans to move quickly to keep the damage from spreading too far and too fast. The reverberations could test whether the global financial crisis officials have put in place the necessary measures to protect the broader area to suffer from the shock. The Bank of England, Britain's central bank, warned that the environment has become *challenging*, noting that there were "tightening credit conditions" in the commercial real estate market. To help provide support for the economy, the central bank cut the buffer rate that British banks need to keep on their books, a move that should allow them to lend more to businesses and consumers. Bank of England Governor Mark Carney stated,"

> When combined with the already strong balance sheets of the United Kingdom's banks, today's action means that UK households and businesses who want to seize value opportunities in a post-referendum world can be confident they will be supported by the financial system/

Mr. Carney also said that "financial institutions, like the citizens, desire certainty in order to plan for the future." Funds hat invested in the British property market look particularly vulnerable in the wake of the BREXIT vote. Real estate, particularly high end properties in London, doomed in recent years as interest rates remained at record low investments, and chased yield creating huge demand for mutual funds that invested heavily in the country's malls, towers, and residential developments. While they represented a small piece of the mutual fund world, such investments have Ł 25 billion in assets under management. The Aviva, Standard Life, and M&G funds account for about one-third of that market, according to Mr. Khalaf of Hargreaves Lansdown. Even before the vote, the signs of stress wee apparent in the real estate market. Ever rising prices prompted concerns about a property bubble; construction activity in Britain posted its weakest performance in seven years, driven in part by a steep decline in investment construction ahead of the referendum. According to the latest market CIPS UK construction purchasing managers' index, which has importance is important. But the sector has been shaken by new uncertainty since Britain voted to exit the European Union. London's future as a regional hub for commerce is in doubt. Cities across Europe are looking to lure companies and jobs. An economic slowdown is an increasing possibility (*New York Times*, July 2016, B2).

The *New York Times* (2016) article stated that mutual funds that focus on real estate face a particular problem in the current tumult. Such funds hold assets that are difficult to trade, but investors can ask for their money back at any time. When investors panic, the redemption requests can quickly exhaust the fund's cash on hand. An American mutual fund run by Third Avenue ran into a similar problem reflecting the portfolio's significant exposure to the riskiest types of high-yield bonds. Rather than unload assets into a difficult market with withdrawals mounting, the managers of Aviva Investors and M&G Investments and Standard Life decided it was prudent to do the same. Investor redemptions in the M&G portfolio and its feeder fund have risen markedly because of the high levels uncertainty in the UK commercial property market since the outcome of the European Union referendum. M&G in a news release said a temporary suspension would allow its managements time to raise cash levels in a controlled manner ensuring that any asset disposals were achieved at reasonable values. On its website, Aviva Investors said that its property trust fund, which was worth Ł1.8 billion and Ł2.4 billion at the end of May, 2016 had been experiencing higher than usual volumes of redemption requests. A day earlier, Standard Life Investments, the asset management unit of the large British Insurance Company also halted redemption requests in its UK real estate fund. It said it had seen an increase in requests for redemptions as a result of uncertainty for the UK commercial real estate market following the EU referendum results. Such funds are already proving a point of concern for the English authorities (New York Times, 2016, B2).

New York Times (July 2016) stated in its article that the Bank of England noted that "valuations in some segments of the market, notably the prime London market had become stretched." The bank has warned that any fall to in commercial property prices could be *amplified* by investors and real estate funds. These even-ended funds could be forced to sell liquid assets. The head of one of the British financial regulators said that so-called open-ended real estate funds forced a structural problem in that their assets did not "revalue naturally" in the market. Mr. Bailey, the CEO of the Financial Conduct Authority was *sensible* to suspend all withdrawable funds because authorities did not want those who "got to the door quickly to get a better deal than those don't." However, he conceded what that the _____ there was a mismatch between such tradable funds and their investments in liquid real estate assets and needed to look "at the dossier of those things," said Mr. Bradley. Officials from the Financial Conduct Authority were to meet with major asset managers to discuss the impact of the BREXIT referendum. The Investment Association, an industry group that represents British fund managers, said that the suspension of redemptions is an important tool that prevents fund managers from being forced to sell too quickly and achieve better results for clients. The group has said that suspension is a mechanism that is laid out under stringent FCA regulations, and when it is employed by one of our members is shown that the regulations are working as they are supposed to do.

London: Britain's Conservative Party Prime Minister is stepping down. The Labor Party leader is clinging barely to power, and now the head of the UK Independence Party, a key architect of the dramatic vote to leave the EU has resigned as well. This has left the United Kingdom with a power vacuum just as someone is needed to step up and own the talks on how Britain will exit the EU. The June 23rd referendum results have ripped through British politics like a buzz saw, and it will like be weeks before some clarity emerges. The new Conservative Party leader will be chosen on September 9, 2016 and will become Prime Minister. The contenders are talking in general terms about BREXIT plans, butt their words are not yet backed by any authority. UK IP leader Nigel Farage said he is leaving his party post because he wants his life back after years of political intrigue. But observers note that he is keeping his seat in the European Parliament and may well be hoping for a formal role when the new Prime Minister takes power and most likely begins BREXIT talks with the EU leaders. "There's always a chance of him returning, but his future relies on other people supporting him and asking him to do something," said George Jones, Government Professor Emeritus at the London School of Economics. On top of Prime Minister David Cameron's and Farrago's departures, Labor Party leader Jeremy Corby is clinging to office despite having lost a vote of confidence by his party's lawmakers. Jones said Britain is gripped by a power vacuum at the top. "There isn't any leadership; there cannot be but in an emergency, Cameron can make decisions," he said. "It's a strange situation. All the parties are in disarray. The unexpected has happened." (*New York Times*, July 6, 2016, B2).

Theresa May, the leading Conservative Party candidate to succeed David Cameron as Prime Minister has pledged to unify her divided party and country behind a slowly negotiated exit from the European Union. Home Secretary May who holds a leader over four party rivals before an initial leadership ballot billed herself as best placed to bridge the gulf between ardent opponents and supporters of EU membership. May has said that under her leadership the United Kingdom would not formally declare its intention to leave the EU until next year, meaning a British exit from the 28-nation bloc might not happen until 2019. Under Article 50 of the EU Treaty, members who formally apply to leave face a two-year deadline to negotiate new agreements with EU partners. "What's important is that we do this in the right time scale to get the right deal for the UK. We should not invoke Article 50 immediately," May said in a BBC television interview. "It shouldn't be before the end of the year. We need to establish our own negotiating position." May officially supported Cameron's pro-EU efforts but avoided campaigning herself. She argued that relative neutrality would help her to build consensus between the 17 million who voted for a British exit from the EU and the 16 million who voted to remain in the EU in the June 13 referendum. May said, "I've been clear that BREXIT means

BREXIT. What we need to do is to bring those two sides together, bring *leave* and *remain* together and bring the country together." Four other Conservatives are competing with May to take the helm of Britain's governing party following Cameron's resignation in the immediate wake of his referendum defeat. These are Anti-EU candidates Michael Gove, Andrea Leadson, and Liam Fox and pro-EU candidate Stephen Crabb (*SF Chronicle*, July 4, 2016, A2).

Commentary

So far I have a sense of what is going on politically in Great Britain, but I have no clue about the economic aspects of the British exit from the European Union. It may be it is too early to know the economic results of the exit. The issue here is that the world knows that the result of the referendum shows those who voted for the exit were 17 million citizens and those who voted against the exit from the European Union were 16 million citizens, which to me indicates a country that is divided. The division may not only be in politics but also in economics because the two (I call them Paul and Barnabas, meaning they are always together; otherwise we are talking miracle). I have also heard about the resignation of the major supporters of the European Union exit, which has caused more chaos like Mr. Nigel Farago. Theresa May herself is talking a _____ and the unity of the country, so we have to just stay tuned.

The European Common Market

In 1947 the International Conference of Agricultural Economists met in Totness, England, and people in many European countries were living on a subsistence basis, rationing of foods was common, most industries were at a very low ebb, and several countries were near bankruptcy. In sharp contrast, by 1961 when the International Conference met at Cuernavaca, Mexico, European industries were booming, the people were buying more meat, more cars, and more television sets, and they had greatly increased their use of newsprint and electricity.

What caused this phenomenal change? Probably the most important factor was the intense desire of a continent of skilled workers and able administrators to regain and improve the standard of living that had prevailed before World War II. This desire was implemented by the following:

a) The development of the Marshall Plan, initiated in 1947 and consummated by the United States Congress in 1948, under which over a period of nine years, $19 billion was given to promote the economic development and reconstruction of 18 countries in Western Europe.

b) The European coal Community formed in 1952 listing a unified mark for coal in Belgium, France, Italy, and other countries.

Looking back at the European Common Market we can see a very successful endeavor, many lives were uplifted, communications made it easier for one country to know others. The European leaders experimented rightly as many European countries were uplifted from poverty to self-sufficiency without the intense rationing of food as people were able to afford what others had to sell. Exchange of products and services was also extended to migrant workers who made costs a little lower than they could have been without the migrant workers. For example, Mexicans were able to buy cars, while car makers were able to afford meat and other food items. In 1947, the movement from one country to another was fairly free because crime was rare, and technologies were also limited. Today, there is crime everywhere in every society, but technological advances offer the world a way of combating crime so that the argument about not allowing other poorer European peoples from Eastern Europe enter Britain for fear of criminal elements or simply taking jobs from British citizens was ill founded because the jobs they took were jobs the average Briton would not do. In the United States, the Mexicans entered the country and did the farm labor, even though some people still reject such entry of Mexican workers into states like California and Texas to do farm labor. Yet, farmers and others who want to pay lower wages to cut costs and increase profits do not understand why Mexican and other laborers should be allowed entry into the U.S. to enable food to be more affordable for all.

The European Union today is making the same arguments on the logic behind not allowing Eastern European migrants into Britain. We still do not know the economic impact of Britain's exit from the European Union will have on Britain if nay. The world is still watching to see what happens because of the BREXIT or British exit from the European Union.

The European Common Market of 1949 was very uplifting for the members and beyond. Countries ceased food rationing, commodities became more affordable, and people learned more from other people. The world became very friendly, the British economy was becoming British, and cars were sold and were very affordable. Today, technology is so advanced that industries enjoy mass production, and yet Eastern European countries became a threat to the British, which is so advanced over and above every product made in Eastern Europe. The fact is that 17 million people in Britain voted for an exit from the EU while 16 million voted to remain in the EU. Is Britain, then, a divided nation? I now believe that the 1947 European Common Market was motivated by economies for the good of all Europeans, while BREXIT was motivated by politics.

Questions

1. Discuss buyers' behaviors.
2. Discuss dynamics of change as it concerns Nigerian independence.
3. Discuss the power of presentations in general terms.
4. What are the anticipated strategies in business for dealing with government?
5. Discuss discrimination and poverty.
6. No access to single-market access without migration. Comment on this.
7. a. Who is Theresa May?

b. What is the BREXIT vote?
8. What is EU? How many member nations does it have?
9. a. What is the largest economy in Africa?
   b. In what part of Africa is Nigeria?
10. Write about a page on discrimination and poverty.
11. Comment on the European Common Market.
12. Mexico and Eastern European countries have what in common?

Answers

1. Buyers behavior may well be motivated by several factors including the following:
   a. The type of product.
   b. The resources of the buyer.
   c. The usefulness of the product to the buyer. I had a friend who saw a product that his high school friend had used, but since he was a very poor student, he let of the love of the product until later. As a young man, he traveled to the eastern part of Nigeria not too far from Lagos City where he found the same product surprisingly but had no money on him at the time.

   The young man became very inquisitive, asking the salespeople if the product was always in stock, how much it cost, and what was the usefulness of the product. So, when he went back home and happened to travel to far western Nigeria he brought money with him and fortunately simply asked the price and with no questions, he paid for the product. Many products usually come up with limitations on the type of product. This man was not by any means a rich man, but he was able to \afford the product because he left out many other products he could have purchased and save his money for that particular product because of its quality and durability, which eventually became an opportunity when the young man could afford the product.

2. Dynamics of Change. The example here is about a young girl who grew up seeing most of her friends graduate from universities as nurses and teachers. She invited both of her parents into her room and reminded them that she was graduating from high school that year, and both parents replied, "Yes, we know." She then told them that she wanted to be a mechanical engineer; the parents responded, "What?" However, her mother retracted her dismay and told her husband that she knew what he was thinking about, and that was that mechanical engineering was for men and a woman had no business in that discipline. She stood up suddenly and said, "Go, girl!" but the father resisted having a concern about mathematics that were required and told her that she only had a "B" average the previous semester. The daughter responded by saying, "I will work harder, I promise." The mother then told her husband to give his daughter the support she wanted. The daughter looked at her father also, and the father looked at his daughter sternly and said, "Young lady, you have my blessings. Your mother and I will do our best to support you, even if that may mean having a tutor in order for you to realize your dreams." Truly, both father mother, and daughter worked together. Mary became the valedictorian of her class, and her father, who had no sons, became very emotional and never thought less of his daughter any more.

3. The Power of Presentations. Presentations, whether academic or just friendly get-togethers, must consist of or portray some sort of an agenda, reasons, what you know about a subject, pros and cons of what you are talking about, economic rationale, political implications of the subject, business reasons, and religious reasons, etc. For some reason, students begin taking presentations seriously because of academic grade; in reality, presentations begin from home. Most parents may not realize what is happening between them and their children. Some parents may think that their children may be good talkers in college; they might be class prefects. However, the young man's professor will subject where the young is headed in his life; even

then, the professor may be wrong. Having said all of that, every person is different; mostly in children, their lives are different change from time to time. Even then, parents may suggest what their children could become in their lifetime, though we are never too sure. The power of presentation should never be underestimated; for instance, in presidential elections with the CEO talking to his or her subjects. The president of a country presents his or her fiscal year budget. Look at two boys talking to their parents; one is more capable than the other in presenting what he wants.

4. What are the anticipated strategies in business for dealing with government? The interdependency principle would support the idea that business has certain obligations. Consequently, it would seem plausible for business to pursue certain strategies in dealing with government. These include the following:

    a.) Pay all taxes when they are due. Pay all taxes when they are due.

    b.) Obey the laws that pertain to the type of business involved.

    c.) Cooperate wiwth government officials who regulate the business.

    d.) Become actively involved in governmental affairs that affect its specific business interest and society in general.

In return, it would seem plasible that the government discharge certain obligations to the business community as follows:

a.) Provide protection for businesses.

b.) Provide the necessary services for a business to flourish.\

c.) Establish a favorable political, social, and economic environment for the conduct of business.

d.) Enforce rules and regulations in providing fair competition among business firms (Hayd & Gray, 1981).

5. Discrimination and Poverty. The preamble to the U. S. Constitution states that all men are created equal and enjoy certain inalienable rights that are guaranteed in order to enjoy life, liberty, and the pursuit of happiness. This political equality concept, however, has not always been applied to all members of society including women and minorities in the United States. People frequently pride themselves on having the ethical concept of fairness in dealing with others. People expect to be treated fairly; however, when people ae not treated fairly, certain; repercussions occur, especially if such discrimination threatens the needs of people to be treated fairly. Those people will seek assistance from the government to ensure that they are receiving fair treatment as guaranteed by the Constitution. Businesses that do not meet the needs of people to be treated fairly will be forced to do so by government laws passed by elected representatives of the people. In the United States such is the case with the passage of anti-discrimination laws dealing with potential employees of a business (Hayd & Gray, 1981).

6. No Access to Single Market Without Migration. European Union leaders drew a line along the English Channel telling Great Britain that it could not keep valuable business links with its former continental partners in a seamless, single EU market if it didn't also accept European workers. The challenge cuts to the heart of the British vote to leave the bloc after a virulent campaign where migration from poorer EU countries was a key concern of the voters. It also set the scene for the complex departure negotiations facing departing Prime Minister David Cameron's successor for which nominations opened in London. Meeting for the first time without Britain, the 27 other EU nations set out a united strategy to face the

next British government that will seek to salvage as many of the EU privileges as possible while reneging on a maximum amount of obligations. The nations emerged from the summit insisting that the *four freedoms* central to unity are indivisible; the free movement of people, services, good, and finances. In Cameron's absence, the most palpable remaining link to Britain at the summit was the English language used. The remaining presidents, chancellors, and prime ministers showed a firm common resolve. Committing to be absolutely determined to "remain united," EU Council President Donald Tuck said the leaders sought to dispel any idea that the referendum results would amount to the EU's Waterloo (*SF Chronicle*, 6/30/2016, A3).

7. a. Who is Theresa May? Theresa May is the favorite among five contenders to lead the British Conservative Party.

    b. What is BREXIT Vote> The Brexit vote was the referendum, conducted on June 23, 2016 where 16 million British voters voted to stay with the European Union and 17 million British voters to leave the European Union.

8. What is EU? How many member nations does it have? The EU is the European Union. There are 28 nations in the bloc, but with Britain leaving, it means the European Union will retain 27 member nations, but the British exit may not happen until 2019 under Article 50 of the European Union Treaty. Members who formally apply to leave face a two-year deadline to negotiate new agreements with EU members.

    a. What is the largest economy in Africa? The largest economy in Africa belongs to Nigeria. Oil and gas are now 15% of the GDP. Agriculture is now 35% of the Gross Domestic Product (GDP). Surprisingly enough, the industrial sector is 50% of the GDP. Industrial progress has helped Nigeria become the largest economy in Africa.

    1. In what part of Africa is Nigeria? Nigeria is in West Africa, which includes the following countries:

    i.   Benin

MAP OF WEST AFRICA

ii.   Burkina Faso

iii. Ivory Coast

iv.   Cape Verde

v.   Gambia

vi.   Ghana

vii. Guinea

viii. Guinea Bissau

ix.   Liberia

x.   Mali

xi.   Niger

xii. Nigeria

xiii. Sierra Leone

xiv. Togo

There are 16 nations in West Africa, but 1990 Mauritania opted out for reasons best known to herself.

9. Comment on the European Common Market. In 1947 the International Conference of Agricultural Economists met in Totness, England, and people in many European countries were living on a subsistence basis, rationing of foods was common, most industries were at a very low ebb, and several countries were near bankruptcy. In sharp contrast, by 1961 when the International Conference met at Cuernavaca, Mexico, European industries were booming, the people were buying more meat, more cars, and more television sets, and they had greatly increased their use of newsprint and electricity.

What caused this phenomenal change? Probably the most important factor was the intense desire of a continent of skilled workers and able administrators to regain and improve the standard of living that had prevailed before World War II. This desire was implemented by the following:

a.) The development of the Marshall Plan, initiated in 1947 and consummated by the United States Congress in 1948, under which over a period of nine years, $19 billion was given to promote the economic development and reconstruction of 18 countries in Western Europe.

b.) The European coal Community formed in 1952 listing a unified mark for coal in Belgium, France, Italy, and other countries.

10. Mexico and Eastern European countries have what in common? Many European countries were uplifted from poverty to self-sufficiency without the intense rationing of food as people were able to afford what others had to sell. Exchange of products and services was also extended to migrant workers who made costs a little lower than they could have been without the migrant workers. For example, Mexicans were able to buy cars, while car makers were able to afford meat and other food items. In 1947, the movement from one country to another was fairly free because crime was rare, and technologies were also limited. Today, there is crime everywhere in every society, but technological advances offer the world a way of combating crime so that the argument about not allowing other poorer European peoples from Eastern Europe enter Britain for fear of criminal elements or simply taking jobs from British citizens was ill founded because the jobs they took were jobs the average Briton would not do. In the United States, the Mexicans entered the country and did the farm labor, even though some people still reject such entry of Mexican workers into states like California and Texas to do farm labor. Yet, farmers and others who want to pay lower wages to cut costs and increase profits.

CHAPTER 19
GLOBAL TRADE

CHAPTER 19

GLOBAL TRADE

Introduction

Over the years we have heard about and seen changes in trade. These include trade by barter, national trade, international trade, and global trade.

Trade by Barter

Trade by barter was more or less a local trade; it was based on an exchange of what you have for what another person had, taking into account the quality and quantity of both commodities. For example, Mr. Tom, the fisherman, wanted rice for his dinner; he went to the market and met with a rice farmer who wanted to cook his dinner with fresh fish and with the type and size of fish that Mr. Tom intended to exchange. Let's call the rice farmer Mr. Bassey, and so both Mr. Tom and Mr. Bassey agreed on the quantity and quality of the rice as well as the size and weight of the fish. Both Mr. Tom and Mr. Bassey had to leave the market if that was the only transaction they had for the day. That was time consuming because one had to find someone who wanted one's product; then, an agreement had to be made on quantity and size. Trade by barter went on for quite some years before the medium of exchange was found including various metals. My grandfather told me that his grandfather told him that the metal was very bulky in that the metals were heavy and the trade could not be canceled easily, but that the pieces of metal created a national trade.

National Trade

National trade is a trade with an entity the size and population of what we call a nation today. The metals were a certain size indicating the quantity and quality of a product; the metals were widely accepted within the particular area. One could buy and sell, but one of the important constraints was inadequate transportation from one place to another, the traders either pulled their own canoe or hired able me to paddle their trading canoes from one place to another for an agreed-upon amount of metal. This type of metal trade gradually became known as the coastal trade. Coastal trade drew people from the inland areas to the coast. Coastal trade lasted as long as it took for trains to make the journey, but still coastal trade was not made also light. Even as I write, coastal trade still exists, but by this time minting metals was invented and metals became less heavy. Denominational minted medium of exchange and paper money were used in the colonies like Nigeria by the British, and this has now introduced international trade.

International Trade

International trade between nations at this point in time has a medium of exchange and rates of exchange, which in English is called money. It Efik it is called Okuk or Okwuk; in Ibo it is called Egol. There are a few of the names in Eastern Nigeria that have come about with the invention of the acceptable medium exchange. Nigeria can now trade with Ghana and South Africa as well as the United States and Great Britain and other countries. However, with the arrival of air transport and other forms of transportation, including accessible roads and larger ships, even newly independent nations are now accessible to global trade today. In today's trade, business people want to buy cheaply and sell high, so wherever they can find cheaper commodities, they go to such a place and buy or sell merchandise. Therefore, global trade is not solely based on friendly nations or allies, but solely on where profits can be made the most and easily. Global business is not only buying and selling; labor is also very important. We have seen many American companies being located abroad to take advance of cheaper labor; for instance, Microsoft and Apple Corporation along with many other have moved factories abroad because of the cheaper labor that enhances profitability. China and India ae two countries that are such locations.

FIGURE 2

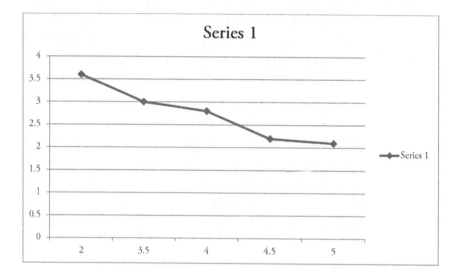

The interest rate that a country pays on its debts can be analyzed as the sum of a country's specified component and an international element. By definition the former depends entirely on the country's (economic, political, and geographical) features. For example, by limiting people's savings choices to domestic instruments, a government can influence the country's component of the interest rate on the debt. In contrast, the international element is determined by the collective borrowing and lending decisions of the participants in international debt markets around the globe. Examples of these players include, among others, individual investors, bankers, multinationals hedge funds, and pension funds. To put it simply, a country is considered a small, open economy when it takes as given the interest rate on its debt.

In principle, the small, open economy can issue as much debt as it desires as long as the country accepts the interest rate and its debt remains within the country's borrowing limits. Figure 1 above plots the interest rate on debt on the vertical axis; and the quantity of debt on the horizontal axis. In this figure, the supply of debt is decreasing because for each dollar the small open economy borrows from the world, it has to pay a higher interest rate on it. In the same figure, the demand for the country's debt is flat at some given interest rate. This means that international markets are willing to buy the small open economy's debt as long as the desired interest rate is paid. Equilibrium occurs at the point at which supply equals demand. In this example, this equilibrium level dictates that the small open economy issue about four units of debt and pay an interest rate of 3% (*Business Review*, 4/4/22016, p. 12).

Business Review (4/4/2016) stated to be precise that Figure 1 is a snapshot of the country's debt market. That the demand line is flat at 3% does not necessarily mean that it will be at that level next month. In fact, demand may most likely change over time. In small open economies, these fluctuations are to a large extent independent of the country's economic fundamentals such as productivity or its labor market. This is because [it?] depends on foreign investors views not only of the small open economy, but also of international markets in. An important feature of debt markets in small open economies is that the demand [schedule?] moves because of domestic as well as foreign considerations. For example, following the Asian Crisis of 1998, international markets became more cautious and demanded less sovereign debt around the world. This meant Mexico [had to?] sell its debt.

What is surprising about this situation is that the spike in interest rates is unrelated to the Mexican economy. In Figure 1, this external component in Mexico's debt market would be reflected as an upward jump on the demand. Figure 2 displays the interest rate premiums paid by some developing countries (Brazil, Ecuador, Mexico, and Turkey. This premium corresponds to the Emerging Market Bonds Index (EMBI) calculated by J. P. Morgan and is expressed in annualized percentages. It is a rough measure of how much foreign lenders request on top of the prevailing international rate to lend to emerging countries. In January, 1995, Brazil's EMBI was 5.82 and the three months treasury bill rate was 5.00. Together those numbers imply that international markets charged a least 10.82 percent for short-term, (three-months or less) loans to Brazil. We can observe that as the Asian Crisis unraveled in

FIGURE 2

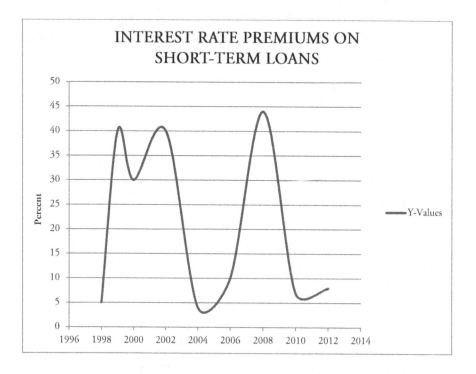

1998, the EMBI for all countries in our sample moved up even though these countries were located in different regions of the world (Brazil's EMBI reached 14.56 basis points in January 1999). This is a clear example of how spreads in emerging economies depend on external factors.

In contrast, interest rates in large-scale economies such as Japan and the United States are determined by their domestic markets. In other words, the demand curve for Japanese or U.S. debt is upward sloping. The higher the amount of debt in the market, the higher the interest rate international markets demand in exchange. More importantly, the interest rate is dictated by the country's fundamentals such as productivity, households, preferences, attitudes toward risk, and technology. This means that unless these factors change, the demand schedule does not change. To rather visualize this effect, Figure 2 also plots the yields on short-term sovereign debt in Canada and the United States during the last several years. In sharp contrast to the yields of some other countries' short-term debt, the U.S. and Canadian yields barely moved during the Asian Crisis or more recently during the 2008 financial crisis.

Another interesting factor of some large economies is that exports and imports play a small role in economic activity. A traditional measure of openness (how much a country trades with the rest of the world) is the ratio of exports plus imports to GDP. A higher number is usually interpreted as a sign of more open (in the trade sense) country. This market is also a rough indicator of how much a country's finances rely on international trade. The more a country imports and exports, the more dependent that country is on international markets. By the end of 2011, this ratio was around 0.30 for the U.S. and 0.65 for Canada. The numbers indicate that the latter country trades more heavily with the rest of the world. Table I presents our measure of trade openness for several countries around the world; whereas Japan and the U.S. are relatively closed economies, Sweden and Germany depend on international trade.

TABLE 2 TRADE OPENNESS AND GDP, 2011								
	Australia	Canada	Chile	Germany	Japan	Mexico	Sweden	U.S.A.
Trade Openness	0.42	0.65	0.75	0.84	0.31	0.65	0.94	0.30
GDP	0.013	0.021	0.003	0.05	0.119	0.017	0.009	0.276

Trade openness is defined as the ratio of export plus imports to output. GDP is that country's output as a fraction of world output. Both are computed using constant 2000 US dollars.

Source: *International Financial Statistics*, April 2013, p. 12.

Among large economies, Germany is the only one that is open. In contrast, economies that are considered small (Australia, Canada, Chile, Mexico, and Sweden) trade substantially with the rest of the world. To further illustrate the distinction between the small and large economies, Table 2 presents the ratio between the countries GDP and the world GDP in 2011. One can see that while large economies such as Japan and the United States each accounted for more than 10% of the world GDP, smaller economies like Canada and/or Chile accounted for only a small share of the total world output in 2011.

Although small, open economies share the feature of being price takers in the international bond markets, that is, they do not influence price in the marketplace, they differ substantially in other dimensions. Consequently, Economists sort these countries into two types—developed (or industrialized) economies and developing (or emerging) economies. This classification was originally proposed in the 1980s by World Bank economist Antoine van Agtmaal. Economy is considered to be developing or emerging if it is in the early stages of economic development characterized by lower income per capita and lower life expectancy compared with developed countries. In spite of this deceptively simple classification, there is no consensus about where the distinction between developed and developing vanishes. Indeed, there are many lists of emerging and developed economies compiled by institutions such as the International Monetary Fund (IMF), Columbia University's Emerging Market Global Project (EMGP), Standard and Poor's (S&P), and *The Economist* (*Business Review*, 2016, p. 12).

To avoid those conflicting views about the definition of emerging countries, we rely on more concrete quantitative measures based on the business cycle. Properties of these economies, to this end, one useful concept is the standard deviation (volatility) of the GDP in a given country. This statistical concept is typically exemplified in percentage units and measures how much the variable in question fluctuates over time around its mean. Higher standard deviation translates into higher dispersion. We also rely on a second concept correlation. The correlation between, say, interest rates and output measures how much the two variables move over time. The correlation takes values between -1 and 1, a positive values means that the two variables (in our example, output and interest rates) move in the same direction over time. In contrast, a negative correlation indicates that they move in opposite directions. Output is increasing and interest rates are declining. With these definitions in place, we are ready to discuss developed and developing small open economies (*Business Review*, 2016, p. 12).

Business Review (2012) stated that developed small open economies have several salient features. First, their business cycle volatility (as measured by the standard deviation of their GDP growth) is usually comparable in size to that seen in large and wealthy nations such as Germany, Japan, and the United States. The second characteristic of developed nation's small open economic is that their consumption follows paths that are smoother than those followed by output. In such cases, economists say that consumption is smoother than output. Consumption smoothing is possible in developed economies because people have access to financial markets. For example, suppose a person is laid off, access to those markets implies that this person can, in principle, borrow to smooth out his decline in income. This means that consumption does not drop by as much as the contraction in income. By the same token, if the person's income increases, he will save part of the extra income for the future. Access to financial markets facilitates saving the additional income overall; consumption save less than output.

Another interesting feature of developed small open economies is that interest rates are pro-cyclical. This means that, for example, an increase in economic activity is associated with an increase in economic rates today and in the near future. Table 3 lists some developed and some emerging small open economies. To facilitate comparison, the table also contains some features of the data for the United States.

Developing Small Open Economies

Business Review (2016, 20B) stated that in contrast to developed small open economies experience substantially more volatile business cycles. For example, the volatility in GDP in Mexico (an emerging small open economy) is around three percentage points. The volatility of Canada's GDP is about half of Mexico's. Consumption in most emerging economies is larger than those of output. As a consequence, the volatility of consumption is greater than the volatility of output. For instance, the volatility of consumption in Mexico is 1.21 times that of output. In contrast, that number is about .79 in Canada.

TABLE 3 Business Cycles Around the World: Small Business Economies

	Emerging Economies				Developed Economies		
	Argentina	Mexico	Thailand/ Philippines	Asia &	Canada	New Zealand	U.S.A.
Standard Development Output	4.22	2.98	.49	1.10	1.39	1.99	1.59
Standard Deviation of ___ to GDP	1.08	1.21	0.93	0.84	0.74	0.82	0.77
Standard Development of Investment to Standard Deviation of Output	2.95	3.83	4.49	4.13	2.91	3.32	4.10
Standard ___ of net ___ to GDP	0.39	8.26	0.30	0.36	0.55	0.66	0.64
Correlation of Output and net export to GDP	0.80	-0.87	-0.48	-0.59	-0.01	-0.06	-0.48
Correlation of Output and Interest Rate	.063	-0.40	*0.53	0.37	0.25	0.07	0.18

Source: Neumeyer and Peyri (2005) for Small Open Economies; Villaverde, Fernandez, et al. (2012) and Gogetti (2008) for the United States.

Business Review (4/2013) has stated that a third important characteristic of emerging economies is that the interest rate on their debt experiences abrupt movements over time. As shown in Figure 2, yields on Brazilian debt jumped over five percentage points in a matter of months during the 1997-98 Asian Crisis. Most developed small open economies have never seen such an abrupt change in their interest rate (at least until the recent European Crisis). Interest rate hikes (arising, for example, from contagion in international markets) in emerging economies are typically followed by a contraction in economic activity; that is, output, consumption, and investment contract. These opposing movements in output and interest rates are captured by the negative correlations reported in Table 2.

FIGURE 3

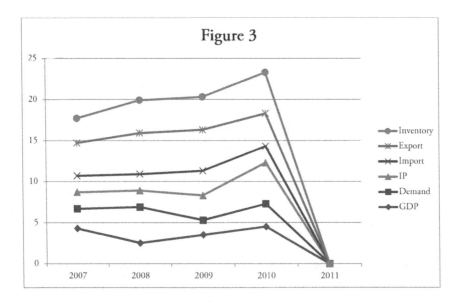

For our three emerging economies, other features of emerging economies are also often emphasized in the book by Paul Krugman and Maurice Obstfeld. In addition to the characteristics discussed above, these countries tend to have high inflation and weak financial systems. Their exchange rates are to a large extent influenced by their local government and their economies rely heavily on commodities, natural or agricultural, resources.

Finally, it seems that there is no clear difference regarding the evolution of net exports. According to Table 2, net exports have been less volatile than output in both developing and developed economies. The exception is the Philippines, which displays more volatility in net exports. A closer look at the data, however, reveals that developing countries display an average strong negative correlation between net exports and output. Furthermore, emerging economies tend to run larger trade deficits (imports are larger than exports) prior to crisis. Subsequently, the trade balance turns into a surplus as the emerging economy reduces its imports from abroad and the weakening of its currency boosts exports. In contrast, developed countries have run persistently large trade deficits, e.g., Canada and the United States (*Business Review*, 4/2013, p. 13.

U.S. Trade and Expenditure

The *Business Review* (4/2013) stated in its article that at the start of the recession, imports fell slightly and exports expanded slightly. From the second quarter of 2009 to the second quarter of 2010 imports and exports fell dramatically about 23% each. The sharp contraction in exports and imports was more than the fall in GDP (5 to 4 percent), demand (14.7%), or industrial production (16.5%) over those in Figure 1.

During the same period, similarly from the second quarter of 2009, the rebound in exports and imports was quite large compared with the rebound in GDP demand or industrial production. To put the dynamics of trade in historical context, the table reports the peak to trough movements to imports and exports in each of the last seven recessions. For imports and exports, the decline downturns are comparable to this in previous downturns. For example, imports fell 4.4 times as much as GDP in 2008-09, which is about equal to the median decline of 4.6 over these seven recessions. Imports fell about 1.5 times as much as demand for tradeable goods, which is a bit smaller than the median decline of 2.4. Similarly, exports fell about 1.3 time as much as manufacturing production in the recession, which is the median decline in these seven recessions (*Business Review*, 2013, p. 3).

Evidence on Auto Imports and Sales

One might be concerned that we have not properly accounted for the different components of expenditures and trade flows; that is, one trade weighted measure of expenditures does not accurately reflect the composition of trade. This clearly explains why trade fails more than GDP since the goods that fluctuate the most over the business cycle are consumer goods (*Business Review*, 2013, p. 3).

TABLE 4 Peak Drop in Trade Relative to Absorption							
IMPORTS							
Median	1971 Qs	1975 2Q	1980 3Q	1984 4Q	1991 1Q	2001 4Q	2009 1Q
GDP 4.62	4.62	4.62	5.25	2.38	2.59	5.92	1.44
IP 1.56	1.17	1.64	2.44	1.17	1.56	2.00	1.42
Demand 2.41	2.50	2.41	2.84	2.39	1.55	5.46	1.47
EXPORTS (Peak to Trough)							
Median	1971 Qs	1975 2Q	1980 3Q	1984 4Q	1991 1Q	2001 4Q	2009 1Q
IP 1.35	0.52	0.86	1.08	1.72	1.53	2.33	1.35

\NOTES: Numbered from start of recession based on the NBER dates. The third panel measures the difference in exports between the peak and trough where the peak is only the start of the recession if exports fall immediately.

All data were HP filtered with a smoothing parameter of 1600 and so the drop is measured relative to the trend (*Business Review*, 1/2013, p. 3).

North American Free Trade Association (NAFTA)

Cross-border trade between the United States and our largest trading partners, Canada and Mexico, continues to grow and cross-border intermodal services offer shippers more options in getting their product to these markets. Transportation economics justify considering rail as an alternative to cross-border truck moves (Buxbaum, *Global Logistics*, p. 44).

Freight moving more than 1000 miles from many U.S. points to Canada or Mexico metropolitans can be serviced via rail two-way. USA and Canada intermodal traffic increased by 38.5% between 2003 and 2013. The southbound leg, where there is more capacity, increased by 353% during the same period. Cross border rail trade with Mexico reached one million rail carloads in 2014. "Typical southbound trade includes grains, plastics, chemicals, and auto parts," says Ixer de Luiza, Director General of the Association Mexicana de Ferracarriles (AMF). Northbound trains transport autos, home appliances, beer, and floor tiles. USA railroads conducting products to Mexico include the Union Pacific, Burlington Northern, Santa Fe, and the Kansas City Southern Railroads. Mexican railroads with cross-border operations are Ferromex and Kansas City Southern de Mexico. A short line railroad from Tijuana, Tecate also operates cross the border on a small scale. Shippers should keep in mind the trade-off between speed and cost and that is inherent in truck versus intermodal choices. "In many cases, intermodal rail transit is expected to be one in three calendar days slower than the over-the-road transportation," says Fox. He continues, "The longer the haul, the wider the gap gets between truckload and intermodal transit expectations; yet, those same longer hauls ae often where the biggest cost savings can be obtained."

FIGURE 4: NAFTA RAIL TIES

Rail carriers are increasingly offering trans-border services in which shipments move on the railroads in both the United States and Canada or Mexico, clearing customs in the interior of the destination country. Rail carriers have been investing in facilities that promote those services. The CSR Transportation, serving Valleyfield terminal 40 miles outside Montreal, has provided shippers additional capacity when shipping freight between the United States and Eastern Canada. Opened in late 2014, the Valleyfield facility achieves intermodal access to Canadian distribution and consumption markets (Fox, *Global Logistics,* 2016, February-March, p. 44).

Bryan Fox (*Global Logistics*, 2016) stated that Valleyfield provided on-site border clearance capabilities facilitated by a 10,000 square foot, secure container processing facility, and access to the Canadian government's VACIS truck scanning system. This equipment is brought on site as required and is capable of more than 25 scans per hour of an entire vehicle to clear freight into Canada. The Valleyfield Intermodal Terminal provides shippers an alternative capacity solution when shipping freight between the United States and Eastern Canada. Wesley Ann Barton, Director of Marketing of CSX Transportation Intermodal says, "Shippers converting from the highway to intermodal rail are able to secure additional capacity and lower transportation costs thanks to the expansive market reach of the CBXT intermodal network." The Canadian National Railway in partnership with Kansas City Southern de Mexico (KCSM) also provides transportation services that allow intermodal shipments to crops in Mexico prior to being inspected. The new inspection point is located in Mexico City at KCSIQ's Puerta Mexico Intermodal Terminal and Terminal Ferroviaria de Valle de Mexico's (TFVM) Panaco Intermodal Terminal. (*Global Logistics*, 2016).

FIGURE 5: Mexico-USA Service. It is like a track across the Gulf. C. G. Railway

Canadian Pacific Alliances and experience are and cost effective transportation solution between Canada, the United States, and Mexico. According to Anthony Chavez, the company's sales director, "On-line tracking and inbound service take the guesswork out of cross-border shipment." He said inbound shipping allows cargo to clear customs after crossing the border. CSXT Intermodal Service between the Eastern USA and Mexico is available via a service called Streamline Passport, a door-to-door solution for shippers to more than 100 Mexican locations. Passport rates include all border fees, fuel surcharge, and container per diem charges in Mexico. CSXT Intermodal ensures that all customs requirements are met when shipping cross-border freight. USA and Mexican customs agencies are working jointly to expedite the movement of cross-border freight by implement a paper rail-e-manifest process. "It is likely that it will be finished on both sides of the Mexico-USA border by 2017," says de Luiza. He adds that Mexican railroad trade is strong and growing and railroads in the US, Canada, and Mexico have the same standards for infrastructure and other operational specifications such as mechanical standards and the use of radio spectrum. According to de Luisa, "it is an integrated network" (Bryan Fox, *NAFTA*, 2016, p. 45).

FIGURE 6: Air Flow (by Ian Puzger)

ASIA: Hong Kong

Hong Kong is one of the world's most densely populated areas. It is home to one of the world's most important financial centers and has more than 1200 skyscrapers lining its horizon. It is mild in the winter months, but very hot and humid with frequent typhoons in the summer. It is relatively easy to travel to Hong Kong; that is, travel for Los Angeles International Airport (LAX) to Hong Kong the service is excellent. Since most flights leave LAX in late afternoon, one arrives in Hong Kong the next day afforded plenty of rest to prepare for your first formal working day. HK "G" is regularly rated one of the best airports in the world. Most Americans won't encounter any major cultural differences when doing business with locals, although Hong Kong people tend to be a bit more formal and conservative. Locals put a strong emphasis on hard work and success, as well as subscribing to long working hours. Formal Western business attire (suits for men and women) is the norm. From a cultural perspective, it is good to practice the usual formalities that one would expect in most other Asian nations such as giving and receiving business cards with two hands. When receiving a business card, handle it with care and look it over for a few seconds before putting it away (Brad Dwan, 2016, February-March, p. 22).

Brad Dwan (2016) has also stated that English and Cantonese are the official languages in Hong Kong. Cantonese is the primary language spoken by locals, but most people, especially the young generation speak English. Not all tax drivers speak English, so it's always a good idea to have hotel or business destination addresses written in Chinese to show them for reference just in case. Luxury business hotels abound both in Kowloon and across Victoria Harbor on Hong Kong Island. You can take the airport express train as soon as you clear immigration at the airport all the way to Kowloon Station. It takes 24 minutes and runs every 10 minutes. The station is right under Elementary Mall where the Waterhole Hotel is located; take the elevator up to the Waterhole and you are there.

Another beautiful hotel is the Ritz Carlton at the top of the ICC Tower in Kowloon. Be sure to go to the very to the Sky Bar at night and look out over the beautiful city lights of Hong Kong. When you get hungry, you will find a wide array of international food options. Local delicacies include dim sum Chinese foods, typically served in bamboo steamer baskets, hot pot, and sushi. When the sun sets, the fun begins. Lan Kwai Fung is the hottest night life spot in Hong Kong, frequented mostly by white collar workers and expatriates. Award-winning dining with more than 100 bars, restaurants, shops, and club makes Lan Kwai Fung a favorite haunt for many. Hong Kong boasts a highly developed public transportation system along with a clean and efficient subway system. There are many taxis and busses moving throughout the city, but be careful when crossing the street. They drive on the left side (the wrong side) of the road. Be sure to save some time for sightseeing. Most popular is the western part of Hong Kong Island. One can take a train to the top for a stunning view of the city and harbor. While you're there, have a bit at the Peak Lookout restaurant and see the panoramic view across Victoria Harbor (Brad Dwan, 2016, February-March, p. 23).

Brad Dwan stated further that the other popular spots in Hong Kong are the Mid-Levels Escalator in the central business district; it is the largest covered escalator in the world measuring 260 feet long and 443 feet vertically; also, almost any spot located on the Victoria Harbor waterfront is a great place to view the *Symphony of Lights*, which is a miniature light show beginning every night at 8:00 p.m. that synchronizes 40 builidngs affixed with light son both sides of the harbor with a musical sccore, creating a fantastic visual experience. Be sure to leave some time available for taking a taxi to the other side of Hong Kong Island on the peninsula to visit Stanley. It is a small seaside area with an array of small shops and street shops and two of Hong Kong's most beautiful beaches.

Last, but not least, if you thrive on chaotic shopping experiences, check out the Ladies Market on Tung Choi Street. One can hone your barbering skills and negotiate with some of the best purveyors of inexpensive clothing, accessories, and more than 100 stalls (Brad Dwan, 2016, February-March, p. 23).

Letters of Credit

Most banks that offer financing to exporters offer export letters of credit that are often used to ensure that an overseas client pays as promised. These are letters that one bank issues to other banks to guarantee that a payment will be made as long as the conditions listed in the document are met. However, many exporters do not realize that letters of credit have another purpose as well; "the Letter of Credit can be used as a financing tool," says Martin Marrow, a Houston, Texas-based international trade specialist with BOK Financial. Marrow explains:

> The way the Letter of Credit is structured allows the exporter to get the advanced payment at certain milestones. For instance, the Letter of Credit might specify the overseas buyer will pay you a portion of what is owed. This can come in hand for US-based manufacturers who are filling jobs that take many months, but let them have working capital while they are manufacturing or producing. Once they meet that milestone, they can get another Letter of Credit. (Paul M. Hietko, *Banking on Export*, 2016, February-March, p. 26).

Hietko stated further than the Letter of Credit comes with fees. Processing fees may range from one-eighth of one percent of the value of a transaction to one-fourth of one percent, depending on the institution. According to Marrow, confirmation fees may range from 1-3% (Marrow, p. 28).

Export Financing

Many businesses who intend to export try traditional bank loans first because these are familiar financial tools; however, export financing can offer more flexibility. According to Marsh, "if they have some domestic and some international business and need more financing, it's to their advantage to choose export financing because it is so similar and more available for them." Marsh also explained that export specific financing often remains more accessible than traditional Small Business Administration (SBA)-backed loans if liquidity tightens, and there is less red tape. Marsh explained, "It is kind of covenant light" (Paul Hietko, *Banking on Export*, 2016, February, p. 26).

Mr. Hietko stated further that EXIM offers several types of financing. In some cases, EXIM will guarantee loans for commercial banks; typically it guarantees 85% of the loan. Banks have a certain *delegation authority* that determines the limit of how much they can lend without getting special permission from EXIM bank's Global Credit Express program, provides six or 12-month fixed rate line of credit of up to $500,000. EXIM Bank provides fixed rate financing of up to 12 years for most projects, financing U.S. corporations' international buyers, and entrepreneurs' local cost of up to 30%. EXIM Bank also provides export credits insurance that insures foreign accounts receivable (Hietko, p. 26).

Traditional Bank Loans

Paul Hietko also stated that if one tried all other options of financing and still needed financing, then the borrower should not rule out getting a traditional bank loan. Acceding to BIZ2 Credit, an on-line matchmaker between borrowers and lenders in New York. City loan approval rates in big banks hit a post-recession high in December; that said, their loan approval rate was only 22.9%, so one has to try another bank as well. Therefore, Hietko found his community bank the most convenient as sources of financing. When Hietko was starting up, community banks had a loan rate of 19.1% in December, up from 18.9% in November. One should be prepared to shop around if you need a relatively small amount of money. Nevertheless, many banks in recent years have leaned toward making small business loans of $1 million or more. "If one is looking for under $100,000, it is challenging to find the financing and loan guarantee," Hietko stated.

New Rules for Foreign Banks

The recent financial crisis has led economists and policymakers to think more carefully about how global banks ae regulated. Before the crisis, foreign banks had operated their US branches and subsidiaries mainly under rules set by the countries where they were based, but as the crisis made clear, financial shocks were transmitted internationally. Efforts to resolve them can be hampered when finances have multiple regulators with opposing interests and different resolution mechanisms.

In response to these concerns, the Federal Reserve Board, in accordance with the Dodd-Frank Act, has approved rules to strengthen the regulation of foreign banks operating in the United States in coming years. The new framework is organizational restrictions and higher regulatory costs may reduce the efficient flow of funds within global banks. These costs and restrictions may also induce global banks to shift activities to other countries, switch from subsidiaries to branches, or take other steps to avoid the full impact of these regulations. However, the new rules reflect international concerns about financial stability that came into sharp relief during the recent crisis. To understand the trade-offs, let us examine how banking become globally interconnected in the years leading up to the financial crisis. How does the presence of foreign banks benefit a country and what are the costs? Why had foreign banks been lightly regulated before the crisis? And post-crisis, what are the new regulations' likely costs and benefits? (Mitchell Berlin, *Business Review*, 2015, p. 1).

The Rise of Global Banking

Global banking expanded dramatically before the financial crisis of 2008-09. The two decades preceding the financial crisis had been termed *the second age of globalization*, a period of rapid economic integration that included a dramatic expansion of international banking. International banks became truly global in the sense that they increasingly had branches and subsidiaries physically located in many countries, performing a wide range of funding, lending, and capital market activities. The share of the foreign banks operating subsidiaries in a sample of 137 countries increased to 14% from 1995 to 2008. The rising share was most dramatic in developing countries. However, the trend may be understated for developed countries because banks often enter foreign markets through branches rather than subsidiaries. For just the United States, we have data extending further into the past and that includes both subsidiaries and branches of foreign banks operating in the United States. This data reveals a rough doubling of the share of all US assets of foreign banks among all banks doing business in the United States between 1980 and 1992. After a modest decline from 1992 to 2004, foreign banks' share of US assets increased again during the period of explosive growth of American banking assets through 2008. Therefore, the dollar amount of foreign banking assets in the US was increasing significantly even as she share increased modestly. Although we observe a slowing and then a quickening in growth of foreign banks assets in the subsequent years, it is too soon to predict future trends (Mitchell Berlin, *Business Review*, 2015, p. 1).

Before and After Regulation of Foreign Banks in the U.S.

(*Business Review, 1/2015*
Before 2014

1. The Federal Reserve oversaw US operations of foreign banks. Their home banks had oversight of their global operations.
2. Foreign banks were not required to meet Fed capital requirements as long as they were deemed well managed, well capitalized, and their home regulations were consistent to US regulations.
3. Foreign banks were free to choose their own organizational structure, subject to approval by the Federal Reserve.
4. Foreign banks faced restrictions on their assets and liability mix.
5. Branches could not take retail deposits.
6. Branches were required to consistently hold a certain amount of high quality assets in the U.S.

Foreign Banks with a Total Combined Assets of between US$10 Billion and US$50 billion Must:

1. Meet home country capital stress test or perform company-run stress tests.
2. Have a risk committee for US operations if publicly traded.

Foreign banks with total combined assets exceeding US$50 billion and combined U.S. assets of less than US$50 billion.

3. Meet home country capital stress test requirements or perform company run stress test.
4. Have a risk committee for US operations.
5. Certify to the FED that they must become country capital standards consistent with the basic accords.
6. Perform company-run liquidity stress for combined operations or US operations.

Foreign banks with total combined assets exceeding US$50 billion and combined U.S. assets of exceeding US$50 billion must:

1. Meet home country capital stress test requirements or perform company-run stress tests.
2. Have a risk committee and a risk officer for US operations.
3. Certify that they meet home country capital standards consistent with the Basel records.
4. Perform company-run liquidity stress for their US operations.

Foreign banks with total combined assets exceeding US$50 billion and combined U.S. assets (exceeding assets held branding companies) exceeding US$50 billion must form an intermediary holding company that:

1. Satisfies capital and liquidity requirements comparable to requirements for requirements for U.S. bank holding companies.
2. Satisfies capital stress tests run by the Federal Reserve.

Questions

1. a) What is NAFTA?

b) Name countries that make up NAFTA>

2. What are the major cultural differences when doing businesses in Hong Kong?
3. Explain Letters of Credit.
4. What is export financing?
5. Explain the rise of Global; Banking.
6. Explain the new rules for foreign banks in the U.S.
7. Discuss developing small open economies.

Answers

1. a. North American Free Trade Association.
   b. United States of America, Canada, and Mexico.
2. Major cultural difference when doing business
   Most cultural differences when doing business with locals, although Hong Kong people tend to be a bit more formal and conservative. They put a strong emphasis on hard work and success, as well as subscribing to long working hours. Formal Western business attire (suits for men and women) is the norm. From a cultural perspective, it is good to practice the usual formalities that one would expect in most other Asian nations such as giving and receiving business cards with two hands. When receiving a business card, handle it with care and look it over for a few seconds before putting it away (Brad Dwan, 2016, February-March, p. 22). The official languages are English and Cantonese.
3. Most banks that offer financing to exporters offer export letters of credit that are often used to ensure that an overseas client pays as promised. These are letters that one bank issues to other banks to guarantee that a payment will be made as long as the conditions listed in the document are met. However, many exporters do not realize that letters of credit have another purpose as well; "the Letter of Credit can be used as a financing tool," says Martin Marrow, a Houston, Texas-based international trade specialist with BOK Financial. Marrow explains:

The way the Letter of Credit is structured allows the exporter to get the advanced payment at certain milestones. For instance, the Letter of Credit might specify the overseas buyer will pay you a portion of what is owed. This can come in hand for US-based manufacturers who are filling jobs that take many months, but let them have working capital while they are manufacturing or producing. Once they meet that milestone, they can get another Letter of Credit. (Paul M. Hietko, Banking on Export, 2016, February-March, p. 26).

4. Many businesses who intend to export try traditional bank loans first because these are familiar financial tools; however, export financing can offer more flexibility. According to Marsh, "if they have some domestic and some international business and need more financing, it's to their advantage to choose export financing because it is so similar and more available for them." Export specific financing often remains more accessible than traditional Small Business Administration (SBA)-backed loans if liquidity tightens, and there is less red tape.

5. Global banking expanded dramatically before the financial crisis of 2008-09. The two decades preceding the financial crisis had been termed the second age of globalization, a period of rapid economic integration that included a dramatic expansion of international banking. International banks became truly global in the sense that they increasingly had branches and subsidiaries physically located in many countries, performing a wide range of funding, lending, and capital market activities. The share of the foreign banks operating subsidiaries in a sample of 137 countries increased to 14% from 1995 to 2008. The rising share was most dramatic in developing countries. However, the trend may be understated for developed countries because banks often enter foreign markets through branches rather than subsidiaries. For just the United States, we have data extending further into

the past and that includes both subsidiaries and branches of foreign banks operating in the United States. This data reveals a rough doubling of the share of all US assets of foreign banks among all banks doing business in the United States between 1980 and 1992. After a modest decline from 1992 to 2004, foreign banks' share of US assets increased again during the period of explosive growth of American banking assets through 2008. Therefore, the dollar amount of foreign banking assets in the US was increasing significantly even as she share increased modestly. Although we observe a slowing and then a quickening in growth of foreign banks assets in the subsequent years, it is too soon to predict future trends.

6. Explain new rules for foreign banks in the United States. The financial crisis of 2008-09 led economists and policymakers to think more carefully about how global banks are regulated. Before the crisis, foreign banks had operated their US branches and subsidiaries mainly under rules set by the countries where they were based, but as the crisis made clear, financial shocks were transmitted internationally. Efforts to resolve them can be hampered when there are multiple regulators with opposing interests and different resolution mechanisms.

   In response to these concerns, the Federal Reserve Board, in accordance with the Dodd-Frank Act, has approved rules to strengthen the regulation of foreign banks operating in the United States in coming years. The new framework is organizational restrictions and higher regulatory costs which may reduce the efficient flow of funds within global banks. These costs and restrictions also induce global banks to shift activities to other countries, switch from subsidiaries to branches, or take other steps to avoid the full impact of these regulations. However, the new rules reflect heightened concerns about global financial stability that came into sharp relief during the recent crisis. To understand the trade-offs, let us examine how banking become globally interconnected in the years leading to the financial crisis?

7. Developing Small Open Economies. In contrast to developed small open economies, emerging small open economies experience substantially more volatile business cycles. For example, the volatility of GDP in Mexico (an emerging small open economy) is around three percentage points. The volatility of Candida is about half of Mexico's consumption. Most emerging economies display fluctuations. The volatility of consumption is greater than the volatility of output. For instance, the volatility of consumption in Mexico is 1.21 times that of output. In contrast to that the number is about .74 in Canada (*Business Review*, 4/2013).

Policy Adjustment

Adjustment of policies is very important in business, economics, and politics, especially in this new world of innovation in technology and the Internet. We do not have to hold on to one idea for years in business, economics, and politics; we have to see what others are doing in the industry in order to compete. We must have visions or dreams about what tomorrow will look like based on our visions of today.

I know that we had feasibility studies when we started the company, but we need a yearly or bi-annual check-up to know where we are now compared to where we were a year or two ago. In some manufacturing companies such as automobiles and clothing, this checking should be done every six months. Policy is a definite course of action adopted by a company's government or even in a household, a family could decide either to go out for dinner one night or to cook whatever they want to eat. A company could decide to train new hires at a certain time or hire already hire already trained employees.

However, let us return to our discussion about the family, which is quite common for everyone. In the past, in most parts of Nigeria, a nuclear family could grow up to any number of members because the children were needed to work on farms and eat whatever they produced and then grow up to become small farmers themselves. Years later, things have changed and responsibilities have mounted.

Nigerians began realizing that having children must go along with having other resources because the children have to go to school and become something better and that the community as a whole. So, people began having fewer children. From ten children, the number was reduced to no more than two or three. That is even more severe with the younger generations who simply want a child no matter what sex and the maximum is based on their resources. This is unlike China which mandated a policy by the government. A policy adjustment individually or even collectively made is always very effective. For example, if you as a parent can encourage your child to study hard for a better grade, the child accepts your vision wholeheartedly, and the child will certainly do more than you anticipated because the person studying made the adjustment herself or himself.

Policy adjustment is the lifeline of any business world must see the competition in its industry and has to follow up to stay in business. When Company A began functioning, the original policy may have been great, but because of tests, migration of people into the proximity of the company, and technological advances that have caused shifts to the right or to the left, whatever it is must be handled efficiently and quickly.

A case in point is I had a mortgage company that I called Metro Loans in San Francisco, California in the United States. I had a few employees in my office working with me, some people in the field, and a telemarketing group in the office. I had an employee who read newspapers in the morning hours, particularly the mortgage section; any information in that section concerning lenders, loans to value, appraisers, and much more he would bring to my attention. I then followed up to see what items were very competitive. For instance, my customers were to pay for appraisals, but when I saw that my competitors servicing loans than I was were paying for appraisals, we began doing the same thing after knowing the loan to value (LTV) and if it was owner occupied or a rental property. I was in the business more than some of my competitors until where we had the training sent out some trainees to find out what I was doing differently. I told them that the training is always a base, the rest is common sense based on what worked for one's business. For example, we were not taught to have a telemarketing division nor what I call policy adjustment. But in my case, here was something different because then I had a MBA. I could be a little more creative than when I had just a BA and a license.

Today, see most of such policies in price adjustments in the supermarkets. Policy adjustments are very important in every business; many businesses thought they could go from year to year without looking on the competition around them in the same industry. That is important and unavoidable in today's global economy. We have to see what others are doing so as to enable ourselves to do the same thing much better. This is a very competitive world we live in. A company may produce whatever it likes, but who is the target audience? Unless one is producing for local consumption, and even then the tests of the product may not be accepted by all community members.

Policy adjustment is not only necessary in business, but it can also be seen in politics. We have just seen women march on Washington demanding respect for women and for Obamacare to remain place. Just as I am writing, middle easterners from different Arab countries are rejecting deportations back to their nations because their nations are regarded as terrorist nations. They are protesting because they feel their detention is against the rule of law. All the demonstrations have called for the President of the United States to review the policy he made in an executive order to be adjusted. In the meantime, some detainees have been let go, meaning the President of the US has adjusted his policy. Policy adjustments can be made during political campaigns, but in politics there may times the political adversary may use such an adjustment as a negative indicating that the candidate's adjustment is case of flip-flopping, which may also mean that such a candidate may not be trusted with his or her campaign promises and that could mean do or don't in politics.

That man has nothing to do with supporters because they know if you make a mistake, you have to correct it quickly. Even very reputable companies make mistakes and so do governments. Sometimes the decision a company has made may not be the problem, but in approaching a problem, a company should make decisions starting with what the employees are comfortable and then continuing on with what they are unfamiliar with or uncomfortable. In other words, a business owner, CEO, professor, principal, president of a country, and any other leader must approach human beings from the standpoint of going from the known to the unknown. Otherwise, if one starts and administration from the unknown you may be giving your students, audience, employees, and voters the opportunity to begin making up their minds about you and your administration and that will affect trust, confidence, and the ability to work harder.

If you're in business or any other human endeavor and you do not feel obligated to adjust when you go wrong or make a mistake, that means you are afraid to fail, and that means you do not belong in a leadership positon. Policy adjustment indicates that the leaders are abreast of changes needed for the company to be current and to be competitive in this advanced technological age. However, adjustments must not be made just for the sake of adjustment. If the adjustment that the company is interested in worked for another company, then one should ensure that it will work for your company by finding out the pros and cons in a costs/benefits analysis. If the analysis is carefully done, the deviation may be minimal and that means your company should go ahead and implement the adjustment. One should make sure the company's niche is protected; otherwise, your products will look exactly like the competition. Your products must be differentiated so as to give you an edge in marketing.

Some political adjustments are made by voters, who call it changes, and that is a way of voting out an incumbent, even though voters often have no way of knowing how good or how bad the change may turn out to be. Such changes may mean that voters are tired of the incumbent for some reason or another. Adjustment is meant to represent something better than the original idea, but if turns out to be wrong, well it is a risk worth taking. Policy adjustment, as the words indicate, in most cases, especially in business and management, not much is expected to go wrong if implemented correctly and if you know that such adjustments are tailored to business like yours.

Excerpts from
IN "NEW NAFTA" DEAL

By Heather Long, *The Washington Post,* October, 2018

On Sunday night, President Trump got his wish for a significantly revised North American trade deal. After more than a year of intense negotiations, the United States, Canada and Mexico reached an agreement to update the North American Free Trade Agreement, the 1994 pact that governs more than $1.2 trillion worth of trade among the three nations.

The new deal won't go in effect right away. Most of the key provisions don't start until 2020 because leaders from the three countries have to sign it and then Congress and the legislatures in Canada and Mexico have to approve it, a process that is expected to take months.

Here's a rundown of what's in the "new NAFTA."

New name. Goodbye NAFTA. The new deal will be known as the United States-Mexico-Canada Agreement, or USMCA. Trump, who had long disdained NAFTA, had suggested that he might call it the "USMC," in honor of the U.S. Marine Corps, but in the end, USMC won out.

Big changes for cars. The goal of the new deal is to have more cars and truck parts made in North America. Starting in 2020, to qualify for zero tariffs, a car or truck must have 75 percent of its components manufactured in Canada, Mexico or the United States, a substantial boost from the current 62.5 percent requirement.

There's also a new rule that a significant percentage of the work done on the car must be completed by workers earning at least $16 an hour, or about three times what the typical Mexican autoworker makes. Starting in 2020, cars and trucks should have at least 30 percent of the work on the vehicle done by workers earning $16 an hour. That gradually moves up to 40 percent for cars by 2023.

While many economists think these new rules will help some North American workers, they also warn that car prices might rise and some small cars may no longer be made in North America because they would be too expensive under the new requirements. There are also concerns that automakers might not make as many cars in North America to export to China and elsewhere overseas costs would be higher in the USMCA region than making the vehicles in Asia.

Trump's victory: Canada opens up its milk market to U.S. farmers. Trump tweeted often about how unfair he thought it was that Canada charged such high tariffs on U.S. dairy products. Canada has a complex milk and dairy system. To ensure Canadian dairy farmers don't go bankrupt, the Canadian government restricts how much dairy can be produced in the country and how much foreign dairy can enter to keep milk prices high. Trump didn't like that, and dairy was a major sticking point in the negotiations.

In the end, Canada is keeping most of its complex system in place, but it is giving greater market share to U.S. dairy farmers. U.S. negotiators say they got a major victory by forcing Canada to eliminate the pricing scheme for what are known as Class 7 dairy products. That means U.S. dairy farmers can probably send a lot more milk protein concentrate, Skim milk powder and infant formula to Canada (and those products are relatively easy to transport and store).

Canada's victory: Chapter 19, allowing for a special dispute process, stays intact. Canadian Prime Minister Justin Trudeau said repeatedly that he wanted to keep Chapter 19 in place, and that's exactly what happened. The U.S. side pushed hard to eliminate this chapter, but in the end, it stayed.

Chapter 19 allows Canada, Mexico and the United States to challenge one another's anti-dumping and countervailing duties in front of a panel of representatives from each country. This is generally a much easier process than trying to challenge a trade practice in a U.S. court. Over the years, Canada has successfully used Chapter 19 to challenge the United States on its softwood lumber restrictions.

Mexico and Canada get assurance Trump won't pound them with auto tariffs. Trump has repeatedly threatened to slap hefty tariffs on car and vehicle parts coming from overseas into the United States. Along with the new trade deal, his administration signed "side letters" allowing the two nations to mostly dodge Trump's auto tariffs.

The side letters say Canada and Mexico can continue sending about the same vehicles and parts across the border free of charge, regardless of whether auto tariffs go into effect down the road. Only parts above that quota could face tariffs.

Trump's steel tariffs stay in place (for now). Canada wanted Trump to stop his 25 percent tariffs on Canadian steel. That didn't happen – yet. The two countries are still discussing lifting those tariffs, but a senior White House official said Sunday that process is on a "completely separate track." Trudeau has called the steel tariffs "insulting and unacceptable" because the two nations are such close allies.

Improved labor and environmental rights. The USMCA makes a number of significant upgrades to environmental and labor regulations, especially regarding Mexico. For example, the USMCA stipulates that Mexican trucks that cross the border into the United States must meet higher safety regulations and that Mexican workers must have more ability to organize and form unions. Some of these provisions might be difficult to enforce, but the Trump administration says it is committed to ensuring these happen – a reason U.S. labor unions and some Democrats are cheering the new rules.

Increased intellectual property protections. The new IP chapter is 63 pages and contains more-stringent protections for patents and trademarks, including for biotech, financial services and even domain names. Many business leaders and legal experts believed these updates were necessary given that the original agreement was negotiated 25 years ago.

Chapter 11, giving investors a special way to fight government decisions, is (mostly) gone. Chapter 11 is eliminated entirely for Canada and mostly for Mexico, except for some key industries such as energy and telecommunications. Chapter 11 gave companies and investors a special process to resolve disputes with one of the governments in NAFTA. The idea was that if investors put a lot of money into a project and then the government changes the rules, there was a clear dispute process – outside the court system – where investors could get their problem resolved.

DEFINITION OF TERMS

Dynamics: The branch of mathematics that deals with the motion and equilibrium of systems under the systems of focus—the motivating or driving forces.

Decision: To settle a dispute; to make up one's mind and make a judgment; to decide on what direction a company will be going and doing business; to decide how the family will function.

Adjustment: To reset; to add more information to had is already written or subtract some information from what is already written. A house that is not well build could be adjusted for more accommodation or for the foundation to be solidified and durable. Congress could adjust the existing laws to either be narrower or broader in scope.

Letter of Credit: Most banks that offer financing to exporters offer export letters of credit that are often used to ensure an overseas client pays an exporter as promised. These are letters that one bank issues to another bank to guarantee that payment will be made as long as the conditions listed in the document are met. Another purpose of letters of credit is that they could be used as a financing tool.

Power of Presentation Presentations, whether academic or just friendly gatherings must contain or portray some sort of agenda or reasons for what you know about the subject, pros and cons of what you are talking about, economic reasons, political implications, of the subject, business applications, religious factors and so forth

An example of political presentations occurred when John Kerry was nominated to represent the Democratic Party as its presidential candidate in 2003. Senator Barack Obama did the presentation and people admired his oratory in his speech, but unfortunately Mr. Kerry was not elected president. When Mr. Obama ran on the Democratic ticket for president and was elected.

In Mr. Obama's second term, Mr. Kerry became the Secretary of State for Mr. Obama. All that originated from the power of presentation by the former Senator Barack Obama.

REFERENCES

Business Review. (2016, June 4). Developing small open economies. P. 2d.

Buxbaum, Peter. (???). *Global Logistics.*

Fox, Bryan Fox. (2016, February-March). *Global Logistics. Journal of Banking on Exports.* (2016, Feb./Mar.). Global trade. P.26.

Hayd, Robert L., & Gray, Edmund. (1981). *Business and government.* Fayetteville, ARK: University of Arkansas and Baton Rouge, LA: Louisiana State University. O, 77,

Heilbroner, S., & Thurow, L (1998). Ergonomics explained: How economy works. New York: Simon & Schuster.

McDonald, C. d., Jr. (1989). *Marketing.* 2nd ed. New York: Harper & Row Publishers.

New York Times. (2016, July 8). *British vote to leave the EU.* P. B2.

San Francisco Chronicle. (2016, July 20). *The EU and the British economy.* P. A3.

Schein, E. (1993). *Organizational psychology: Foundation of Psychology Series.* NJ: Prentice-Hall.

DEFINITION OF TERMS

PHRASE	MEANING
ANC	African National Congress, South Africa's ruling party
APWU	American Postal Union
Approaches to Discipline	Approaches to violation of company rules can be handled in many different ways. At one extreme supervisors seeing a mistake may scream at the offender in front of other workers and issue snap decisions aimed at punishing the offender and at deterring others from wrongdoing. The other extreme a supervisor upon seeing a mistake may respond in a calm and considerate manner with the intent of improving future performance not at punishing past performance.
BBC	British Broadcasting Corporation
BPD	Barrels per day

Biase	Biase is a local government area consisting of five clans, each of which is made up of about 5 million people. Biase is endowed with academicians, medical doctors, engineers, lawyers, teachers, civil servants, as well as business people, which is a very fast growing segment. Others include farmers, civil servants, and private palm and rubber estates. With lights all over Biase, manufacturing of assorted products are springing up. I think that contributions from places like Biase from most local governments in Nigeria make it the largest economy in Africa.
COD	Cash on Demand or pay on delivery
CPO	Community Post Office
DMD	Deputy Managing Director
ECOWAS	Economic Community of West African States
EEC	European Economic Community
EFTA	European Free Trade Association
Employee Relations	In unionized organizations, the personnel department takes an active role in negotiating and administer-ing ;labor agreements. Gathering information and helping to prepare the company's bargaining position is normally the responsibility of the personnel department prior to negotiations. After an agreement has been reached, the personnel department typically instructs supervisors about administering the labor agreement and avoiding excessive grievances and unfair labor practices.

Environment and Structure	Actually organizations exist in different environments. We recognize, for example, that steel producers, residential builders, private universities, and public utilities fact substantially different external situations. Some environments are described as stable, whereas others are characterized by shifting conditions, uncertainty, and difficulty in predicting the course of events.
Exchange Control	This is another means of regulating foreign trade, a government monopoly on dealings in foreign exchange.
Exporting	Exporting is usually the lest complicated of those opportunities. A buyer for export is usually treated as a domestic customer and served by the domestic sales force. The buyer for export is essentially a middleman who assumes all the risks and sells internationally for his own account. Direct exporting is the preferred alternative for the firm that intends to maintain control over its export activities and also avoid middleman fees.
FED EX	Federal Express
Financial Control of Operations	This is facilitated because managers can prepare a separate income statement for each geographic area and determine its contribution to corporate profit.
GATT	GenerGeneral Agreement on Tariffs and Trade
GDP	Gross Domestic Product
IMF	International Monetary Fund that makes loans to needy countries

Incentives	Biase Lumber Company is a very strong union company. I suppose it was strongly unionized because it received help from the government in receiving free trees, and as such, the company wanted to show its appreciation to both the public and the government and became role model for the future of others receiving government assistance. Among the incentives for workers, the company pays over time and double-time workers for work over 8 hours a day, vacation time with pay, health insurance for workers, and life insurance up to $30,000 naira with a minimal premium from workers. Day care for employees, interest-free loans, and scholarships for employees' children are other incentives provided by BLC.
International Franchising	This is a form of licensing. Franchising has been most successful in developed countries that have full-fledged service economies. In addition to the traditional products that are franchised such as fast food, restaurants, and automotive products, service franchises have been growing rapidly in industrialized nations.
Joint Venture	This is quite similar to licensing agreements except that the domestic firm assumes an equity position in a foreign company. Naturally, this type is riskier.
LAFTA	Latin America Free Trade Association

Law Enforcement Agencies	The United States Postal Inspection Service is one of the oldest law enforcement agencies in the United States. Founded by Benjamin Franklin, its mission is to protect the postal service, its employees, and its customers and to protect the nation's mail system from criminal abuse. Postal inspectors enforce over 200 laws providing for the protection of mail in investigations of crimes that may adversely affect or fraudulently use the postal service, the mail, and the postal employees.
LEA	Law Enforcement Agencies
Licensing	Licensing is a more aggressive move into the international marketplace without direct manufacturing. The licensor agrees to let another firm use its manufacturing process, trademark, patents, trade secrets, and in turn to pay the licensor a royalty or the fee that is agreed upon.
MBA	Masters of Business Administration
Mail Carriers	They are also referred to as mailmen or letter carriers and prepare and deliver mail and parcels.

Market Groupings	Trade is also encourage through market groupings. Countries creating common trade alliances integrating several markets into a common unit have severed; advantages"

1. Increased growth for the region;
2. Growth in income within the region can lead to increased exports for both member and non-member countries;
3. Trade creating and diversion possibilities may lead international businesses to invest in production and marketing within a region in order to get behind the tariff wall and to minimize non-tariff barriers. The best known market groupings are the EEC and ECPWAS.

NALC	National Association of Letter Carriers
NCNC	After WWII, Cameroon became a mandated territory to Nigeria because Cameroon was defeated by Hitler. A political part was born in Nigeria founded by Dr. Nnamdi Azikiwe, and was known as the National Council of Nigeria and Cameroon. A few years later, there was a plebiscite in Cameroon allowing them to choose between forming their own country or staying with Nigeria as Nigerians. As a result, Dr. Nnamdi Azikwe became the premier of Eastern Nigeria. Later Dr. Azikwe was succeeded by Dr. M. I. Okpara as the premier while Dr. Azikwe became president of the country, but by then, Nigeria used a parliamentary system of government. So, Alhaji Abutoakar Tafawa Bellewa became the prime minister and the leader of the Federal Republic of Nigeria.

NPNHU	National Postal Mail Handlers Union
NRLCA	National Rural Letter Carriers Association
OIG	Office of Inspector General
OPEC	Oil and Petroleum Exporting Countries
P&DC	Processing and Distribution Center
PTF	Part-Time Flexible
Patterns of Organization	This explains the way in which individual jobs such as machine operators, engineers, accountants, sales representatives, and others are grouped for purposes of management. We accept that jobs themselves as given and concentrate upon relationships among them. (See page 397).
Performance Evaluation	Evaluating the performances of both managers and non-managers is generally a shared responsibility between the personnel department and other department managers. Department managers and supervisors assume the primary responsibility for evaluating subordinates since they observe job performances and are best able to more accurately assess the individual.
RFD	Rural Free Delivery

Social Satisfaction	Employee derive social satisfaction from the work group. They feel themselves a part of a social group and enjoy the contacts and friendships involved in their association with others. A change in the organization may disturb the social group and social relationships of affected employees. It is apparent that the change might be viewed as negative and threatening to existing satisfactory social relationships or the changed situation might be welcomed because of a promised improvement in social relationships.
Staffing	This involves three major activities—human resource planning, recruiting, and selection. Typically, anticipating human resource needs is the responsibility of line managers as organizations grow in terms of size and complexity. However, managers become more dependent on the personnel departments to gather information regarding the composition of the work force and the skills of present employees.
TES	Transitional Employees
Trade by Barter	Exchange of goods, lack of medium of exchange such as money
UNCTAD	United Nations on Trade and Development
USPIS	United States Postal Inspection Service
USPS	United States Postal Service
WTO	World Trade Organization

ABOUT THE BOOK

There was a young high school graduate whose ambition was to succeed like anyone else, but he had no opportunities at all. His parents barely paid their rent and have food on the table.

While he was in high school, he found a security job from which he earned funds for his books and transportation costs. His name was Johnson, and was very respectful of his parents. He always told himself that it could have been worse without his parents. After high school, he promised himself that if he found a job and had a child or children, that they would have to finish high school and college. He was lucky enough to find a job in a manufacturing company where he could move up the corporate ladder.

Mr. Johnson made sure that he was conversant with what his duties were, got a raise in salary, got married, and had children soon afterwards, and began saving for the university education of the children.

Soon, he had a raise, then a catastrophic incident struck the company, and production went so low that they hired engineers from a private company to remedy the situation, but to no avail. The next step was to begin laying off employees. This was a scary situation for Mr. Johnson who began thinking that he might have been hoping against hope about his position.

Later, Johnson heard that participative decision making was going to take place in the company, but he was not selected as a participant.

Already, he found that at about 2:00 p.m. the machine he was working with would sound normal but productivity would be very low. He knew that if he told his supervisor, the supervisor would just brush it off because he would just think only university graduates could think like that and because of the company's belief in university graduates.

One day, all the executives and some investors gathered together to figure out what to do next as the company was headed for liquidation. Apparently, Johnson walked into the meeting, but his supervisor asked him to leave; he shouted in desperation. "Please do not ask me to leave or go away because I made a discovery." The Chairman of the Board of Directors asked Mr. Johnson about his discovery. Johnson told the group he had been observing both the plant engine and productivities. Since the productivity problem started and that about 2:00 p.m. daily the engine would be sounding well, but the productivity would be very low.

The Chairman adjourned the meeting and asked Mr. Johnson to show them where he stands to observe and then asked the representatives to be back at or before 2:00 p.m. the following day. The Chairman and the participants turned up the following day and found that things were as Mr. Johnson had told them. The Chairman then ordered breaks and lunch hour policy to be adjusted. Apparently, Mr. Johnson was promoted to an executive position.

INDEX

barter. *See* trade, by barter
BART policeman, 22–23
Bassey (Mr.), 276–77, 279–82, 295–97, 299, 492
Bassey, Uno, 294, 296–97, 299–300
Bassey, Victor, 294–99
Bassey and Sons, 16
behavior, 130, 171
  accumulative, 173
  causes of, 289
  disruptive, 128
  incremental catastrophic, 173–74
  individual, 290
benefits, 273
Bettel, Xavier, 473
Biase Lumber Company (BLC), 354–55, 357–60, 362, 388–93
  competitors of, 363–64
  customers, 371
  financial growth of, 372–73
  human resources of, 368
  incentives of, 369–71
  internal growth of, 374–75
  management of, 378–80, 382–84, 386–87
  mill, 380, 383
  operations of, 365
  products of, 356–58, 360, 366–67
  sales and marketing of, 367–68, 388
Board of Directors, 51, 54, 145–47, 155
Board of Governors, 325, 348, 352
body language, 218, 223
Bohm, David, 1, 5–9, 73, 81, 115–18, 121, 217
bonuses, 370
BREXIT, 476, 480–81, 483
BREXIT Vote, 477, 484, 488
Britain, 448, 473, 476, 478, 480–83, 488
bulk mail center (BMC). *See* Network Distribution Center

Bush, George W., 434
business
  global, 138, 161, 454, 494
  mail order, 205, 318
  private, 323
business cards, 508, 515
business cultures, 7
business organizations, 453
  customers of, 454
  teamwork in, 113, 147
business owners, 179, 437, 521
business partner, 198, 207, 215, 222–23
business policy, 131, 315
business presentations, 442
business scientists, 137, 244, 399
business team, 19
business transactions, 74, 161–62, 205
buyer, 229, 356, 392, 427, 429
  product usefulness to, 429–30
  resources of, 428–29
buyer behavior, 427–28

C

Cameron, David, 472, 480–81, 487–88
Canada, 524–25
capital, market in, 420–21
Carney, Mark, 474, 477
Carter, Jimmy, 9–10, 113, 221
case study
  on the Bassey brothers, 294
  definition of, 25
  of a village, 275
change, dynamics of, 430, 432–34, 438–40
Cherrington, David J., 267–75, 289–90, 292–94, 301–5, 309–12
Chief Executive Officer (CEO), 34, 41, 49, 88, 95, 113–14, 145
Chief Financial Officer (CFO), 100, 145–47

China, 184, 205
Chinatown businesses, 405, 418
Civil Service System (CSRS), 324
clerks, 343, 351
  for deliveration, 99
Clinton, William Jefferson, 65, 226, 394, 438
collective learning. *See* dialogue
collective thinking, 59, 76, 81, 84, 147
communication, 6, 184, 186, 213–14, 449
company rules, violation of, 301
compensation, 271, 273
competition, 192–94, 424, 458–59
  of Biase Lumber Company, 363–64, 375, 380
  price, 424
  of USPS, 333, 347–48
  worldwide, 100, 199
competitive advantages, 160, 261–62, 356, 363, 367, 393
Congress, 316, 318, 324, 326, 339, 348, 453, 460
consensus, 2, 30–31, 90, 211–14
consumers. *See* buyer
costs, 361, 512, 517
credit, 429
  letters of, 509–10, 515–16
crime, 482, 490
Cross River, 387
Cross River State of Nigeria, 205, 393
cultural conditions, 405
cultural sensitivities, 183
culture, 75, 181–85, 191, 197, 232, 405–6, 467
  African, 259
  economic, 185
  insensitivity about, 120–21
  and language, 186
currency, devaluing, 67–68
customers

needs of, 460
rural, 317, 322, 346, 348

D

debt, 494–95
decentralization, 402, 411
decision-makers, 19, 49, 90, 100, 110, 129–30
decision-making, 113, 145, 147–48
  benefits of, 124
  clarity in, 155–56
  dialogue in, 92
  group, 113
  by one person, 43
  participative, 12, 19–20, 98, 112, 123–24, 136, 140, 142, 147, 163
  team, 14–15, 33–34, 48–49, 95
  tribal group, 113
decision-making chambers, 145–46, 148–49
decision-making process, 14, 92, 127, 137, 143–44
  autonomy in, 127
  participating in, 53–55, 129, 139–40
decisions, 109, 113, 131, 152, 413–14
  participative, 127, 140, 155, 538
  political, 109
  See also decision-making
deliberations, 30–31, 56–58, 72–73, 90–91, 94
  short-term, 99–100
delivery, 327, 340, 422
  free, 360
  proof of, 331
  restricted, 331
  special, 341
delivery services, how they work, 314, 328
demography, 209, 224, 238
Deputy Director, 253
DHL Express, 327

V

village post office (VPO), 322,
    335, 348

W

Wall Street, 130, 195 96, 226
wealth, 238, 420, 422–23
Webber, Alan, 76, 79, 81
West Africa, 225, 250–51, 255, 264,
    488–89
West African Common Market
    (WACM), 237, 264

West African Economic Community
    (WAEC), 237
West Africans, 254, 264, 307
Wilson Maintenance, 86, 169
wood products, 354, 356, 361, 365–
    66, 391
workers, postal, 318, 344–45
work force, competitive, 156, 158
workshop, 101–3, 294–95, 297–300
Wright Brothers, 184–86, 226
WTO (World Trade Organization),
    253, 260–61, 263

CPSIA information can be obtained
at www.ICGtesting.com
Printed in the USA
BVHW030847240719
554204BV00008B/27/P